Cinderella After the Ball

OR, JUST KEEP GOING

Barbara Redzisz Hammerstein
a.k.a. Basia

Peppertree Press
Sarasota, Florida

For information regarding permission,
call 941-922-2662 or contact us at our website:
www.peppertreepublishing.com or write to:
the Peppertree Press, LLC.
Attention: Publisher
1269 First Street, Suite 7
Sarasota, Florida 34236

ISBN: 978-1-936051-04-5

Library of Congress Number: 2009925089

Printed in the U.S.A.

Printed August 2009

To Linda
with much
affection from
Paula
Hawkins
2/22/11

Barbara Redzisz Hammerstein, a.k.a. Basia

Chapter 1

In the early winter of 1954, Ray's single-story diner stretched across the center of the block on the east side of Eighth Avenue between Forty-Fifth and Forty-Sixth Streets in New York City. Rusty chains, suspended from protruding brackets on the parapet of the diner, partially restrained the movement of a large white sign that had RAY'S DINER printed in large black letters across it.

Because the diner occupied a double lot, it became apparent, even after a cursory glance, that it had been constructed from two adjoining spacious and disparate, if not totally related, stores. The retaining wall between the two establishments arched upward at the center, creating a crest from which the relatively flat, black tar roof journeyed to the edges -- sagging, bowing and hammocking its way sideways, to rise, as if on bent elbows, up against the cracked soot-covered walls of the encroaching flophouses. Like crumbling book ends, the flophouses not only flanked the diner between them, but framed the entire decrepit block itself. The central hump on the roof furthered the unsettling image of something squatting, something poised ominously, like a large spider, waiting not necessarily to pounce on the unwary traveler but, more to the point, to surround within its culinary web the chomping occupants within.

Well-choreographed activity seemed to pervade the diner. The blue and white glare of bright neon lights inside exposed its barely patched walls and peeling ceilings. They cast an eerie glow on the unwashed faces and tattered clothes of the local street bums who nodded over their endless cups of coffee. The waitresses were friendly and loud, in contrast to the more selective and seductive, swishy blond waiter who was eager to please the local chorus boys as they minced in and out with their cups of coffee held high.

I sat on one of the stools by the counter waiting for my coffee "to go." Debbie, my roommate, with whom I took the cross-town bus from Tudor City on the east side of Manhattan where we lived, sat next to me complaining about her latest unhappy love affair. She bemoaned the often-repeated litany that her mother had been prodding her to get married.

As her fresh squeezed orange juice arrived, she leaned back from the counter and beckoned to someone outside, someone whose face she saw peering through the diner window. The door opened, and a very tall young man stepped out of the chilly twilight into the brightly lit confusion of the diner. He slammed the door behind him, catching in it the tail end of his short and apparently ill-fitting coat. As he did so, he smiled at Debbie. All this was accompanied by his bumping an overhead fixture, which sent dust and dead moths drifting downward upon him and the nodding bums at the counter.

A pushing up of his glasses, which immediately slipped down to the front part of his nose, and a hiking up of his shoulders, like prize fighters do when they face an opponent, completed his grand entrance. Long arms hung down past the short cuffs of his coat, revealing the lower half of his shirt sleeves. His armpits curved at my eye level, as did a thread which once held a button. At the end of his long legs, a pair of desert boots curled up at the toes. White socks barely contained his skinny legs, and a pair of corduroy pants softly cupped his flat behind. He smiled at Debbie and brushed the dead moths off the front of his coat and onto the lid of her freshly squeezed orange juice.

"Hi there, Debbie! Long time, no see!"

"Not my fault! How've you been?"

She peered up at him, at first apparently surprised at seeing him, then becoming instantly resentful. "I'd like you to meet my roommate, Basia. Basia, this is Jimmy Hammerstein, our stage manager. Jimmy, this is Basia Regis, and I hope she ruins your life, like you ruined mine."

Well, that certainly was to the point! Debbie thought I was a bit of a femme fatale, more because of the way I looked than who I was. Gingerly picking the moths off the lid of her orange juice, she disappeared into the night, in the process releasing the edge of Jimmy Hammerstein's ill-fitting coat, which had remained trapped in the door. He stepped aside to let her pass, oblivious that for a few minutes he had been immobilized by it. With an exaggerated bow and a sweep of his arm, he ushered her out into the dark and windy street.

He then turned to me. "You work around here?"

"Yes, in Can-Can."

He looked me over. "You a dancer?"

"No, but thank you. I'm a singer." I puffed myself up, standing straight and tall, knowing that dancers were usually in better shape than singers.

"What're you thanking me for?" He stared down from his great height. I couldn't see whether his eyes were twinkling or not. The diner lights bounced reflecting squares off his glasses.

"That you thought I was a dancer." I smiled.

"What's the big deal about being a dancer?" His lips puckered up, and he looked puzzled.

"Singers are usually lumpy."

In those golden days of the musical theater in the Fifties when choreographers were kings, they and their dancers held singers in great contempt. The general belief was that singers couldn't move and had soft lumpy bodies. When I was in Two's Company, Jerry Robbins, our choreographer, did an impersonation of singers. He lumbered stiffly across the stage like a little toy soldier. His left arm and left leg shot forward; then his right arm and right leg also shot forward. Back and forth he marched, urged on by the hysterical hilarity of his dancers. When he couldn't keep the singers off the stage altogether, he usually compromised by having us swaying like trees in the background. Singers to him were off-stage voices, disembodied spirits, to be heard and not seen.

Jimmy Hammerstein laughed. As he opened his mouth, I became aware of the horrible condition of his teeth. I wondered if anyone had ever taken him to a dentist. The top row of teeth bay-windowed out, while the bottom row leaned erratically all over itself, like crowded broken matchsticks.

Half-jokingly, I asked him, "Is your father Oscar Hammerstein?" Debbie had kept her relationship with him pretty much under wraps. He looked at the floor and then at me.

"Yeah," he said, staring at an area just past my ear, apparently resenting he had been asked. His answer stopped me in my tracks. Not knowing how to extricate myself with some grace, I barreled on.

"Is he as tall as you are?"

"No, I'm much taller than he is." He drew himself up to his full height of six feet, five inches and asked me, "How'd you like to have din-din? I'll call you."

He raised his hand to quiet my offer of the telephone number. "Groovy! I have the number. It's the same as Debbie's."

"Oops!" I slid off the stool. "I've got to go, or I'll be late. Nice to have met you."

I extended my hand and shook his. He had a nice solid handshake. Din-din! I was going to have din-din with Jimmy Hammerstein. I gazed up at the tall unnerving apparition before me and realized, as my heart began to race, that I had met my Prince Charming.

The next Saturday, between shows, we had dinner at Sardi's. I had gone there before with some of my friends in the chorus. We usually wore heavy stage make-up on matinee days between shows and therefore felt comfortable in only a few of the restaurants in the immediate vicinity, one of which was Sardi's. When the girls and I dined between shows, no great fuss was made over us. We would be politely welcomed and neatly tucked behind a post, or filed away at a table in the back, near the kitchen. Our dinners were usually spent shouting over the clatter of dishes and the rush of waiters, as they slammed in and out though the swinging galley doors that led to the kitchen.

When I walked into Sardi's with Jimmy Hammerstein, the whole world changed. The <u>maitre'd</u> swept so low to the ground that his bald pate flashed before my eyes, catching the soft glow of the lights. With a continuous extended movement, he plowed forward, tucking us not only into the lefthand area where only celebrities were seated but then into the corner banquette reserved strictly for the <u>creme de la creme</u>.

I felt my face glowing beneath my heavy stage make-up from all the fuss and bother because my date just happened to be the son of Oscar Hammerstein II. Young Jim seemed uncomfortable, bumping into the table, stumbling aside, letting me slide first into the banquette, pushing up his glasses, which insisted on sliding down his nose, and cracking his knuckles before he finally settled down and flicked the napkin across his knees. Nice gesture. We never did that at home. In restaurants I had to remember to cover my knees with a cloth; otherwise I not only wore the meals I ate on the front of my chest but also on my lap.

It didn't make any difference where they placed us when I was with my gypsy theater friends; I still loved Sardi's. It was the "in" place to go. When I wanted to share the life of the theater with my mother or my nieces, I took them to Sardi's. Sardi's was convenient and special, located right off Shubert Alley, across the street from <u>Can-Can</u>, where I worked. It was frequented by all the theatrical celebrities. You stepped out of the hustle and bustle of Forty-Fourth Street into a sanctuary of privilege. The tables down front were often filled with the familiar faces of Ruth Gordon, Gwen Verdon, Mary Martin or Alfred Drake, echoing the caricatures of theater celebrities on the walls.

I barely recognized some of the drawings. Most were strange to me. In my youth, I had been exposed to the movies and knew the movie stars, but the stars of the theater were unfamiliar to me. As I studied the faces on the walls, with their heightened imperfections caught by the artist's hand, I wondered if I would ever have my picture hanging up there. Would it be a flattering likeness, or would Hirschfeld, who did most of the caricatures, find and magnify some hidden flaw of mine? Would he make my nose too long? I already began to be concerned, overwhelmed by my imperfections.

On my first date with Jimmy Hammerstein, we talked a great deal. At least I talked a great deal, entertaining my new date, whose name carried so much theatrical baggage, with local gossip. He was relatively quiet, looming over me with his buck teeth and his crew cut, which exposed his ears and encouraged them to stick out, in the process giving me their undivided attention.

People stopped at the table and greeted him with great enthusiasm. He seemed ill at ease over their effusiveness, and as he introduced me to some of his apparent, if not too close friends, he stumbled over my name.

Finally, after all the introductions were over, he asked, "Where the hell didja get Basia from? What kind of name is that? You Russian?"

"No, I'm Polish! I was born in Warsaw and came to this country when I was nine."

"Wow! Top drawer, a real foreigner. Ha! You still speak Polish?"
"Yes."

"Say something in Polish."
"Chszaszcz brzmi w tczcine."

I had dredged up the Polish equivalent of "She sells sea shells at the seashore." That should impress him.

"What the hell is that?"

"The beetle is buzzing in the rushes."

"The what?"

"The beetle, a kind of bug found in Poland!"

"Then why didn't you say so!"

"It sounded more exotic my way."

"Great conversation stopper!" He shook his head and looked vaguely unsettled.

"Au contraire! Look how much mileage I got out of it."

"That's what I thought!" He laughed. I watched his hands as he ate, beautiful hands with long fingers that knew how to navigate the food that went into his mouth. Not only that, he knew which utensils

10

to use. As I watched, I made mental notes, interested in learning a necessary and elegant new skill.

After that first dinner at Sardi's, Jimmy Hammerstein became a part of my life. He loved skindiving, and I wanted to learn. It surprised me that he frequented some of the same areas on Long Island that were familiar to me. I thought the North Shore would have been his place to hang out, but, no, it was the less impressive South Shore that he was drawn to. Breezy Point, Point Lookout and the Rockaways were the beaches to which we journeyed to stalk and spear unwary fish.

We'd rent a rowboat with a motor on it. I'd help him lug the scuba gear and the picnic baskets on board; then I'd spend the day bobbing above the waves as he appeared beside the boat, spitting and spluttering in the chilly ocean, more often than not waving a speared bluefish in the air. As I watched the blood spreading along the white underbelly of the stricken creature and trickling down Jimmy's arm into the dark water, I dreaded to catch the look of reproach in the fish's panicked eyes, wondering, as film glazed over its eyes and it surrendered its last remnants of life, when the being inside departed and where it went on its last journey.

Given the great disparity in our backgrounds, ours was a bumpy relationship from the very beginning. We had many misunderstandings, punctuated by a great deal of mutual silence that I tried to fill with stories: stories about Poland, about school, the courses I was taking at Hunter College, how proud I was of having gotten so close to my degree (even though it had already taken me five years and I had one more year to go), and all the other anecdotes I felt he might find entertaining.

"What you want to get a degree for?" He scowled when my classes interfered with our spending time together.

"I think it's important to be educated. Don't you? Did you go to college?" He shot me a look and cracked his knuckles.

"Nah, well, two years, but that doesn't count. Hated it, a drag. A boring, bloody nuisance!"

11

How could anyone find school boring? I was in the middle of anthropology, Russian history, perspective drawing and music, always music.

"What did you take?" I asked him.

"Music and tennis."

"You studied tennis?" I couldn't believe my ears.

"Why not? I wanted to be a pro."

"What's a pro?"

He looked at me and laughed. "A <u>pro</u>fessional tennis player." He laid it out very carefully. "You know, pro, as in <u>pro</u>fessional, do the tennis circuits like Wimbleton and Forest Hills."

"No, I didn't know that." I shook my head, feeling foolish. The only thing I knew about Forest Hills was that it was an express stop on the Independent "E" and "F" subway train. "What's at Forest Hills?"

"A tennis stadium. Haven't you ever been there? Don't you play tennis?" He was incredulous.

"No." I felt inadequate.

"Don't worry." He patted me on the hand. "You can learn."

I decided to learn as soon as I could and made a mental note to see if Hunter College gave courses in tennis. Somehow I doubted it. Still, if I needed to learn tennis to be a part of the new life that was spreading before me, then I would learn to play tennis.

On one of our early spring skindiving forays, I dragged him to Farmingdale, Long Island, and introduced him to my mother and father. Mamma was shy. As we banged our way into the house with some of the skindiving gear, she tentatively peered out of the kitchen and blushed. Coming forward, while wiping her hands on the apron around her waist, she shook Jimmy's outstretched hand and seemed overwhelmed by his size.

"My, but you tall!" She craned her neck up and patted his beautiful hand. She was hopeful that I would marry him. To her, a woman without a husband had no status and her life was suspect. My younger sister had married at seventeen, had twins at eighteen, while I at twenty-four, was the maiden-aunt sister Barbara from New York.

More often than not, the <u>big shot</u> maiden-aunt sister Barbara from New York.

Jimmy's family, the theatrical Hammersteins, had little meaning for her, except for the fact that she had heard they were probably very rich. Eyeing Jimmy's disheveled clothes, she found that difficult to believe. She couldn't understand why, if they were rich, he drove a car that was literally held together by ropes and why he was so shabbily dressed.

On his first visit to Farmingdale, she surreptitiously took his tattered overcoat, mended the frayed elbows with corduroy patches, tacked up the hanging lining, and sewed on some buttons that matched amazingly well, buttons she picked out of a large tin button box. I shook the box and remembered how, when we were children, I loved the rattling sound the buttons made as we rummaged through them.

Poppa was already tipsy when we arrived, paler than I remembered him when I lived at home. A kind of yellowish green paleness hit all of us when we weren't feeling too well. The Tatar blood in us, I would proudly tell people, picturing Oriental hordes on horseback sweeping across Eastern Europe and ramming their seed into screaming reluctant women. The sallow skin and slanted dark eyes were more intense in some of the family members back in Poland. Every time we looked through the family picture albums, Poppa glossed over them and shoved them out of sight, but they were a source of pride to me. My Tatar blood gave me a distinctly foreign look: high cheek bones, thick smooth skin, wide dark eyes. I played up the romance of the idea.

When we landed in Jersey City many years before, being foreign was like a curse. Among the theater folk, it was intriguing. I capitalized on my apparently newfound mysterious past. The reality of what my life might have been seemed to be irrelevant. What mattered was the romantic idea, the peripheral innuendo. I was more than just a foreigner, more than just a Polack. I felt I was a combination of unknown factors, maybe not as socially impressive as Jimmy Hammerstein and his family but nonetheless interesting.

At the moment when I met Jimmy Hammerstein at Ray's Diner, one part of me was preparing myself to be another Ilona Massey, a gorgeous Hungarian singer who droned along with Nelson Eddy in <u>At the Balalaika</u>. Surrounded by a halo of glistening white hair, I, too, pictured shimmering stars around my face, stars that sparkled like fairy dust. I didn't know then, in the early Fifties, that photographers used a silk stocking on the lens to get that magical glow! When I was a Copa girl a few years before, I bleached my hair platinum blonde at the request of Doug Coudy, our choreographer. Most of it fell out, and I had to wear a fall to continue in the show.

At that time, the idea of a career in the theater still held great magic for me. I had been in <u>Top Banana</u> with Phil Silvers and in <u>Two's Company</u> with Bette Davis. When I met Jimmy Hammerstein, I was one of the laundresses in <u>Can-Can</u>, with Gwen Verdon, and I was preparing to star as Suzie in <u>Sweet Thursday</u>. I was beginning to realize what some of the theater was about.

Show biz was not the classless talent-determined meritocracy I first thought it would be. Indeed, I soon found it was a hierarchy as rigid as any military organization; only on Broadway it was based on pink and white contracts. White contracts defined principal players and stars. Pink contracts were for the chorus members. They were just a peg above the stagehands who swam at the bottom of the theatrical barrel.

Being in a Broadway show no longer held the wonder for me as it did when I first started out a few years before as a young naive, rather eager, hopeful. Stardom was still that glitter in the distance, but the reality of achieving stardom had become tarnished for me. At twenty-four, I knew I would never learn to play the games that a pretty young, dumb blonde had to master to advance her career. Turning on the charm and telling interesting stories were one thing, but keeping it up all evening to wear out my dates so I wouldn't have to come across sexually and not incur their wrath was another. Often when I got home and finally closed the door behind me, my cheeks ached and twitched in my sleep from all that smiling.

14

No one told me as I pursued my education at Hunter College, raced around fitting singing and acting classes into my busy schedule, that part of the preparation for getting a job in show business, talent notwithstanding, was to know how to service men sexually. "Down, boy!" was more than a phrase in obedience training for dogs. It was a command that often set the stage for potential employment. My future as a budding theatrical hopeful faced a perilous journey on the jagged shoals of a high gagging reflex.

I thought that if I could become a star, then it would change, so I pursued stardom. Things seemed to be falling into place. Arthur Lewis, casting director for the producers Feuer and Martin, had seen me in Two's Company and felt I would be perfect for the leading role of Suzie in Sweet Thursday, a musical based on John Steinbeck's novel, Cannery Row. Lewis put me in Can-Can as one of the laundresses and sent me to a voice coach to work on my chest voice.

With the possibility of achieving stardom as Suzie in Sweet Thursday, I would no longer have to put up with men like Jack Entratter, who hired me to be one of the showgirls at the Copacabana. During my first week on the job, he showered me with flowers and mandated that I join him at the Hotel Fourteen above the Copa between shows for the mandatory medium-rare steak and baked potato. When I wouldn't come across sexually, with his six-foot, eight-inch frame wobbling in his space shoes, he wedged me up against the wall and came all over my legs. The smell of semen stung my nostrils, and I threw up on the way to the door.

That was my first and last stint at the Copa. Entratter spread the word around that I was a great lay. The gangsters gracing his table at ringside leered at me. Smiling my ever practiced smile, I sashayed jauntily on and off the dance floor as the band played and the vocal duo sang.

"When skies are blue and grass is green,
my heart's a strumming tambourine.
Summer makes a Gypsy out of me."

15

With stardom and its accompanying importance, there would be no more directors panting after me in out-of-town hotel rooms and no more producers dangling roles in front of my nose, along with keys to their hotel rooms.

If I didn't become a star, then to please the other more reflective side of me, I would become a philosopher, whatever that was, as categorical imperatives spun around in my head. Thinking all those sages that I had to read as part of my philosophy major would give me some answers to life, along with academic status, I read avidly but with growing disenchantment. All that the philosophers seemed to do was to redefine old words, coin new ones and rearrange them in different combinations. They contained few new insights, few new possibilities. It was just the same old stuff rehashed. Even in philosophy I realized there must be something else, so I plowed on.

The fact that I went to college during the day and worked in the theater at night gave me points in both areas. In the theater I was an oddity, a chorus girl with academic aspirations. At Hunter College I led a glamorous life beyond the reach of most of my friends.

Then without any warning, two major changes rerouted my whole life. Like a train racing along one track, I was suddenly detoured, shunted over to a new and unfamiliar direction. The tangent took me at right angles to the trip for which I had prepared myself, away from the dreams that had begun to sustain me, for which I had all the accumulated knowledge. When the shunting occurred, it was only my private car that had changed course, leaving me without my baggage, my props, the accumulated experience of my life. Nothing to which I had been exposed to prepared me for the new journey upon which I had embarked.

It was during the period of one week that two seemingly unrelated events changed the course of my life. One was that Jimmy Hammerstein proposed to me, which was becoming more and more predictable from the amount of time we had been spending together. The other was that Feuer and Martin, the original producers of Sweet Thursday, sold the property to Rodgers and Hammerstein, in the process giving up all their casting and directorial rights. Richard Rodgers, the new partner and co-owner, visualized the leading lady, Suzie, the part for which I was being groomed, not as a vulnerable blonde, displaced European chanteuse, a la Ilona Massey, but as a tough, motorcycle gang type of prostitute with a heart of steel. Judy Tyler, short, dark and tough, became the new Suzie, and I married Jimmy Hammerstein, six months after we had met at Ray's Diner.

He proposed to me four months into our relationship, one cold lingering winter day, as we were driving across Fifty-Fourth Street in his patched-together car. The wind was blowing stray snowflakes through holes in the roof and through the broken window. I sat next to him, still "up" from the show, looking into the gently falling snow melting on the black glistening pavement outside and on my folded hands where the flakes landed and remained for scant moments before they disappeared. The warmth of my body melted them, and they rolled out of sight down the sides of my coat.

"Will you marry me, Basia? I love you."

I knew it was coming, for we had skirted the edges of marriage before, but he had never proposed to me directly. As my heart pounded in my throat, thoughts ran through my head. I had never planned to marry and was still hoping to find the "truth and beauty," as the Romantic poets had promised, somewhere out there. The search seemed to have become more and more fruitless, as both seemed to evade me. We jostled forward as the traffic moved again, and I felt his eagerness next to me. Through the thumping in my chest, I rationalized that we'll both be in the theater. I'll sing; he'll produce and direct. We'll have a garden apartment on the West Side and live happily ever after.

"Yes, I'll marry you." I leaned over in the cold car and kissed him. "Have you told your family about me?"

"Nah, not yet."

"Why not?" An edge of resentment rose in me to join my thumping heart, along with my fears. Call it the panic of an immigrant. He's afraid I'm not good enough for them, that they won't like me.

"Mumsie and dad have been at The Farm, and I haven't had a chance to talk to them." He stared forward into the traffic.

"Your parents have a farm?"

"Not a farm. It's called The Farm. When they want to get out of the city, they go to The Farm. It's over in Bucks County, Pennsylvania."

"Do you think they'll like me?" I stuffed some Kleenex into the crack of the broken window.

"They'll love you. Wait and see!" He gunned the old car forward. "Mumsie was a show girl when she came here from England in Chalot's Revue."

That took me a bit by surprise. I didn't know that the imperious lady in the silver picture frame in his apartment had been a showgirl.

"Do you spend a lot of time with them? I mean, your mother and father."

"Nah, not much."

"Do you see them at all?"

"Oh, yeah, once in a while."

"Don't you miss them?" He looked at me as if I were crazy. "I mean, I'd miss my mother if I didn't see her on the weekends."

"You're too attached to her."

"I love her! She's my Mother!" Somehow he made me feel defensive and not altogether right about the fact that I loved my mother and missed her when I didn't see her. "I mean, I need to check in. It kind of recharges my emotional battery to see her." I tried to explain it in terms he would understand. "I like to plug into her from time to time because it makes me feel good. You don't feel that way about your parents?"

"Nah."

"What about your father? What's your father like?" He continued to look ahead into the falling snow.

"He's a great guy."

"What kind of a man is he?"

I persisted in my questioning, wondering about Oscar Hammerstein II, one of the giants not only of the musical theater but of my youth. His songs had punctuated many of my crushes and lost loves.

"He's just a great guy." As he said this, he shrugged his shoulders. I wanted to hear something more personal, maybe even gossipy.

"What's he like? He doesn't seem to have any faults?" I didn't much believe in human perfection, even then.

"Nah, he doesn't."

"Then why doesn't he buy you a car that runs and has no holes in it? And what about a coat that fits?" I looked over at his patched sleeves. "Where did you get that coat, the Salvation Army?"

"Dad gave it to me. That's not the way it works with us. My old man may be rich, but I don't take any money from him. This happens to be real fur!" He yanked at his collar.

"Oh, I couldn't figure out what that was. Real fur, huh?"

The threadbare area of collar around his neck belied the fact that it once graced the body of some small furry live creature. I pressed on. "What's wrong with your father helping you?"

"It's his money. He made it, so I have no right to it! Why should he share it with me?" He seemed incredulous at my question.

"Because you're his child. Because you're struggling to get on your feet. Why not? My God, when I worked in the garment center, all the fathers helped their kids. They took the sons into the business and gave their daughters dowries, although they don't call it that."

"My parents aren't from the garment center." A distinct edge crept into his voice.

"But isn't your father Jewish?"

"For your information, my father was baptized Episcopalian by his mother. Grandma Allie baptized them both."

"Both? Who else?" He rarely spoke of his family, so I knew little about them. "She dunked both dad and Uncle Reggie," he answered irreverently.

"Your father has a brother?" I had never heard him mention that he had an uncle who happened to be another Hammerstein, so I was surprised that one existed, wondering if he was also in the theater.

19

"Yes, a great guy, a sweetheart! You'll meet Uncle Reggie. He'll like you."

"I thought you were Jewish, a German Jew." I wondered how come everyone thought that Oscar Hammerstein II was Jewish.

"Well, partly that's where the name come from. Somewhere in Germany. Pomerania, I think. My great-grandfather was the kosher Hammerstein. His mother was a French Huguenot, but they were very Jewish. I don't know how it works. Dad's grandmother came from Glasgow. That's where the Episcopalian dunking comes from, and also from my mother, who was born in Tasmania, you know, Australia."

He nodded to me. I was delighted to hear that he wasn't such a purebred, after all. He wasn't pedigreed stock as I had anticipated, but a mixture of Scotch, Irish, English, French, German, Jewish and Australian. A mutt! A Goddamned mutt! Somehow I felt warmer toward him and glowed with pride at the perfection of my pure Polish heritage.

"Do they go to church?" I wondered.

"You kidding?" He looked askance at me.

"No," I had to admit. "How about you? You go to church?"

He looked at me. "Not anymore, but I had to as a kid. If it makes you feel any better, I was also baptized." He patted my arm.

"You were?" I was disappointed, thinking that he was a freer spirit, not saddled with the trappings of organized religion. "Did your father ever go to church?"

"I don't think so. I don't know. I think he once said that he was an acolyte, an altar boy. But I don't really remember."

"I know what an acolyte is." I grew a bit defensive.

"Anyway, he became an orphan when he was young."

"Your father was a poor lonely orphan?" Jimmy laughed, and his head bobbed up and down.

"You might call it that, I never looked at it that way."

The light changed, and we finally made it through the Lexington Avenue intersection. Emotions welled up inside of me for this famous man whom I had never met. An orphan, the word stuck a pain my heart. I felt my chest constrict. An orphan, a child bereft, left without mother or father. Along with the fear of desertion, all the fairy tales of my youth flooded back to me. Poor Cinderella, Hansel and Gretel, all those parentless princesses locked in towers, braiding their long blonde hair.

"Who raised him?"

"His aunt, Aunt Mousie. That's what he called her, Mousie. She had tattoos on her arms." He laughed almost to himself. My heart went out to this orphaned millionaire. Tattoos on whose arms, his father's? No, Aunt Mousie's. But I found it difficult to believe that he wouldn't help his son. There must be some other reason. I egged him on.

"Do you get along with him?"

"Yeah, why?"

"Then I don't understand why he doesn't help you."

"You don't have to understand! It's none of your business! You're marrying me, not him!"

I recoiled as if I had been slapped, realizing that his family seemed to be a very touchy area for him. He usually left them out of our conversations altogether. As gently as I could, I tried to explain.

"Since you just asked me to marry you, I think it's my business to know how you get along with your family and how I'll fit in."

"Look, I get along with them fine. They brought me up to be independent. That's how it is. You'll fit in O.K. Groovy!"

His knuckles gripping the steering wheel turned as white as the snow that was melting off them. He cracked them, using the thumb against the pinkie, then against each successive finger. When we stopped at Third Avenue, he put both of his hands on his head and cracked his neck, first in one direction, then the other. It wouldn't pop immediately, so he whacked his chin with his free hand. It finally snapped. Realizing that he had a thin layer of snow on his shoulder, he flicked it off while pulling on some gloves he had discovered on the floor under his seat.

"Where's your Chevy?" he asked, closing the subject he didn't feel like pursuing.

"I left it in Long Island City, just off the 59th Street Bridge."

"I'll drop you off there and follow you to your mother's house, O.K.?"

The conversation was over. He rarely spoke of his parents and didn't seem to spend much time with them. I was curious to know more about their relationship. It didn't seem to be the right time, so I backed off. I didn't like the fact he told me that it was none of my business. If I were to share my life with him, then whose business was it?

Something nagged at the back of my awareness about repetition of cycles and people getting along with their husbands and wives the same way they got along with their parents, but I pushed it out of my mind.

Marriage would be good for both of us, I felt. I would create a home for Jimmy and shower him with affection. He would protect me against the rampant sexuality of the theater, which had grown repugnant to me. I would be safe from the revenge of rejected men. This scarecrow next to me, driving his beat-up Austin, cracking his knuckles and his neck, would shield me from the outside world. I would feel safe and protected with him. Someday we'd get him a coat with longer sleeves and a car that was sealed against the elements, and everything would be all right. I leaned up against him and held his gloved hand. He kept his gloves on but didn't pull his hand away.

Part of me was jubilant. Another part of me had misgivings. Contrary to the general propaganda that it was women who hankered after the security of marriage, I always felt that marriage was made for men. Men got the better end of the deal. They got a mother whom they could take to bed, and they also got a servant. What did women get? A stranger they had to deal with like a child, because some part of that stranger never grew up. I had watched Momma and Poppa and swore I would never marry; and here I was being caught up in a situation I could not refuse. To the outsider on the periphery, the center presents great comfort. Jimmy Hammerstein was smack dab in the center on so many levels. His family was the theater, the musical comedy world. It was all that I, an immigrant child grown up, standing outside with my nose pressed against the window, could have hoped for. He had said he loved me, and that had made all the difference. I would make him happy. He would make me feel safe.

Poppa was ignorant, and I blamed this on his lack of education. Jimmy came from an educated, enlightened group, which I felt had transcended the primitive marriage arrangements of my background. I felt things would be different. We would share our lives together. Wasn't that the function of education? To set us free, women, too?

I had already taken him home to meet Momma and Poppa, but as yet he hadn't told his family about me. We got engaged, and his family still hadn't met me. I wondered about that, realizing that the rules guiding his life were different from mine. Since he came from the "rich" and since we all assumed that the "rich" knew better, I started to go along with him. But different backgrounds or not, I had to meet his family.

"Why haven't you told your mother and father about me, that we're engaged and living together?"

"I have to find the right time. Muz is not well, and I'm the last child in the nest. It's hard for her, you know." He was repeating some of the old familiar excuses.

"When are you going to tell them? Listen, I have to let my mother know. She keeps calling me and can't get me at my apartment. I'm running out of excuses as to why I'm never there."

"I'll tell them. Dad and I will have one of our Lord Chesterfield talks." He laughed, and his buck teeth sparkled.

"What's that?" I hadn't heard that one before.

"You'll see."

The next time I saw him, he had spoken to his parents. "I have some good news and some bad news," he announced.

"Oh-oh, how did they take it? What's the bad news?"

"Mumsie started to cry that her baby was getting married."

"And your father, what did he say?"

"He asked me how old you were."

"What difference does that make?" I was two years and four months older than Jimmy. I felt a clutch at my heart. Twenty-eight months was twenty-eight months. Not only that, it was in the wrong direction. Men had to be taller, older, darker, richer, and smarter. Women had to be shorter, younger, blonder, poorer, and dumber. Well, I fit three out of five: shorter, blonder and poorer, barely a majority. Who made up those rules, anyway?

"What else did he say?"

"He asked me if I could live without you, and I told him that I couldn't." His warm look embraced me. It spread through me like melted butter.

"Anything else?"

"He told me to reconsider our age differences because he said there would come a time when I would want younger flesh."

Younger flesh! I was only twenty-four, but it seemed to his father, sight unseen, that I was already over the hill. The phrase cut through me like a knife. Younger flesh! And this was from the man who wrote "All the Things You Are," "My Romance" and "If I Loved You." He certainly never wrote about getting older and wanting younger flesh! Something in me yelled, "Go slow. Think this thing through." Another part of me, a quieter, colder voice was asking, "Why did Jimmy tell me that?" It was unkind. I wondered if that was the good or bad news.

"And the good news?" I asked hopefully.

"Well, that was the better of the two. Mumsie made a date for me to take one of her friends' daughters to a debutante party."

"Didn't you tell her we were engaged?"

"Yeah, but she didn't think you'd mind. She made the commitment months ago and forgot to tell me. Now I'm stuck."

He cracked his knuckles. I felt a wave of resentment, not fully believing that the date had been made months ago. His mother feared my being Polish, an immigrant from the wrong side of the tracks, that I wasn't good enough for her son. She had made the date to put a wedge between us.

"Can't you tell her you can't do it?"

"That would bug her, and I don't want to bug her."

"But it's O.K. to bug me?"

"Look, you're making a big deal out of this. If I dug Buffie, I'd be engaged to her, not you." His lips curled down.

"Is that her name, Buffie?" He nodded.

"What does it stand for?" Buffinda? Buffancy? Buffeldrid? Buffary? Bufferyn? Possible proper names ran through my mind.

"I don't know. It's just Buffie."

"When is it?"

"Next Saturday night."

"Great." I felt foolish for being jealous and resentful. Emotions raced wildly inside me; all the feelings of being left out, of not being good enough, of being replaced, surfaced again. I had no way to express them without making a big scene. He was not into big scenes; I already knew that. Expressions of emotion were illogical to him. So the next week when he took Buffie to her debutante ball, I talked to myself, trying to work it out. It kept bothering me. I knew I was capable of becoming very emotional, so maybe it was good for me to restrain myself and put a damper on my feelings, but something else clamored for my attention. Something else was trying to nudge its way to the surface.

Chapter 2

The slush of winter receded into the background, and the trees in Central Park flushed pink with the maple buds and pale green with the weeping willows. Finally, in April 1954, I was invited to have dinner with Jimmy's parents. Not only was I in awe of his father's success and his mother's beauty, but also fearful of the subtle rejection I had already received from them.

Beside the fact that they were Jimmy's parents, great curiosity propelled me to meet the two people who had stayed in love for twenty-five years and, as Jimmy told me, had a marriage "made in heaven." I wanted to see it for myself. I had never seen any of those marriages except in the movies, and I wondered how they did it. I also wanted to do it, to have a marriage not only "made in heaven" but one that would last forever.

I'll never know why we chose a Wednesday matinee to have dinner with them. It seemed the only day we could all get together. I removed most of my make-up before the last number, as we all did, leaving only my eyes, so that when the curtain came down after the matinee, we could bolt out of the theater and not lose any time from our dinner breaks by stopping to put on street make-up. The secret to not being discovered while doing the finale was to smile a lot and to keep moving; then the pale face devoid of make-up wasn't so apparent. We were often called on the carpet by our stage manager, but it didn't do too much good. Sometimes in the last number only the stars had on full make-up. As a result, they looked orange next to the rest of us, with our pale but frantically smiling street faces.

Jimmy was the assistant stage manager in the theater next door, in <u>Me and Juliet</u>. All he had to do was grab his coat and run. As I picked some of the beading off my lashes, I prayed I wouldn't do anything stupid or out of place. I hoped that the table silver place setting didn't look like the display window at Tiffany's and that I wouldn't make too many mistakes trying to navigate it. My hands shook as I applied my light street lipstick. As I looked at them, I wished that I had done my nails, too.

We had two hours to get acquainted. Jeannie, one of the other singers in the show, lent me her long black gloves, and Mary, her strand of real cultured pearls. Before I thundered down the metal back stairs of the Shubert Theater, I surveyed myself in the full-length mirror on the landing. Waves of inadequacy washed over me. My dress seemed too short, my hair too light, my stockings too dark, my heels too high, my small hoop earrings, too jazzy. In spite of my efforts to tone it down, my face looked too made-up.

Phil Leeds, a co-performer and stage partner who played artist to my laundress, poked his craggy face out of his dressing room and gave me a big hug, along with a piece of advice.

"Don't spill any wine on the tablecloth."

"Thanks loads."

"Good luck and <u>merde</u>!" The opening night wish. As he smiled and patted me out of the stage door, his face broke into deep affection-filled folds. I plowed my way through Shubert Alley, past the autograph hunters waiting for Gwen Verdon, one of the stars of my show. After spotting Jimmy in the crowd, we clasped hands and chased the snaking line of yellow cabs until we found an empty one, which whisked us east on Forty-Fourth Street and then uptown.

Since it was early Spring, the sun had already disappeared behind the surrounding buildings and cast long shadows around us as we settled into the smelly, smoky cab. I looked over at my soon-to-be husband as we both reached over to hold hands. For the first time since I had known him, he looked immaculate, encased in a dark blue suit, which I didn't know that he even owned. His sharply starched white shirt sported a dark blue tie. His smooth face was freshly shaven and just as freshly nicked. He held my hand and for the first time since I met him, as the perspiration darkened my gloves, I saw that his palms were wet. Without being asked, he reassured me that his mother was the most wonderful woman in the world. After a small reflective pause, he added, almost to himself, "She means well." I remember wondering what he meant by that.

By this time, I had almost gotten used to the fact that he was never prepared to pay for the cab until we got to our destination. When the cab stopped in front of the brick building at 10 East Sixty-Third Street, he started fumbling for his billfold. The traffic behind us backed up, and the cabs honked their horns. I became more and more agitated as he searched through all of his pockets, finally finding some crumpled bills and paying the by-now equally impatient cab driver.

"You should clip your wallet to your cuffs," the cabby barked out at Jimmy, after getting an indifferent tip. "Like my mother did to our gloves when we were kids," I heard him yell, as we slammed our way out of the cab.

We stood in the relatively peaceful block of the East Sixties, far from the crush and noise of the theater. The brick townhouse stood right off Central Park. Cherry tree blossoms floated like white puffs in the distance. The sound of horses slowly clopping along the park drives came back to us along with the sound of the traffic. In the distance, I could faintly hear the soft bellow of a lion in the Central Park Zoo. It must be his dinner time, too, I thought.

We entered through the glass doors of a neat five-story brick building. Boxwood hedges softened its lines as it met the street and shaded a splash of daffodils and tulips. There was no stoop here, just two discreet steps leading down. The buzzer let us through the click-click of a wired front door. Black and white checkered inlaid squares on the floor of the vestibule surrounded a linoleum cutout of an English lion with its tail arched over its head. Jimmy had a pinky ring with a crest of the same lion. I wondered if it meant anything special, if they were not only the theatrical Hammersteins but also English royalty. They might have something in common with Poppa after all, who claimed lost estates before the third partition of Poland.

There were plants around the door and around the gilded mirror that hung in the foyer. Upon a closer look, I realized that the plants were plastic. As the massive street door closed gently behind us, we were partially cushioned from the sound of the traffic outside. A second buzzer opened the inside door to the inner sanctum, which was graced by a circular marble staircase winding its way up four flights of stairs to disappear under the roof. The inner door cut the sound of the street completely, and we were enveloped by a thick carpeted silence. A thought flashed through my mind. The moment reminded me of the All-City Chorus auditions in high school: Once you got to the stage, there was no turning back.

I reached for Jimmy's hand again and held on to the railing with the other, following him up the moss-green carpeted curving staircase. The white marble railing felt cool and smooth even under my gloved hand. When we reached the second floor landing, the homey smell of roasted chicken came from somewhere to the right.

A woman's voice called down from above. "Is that you, Jim Boy?"

A strange British accent cut through the silence. Jim Boy! My big tall silent future husband was called "Jim Boy," all six foot five of him.

Before he had a chance to answer, we heard, "I'm in the bedroom, darling." The voice wasn't Cockney, but it had a vaguely British sound to it. Jimmy had said she was Australian, but I wasn't familiar with the strange accent.

"Yes, mother." Jimmy quickened his stride and took the carpeted stars two at a time, jerking me along with him. We passed the second-floor landing, which had more of the black and white tiles, shiny and waxed, like a gleaming enormous checker board. A glass closet spanned the expanse of the back wall, which contained in it backlit pink plates. Dozens and dozens of pink plates stood on edge and didn't seem to be used for eating; they were more like displayed museum pieces. A crystal chandelier floated in the center above a love seat constructed in the round to seat three people. In front of the long glass closet and under the love seat was spread a large round scalloped rug, echoing the pattern of the plates: pale pink, with touches of Spring green at the edges, reminiscent of a large flower, like a lotus or a water lily, floating on a checkerboard sea.

To the left, toward the street, where the early twilight glow filtered softly through organdy curtains stretched tightly over French doors, was a huge sitting room, what we called a parlor when I was a child but which was much more fancy and elegant. The couches were satin and the color of elephant hide. What looked like a hand-embroidered rug covered the floor. An Aubisson, I was to learn later. A shiny black Oriental screen covered the wall behind the couch. Its image was reflected in a filigreed mirror hanging over the fireplace on the opposite wall. The smaller chairs in the room were covered in beige brocade, as were the walls. Cascading arrangements of fresh flowers were everywhere. On every table top stood dozens and dozens of silver framed pictures of the family I was about to meet.

Jimmy bumped into one of the rickety little tables covered with those silver frames, and they jostled around, threatening to fall down. He tried the liquor cabinet, but it was locked. As he was about to bolt out of the door to find a key, I implored him,

"Please don't leave me alone."

He stayed, holding onto my hand as I surveyed the other side of the landing. To the right, glittering with silver and crystal, was a dark blue dining room containing a highly polished mahogany table set for dinner for four. Large Early American paintings of stern faced forefathers hung on the walls. When I was a child and just a new immigrant, the intricacies of the English language were still a mystery to me. I thought it strange that people in America had "four fathers" and were so proud of them. I had only one, and that was enough. Four seemed to be three too many. "Forebears" left me in a similar quandary, until I began to sort it all out.

Beyond the dining room were the kitchens from which came the sounds and smells of dinner being prepared. We left the promise of something delicious behind and climbed another carpeted staircase to a smaller landing with another crystal chandelier. The door to the right was closed, and we followed the female voice to the front bedroom, on the left hand side of the circular staircase.

"I'm in here, Jim Boy." At this point and when I needed him the most, old Jim Boy dropped my hand, and I stood there alone. It was too late to bolt, "Mumsie" was so close I could smell her perfume.

Dorothy Hammerstein turned out to be a tall handsome woman in her middle fifties, with a bosomy figure that her lemon- colored hostess gown could not fully disguise. She swept over to us, her red hair bobbing around her face, a face that seemed to be a cross between Joan Crawford's and Dorothy Lamour's. She, too, seemed nervous, and her pale blue eyes looked not only watery but anxious, darting from her son's face to mine, not quite sure whether to smile or to be imposing, or both.

"How are you, darling?" She pecked at the air over Jimmy's right ear, just beyond his cheek.

"Fine, mother." He pecked at the air over her right cheek. Her watery blue eyes darted to me again, in expectation.

"Mother, this is Basia. Bash, this is my mother."

"How do you do?"

I extended my hand, realizing too late that I should have removed my gloves. She leaned over and pecked at the air above my right ear, just beyond my cheek. No contact was made; just a bobbing forward, like two geese meeting. I kissed her on the cheek and left a smudge of lipstick. She had not left a mark on either her son or on me, when she pecked at us, but I had left a smudge on her perfectly made-up face. The impulse to wipe it off was checked by a stronger one: <u>Don't dare!</u> As she spoke to us, she held her chin very high, which made her appear as if she were constantly retreating from a bad odor.

Age had left its traces on her face, but she was still quite beautiful. As she turned away from me to address her son, her profile was reminiscent of Greek statuary and took me back to my days at Washington Irving High School, with all those art classes and art books I had devoured so avidly. I looked at both of them and tried to detect some resemblance. Jimmy didn't look at all like her. Her hands smoothed her neck, which was aging faster than her face, and they were covered with the ubiquitous liver spots. Would I get them, too?, I wondered, as I pulled off my gloves and looked down at my smooth white hands. Her spotted fingers, covered with an array of rings, fluttered about her face. She arranged her pearl necklace, twisted a jade ring, reset one jade earring and repeated the pattern again. Her watery blue eyes seemed to betray the fear of some kind of discovery. What was she so afraid of? Certainly not of me. The fear in her face was a tenant with a long lease and was not of recent origin.

"Ockie's in the pantry getting something to drink." Surprise again; she called Oscar Hammerstein II "Ockie."

"Won't you sit down, Bawrsha." Her bejeweled hand pointed to a lemon-colored chair. She had a strange arched way of pronouncing my name that took away its soft Slavic quality. When my mother called me Basia, it was like rose petals falling around my ears. There was a loss in the translation, and the name fell awkwardly from foreign lips.

"You're a showgirl, aren't you?"

"Oh, no, I'm a singer."

Didn't Jimmy tell her? There was a great difference between a showgirl and a singer. A singer had more status in the theatrical community. At that very moment, I needed all the status I could get. Having been a showgirl herself, she should have known better. I felt a slight putdown. The idea of fixing her son up with Buffie, the debutante, after she knew he was engaged to me, surfaced on the wave of newly activated resentment.

"Mother, I told you Basia was a singer!" Jimmy interjected.

"She doesn't look like a singer, dear. She looks more like a showgirl. Singers are usually sloppier." She looked me over as I relaxed a bit. I guess it was a compliment to be a showgirl.

"Your name is Bawrsha?" She repeated my name with her strange Americanized pronunciation. "Is that Russian?" Didn't Jimmy tell them anything about me?

"I'm Polish. I was born in Poland, 'Baa-shah' is a diminutive of Barbara. All names in Polish have diminutives. My sister's name is Janina, and we call her Jasia. Stephanie would be Stasia. My mother is called Juzia because her name is Josefa, or in English, Josephine. Anyway, I never liked the name Barbara, so I decided to use Basia when I went into the theater. I want people to know I'm Polish. 'Baa,' as in baa, baa black sheep and 'shah' as in the Shah of Iran. 'Baa-shah.'" I clarified it for her, as I gasped for air.

"Polish, my dear, you're Polish. How wonderful, Bawrsha. Our maids on The Farm are Polish. They raised Jimmy, you know. Mary and Josephine. So Josephine would be called Yooshah. What about Mary? What would you call her in your way?"

"Marisia." I felt stupid, with an uneasy sense of having been put down.

"And my name, Dorothy. What would you call me in Polish?"

I had never heard anyone called Dorothy in Polish and wracked my brain trying to come up with something.

She didn't wait for me to answer, continuing on her own nervous roll. "Wonderful clean women, those two, but is there that much difference between Polish and Russian? I mean it sounds very similar to me, dear." She smiled apologetically at Jimmy.

About as much difference as between the Scots and the English, I felt like adding, knowing that she had Scottish ancestors and would appreciate the subtlety of the difference, but I was determined to keep the peace and kept my mouth shut. Jimmy must have caught the drift, for he gave her a look. She stiffened a bit, drew her head back as if the smell had gotten stronger. As she did so, she revealed yellowing capped teeth with black roots. Interesting, I speculated to myself, to have teeth with black roots. Usually the hair has black roots. Her finely coiffured red hair had snow-white roots. As we struggled to make some civilized contact, her watery eyes took me in. I wished I had

33

ironed my black dress more carefully and brushed my none too black suede pumps more vigorously.

"You're right about Polish women being clean. At least my Mother is. She's also a fine dressmaker," I interjected into the moment of silence.

"Really! How clever of her. What does your father do?"

"He's a mechanic." I wished I somehow could have made that sound more impressive. "He makes airplane parts. He's a tool and die maker. In fact, he's a bit of an inventor. When the war came, he had to go to work for Grumman Aircraft on Long Island. Grumman gave him a medal for helping to design the ejector seat in a new Army jet plane. He wears the medal all the time." He even pins it on his pajamas at night when he goes to bed, I wanted to add, feeling dumb that I had to embellish the importance of my family.

"How marvelous! There's such nobility in working with your hands. I envy people who work with their hands. Your mother's a dressmaker? Do you sew?"

"Why, yes." I again jumped to, and smoothed my dress proudly. "I made this!" I said, showing my dress off to its best advantage.

"How clever of you. It must save you a great deal of money. I wish I could sew." She looked around her lemon-colored bedroom. "I have this dressmaker . . ."

Jimmy was backing out the door. "I think I'll go find Dad." He left the room, followed by the sound of knuckles being cracked as he clacked his way across the landing to the back of the townhouse.

Dorothy lit a cigarette, sat back on her lemon-colored chaise lounge and almost disappeared into her enormous down pillows. Everything in the room matched; her lemon brocade hostess gown matched the lemon-colored rug, which matched the lemon-colored wallpaper, which was the same color as the bowlegged velvet chairs. The rest was white. Stiffly taut snowy organdy curtains stretched across the French doors matched those in the parlor below. White pillows and white sprigs of Baby's Breath floated on the wallpaper, matching the white pearls that hung around her neck.

On every available piece of space, ledge, shelf or table top, arranged according to size and with studied casualness, like soldiers waiting for some command to attack, stood the ubiquitous silver framed pictures. Dozens and dozens of photographs of smiling faces, framed in shining silver, looked back at me. Some I had seen only in magazines. There was one of Mary Martin with her son, Larry Hagman, and a little girl, then another one of Richard Rogers with a thin woman.

The rest must have been family members, but I didn't recognize them. In one, recognizable only by the look of defiance on his face with long arms hanging from a shirt that was much too small for him, was a young Jimmy. He hadn't changed much. Even at that age, he looked uncomfortable, and his clothes didn't fit. I was tempted to pick up the silver frame to get a closer look at his gawky youth, but the other frames were so tightly packed and carefully arranged that I feared my shaking hands would only knock them down.

Dorothy had a portrait of Oscar over the marble fireplace mantle across from the bed and one of herself over the bow-legged dresser. She was very beautiful when her picture was painted some twenty-five years before, yet the eyes had the same look of fear in them, but not with the intensity I saw there now.

"Do you make all your own clothes?" Her voice cut in on my observations as she gazed at me through the smoke drifting around her head. "Or do you also shop?" She expected no answer as she continued. "Susan, my daughter by Henry Sr., my first husband, now married to Hank (Henry Fonda whom I was to meet at a later date), and I, shop with Mahm-boo-shay. We also have garment district connections through Sondheim and some of Ockie's other backers," she explained.

I wracked my brain trying to be with it. Mahm-boo-shay? All the years I spent in the garment center, I never heard of Mahm-boo-shay. Must be foreign, maybe French, I reasoned. She got up and rolled back part of a mirror, revealing a closet that covered the whole wall, from which she removed a finely tailored tweed suit. My years in the garment center and my mother had taught me good tailoring. On

35

the label I saw the imprint, MAINBOCKER. Who pronounced it Mahm-boo-shay? Obviously the cognoscenti, not stupids, like me.

Dorothy's voice continued behind my shoulder. "It doesn't make much sense to buy any other suits than from Mahm-boo-shay, don't you think so?"

I looked at the price tag still dangling from the sleeve. The tweed suit cost one thousand, two hundred and fifty dollars. I spent less than that on my wardrobe for the whole year and not on one suit. Suddenly, I became aware of my homemade basic black dress and wondered if she were trying to tell me something.

"With school and work and all my lessons, I don't have to much time to shop." I tried to make it as simple as I could. She carefully rehung the suit in the closet, in the space neatly provided for it, and rolled the doors shut across the side of the room. The closet disappeared, and the mirrors reflected us again.

As I gave my attention to each piece of furniture, she pointed out its provenance. An eighteenth-century English dresser and the seventeenth-century French chairs were flanked by an "ahmpeer" bed and the candelabra. I made a note to look up "ahmpeer," never having heard of that particular name before.

The sound of voices floated up the stairs. Jimmy came in carrying a glass of port wine for me.

"Is that port, dear?" Dorothy arched her head back.

"Yes, mother."

"But, dear, nobody drinks port before dinner. I mean, we don't drink port . . ."

He handed me the glass of tawny liquid, sticky where it had spilled on the side.

"I know, mother, but Basia likes it." He smiled at me.

Behind Jimmy, hunched up, came the stooped figure of his father. I had seen his face in countless magazines and newspapers, on sheet music and record jackets and even once on television. Before that moment, he had seemed to be a figure out of a fairy tale, and yet there he was, following his son up the stairs with drinks in both hands, a vodka for Dorothy and a glass of white wine for himself. His brown hair was closely cropped, almost shaven, in the shape of those little statues in flower shops that grew green hair and were called "Paddy." His face was not unlike them either, deeply furrowed, with lines around his mouth and across his forehead. The heavy case of acne had not been apparent in his pictures. I could see that the pockmarks went clear down his neck. Both he and Jimmy had receding chins, and it made both of them look a bit like turtles. I wondered if Jimmy would age in the same way. He, too, cropped his hair like his father, but at least his skin was clear and his eyes were a sharper blue.

Oscar was not as handsome as his wife. It was only the women who had to be young and beautiful. Anyway, he could write. His hands were graceful and soft like Jimmy's. As he came over to me, he stooped to peck at the air above my ear. I grew rigid with awe.

"Jimmy told us a lot about you, ah . . . ah."

I wondered how much Jimmy had told them, since Oscar didn't seem to know my name. Dorothy came to his rescue.

"Bawrsha is Polish, dear."

"Ah, yes. Really, what a lovely name. Do you use it professionally?"

Before I could answer, he remarked to Dorothy, "You have a red smudge on your cheek, dear."

She brushed off the lipstick and gave me a look. He then settled down on the lemon-colored couch, while Jimmy cracked all of his knuckles. Then Jimmy cracked his head, whacking it when it wouldn't give. When it finally popped, the crack filled the room like a pistol shot. No one seemed to notice.

Almost soundlessly, a little colored maid in a black outfit with a starched white cap and apron appeared from the landing and nodded to Dorothy, indicating that dinner was ready. We filed down the deeply carpeted staircase to the dark blue of the dining room, brightened by an airy chandelier of blue and gold metal, holding the bulbs of light like flower buds above the table. I paused at the dinner table, surveying the sparkling display of silver and crystal, waiting for Dorothy to sit down. As Oscar pushed her chair forward, she gestured for me to sit on her left.

I had already learned that you have to lean forward as the chair seat is pushed in under you. If you don't wait for it to bump the back of your knees, you can either land on the floor or get a rough push forward. In the process, the table gets jostled as you get a bumpy ride. The men I knew, and especially my father, never pushed a chair in for me or my mother, so I had to watch for the right moment and to rely on my thigh muscles to hold me suspended, then with great dignity finally settle back when the chair was in place. Jimmy, with casual elegance, folded me into my Chippendale chair.

They slipped napkins from silver napkin rings engraved with DHB (Dorothy Blanchard Hammerstein). Then they flicked them neatly across their laps. I did the same. The soundless little colored maid came in and, one by one, removed the plates with Chinese designs on them, leaving in their place simpler white dinner ware. My dinner companions all surveyed their China before it was taken away.

"The lucky person gets the plate with the Chinese figure on it," Dorothy leaned forward and confided to me.

I checked my plate before it was taken away, and there in the center under a pagoda stood a little Chinese man. We smiled at each other, and she nodded, letting me understand that it was some kind of a good omen. I felt relieved.

Another colored maid, this one bigger and rounder, returned with glasses of hot brown broth, in big chunky glasses, glasses in which I usually had highballs. What do I do now? They all picked the glasses up with both hands and drank the beef bouillon as if it were a martini. I followed suit. Oscar gulped his soup down first and sat waiting for us, making a pyramid out of his fingertips. When we had all finished drinking and our squat glasses sat empty, Dorothy rang a little silver bell sitting next to her plate. Oscar arched his eyebrows in surprise and looked at her.

Fear sprang back into her eyes, as she blurted out, "The bell under the table doesn't work, dear. I'm having it fixed."

She pumped her leg up and down on the carpet, but nothing happened. I discreetly craned my neck to see under the table and spotted a button emerging from the dark blue carpet next to her right foot. She kept pressing it. It made no sound. Her hands fluttered to her neck and to her pearls. The watery blue eyes looked stricken. Oscar dismissed her and turned to me.

"You're a singer, aren't you?" I felt presumptuous even to admit that I could sing. He had heard the best singers the theater had to offer. "You must sing for Dick and me one day. We're casting <u>Sweet Thursday</u>."

I wanted to tell him that Feuer and Martin had been preparing me for the part of Suzie, the leading lady in <u>Sweet Thursday</u>, before he and Richard Rodgers bought it from them. I also wondered if the gossip was true that the role of the leading lady had already been cast. It might have sounded like a reproach, so I left it alone.

As I thought of singing for Oscar Hammerstein II, my palms began to sweat, and my heart began to pound. Singing was becoming a burden to me. I wanted to share my soul when I sang, but I naively feared that the sharing of my soul while singing precipitated some kind of sexual turn-on for men. How could I share my soul with the world, bare my passions and not have men grabbing at me?

My thoughts returned to the dinner when I heard Oscar asking me, "Do you have a cold?"

"No, it's the way I always sound. A bit nasal. My whole family sounds this way."

Dorothy's voice cut through my answer. "Dear, I went to see Ben (their doctor) today. I've lost my sense of smell, but he can't seem to find anything wrong." Her voice trailed off.

"What's the matter, Mother?" Jimmy bent toward his mother, apparently concerned.

"I don't know, dear. I can't smell anything."

The small soundless colored maid came back and cleared the soup glasses away. We continued the conversation as if she weren't there.

"It's probably just a cold," Jimmy added.

"Or an allergy. It's pollen season," I ventured, trying to be helpful.

"No, it's not a cold, but I have been very tired lately. The trip to The Farm is very... I mean, it does tire me out."

She shot a reproachful look over to Oscar. He suggested a second opinion, then again turned to me.

"I hear you're going to Hunter College."

"Yes, I'm trying to get my degree." I now felt I was on firmer ground.

"What is it? A master's in Music?"

"Oh, no, I'm not that old." "Younger flesh" jumped into my mind. "It's just my B.A." I felt as though I had disappointed him.

"Oh, my, I thought you were working on your master's." He looked over at Jimmy as Dorothy jumped in.

"Well, then you're not really that much older than Jimmy. We pictured you as some kind of brain or something, working on your master's."

She fumbled for words. "My son Henry is a Phi Beta Kappa."

Oscar shot her a look across the table. I didn't know what to say, so I said nothing.

Oscar turned to me again. "What are you studying, Basia?"

"Philosophy. Primarily philosophy."

"Really? What will a pretty girl like you do with philosophy?"

"Perhaps understand what life is about and what others think it's about." I wondered what being pretty had to do with it.

"Has philosophy helped you to understand what life is about?" His eyes twinkled, and I felt that he was pulling my leg, but I plowed on, determined to explain myself.

"No, all I do is argue with my professors. They seem to miss the point. I'm not quite sure what the point is, but it's not in what they are saying. When I left the Church, I hoped to find a system of values based on human behavior, I mean, what is best in human behavior. I thought I might find some of the answers in philosophy."

"Did you?" Not only were his eyes twinkling, but he was openly smiling.

40

CINDERELLA ❧ AFTER THE BALL OR, JUST KEEP GOING

"No. I just have a sense that the glorified philosophers are all dealing with half a deck."

He laughed, and so did Jimmy. As they remained smiling, they broke their slices of bread into little pieces and buttered each piece individually before popping them into their mouths. While talking philosophy, I had taken my whole piece of bread, spread butter over it, and after I had taken the first bite, I realized that I held the slice of bread, unbroken, up to my mouth. As I held it before me, it felt like a large platter in front of my nose. I put it back on the plate, hoping no one had noticed. No such luck. Dorothy took a deep breath and lifted her head even higher in the air. From then on, all I needed to do was to listen for that sharp intake of breath to know I had committed another <u>faux pas</u>.

The maid returned with an enormous sliver tray filled with chicken and carrots. On either side of the chicken lay a large silver spoon and a large silver fork. I had never maneuvered serving myself from a tray over my left shoulder. The fact that I'm left-handed made the job even harder. With the maid bending over me and the rest of them watching, the chicken kept slipping out of the grip of my fork and spoon. I became wet from perspiration. Finally, I got some carrots and gave up.

"Are you on a diet, Bawrshah?" Dorothy inquired as she deftly piled her plate high with the steaming succulent bird.

"Oh, no! I just don't want to eat too much before the show," I lied.

"I diet all the time," she confided as she smiled, and the black roots of her teeth appeared and disappeared as pieces of chicken vanished behind them.

After she picked up her fork, I, too, started to eat, copying her choice of silver. Gingerly, I nibbled on my carrots, and I was able to spear some lettuce leaves when the salad came around. Jimmy could serve himself deftly, moving both spoon and fork around the chicken, vegetables and salad with one hand. I admired his facility and vowed to master it.

Then the finger bowls arrived. I sat frozen in my seat, waiting for someone to do something. Jimmy did. He took the spoon and fork that flanked the sides of the bowl and laid them neatly on his place mat, if you could call the lace hand-embroidered place settings place mats. Then he picked up the crystal bowl with its individual lace doily and put it before him off the place mat. I followed suit, remembering stories of people who committed a cardinal sin by drinking water from their finger bowls. Jimmy flicked the tips of his fingers in the bowl and then wiped them on his napkin. As a last flourish, he also wiped the corners of his mouth.

Dessert came, strawberries with Devonshire cream that Dorothy had flown over from England. I passed it and then watched them each scoop up the strawberries and dollop them with the cream. Feigning a change of mind, I had some. Watching them gave me some confidence.

Every course seemed to need at least one fork and one spoon. I watched with my stomach grumbling. At home we used small spoons for dessert. We never used forks. Forks were used for cakes and pies. The Hammerstein spoons were as large as the forks, and somehow you had to learn to use both of them at once. You held the strawberry with the fork and then scooped up the fruit and cream with the spoon.

Again Oscar finished first, made a pyramid with his fingertips and waited. It was his way of expressing his impatience with slow eaters. My own father drummed his fingers on the table, lending an accompaniment of sound to his impatience.

We had coffee in the living room, I settled for black, not daring to deal with the tiny filigreed silver spoon that would carry the colored sugar to my cup, or the tiny milk pitcher, which only I seemed to want to use.

Dorothy ventured, "I'm going to give up smoking. Maybe that will help my sense of smell."

Oscar turned to Jimmy. "What have you been doing, son? We haven't heard from you in a long time."

Jimmy cracked his knuckles again, jostling his cup of coffee and blurting out, "Buddy and I have a sport short pre-sold."

42

I looked at Jimmy. He looked away. Oscar slowly nodded his head.

"Really? Pre-sold? With Buddy? Even Dick and I don't have our shows pre-sold."

He turned to me. "We had to hold backers' auditions for <u>Oklahoma</u>." He paused, then said, "But that was when we started." I was grateful for the clarification.

"Yeah, well, we got this guy, and he guarantees us distribution," Jimmy said. "We'll make a cool fifty thou with it."

Oscar again nodded his head slowly. "Why don't you have Howard look at it? Howard is our lawyer." He glanced in my direction. "It's always good to get a solid legal opinion."

"I don't need a solid legal opinion!" Jimmy's voice carried an edge in it. "We have the deal all sewed up."

I looked up at Jimmy, and he again looked away. There was no deal all sewed up, at least no deal that I knew about. My only knowledge of Buddy was that he and Jimmy played squash at the health club. Where I came from, squash was an Italian vegetable, but in America men played it in a gym. Looking across the table, I saw the competition between father and son, suspended like a physical mass between them. As they spoke about Jimmy's deal, I began to realize my future husband's awesome need to impress the "Old Man," as he called his father.

Oscar continued, and a strange ambiguity crept into his voice, as his eyes began to twinkle with shafts of steel. "Sammy Goldstein would get a solid legal opinion from Howard. He wouldn't do anything foolish."

Jimmy became rigid, and his face turned beet red. He dropped his spoon and was about to blurt out something, when the clock on the landing chimed seven-thirty. It broke the mounting tension around the table, and we rose to leave. Eight o'clock was sacrosanct in the theater, and neither of us could be late. I felt a wrench of nerves and hunger in my stomach and wanted to get out of the house as fast as I could. Who was Sammy Goldstein?

Dorothy asked, "Bawrsha, would you like to come to The Farm next weekend? Jimmy?" Jimmy looked deceptively blank.

"I'd love to, but we both work on Saturday," I answered. Jimmy shrugged his shoulders.

"Come up after the show. We'll have the doors left open for you and some of the lights on."

Dorothy busied herself around the coffee tray, stacking cups and saucers for the maid to take away. We were edging toward the staircase.

Oscar turned to Jimmy. "Bring your racquet. We'll have a game of tennis after breakfast."

As we started to descend, my future father-in-law leaned over the railing and whispered to me, "It wasn't so bad after all, was it?"

I smiled back at him and shook my head gratefully. I was still shaking when we got into a cab and raced through the enclosing darkness to our theaters downtown. The street lights lit up our faces in the cab, and I could see the pulse throbbing on the side of Jimmy's jaw. He clenched his teeth, and the line of muscle stood out. As he cracked his knuckles, his hands shook. What had upset him so? Who was Sammy Goldstein? Jimmy made no attempt to answer me when I asked him, so I left it alone.

Outside the theater, I had a hot dog and an orange juice from the umbrella stand on the corner. Upon returning to our dressing room, my friends were dying to hear what had happened and how the dinner went. I extolled the virtues of the cook, the silent efficiency of the maids, Dorothy's beauty and Oscar's regal Lord of the Manor calm. In my exuberance to make it all seem perfect, I left out all the discomfort and tensions that had enveloped us throughout the dinner.

With the meeting of my future in-laws behind me and the possibility of auditioning for Rodgers and Hammerstein ahead of me, I continued in my role as one of the laundresses in <u>Can-Can</u> at night. During the day, I took a bus uptown to Hunter College to earn enough credits to get my B.A. It was hard for me to get all the reading done and to write all my papers, but the biggest problem was to earn enough credits in the required areas in order to graduate. The courses I could take had to fall on Monday and Thursday or on Tuesday and Friday. There could be no classes for me on Wednesday because of the matinee. At all the registration days, with beating heart, I surveyed the offerings in the catalogue, hoping that enough subjects were offered on the days straddling Wednesday so I could fulfill the general requirements.

I felt that the general study of the world's philosophers would not only give me some answers to the questions of "being" that had begun to plague my life but would also provide me with a well-rounded academic education. By the time I got into studying philosophy, I was working in the theater at night because it was one of the few jobs which would leave my days free to pursue my studies. I could also have been a hatcheck girl, but the hours that hatcheck girls had to put in were longer and the nightclubs where they worked hung heavy with smoke, which hurt my voice.

Once I started the round of Broadway shows, the theater bug got to me. Questions about the nature of "being" didn't pay for my lessons or my rent. Singing in Broadway shows did.

Momma kept saying take steno n'typing (it was one word for her), but I had my sights set higher. With philosophy, it was a kind of ambiguous wise sage distributing wisdom. With singing, the thrust became stardom; to star, to shine, to glitter, to break free, to soar, to experience ecstasy and in that soaring to share it with others. When I was offered the part of Suzie in Sweet Thursday and given a job in Can-Can until Sweet Thursday was ready for production, I had begun the climb upward out of the pink contracts and out of the chorus. I felt I was on my way.

After Abe Burrows, one of the writers of Can-Can and Sweet Thursday heard my audition for the show, he said to me, "You have a quality on the stage. I mean, you're great off stage, too, kiddo, but on the stage you have something else. You know, there are the watchers and the ones who are watched. In all relationships there is always one person who does all the watching and the other one who accepts it.

You're one of those people. You're one of the watched. I couldn't take my eyes off you up there. You're a pretty girl and you sing nice, but I'm talking about something else. Lots of broads are gorgeous and have better voices than you, but you have a quality. Boy! If I just didn't get married, you'd be in trouble. It's rare. A kind of glamour and star quality like Dietrich or one of the Gabors."

He laughed. "Anyway, when we get the show together, you'll add a nice touch to Suzie. If not a heart of gold, then a heart of foreign intrigue and glamour. Anyway, kid, the world's your onion. Don't peel it too fast," he added reflectively. And he laughed again as one of his eyes looked over my shoulder and his fat body wobbled around him.

Chapter 3

One's life gets shaken up from time to time. Up to that point, I had great luck when the shaking occurred. When the dust settled, I seemed to end up near the top of the heap every time. It was happening again. There I was at twenty-four, with most of my dreams answered, a year away from my degree, a career in the theater, marriage in the future to my Prince Charming that would bring me safety and security, and protection from the constant and never-ending sexual humiliations from men. No more photographers playing with themselves while taking pictures of me. No more having it put on the line: job and sex; no sex, no job.

Max Kolmer, my boss in the garment center who hired me as a model when I was sixteen, used to say to me, "Honey, all men want is one thing."

And he lifted his eyebrows high up on his forehead so that his eyes popped open. "You know, just one thing. You want to talk philosophy, they'll talk philosophy. You want to go ice skating, they'll take you to Rockefeller Center. You like poetry, they'll compose poems. Anything, just to get you in bed."

On the one hand, he was like my Jewish Dutch Uncle, giving me good advice, having me gather up all the discarded suits and fabrics and letting me schlep them home on the subway for my mother to pack and send off to Poland. On the other hand, he would stand there before me as I modeled one of his suits.

"Good hand-pricking on these lapels," he said. He rolled the "r" in pricking, to be sure I knew what he meant, as his fingers ran up and down the underside of the lapel, brushing my breast as he did so. I would stand there with beads of perspiration gathering on my chin and under my nose, the cigar smoke and smell stirring nausea in me, psychically raped, humiliated, intruded upon, but needing the job to pay for my schooling and my rent, not being able to say anything.

I wouldn't have to put up with that anymore. I'd get married, and no one else would touch me. I'd be Mrs. Hammerstein, a married woman, if not altogether safe, then at least safer. I'd attain social stardom. I'd become a wife, give up my name, my identity and follow my husband, who now sat next to me late at night as we drove through the gentle rolling hills of the Pennsylvania countryside, looking for a road that would take us to The Farm.

He had driven there dozens of times before, but he was so unnerved with me beside him that he got lost. Most of the back roads in Pennsylvania have no signs on them. It took us two hours of driving in circles to find a familiar farm house and then to head west through Bucks County, just this side of Doylestown. At first we confidently followed the double yellow line through the night as it rolled out before us, with the patched-together Austin rattling along. Apple blossom petals flew past our headlights and created a wonderland of snowflakes. We stayed silent, vaguely agitated by our meanderings but enchanted by the beauty of the night. Along the way, the double yellow line changed to a modest single white ribbon, leading us through the dark. Then roads with no lines on them unfurled before us, just dark country roads with the smell of cow manure spilling out from the dark and silent barns that we passed. Jimmy drove in silence, and I wondered what deep thoughts were occupying his mind that he might someday share with me.

One moment we were on a dark country road at three o'clock in the morning, and the next, after a sharp turn to the right, a brilliant white Southern mansion loomed into view and grew larger before us. As we crunched our way up the curving driveway, neatly trimmed, ten-foot-tall privet hedges flanked the sides of the property facing the road. Eastern pines towered over the sprawling colonnaded house, gentle dark giants swaying against the midnight blue of the moonlit sky. Cut white stones of the driveway glistened as our headlights flashed by them and skimmed past the cotton puffs of blooming apple trees on a smooth and shadowed lawn.

We had arrived at Highland Farm, built in 1790 as a farmhouse and expanded over the years by its many subsequent occupants. Oscar had bought it in 1940 to get away from New York City and the possibility of war. He had little faith in air raid shelters and once mused that they should invent a bomb that would spare the buildings and cultural artifacts of civilization but just kill the people. People could be replaced, he continued, but art works and the fine buildings that rose into the sky could not. In time, I came to realize that the antipersonnel bombs of the future would have warmed his heart.

Large white-painted boulders edged the driveway. The equal signs of white fence rails stretched far into the distance to circle the seventy-two acres of rolling fields. The soft mooing of cows and the flutter of newly awakened birds barely disturbed the stillness of the night. Jimmy flicked the ignition switch off, and the beams of light disappeared. We sat in the darkness getting accustomed to the eerie shadows cast by the great lunar disc. The whole setting reminded me of motion pictures I had seen in my youth. Still, dark enchantment surrounded us, lit by a round silvery moon. Only the wreck of Jimmy's car didn't belong to that close-cropped, neatly traced pristine perfection.

After we had folded ourselves and our baggage out of the old Austin, Jimmy gave the jalopy a kick, and it crunched its way down the gravel path, coming to a stop against a log under a massive canopy of blooming apple trees. Later I learned that Arnie, the family chauffeur, always washed it in the morning and applied duct tape and new ropes to keep the doors from swinging open.

As we stumbled our way through the dark, kicking up the gravel on our way to the veranda, Jimmy in his sneakers and I in my high-heeled shoes, I valiantly lugged one of those large round patent leather hat boxes that were "in" with all the models in town. With it, I felt chic and ready for the weekend.

As we approached the house, a dark shape stirred on the veranda between the columns in front of the main door. It growled as we plowed on. The moon caught the gleam of white teeth. Jimmy bent forward.

"Luther, it's me, Jimmy!" Another growl. "Come on, Luther, get out of the way and let me open the door!" The growl got louder. I moved back behind my husband-to-be and protector.

"I don't think you should go near him."

"Nonsense. Luther never bit anyone in his life."

"Well, there's going to be a first in Luther's life tonight."

As Jimmy moved toward the door, Luther snarled, and the hair on his back bristled in the moonlight. The shadow stretched taller. We decided to find another door and moved around the house, trying all the windows and yanking at all the patio doors. Everything was tightly secured.

"What kind of a dog is that?" I asked Jimmy, pointing at the growling dark mass.

"He's a Standard Poodle."

"But he looks bigger than a Standard Poodle," I insisted.

"We don't cut his hair. He doesn't like it."

"Does he like anything? Whey do you call him Luther? After Martin Luther?"

"No," Jimmy said, laughing. "After Luther Billis in South Pacific."

The back of the house had a patio facing a glistening pool, guarded over not only by Luther but by two enormous white metal swans. My eyes lingered on them, and I wondered if water lilies floated in the pool. Of course not! Don't be silly. Lilies and white swans floated only in the fairy tales of my youth. We circled around to the front, just in time to see Luther's massive bulk loping away in the distance, probably chasing a stray rabbit. Jimmy tried the door. Luther need not have guarded it with such ferocity; it was locked anyway.

"What do we do now?" I looked at Jimmy, vaguely discomforted by the situation.

"Throw pebbles up to the maids' window. That'll wake them," he answered, obviously having done that before. "Uppy-duppy!" he yelled up to one of the dark windows as he flung the first pebble. It was a curious welcome to find ourselves locked out on our first visit to The Farm together. After a few more rocks bounced off the glass pane above, a light flashed on.

"I'll be right down!" came from the air above us. The voice had the strange familiar Polish catch to it. As the maid descended down the stairs to let us in, the darkness of the house became illuminated by lights that followed her journey toward us. A little lady with dark brown hair in curlers and a round face opened the door. We were momentarily blinded by the brilliant lights of the foyer. She apologized for her curlers and her bathrobe and pumped the hand of the enormous boy she had raised.

"Hello, Master Jimmy! How are you? My, you look well!"

"Mary, this is Basia."

"Ah, Miss Basia, you're Polish too. My, you're a pretty girl. Did you have a nice trip? Are you hungry? I have some lovely cold roast beef and some salad. Would you like to have some?"

We both nodded. As she chattered on to Jimmy, I surveyed the splendor of the lush interior. We stood practically knee deep in crimson carpet. The shining furniture in the dimly lit room to the right contained English antiques with touches of gilt, like those in the New York City townhouse. The foyer in which we stood had a busy wallpaper of trailing fuchsias. There was a throw rug on the floor that was woven in a pattern to match the wallpaper. In one corner of the foyer stood a brass baker's stand filled with real live blooming fuchsia plants.

We passed through the dining room containing a highly polished mahogany table reflecting a gleaming silver candelabra. It was a large room, and the table filled most of the area. It could have sat a dozen people and even more, when on holidays it became extended. I slipped along the sparkling shiny floor, past the starched organdy curtains,

51

and through the white swinging door of the gleaming kitchen.

My mother may have been neat and clean, but the rooms we lived in reflected their purpose. At The Farm you really couldn't tell that it was a kitchen because all of the utensils and cooking apparatus were out of the way, out of sight. The kitchen was just a beautiful gleaming white room with butcher-block counters and banks of highly polished silver trays. Black marble Grecian busts, which in profile looked a lot like Dorothy, stood on carved pedestals. Ivy plants cascaded down the walls forming dark green waterfalls. The white wallpaper fluttered with pale blue butterflies. They also fluttered pale blue on the crisp organdy curtains.

Mary took out the roast beef and in a few seconds had a small meal ready for us. Jimmy rummaged under the counter for his favorite mustard and soon found it.

"Have you ever tried Bahamian mustard?" He waved the tawny bottle at me.

"No." I shook my head.

"Here, have some."

I spread it on the cold beef. Oh, my! The mustard had a rich sweet taste and heightened the flavor of the beef. I savored the cold pungent sandwich and the still colder glass of milk. Mary peeled away the cover to a large plastic box. A series of bowls and berries appeared: purple blueberries, crimson strawberries and red raspberries, swimming in their own juices. We wolfed them down, thanked her and helped her to clean up the kitchen, returning it to its pristine, apparently untouched state.

I picked up my round plastic hat box, and we tiptoed past the second floor where Jimmy's parents slept. The crimson carpet on the second floor landing was replaced by teal green. On the third floor, we found handwritten notes pinned to two tiny attic doors. One had "Baschia" on it; the other had "Jimmy." So they knew we were coming. Then why didn't they leave the downstairs door open?

Jimmy had to duck to get into his room and, as always, bumped his head. The old-fashioned four-poster had been his bed when he was small. Now it seemed too short for him. We again entered a lepi-dopteran room, with butterflies fluttering on all the walls, on organ-dy curtains and, arrested in their flight, on the lamp shades. I later learned that Dorothy was in her butterfly period.

Jimmy's half-sister, Susan (Dorothy's daughter from her first marriage), who came to visit her mother one weekend, after seeing all the fluttering butterflies and the large Japanese paper butterfly on the lawn with its movable crepe wings, remarked in her understated manner, "It takes a heap of living to make a house a home!"

My tall intended looked out of place in the frilly room. When he stripped to his boxer shorts and got into bed, his long legs and big feet hung over the edge. I tiptoed over to the pink room where I was to spend the night. There I was confronted with more frilly curtains and bedspreads, more butterflies and a pitcher of cold water. A bookshelf in the corner held a set of Pollyanna books.

The bed was covered with lacy pillows and a lacy bedspread. Un-derneath all that starched lace, stark in its inhospitality, was a bare bed, no sheets or blankets, just a mattress covered with a mattress pad. I had brought a cotton robe with me and realized that it had to be my salvation for the night. I had never been away from home for a weekend before and was at a loss. Did I have to make my own bed? Then where was the bedding? The room looked unlived in and unused. What to do? I shuddered in the chilly night air. A hot bath seemed like a good idea. I put some of my Abano Oil into the water. As the heavy rich sweet scent filled the room, I began to feel more comfortable.

There were no towels in the bathroom, only those little embroi-dered doily things that clung to the wall for show and which were never, never to be used. Even the butterflies on them looked at me with disdain. The only thing in the bathroom remotely possible to use with which to dry myself was the toilet paper. After I soaked myself in the hot water, I dried my oily flesh with miles and miles of toilet pa-per, which stuck to my wet skin and remained in soggy tatters all over my body. I blotted myself and peeled them off, flushing them down the toilet, freezing in the cold, damp bathroom, waiting until the tank filled up, so I could flush new wads of wet separating paper down the drain. Then into the comfort of my familiar nightgown, with my robe over me and no sheets or pillowcases under me, although chilly, I slept the sleep of the innocent.

The next morning, Mary, the Polish maid, who had let us in the night before knocked on the door and asked me if I wanted breakfast in bed. Through the closed door I asked her, "Where is Jimmy having his?"

She informed me that he had already eaten and was playing tennis with his father. It was barely nine o'clock, and I had hoped to share our first meal at The Farm together. I settled for breakfast at the tiny wicker table in front of the windows. Before Mary returned with the tray, I put the room in order and made the bed. On opening the closet in the hall, I found a stand holding sheets and towels. They should have been out, I thought. The bed should have been made. The towels should have been hung in the bathroom. Jimmy's bed was made; why wasn't mine? Names were pinned to the doors to make sure we didn't sleep together. The maids must have known I was coming. Didn't Dorothy tell them? Then why the full pitcher of water? Maybe it had been left over from the last occupant. I smelled it. It had that stale old smell of standing water. I realized the maids had not been told that Jimmy was bringing his bride-to-be to the family home that weekend.

Breakfast was an elegant affair with scrambled eggs made with the mustard I had tasted the night before, giving the eggs a slightly sweet spicy flavor. Toast was secreted in a covered silver dish. Jam came in a crystal jar. Hot coffee flowed from a silver pot. No colored sugar here, just white crystals in a tiny silver bowl with a tiny silver spoon. After finishing my breakfast, I brought the tray downstairs into the kitchen and was gently rebuked for having done so, by Mary. She apologized for not having prepared the bed. A terrible oversight. She seemed embarrassed. I cheerfully assured her that it hadn't been a problem, as the memory of all that sticky wet toilet paper separating in shreds over my cold, wet body flushed over my skin.

From the front of the house came the sound of popping balls. Jimmy and his father were having their game of tennis. I wondered what to do, so I went back upstairs and knocked on Dorothy's door. Her voice summoned me to enter. In the city, her bedroom had been lemon-colored. In the country, it was purple with touches of pink. The purple carpet flowed under the purple chaise lounge that was aflutter with pink butterflies. The same pattern was echoed on the walls. The highly polished tables were again covered with neatly arranged silver frames. Dorothy's writing desk of inlaid wood, edged in brass, was covered with mounds of letters in the process of being answered. The four-poster bed with its canopy and curtains was filled with organdy-covered pillows and flanked by the same bowlegged dressers as the ones at the townhouse in New York City. Over them hung portraits of Victoria and Albert, instead of Dorothy and Oscar, king and queen of another era.

Should I sit on the chaise lounge? It looked unused. It would never do to perch on the edge of her bed. So without making a commitment as to place, I began to inspect the photographs in their frames. The faces in the photographs at The Farm were less famous than the group in the New York townhouse. One simple frame contained a much younger Dorothy with her two small children, Susan and Henry, from her first marriage. On the other side, in a more ornate frame, stood Oscar with his two children by his former wife, "Mike" (Myra). Then, in the center, in a wider display, was the whole family looking awkward, with the children sullen and the parents gazing out hopefully.

My father had lined us up against the wall almost every Sunday when we lived in Jamaica, Long Island, grabbing any unsuspecting passerby to snap our pictures. In our family album, not unlike the pictures I was inspecting in Dorothy's bedroom, all those posed family pictures seemed to look alike: uncomfortable and strained.

The bathroom door opened, and the reigning lady of the manor, preceded by a glorious perfume, swept out in her starched organdy peignoir. It looked like a summer bathrobe to me, but she called it a peignoir, as she apologized for being in it, and not fully dressed. Without her make-up, she looked softer and less imposing. She rolled back another mirrored wall and selected her attire for the day. The whole outfit hung on one hanger: pink slacks, covered by a pink blouse under a pink sweater. Pink loafers neatly pointing forward, waiting to move on command, stood beneath them.

How I envied having everything that matched. When we came to America, it was a Spring ritual that every Easter we were fitted for a new outfit. Momma would usually buy navy blue material and make my sister and me matching suits and white blouses with white lace on the cuffs and collars. Sometimes we got a pair of shoes that matched the newly made suits. If we were lucky, a pocketbook and gloves completed the picture.

We went to church on Easter Sunday to show off our finery. All the kids in the neighborhood came with their matching outfits, all sparkling and clean. As I got older, I refused to wear homemade clothes. It smacked too much of the old country. Factory-made outfits were the rage. My mother stopped sewing them for me, and I had to pay for my subsequent wardrobes. It became a problem to get the whole outfit to match at the same time. If you got the shoes, then you had to wait for the pocketbook. By the time you got the pocketbook, the shoes were no longer new, your feet grew, the old foot wear needed to be replaced. To go to church, we had to have a hat, which took most of the available money. We saved on that, too, hunting through the fashion magazines and buying the straw shells. Roses, ribbons and veils, added in stages, saved on the cost. No matter how diligently we put those Easter hats together, they never looked as good as the ones in the magazines.

Before my eyes hung Dorothy Hammerstein's outfits, all lined up in the closet and all matching. Even the skirts had their own matching blouses and sweaters. She didn't have to interchange them with the slacks. She just took the hanger out of the closet, and everything hung there for her to enjoy. Even the expectant shoes looked new and barely used.

"Jim Boy told me I forgot to leave the door open for you. I am sorry. I forgot you were coming this particular weekend, time goes by so quickly, but I did remember to put your names on the doors, didn't I?" she contradicted herself. "Did you sleep well?"

As she leveled her gaze at me waiting for an answer, I realized that their master bathroom was directly under my guest bathroom on the floor above. They must have heard me flushing all that toilet paper with which I had dried myself the night before. There was no way comfortably to explain what had happened, so as the discomfort spread through me, I looked away.

"This is a lovely home. Jimmy calls it The Farm, but it looks more like a Southern mansion."

Since I was standing close to the fireplace, my eyes rested on a purple candle holder, "This is a very pretty candlestick." I nodded in appreciation.

"Yes, it is a nice house. We had to do a great deal of work on it. Did you see the porch around the second story?"

I nodded. It framed the gleaming windows in the moonlight. "Well, I had it built for Ockie for his birthday. He likes to walk around the house when he writes. And this, oh, my!", she fingered the candlestick, "is an old Polish heirloom, this candelabra. Imagine that! I bought it at an auction in New Hope, from the estate of a defunct Polish countess. Of course, our <u>home</u> is in town; this is just a nice <u>house</u>. Ockie likes it. He writes better here." Her voice underlined the difference between <u>house</u> and <u>home</u>.

"We bought it in, when was it? 1940? Yes, 1940 or '41. Anyway, we were looking for a place where we could grow our own food during the war. They said there would be rationing, so we decided to get a working farm. As we drove up the hill I saw a rainbow over the house and knew that it was a good omen. So we bought it, and Ockie's been writing here ever since."

It surprised me to hear that she saw a rainbow over The Farm. It seemed to me as if a swarm of butterflies had pinned her to the spot.

"Would you like me to leave the room while you dress? I'll go and watch Jimmy play tennis."

"Oh, no, I don't mind, I'll use my dressing room. Do you play?"

"No, I don't."

"Didn't they teach it at your school when you were a child? It's best to learn these things when you're young," she added.

"No, the only games I learned were 'Hide-and-Seek,' 'Ring-a-le-vio' and 'Kick-the-Can.'"

"'Kick-the-Can'? I never heard of that game. Is it a group game or a partners game?"

"I guess group. You play it in the street . . ."

"Isn't that dangerous?"

"Yes, I guess so, but when you're a kid, you don't care too much. You learn to duck between the cars. It's part of the game. One of the kids kicks the can . . ."

"A can?" She seemed incredulous.

"Yes, an empty tin can . . ." I continued to enlighten her.

"Was this taught in the schools? I mean, did they let you play in the streets?"

"No, we played 'Farmer-in-the-Dell' in the school yard. After school we got the kids together and played a game of 'Kick-the-Can' in the street."

"Was this an underprivileged area?" She seemed to grow a bit straighter as she asked me the question.

"I guess that's what they call it now." I realized I had gone too far and let her know too much, too soon. "It was just an area of tenements, houses strung out along the sidewalks, with backyards running the length of the block behind them."

"God must love poor people," she chuckled.

"Why is that?" I bit at the bait.

"Because he made so many of them." She laughed heartily, exposing the black roots under her white caps. "Poverty must be so ennobling."

This time I baited her. "Why is that?"

"Because it's so good to work with your hands." She repeated the observation she had made before at our dinner in town. "Very ennobling . . ." She inspected her spotted hands before whisking them out of sight. The subject needed changing.

"Does Jimmy get up this early every time he comes here?" I asked.

"Only when he has a game of tennis with Ockie." She stood before me, resplendent in pink, with her red hair brushed softly around her face.

"I was hoping to have breakfast with him this morning."

"My dear," she leaned conspiratorially over to me, "tennis is the only thing besides chess at which Jim Boy beats Ockie. He <u>never</u> misses a chance to do so, even sometimes at the cost of breckie."

"He competes with his father?"

I had seen a touch of it at the dinner in town, but the idea still seemed preposterous to me. How could you compete with Oscar Hammerstein II at anything, even if you were his son?

"Oh, yes, he never misses a chance," Dorothy assured me.

"I mean, does he ever win?"

"Now that Ockie's getting older, Jim Boy is getting his licks in." I wondered if she used the colloquialism for my benefit.

"Is Sammy Goldstein a friend of Jimmy's? I never heard him speak of Sammy." My curiosity surfaced with the question and the memory of Jimmy's silent and painful discomfort when we had dinner with them at the town house the week before.

"Oh, no," she laughed. "Sammy Goldstein is a fictitious friend that Ockie invented for Jimmy. He calls on him whenever he wants Jim Boy to do better. It gives him an image of perfection to aspire to. It's a joke that Ockie plays on him. He's been doing it ever since Jimmy was a little boy. You know, 'funzies' at the dinner table."

She chuckled. I wondered if she had ever looked at her son when her husband brought Sammy Goldstein into the picture. Why would Jimmy need Sammy Goldstein as an image of perfection to aspire to? Wasn't Oscar impressive enough?

"Did Jimmy ever do anything on the creative side?" I tentatively inquired, for I had read a short story he had written about himself and Bob Fortier, a skin-diving friend of his, and knew he played a kind of loud and indifferent piano, but nothing more than that.

"He studied music at Chapel Hill in North Carolina, but he made such a racket on the piano when he visited home that I asked him to stop, especially when he played those modern composers. You know Strinberg, and those others . . ." She searched for some names.

"Poulanc?" I ventured, ever helpful.

"Yes, something like that." Jimmy had played some Stravinsky for me and grew pensive as he recalled how his mother had yelled for him to stop the noise. The modern composers were the only ones with whom he felt any affinity. He had never again played the piano at home, taking it up again only when he had moved out on his own.

"It must be very difficult to have a famous man for a father," I interjected. She bristled a bit at my observation and got somewhat defensive, as if she thought so, too, but wouldn't let on.

"I would think that it would be marvelous. It's not as though Ockie was a drunk or a criminal or something." Her hands fluttered around her face. She sounded like my mother. Anything short of criminal behavior and alcoholism was acceptable in a husband or a father. You could ignore all the rest of the stuff, if he didn't drink, beat you up, or kill people. As my mother never got tired of repeating, "Poppa not drunkard, he not kill people, he your father."

"How can you compete with a father like Oscar? I mean, how can a son overcome that?" I wondered what the repercussions of that competition were, on a deeper less apparent level.

"I think it's a wonderful thing for a son to copy his father. Why, Jim Boy even walks like Ockie."

"Yes, I noticed. He stoops over."

"Well, Ockie loved baseball when he was young, and his favorite baseball player stooped over, so he copied him. Now both of his sons do it, too."

"It's a shame that Jimmy didn't pick another area in which to excel, and not the theater. Why did his father offer him a job in a show even before he finished college?"

"Well, he didn't really offer it to him directly. Ockie called Jim Boy when he was half-way through college to ask him if he had any friends who would like to work as third assistant stage manager on the revival of Music in the Air. Jim Boy jumped at the chance."

A strange coincidence surfaced with her remark. My first small part in a bona fide legitimate show had been as Marthe, the secretary to Ernst, in Music in the Air in summer stock in Hyannis, Massachusetts. I sang the closing bars of a song that ended the first act, "Egern on the Tegern See." At the time, the fact that Oscar Hammerstein II wrote the lyrics to this show meant little to me. I marvelled that the show had been a springboard for Jimmy also. We shared something. We had something in common. I felt a wave of affection for my husband-to-be. Dorothy stopped for a second and listened to the sound of popping balls in front of the house.

"He has been a fine tennis player. He could have been a pro," she continued. At least I didn't have to ask her what pro meant. Out of my Eastern European roots, it seemed strange to me that a grown man could make a career not only out of sports, but also out of chasing a ball around a court. So that's how Jimmy got into the theater. His Old Man, as he called him, offered the job generally. Jimmy jumped at it specifically.

"Does he ever discuss with you what he would like to do?" She barely touched me with the question. Her inquiry hung tentatively suspended in the air between us.

Feeling on safer ground, I plunged in. "Well, right now he wants to produce a record with all kinds of different sports people, like announcers and baseball players doing and saying memorable things. He has a partner, and they seem to be working on that. I don't know; I don't see him much during the day."

I flushed crimson because the statement left an implication that I saw him only at night. Other than taking a louder than usual gasp of air, my future mother-in-law made no comment.

"Who is this partner of his? What kind of a boy is he?"

"I don't really know. His name is Buddy. He sweats a lot, and he shaves his balding head."

"Yul Brynner shaves his head bald, and he's quite attractive, in a foreign kind of way," she confided.

I picked up the cue. "Buddy makes me feel vaguely uncomfortable when I'm around him."

What a strange statement to make to her, I thought. Since I stumbled into Jimmy's life at Ray's Diner, I had been uncomfortable with most of the people I had met through him. As I rambled on internally, Dorothy kept the conversation afloat externally by going off on a slight tangent.

"Oscar doesn't really have any close friends. Maybe some old cronies like Milton and Harold, but they've never come between us. We've always had each other."

She leaned over and looked at me as levelly as her watery eyes could manage. "I hope you have the same kind of marriage that I've had with Ockie. I could wish you no more with my son."

We smiled at each other. A tentative bond had become established. She picked up her glasses and the <u>Times</u> crossword puzzle. The conversation was over. The newly established bond sagged somewhat. I followed her down the silent carpeted stairs. Lord Nelson prints stared down at us as we moved past the fuchsia foyer and into the parlor. She settled into one of the voluminous crimson couches. I headed through the sun-filled foyer out into the open air.

Following the sound of popping tennis balls, I pushed my loafers through the still damp grass to the tennis courts. They were sheltered from the house by a natural drop in the land, which was framed by a rock garden filled with daffodils and tulips. Huge hemlocks hid the barn from view. Closely cropped yews camouflaged the farmer's and caretaker's house.

I waved to Jimmy and his father. They waved back and started another set of tennis. The shade of the huge beach umbrella flanking the court still held the chill of the night. I moved out from under it to enjoy the gently warming spring sun. The apple trees that looked like giant cream puffs in the moonlight the night before now hummed with bees. Beyond the apple trees, the giant pines swayed, spreading their scent and murmur out upon the gentle wind.

Chapter 4

My education in the streets of Jersey City or South Jamaica in Queens may have given me street smarts but didn't offer courses in tennis or the finer points of etiquette, so after watching the players for a while, I decided to explore The Farm. The Black Angus were mooing in the field. I passed a stand of lilacs and climbed the fence to watch the peaceful herd. Here I was in Bucks County, and there was the ever present Spring mud. The cows plodded slowly through it, their hooves disappearing in its softness.

A solitary bull stood in the distance protecting his harem, threatening the veil of peace. Memories of another bull in Poland came flooding back to me. I remembered the way that ancient icon had chased me, when I inadvertently made a shortcut through his domain. My fear of those horns and the hooves pawing at the ground behind his fence always quickened my step as I ran faster and faster. Then came the stifling panic that the fence wouldn't hold him. The memory turned into dreams of running away from him, across the fields and up circular staircases which ultimately had nothing to do with the field in which the bull stood glaring at me with lowered head and blazing eye.

How I hated to pass that field every day on my way to the little private school where Momma sent us. I never knew how she prevailed upon my father to pay for the tuition. She must have appealed to his sense of self importance and his need to impress the neighbors.

The stocky black bull was there again, the nemesis of my youth, lowering his head and slowly, deliberately pawing the ground. Like a locomotive building up steam, his snout exploded with an occasional vapor-filled snort. I had no intention of invading his territory, until I saw a glimmer of water in the distance and realized that a brook flowed at the bottom of the sloping field, in between a line of trees.

The look and sound of water have always been like a magnet for me. Carefully keeping the bull in my field of vision, I took off along the fence and edged my way down to the shimmer of water. The peaceful herd of black cows stirred as they saw me move along the fence. Their square bodies grew a bit restless and swayed on their short tapered legs. The bull lowered his head even more, carefully watching me. After getting my loafers stuck in the mud, I finally reached the bottom of the field. Under the trees, the brook flowed gently by, with the same movement, as when I was smaller and my eyes were much nearer to the ground.

It wasn't until I got very close that I realized how much damage the cattle had done to their watering hole. The newly sprouting green plants had been crushed under the repeated pounding of heavy hooves. The trees were stripped of bark. Young birch saplings, their trunks shining and bare, trailed their still green leafy branches in the stream. In dismay I looked around. I should have stayed away. It looked better from the distance. I made my way up the muddy bank and edged carefully back along the whitewashed fence that powdered my slacks with chalk. The cows and the pawing bull had moved down the slope away from me. At the servants entrance to the main house, I took off my muddy loafers and made my way up the back stairs to clean up and to wait for lunch.

What had I expected down there by the brook? Some of the same kind of joy that had filled me when I was a small child? I was feeling less and less of that fresh and exuberant wonder. With sadness, I tried to figure out where it had gone. Was this what growing up meant? Was the brutalization of a sensitive spirit synonymous with maturity? Was this what facing reality meant? A world without joy or ecstasy, a world devoid of wonder? I shuddered at the thought and saw an abyss yawning before me, an abyss which I hoped my impending marriage, with its promise of love and affection, would deflect.

The wonder of Spring in the country, how I missed it when we left Poland. It seemed like ages ago, but in reality only fourteen years had passed. There I was, after the tin-can-filled lots of Jersey City, the muck-filled back waters of Bayonne, the riot-prone streets of South Jamaica, Long Island, the fetid subways of New York, and the panhandling bums in Union Square. How I missed the trees, the flowers and the rolling fields ending along the horizon in dark swaths of forest. There I was after all those years of endless narrow staircases in crowded tenements, enjoying the simplicity of the natural life, out in the open, in the sun, among the sounds of birds and bees and the murmuring pines, punctuated by the popping of tennis balls. It took a great deal of money to create such simplicity. In Poland, only the poor lived in the country. In New York City, only the rich could afford to do so.

In Poland, Spring was a season of drying off. The melting snows of winter brought mud oozing out from under the hooves of horses and wheels of carts, leaving deep ruts that ultimately dried and left long crusty trenches along the road. After each warming rain, I loved to squish my way through that yielding mud, plopping each buckled galosh in and out of the muck. It usually took me an hour to get to school. I inspected tadpole eggs trembling under the melting water in the brook. The long streams of yellow duck flowers bobbed up and down on the gently meandering current that trailed behind me, as I stuffed their golden faces into my pockets. I picked bunches of white and lavender violets. I marveled at the muddy underside of newly green moss that revealed scampering brown insects and an occasional tiny red spider. The rocks and beetles, flowers and snails that filled my pockets caused my mother to throw her hands up in despair. The perplexed shaking of her head never dampened my ardor at the discoveries I made on my way to school each day, across the railroad tracks and past the deep dark, pine forest.

66

I had a favorite place in the field a mile or so beyond the house, past the lake and the winding stream. Two small hills came together and formed a depressed triangle. Each Spring the melting snow transformed the area into a shimmering lake, flooding the moss that lay like a carpet on the bottom. I saw kingdoms reflected in those waters, other lands that I could only dream about, places that existed only in the fairy tales read to me by Momma.

As I searched for swans and for water lilies, bugs skimmed across the surface of the still pond and frogs burped on the edges and plopped into the reflected sky below, shattering its mirrored stillness. I felt myself part of it, a fairy child, wedded to it all by my wonder. If I sat still long enough, the white stork flopped by, his feathers tipped yellow with age. After arranging his wings around his body, he joined me in my vigil. I'd sit as still as the boulders around me and watch him as he stood with one leg bent under him, balancing on the other, all the time keeping a wary eye on the frogs leaping around him. Then, with the flash of his red beak slicing the air, the frog was gone, leaving a wriggling lump slowly descending down the stork's skinny neck. My heart ached for the frog, but I sat there transfixed, warily watching, as silent as the stones.

Chapter 5

Jimmy and his father were breathless from their game when they arrived back at the house for lunch. My intended had won, and the Old Man was scowling. Lunch around the shining oval dining room table was a simple affair of cold beef, the final destination of the Black Angus who were now munching their way across the fields, oblivious of their fate. Salad accompanied the main course, followed by fresh fruit. I used the silver spoon from the sugar bowl to stir my coffee. <u>A major no-no!</u> As it touched the hot brown liquid, I stiffened at the intake of breath that came from across the table. With deliberation, I dried the spoon with my napkin and placed it carefully back in the bowl, wedging it straight up in the sugar, like a flag on a white sand dune.

After lunch, Jimmy left to play another set of tennis with people who came from a neighboring farm. Oscar invited me to join him upstairs in his study. The Polish maids soundlessly cleaned off the table. I pattered up the stairs behind him, shaking whenever I had to speak to him. Every time I wanted to sound erudite and tried to impress him, I felt awkward, impatient at my need to do so.

I remembered the time Jimmy took me to the ballet. The program stated that what we were about to see was a "<u>pas de deux</u>." I tried to impress him by saying how delighted I was that a light piece was coming up.

"How's that?" he inquired.

"Well, it must be a light piece, since the title implies that it's about just passing the day. You know. 'Pas de deux,'" pass the day?" He laughed so hard that spittle formed on the corners of his mouth. People sitting in the seats around us turned around to shush him.

In Oscar's case, I tried even harder, but I was much more careful with foreign words.

My future father-in-law opened the door to his study and asked me in. The view through the windows fell upon softly rolling green hills of Pennsylvania with the blue sky meeting the far line of dark trees. One of the fields was planted with corn that one day would be "as high as an elephant's eye," a line he may have written while looking out of his second-story window.

On one of the walls, a framed <u>Time</u> magazine cover caught my eye. There was Oscar holding his head with his hands as if the hits he had created had also amazed him. He had gotten the cover in 1947 and the artist who painted him for <u>Time</u> had been kind to him. None of his pockmarks showed. Hanging next to the picture was the <u>Time</u> magazine article. It extolled the "New Look" that he and Richard Rodgers brought to musical comedy. Since he and Richard Rodgers were partners, I wondered how the musical half of the partnership felt about being left off the <u>Time</u> cover.

In Oscar's study, I stood surrounded by awards and plaques. His output was prodigious and overwhelming. Something else nagged at me. I wanted to know how the process of creativity affected him. Was he covered by goose pimples every time a beautiful rhyme flowed onto the paper from his pen? Was he transfixed with joy when he wrote his lyrics? How was it with him? I groped for words to express what I wanted to ask him, feeling awkward at revealing the passions that creativity awoke in me.

"Do you wait to be inspired, or does Mr. Rodgers give you a melody to work with first?" I plunged my oars into the water through which I wanted to navigate.

"Oh, no, I never wait to be inspired. Usually I write the lyric first; then Dick writes the melody. Inspiration is a tricky, overrated business. A 'dairy' business, as Jimmy would say."

Jimmy made that remark many years before when he was a little boy, after Oscar declined to float a loan for a chicken-growing operation. He called it a "dairy business," meaning "daring business." The family thought it charming and subsequently used it as a phrase describing a perilous undertaking.

"You can't wait for inspiration," Oscar continued. "They're right, you know, when they say it's ninety percent perspiration and ten percent inspiration. You have to get the seat of your pants into a chair, or at least you have to face the problem and gather your thoughts in trying to solve it. The muse is unpredictable. In trying to solve the problem, you have to make yourself receptive to an answer. You have to focus on what you want to say. Then it starts coming through." He paused.

I jumped in. "What is it that you tune into?"

"I don't know, but something always comes through. The chances of good ideas to get through are better when you are trying to get them. If you don't make yourself available, if you don't try, then even if they come through, you might not be there for them."

I still wondered how he <u>felt</u> when he wrote. "How do you contain your feelings when you write?" I was almost embarrassed to ask him the question. He looked surprised.

"I get a great deal of satisfaction when a song is right and works, but I'm not overwhelmed by my feelings when I write. You sound like a bit of a romantic." He smiled at my naivete. As I blushed, he continued. "See, I do the trying and the thinking; the audience does the feeling. What I try to do is to establish a presence of intangibility that touches some deeper core than thought."

"Emotion?" I wanted to stay on the track.

"Yes, perhaps emotion, that sense of fresh discovery all of us yearn for. The possibility of always discovering something new."

"A cockeyed optimist?" We both laughed. "Does writing make you cry?" He looked at me as if I were crazy. His eyebrows arched up into the furrows of his forehead.

"Do sad songs make you cry?" I pushed on. He looked vaguely uncomfortable and rearranged some papers at the lectern at which he stood while writing. I was apparently treading on an area of "intangibility." My sense of curiosity was greater than my sense of caution.

"No, I never cry out of sadness. I don't allow it. It's maudlin, sentimental, an indulgence. If I've ever cried over a lyric, it's more because it awoke in me a sense of..." He looked up to find the appropriate word and then presented it with a grace born of confidence, "Naive happiness. Like 'Surrey with the Fringe on Top.' That song makes me cry every time I hear it. It's one of my favorite lyrics."

I wracked my brain trying to remember the words to that <u>Oklahoma!</u> standard, but memory failed me and didn't rekindle memories of aching sadness that my beloved Polish melodies evoked in me.

He continued. "Writing lyrics is hard work, a craft. I love it. It's my job. All you can do is the best you can. Certainly you can never be careless with your art." I listened avidly.

"You can't be sloppy. You have to be very careful, or you may be found out."

His eyes twinkled, and he grew conspiratorial, as if he were telling me a secret. He even leaned forward toward me. "I remember once I saw a picture of the Statue of Liberty in a Sunday magazine section. It was obviously taken from a helicopter and showed the top of her head. Every hair on Miss Liberty was in place. Now, the man who made her must have been a great artist. Except for some seagulls or migratory birds, he knew that no one would see the top of her head once the statue was in place. That made no difference to him. He made it perfect. He was right, of course. Years later when they invented the helicopter, everyone would have seen his cover-up. Had he been sloppy, he would have been found out."

He leaned back away from me. "I never forgot that picture. It taught me a great lesson. You can't be careless with your art."

His words resonated in me, and I understood what he was saying. The psychological dogma of the day was that perfectionism was obsessive and neurotic. Freudian analysts called it anal behavior. I looked at my future father-in-law, not only with awe, but with respect, based on commiseration. I, too, had a sense of perfectionism and felt a growing affection toward him for sharing his thoughts about it with me.

But where was the passion of creativity? Was it all a mental exercise? Was he never consumed by the goose pimples that consumed me when I sang or wrote some poetry myself? I marveled at his apparent self-control and objectivity. Fearing another rebuke for being "a bit of a romantic," I kept my own counsel.

We both were silent as I explored the study. Beyond the French doors was the porch that Dorothy had built for him so he could walk and create. Early American furniture filled the room. The table tops were covered with more silver framed pictures. I wondered if my face would ever gaze back at me from that assemblage as I had wondered at the caricatures on the walls at Sardi's. Neatly stacked books and magazines filled the shelves. In one corner stood an enormous glass and mahogany display case. It was filled with awards and statues. A mounted medal attracted my attention because of its elaborate pedestal and down front center position. I leaned my nose against the glass and read the inscription:

Oscar Greeley Clendenning Hammerstein II
GOOD BOY
CITY OF NEW YORK P.S. No. 9

What a surprise! It seems that the good conduct medal was very important to Oscar, as important as all the trophies and theatrical awards. He saw me looking at it and proudly explained,

"When I was seven, I heard my mother tell a neighbor that I never lied. Because my mother believed in my immunity to falsehood, it never occurred to me to fib, even a little bit."

I was impressed. I had tried to tell the truth, but it wasn't always possible, practical, or kind. I made some complimentary comments about the trophies for Oklahoma! and Carousel, Allegro, The King and I, and South Pacific. Words seemed inadequate, almost irrelevant, in view of his accomplishments. He nodded and took my admiration gracefully in stride, seeming just a bit uncomfortable about the praise, but nevertheless accepting.

He changed the subject, turning to the window and to the wide expanse of land beyond it. "I'm trying to buy the farms surrounding us, so we can maintain our privacy. Over that hill is a village that is sprawling with building projects. I'd like to buy the farm on the hill to keep them from building there. I own all the land at the back of the house where my brother Reggie lives. The barn is protected by the golf course." He pointed to the brilliant green fairways in the far distance.

"The only piece that bothers me is that bluff down there and the farm across the road. The man who owns it is a school teacher. A builder has offered him a handsome price for it. I'm willing to match it, to keep the land away from developers. He may sell out anyway, just to be vindictive." I remember wondering what his neighbor had to be vindictive about.

He chatted on, inquiring about my career. I finally told him about <u>Sweet Thursday</u> and how the show that might have made me into a budding star had been sold to them, to Rodgers and Hammerstein, and how I had lost the leading-lady part of Suzie. He listened carefully, watching me and nodding, apparently surprised at the ironic twist of fate. He again encouraged me to sing for him and Dick. A small tremor of panic rumbled in me at the thought of auditioning for them. The bond we had established after the dinner in the city, on top of that majestic staircase, when he leaned over the railing and whispered to me "It wasn't so bad after all, was it?" seemed to grow and to deepen.

There was a moment's pause in the conversation, and I felt that subtle inner beat of dismissal. Closing the door soundlessly behind me, I went downstairs into the silent house. Dorothy was gone, probably writing her endless letters. I had already learned that she acknowledged all the birthdays and anniversaries, opening nights and holidays for all the family and friends. She also cherished all the moments she and Oscar shared: when they met, when he proposed, when and where they ate their first meal, etc. All the "whens" got a little personal note of acknowledgment on her monogrammed blue and gray stationery. She was an avid correspondent.

Coming out of a ball at the St. Regis. Dorothy Hammerstein with cigarette, Oscar Hammerstein at bottom, Jimmy Hammerstein at right, Basia is at center

Chapter 6

The house was deathly still. The bouncing tennis balls popped like small Fourth of July firecrackers in the distance. I skimmed along the crimson carpet, toward the library, with its banks of books and the cavernous fireplace. Surveying the shelves, I picked out something about natives in New Guinea. After I sank into the down-filled pillows of the couch, I had to slit open the pages to read it. I learned later that to achieve a literary effect decorators filled the library shelves with unread books. The phonograph in the corner was silent. The books on the shelves were unread.

Time passed quietly as I read my book, growing more and more engrossed by the headhunters of New Guinea and their primitive cannibalistic customs. Eat the brains of your enemy, and you got his smarts. What could you eat to get a crash course in etiquette? In what part of the body does that reside?

The silence was broken by the subdued clatter of a tea tray being brought in by Mary. As if by magic, both of Jimmy's parents materialized from their respective rooms. The lady of the house played "mother" and poured tea. Having grown wary around them, I carefully drank my tea straight, hot and bitter. No fooling around with those tiny silver spoons with the colored sugar and the treacherous porcelain pitcher of milk that seemed to be wedged between the teacups. We drank in silence until Oscar noticed the book I had been reading.

"What are you reading?"

"A book about aborigines, New Guinea aborigines." I held it up to show him the title.

"Oh? You're interested in natives?"

"Yes, I'm taking anthropology this term at Hunter College, and these people seem to have one of the most primitive cultures on the planet."

"What else do they teach you in anthropology at Hunter College?" His blue eyes betrayed the familiar friendly twinkle.

"Mostly about evolution and Darwin's theory of natural selection."

"Really? Do you believe in Darwin?"

"It seems to make sense. If I believe anything, yes, his theory lies within the realm of possibility."

"Doesn't Darwin explain that giraffes have longer necks because they have to stretch them to reach the top branches?" The other way around, I wanted to tell him, but I didn't dare to be impertinent. He continued, "The higher the trees grew, the more they had to stretch their necks to get at the leafy branches on top. Certainly that got translated into their genes, and giraffes evolved with longer necks." He sat back self-satisfied that he had clarified Darwin's theory. "It's only logical. If you change the environment, the creature will change to adapt itself to it."

I wanted to tell him how genetic change actually occurred, but hated to stop him while he was on a roll. "If you make the environment better, then the creature will change itself for the better. If the environment is made worse, then the creature becomes worse. Man is the product of his environment. If we improve the environment, we will improve man."

He leaned forward as he made his last point. As I listened, he continued. "I think that my sons, Jimmy and Billy, grew taller because I installed a basketball court and they had to reach up for the basket. In that way, they stretched upward like the giraffes, and a change in their environment caused a change in their height."

He sat back smiling and nodding, self-satisfied as if he had shared something profound with me. I decided against explaining the most current laws of natural selection to him. It might have been interpreted as a put-down, and I was in no position to put down my future father-in-law, especially since he was Oscar Hammerstein II.

He continued with a further furrowing of his already furrowed brow. "You don't believe that environmental change affects genetic mutation?" He smiled, catching my hesitation.

"I think that better food makes for healthier people who are more apt to deal with life better, but I don't think that it changes their genes. No, I don't think so."

"Then how come my sons are so tall?" He leaned forward and again asked me directly.

Dorothy, who had been listening to the conversation while doing a crossword puzzle, added, "Well, dear, maybe Jimmy is tall because my Scottish ancestors were tall."

Oscar shot back, "But Billy is also tall, and he's not related to your Scottish ancestors."

Billy was obviously not Dorothy's son, but Oscar's by his first marriage. An edge of harshness had crept into his voice. Dorothy looked a bit startled, and the fear returned to her watery blue eyes.

I jumped in. "Well, you're tall! In the United States, children seem to be taller than their parents. I don't think it has to do with basketball courts. It seemed to have to do with all the pasteurized cows milk they drink. Cow's milk makes the calf double its weight every few months. It's a change in nutrition, not in the genes."

They laughed at my apparent earnestness. I was dead serious, having read it in a nutrition article by J. I. Rodale, a contemporary advocate of milk reduction in the American diet. It seemed to ease the tension.

"If what you say is true, then no matter what we do to make the world better, human beings won't change." He shifted in his seat, as if the thought had made him uncomfortable.

"Yes, I believe that."

"Then there is no hope for the human race. It seems pessimistic, a bit cynical. Why would people join organizations to make the world better, if the world never got better? I belong to the Fund of the Republic, and we believe in the perfectibility of human beings and the dignity of man."

I had heard of the Fund of the Republic and the prestige it carried, so I dared not argue further. You either believed in the environment, or like me, you believed in heredity as the primary shaper of humanity. The reality of history allowed little room for hope.

Oscar pursued his argument. "If we can have perfectibility in our art, then why can't we have perfectibility in human nature? It seems all we have to do is put our minds to it."

He nodded to himself as he formed the answer. I wondered where that great "mind" that caused this development would come from. I hadn't seen it at work in the human life around me. Still I liked the thrust of the conversation and turned up the flame, interjecting, "Then you must believe in God, the invisible mover, the mind behind matter, the passive manipulator, and that we were born for some reason." I leaned forward with growing confidence.

"I don't know about that. I do think that certainly we were born to advance life in the universe. How else can we do that if not through our minds, our wills? You can't stop it, can't halt it, that movement forward. It goes on. Lands up as the same thing, like drops in a river or an ocean."

There seemed to be a contradiction in his logic, so he shifted gears, pausing for a moment. "I guess I believe that oneness on earth with man is God. We have to have faith in ourselves, in one another."

"Then you love humanity?" I thought of his lyrics and their boundless good will.

"I don't idealize people. We don't have to love one another; we have to understand each other. Understanding precludes hate, that's all. I'd settle for that."

I realized that as he spoke where the lyrics to the song "You've Got to Be Taught" came from. It was a deep part of his personal philosophy.

Dorothy, who had been fidgety since Oscar had zinged her with the put-down about the height of his sons, and who had kept silent, now ventured, "If you don't believe in environmental change and that people expand to the circumstances around them, then how do you explain the fact that Jews look like the people of the country they come from? I mean, I know Irish Jews who look Irish, and I know Italian Jews who look Italian. If the change in the environment didn't change their genes, then how did that happen? I mean, even Norwegian Jews look Scandinavian."

Her question caught all of us off guard. With a look of perplexed patience, Oscar grew condescending. "Dear, I don't know if it works that way. Jews are Semitic, and they look like Semites, generally darker, with a Mediterranean complexion. Look how many are called Schwartz. It's German for black, or dark, so it must mean that Jews are darker than their European counterparts."

"But, dear, I know so many Jews who look like the people of the country they come from!" she insisted. No one mentioned the fact that intermarriage occurred among the Jews as well as with the Christians in Europe. Intermarriage with non-Jewish women was common, even among the Hammersteins.

"There seems to have been a great deal of intermarriage and inter-mating," I offered, "even among the Jews."

"Inter-mating! Ha!" Oscar laughed; so did Jimmy.

Dorothy looked surprised, as if the double entendre of the word had put her off guard. Oscar interjected, "I think you've given the word a new meaning. Are you intimating that 'inter-mating' is the only cause for genetic change?"

"Yes, anyway partially."

"Then we're doomed to go round and round, never upward, never toward perfection. I can't accept that," he ventured.

"Do you believe in God?" Oscar asked me across the coffee table. The directness of his question startled me.

"I don't know. I don't think so. I believe in Mother Nature. As for God, if I have any belief at all, it's the definition that Spinoza gives to the problem, or maybe Walt Whitman's idea of the soul."

"Really, what does Spinoza say?" I felt a slight tease in his voice, but I plowed on earnestly.

"Benedictus de Spinoza explains it this way," I tried to remember the exact words of the passage that made such an impression on me. "He says that we, each one of us, cannot ever know who or what God is. We are like a blood corpuscle in the bloodstream of an enormous beast. As a blood corpuscle we can never get out of the vein or artery to see the whole animal. That is not possible for us. We are forever doomed to course on the inside, never allowed even for an instant to get a look at the whole creature. If you believe that God is infinity, we can't grasp infinity. Our finite minds can only grasp finite ideas. We are limited not only by our perceptions but also by the situation in which we find ourselves."

"Sounds like a good man, that Spinoza. What does Whitman say?" Oscar was smiling. Jimmy was looking uncomfortable. I plodded on.

"He has a slightly different focus in understanding the problem. We are all part of a great big soul, a pulsation of life. We are all in it together; plants, animals, humans, segmented sparks of a bigger mass called life. I think I agree with both of them."

"You don't believe that man was created to lord it over the beasts?"

"No I don't!" I answered vehemently.

"Neither do I." He leaned forward and placed his tea cup on the table. "Well, that was quite a tea. Does Jimmy know what he's getting into with you?" His blue eyes twinkled, but there was a steely glint in them. Now Jimmy seemed to have been caught off guard.

Without waiting for an answer from either of us, Oscar turned to Dorothy and added, "Well, dear, I have work to get back to. We'll change for dinner."

He rose. Using his fingers with great delicacy, he wiped the corners of his mouth with his tea napkin.

"Yes, dear, I'll lay your clothes out for you," Dorothy answered as she busied herself stacking the China dishes on the silver tea tray.

I realized that Oscar's beautiful hands did nothing but write lyrics. All his other needs were taken care of by his wife and two or more staffs of servants. That seemed O.K. if the wife had nothing else to do and nothing to say. What happened if the wife wanted her own life? I had often wondered about that. From my background, it was a given that men were the bosses and had to be waited on. I had hoped that among the rich and educated there would be more freedom for women. I began to realize that it wasn't necessarily so. Wives and mothers still acted like servants, not doing the menial jobs. Maids were hired to do that. But they still did jobs of service that made them hirelings, if only on a higher level and for more base pay.

Oscar disappeared up the stairs, his hunched-up shoulders almost absorbing his cropped head. I had tried to get Jimmy out of that habit, but realizing it meant too much to him to look like his father, I backed down and left him alone.

The talk left me in a good frame of mind. It showed them that I was more than a pretty face from the wrong side of the tracks. I was educated, and my education might balance out my lack of social graces. At least it might gain me some time until I learned the new rules. If I didn't impress my future father-in-law, at least I amused him, which was an old standby for me with men.

I took the tea napkin and wiped the corners of my mouth as Oscar had done, and a lipstick stain appeared on the pink cloth. Dorothy reached for another cigarette after her louder than usual audible intake of air. Education or not, if I left lipstick stains on her tea napkins, I was not going to pass muster. She pushed her glasses up onto her forehead, into her red hair and swept upstairs to her bedroom. The maid silently appeared and then just as silently disappeared with the tea tray.

I stood up when Dorothy did, a reflex action I had learned from Jimmy. After she left, I sat down again, feeling vaguely confused. Not much of me was gaining much ground here. One step forward, one step back. Stasis, if not status.

When I told Momma that I was marrying Jimmy, she suggested that I go to finishing school. She understood that I would need some new social graces in order to fit in. I bristled at the idea, feeling and insisting that I was as good as anybody. Momma was right again. I should have considered finishing school.

The elegant silent house was stifling, so again I went outside. New games of tennis were being played, doubles this time, with Dorothy joining the men on the courts. She moved well but was self-deprecating, fingering her neck every time she missed a shot, proclaiming loudly what a wretch she was.

Later that afternoon, we shared a glittering, if muted, dinner to which Uncle Reggie and his wife Mary were invited from the farm next door. They both staggered in. Reggie was Oscar's brother, and Jimmy had spoken of him with great affection. He had been more active in the theater as a younger man, having been the great love of Helen Morgan in his youth. He lived a life of relative seclusion, partially dependent on his brother, and partially on drink. His large shiny, raspberry nose bore witness to many years of putting away large quantities of alcohol, giving Reggie an uncanny resemblance to W.C. Fields.

Mary, his wife, had grown in size, if not in color, due to her unhappy habit. As a younger woman, she had been a great beauty, one of the stunning John Robert Powers models that I myself had aspired to be, but failed, due to hips that were wider than the fashion world prescribed. The traces of her beauty were still there: fine small features, straight white teeth, delicate skin. Now too much of it hung in folds around her face.

She and Reggie lived to argue. One of their arguments preceded them into the living room as they bumped their way in through the furniture. With a drink in one hand and a cigarette in the other, Mary weaved her way in, trying not to jostle any of the picture frames that were marching across the table tops. Dorothy eyed her archly and sighed a sigh of relief when her sister-in-law finally plopped into one of the chairs, almost disappearing into the feather cushions. Reggie staggered into a soft satin settee opposite mine and proceeded to stain the mahogany table top with his Scotch. Dorothy slipped a coaster under his glass almost before it hit the highly polished table top again.

Reggie bellowed, "So you're Basia! Well, I hear you're a singer. Why don't you sing me a song?"

With that request from his brother, Oscar turned to Dorothy.

"Dear, did you have the piano tuned?"

"No, dear, I couldn't get the tuner. I didn't think we would need him. It's been unused for so long," she rattled on, but it took me off the hook. No one would make me sing with an untuned piano.

Jimmy burst through the door, and with obvious affection he pumped Reggie's hand, kissed the air over Mary's chubby ear and settled in to discuss the tennis game he had been playing. The talk turned to the theater and the new show that Oscar had bought from Cy Feuer and Ernest Martin. It seems that they didn't like the title Sweet Thursday and were considering other alternatives. The name Pipe Dream was brought up. They discussed the cast and who might play the madam. Reggie suggested Helen Traubel. Henry Fonda -- Susan's husband and Dorothy's son-in-law -- was discussed for the part of Doc, the leading man, and was rejected. He didn't get the part even though he had been taking singing lessons daily. It went to Bill Johnson, just as the part of Suzie, for which I had been slated, had gone to Judy Tyler.

Old Hank and I had something in common. We both lost out on the leads in Pipe Dream. It was ironic that Judy Tyler and Bill Johnson both lost their lives in separate auto accidents within a year after Pipe Dream closed. Perhaps Hank and I should have considered ourselves lucky.

Chapter 7

I wasn't aware of it at the time, but patterns of destiny were being formed during those months that would become apparent only with time, patterns that would affect my life, as well as the lives of Jimmy, Dorothy and Oscar.

One of those patterns included a singer who had been hired to play the role of one of the prostitutes in the newly renamed <u>Pipe Dream</u>. I wouldn't know how deeply it would affect my life and how radically it would change it until after I was divorced, raising my son and singing in the chorus of <u>Fiorello</u>. At the time I dealt only with the immediate disappointment of having lost the lead in <u>Pipe Dream</u>. The ramifications became more obvious to me the farther I distanced myself from the Hammerstein family and from my subsequently changing marital situation.

I was becoming aware that the tensions and violence that existed between my mother and father, spilling down over to my sister and me, were not the result of poverty or of merely being foreign, or Polish, or Catholic, or anything like that. The problems we shared were universal and common to the human condition. Even surrounded by the great wealth of the Hammersteins, I became aware that the tension was not only my tension. The tensions existed among them as a family long before I came on to the scene. My naive assumption that status and wealth made it possible for happiness to flourish was an optimistic dream that I had harbored all my young life and that I was not yet ready to give up.

If I quailed at the initial dinner and felt out of place at The Farm, I had a surprise in store for me at Dorothy and Oscar's twenty-fifth silver wedding anniversary that was coming up in May. It was going to be celebrated at the roof garden of the Hotel Pierre. I knew that all the greats and near-greats of the theater would be there.

Buffie had had her debutante ball. The Hammersteins' anniversary celebration would be my coming-out party in their society. I would have to meet all of their friends, all of the people in those silver frames marching across those table tops. Some were famous in ways I had not as yet grasped: writers, directors, musicians, producers, backers from the garment center, mostly unknown faces to me, respected in the theater community and part of the Hammerstein circle, if not close friends, then acquaintances and co-workers.

So I started to sew. I had always wanted a bronze-red taffeta dress. As a young girl, I had seen one of my favorite actresses twirling away on the screen in the arms of a tall, dark and very handsome man, who guided her deftly across the floor. The bronze-red taffeta swirled around her as she pulsated to the beat of the music.

Momma fitted me. I stood quietly without twitching as she pinned the flaring gored skirt into small tucks around my twenty-three-inch waist. It billowed out around me like an enormous flaming poppy. The strapless top was kept up by bone stays. A cuff-like fold hugged me under the arms and plunged precariously between my breasts. Momma filled the cleavage with a large velvet black cabbage rose. I had long black gloves with small pearl buttons and a six-strand pearl choker to wear around my neck. One of the girls at the theater insisted that I wear her black fox stole. She felt it was imperative, if I were to fit in with the rest of the guests. I hoped it would be in good taste, since I looked like someone out of a movie musical.

I had not as yet learned that for rich women, taste on that level, in the middle Fifties, lay in drabness and in self-obliteration. New things were frowned upon. Old used leather that had seen a great deal of polishing was valued. Cashmere sweaters, ever so barely frayed at the elbows, were in good taste. Things worn or slightly aged, things having a fashion pedigree, had value, like antiques. New things did not. New things were possessions of the <u>nouveau riche</u>, bought with new money. Only old things were good, representing old money, which was the best. Where I was standing, money was money. I had not learned to make the distinction between old vintage and new mintage.

I dressed in the theater after the curtain came down on <u>Can-Can</u>, and with shaking hands, I put myself together. My good looks would be a limited asset here. I hoped my coming-out get-up would establish me as a woman of taste and beauty in the eyes of the Hammersteins' friends.

At home no one ever told me that I was beautiful. Once I hit the theater, all I heard was how "gorgeous" I was and how lucky I was to be that gorgeous. My gorgeousness was never important to me. As I grew up, I began to realize that it not only opened doors for me, but was getting me into a lot of trouble with men.

For the anniversary party, I toned myself down, wearing a light base on my face, bronze lipstick to match the dress, with light mascara on my eyes. Too much eye make-up seemed to be in bad taste. I had my hair styled by a hairdresser. He cut it softly around my face and gave me a permanent, telling me I looked like Claudette Colbert. He was right; with my new hair-do, I <u>did</u> resemble Claudette Colbert. But I preferred to look like my most favorite Hungarian singer and look-alike, Ilona Massey.

I checked my hands. They were clean. The gloves were mended. My black suede pumps were brushed. I slipped on the vibrant taffeta dress and snapped on the wide pearl choker. I looked like something not only out of a musical, but also out of an old Russian movie. No matter what I did, I always looked like something out of an old Russian movie. I felt regal and beautiful. My youth and excitement lent me radiance as I skipped down the back stairs of the theater to a chorus of "<u>merdes</u>" and popped out into Shubert Alley, into the arms of my waiting Prince Charming. We made a handsome couple as he strode and I billowed beside him.

Then we rushed for an empty cab through the crowd of autograph hunters. People asked me if I were "anybody," and I answered "No, not yet!" I felt wonderful because I knew that's how I looked, like somebody important. Not yet! I would not sign any autographs yet!. But there would come a time when it would be honest for me to scribble my name on theater programs or restaurant napkins. We ducked into a cab heading east and sped away from the teeming crowds of the theater district.

It was always much quieter uptown. Few people were out on the streets as we got out in front of the Hotel Pierre. Even though Jimmy fumbled for his wallet, I was grateful that he was with me. We were just a few blocks away from the Hammerstein townhouse on Sixty-Third Street. Central Park looked dark in the distance. The hansom cabs, with munching patient horses, were standing in front of the Plaza Hotel across the square. The silence was broken by an occasional shake of a blinkered head, filling the spring air with the tinkle of tiny bells and cymbals.

The doorman at the Pierre swept the door open for us, and we entered the brilliantly lit lobby. To Jimmy, the anniversary of his parents' marriage was one of many such affairs he hated and dreaded. Although he loved being tall, his height made other men uncomfortable. Short men usually did Jimmy Cagney imitations around him. His height elicited questions even from average- sized men. He managed to cover his own often growing discomfort with an air of detachment and apparent indifference.

I realized, too late, that I should have practiced walking in a long dress. I found there was an art involved to it. You couldn't bend over, or you stepped on the front hem and stumbled. That's why women in long dresses, if they knew what they were doing, looked regal. Not only did I have to remember not to bend over, but how to manage my bag, gloves and fur wrap. I read somewhere that a sign of a truly chic woman was how she managed her stole. Careless nonchalance was the key. I was neither careless nor nonchalant, needing two more hands to manage all the paraphernalia that was slipping and sliding around me.

In the lobby, we worked our way past people leaving other parties and took the elevator up to the Hotel Pierre roof. As we entered, the anniversary celebration in the penthouse ballroom was just past its peak. The elevator deposited us on a landing located above the rest of the assemblage. We had to descend a small flight of stairs to get down to the dance floor and its encircling tables. People waved to Jimmy and discreetly looked me over. Features swam before me; some of them were on familiar faces of performers in the theater, looking older than their pictures. Couples were dancing. An orchestra was playing "Blue Moon." Others were sitting around the tables in groups, dazedly talking. Many were drunk. They had all eaten dinner, and a buffet was prepared for the stragglers, family and friends who were in shows and who would show up after the theater. We were the first of that crowd to arrive.

Dorothy spied us and sailed over in her very tight pink brocade. In every dress she wore, her large bosoms seemed to be strapped down and flattened. The look was reminiscent of the Roaring Twenties. Although held down, her breasts rebelled and managed to bulge over the top of her dress. Subsequently, I noticed that all her dresses had that same look, pale in color, rich in texture, with her breasts flattened down and bulging over the top.

"Hello, Bawrsha!" A peck over my ear.

"Hello, Mrs. Hammerstein." A careful peck over her ear.

"Call me Dorothy, dear! Hello, Jim Boy!" Pecks over both ears.

"Hello, mother." A returned peck.

I was getting better at not leaving any of my lipstick on the other person's face. No contact was made, since the air was pecked at the hair line, the space just off the edge of the cheek. Powder to powder, base to base, perfume to perfume, nothing more. After the first series of encounters, I was getting good at it, but it felt strange. When I met my mother, I always grabbed her and planted a juicy kiss on her face and she on mine. Then we hugged, a real hug so that I could feel and smell her body. But not in this new world. All was furtive and passing. No physical contact was ever really made.

The greetings went all right, and I wondered if I dared to have anything to eat since the gloves, stole and bag were sliding around my body on the slippery taffeta. The dress itself wasn't as securely anchored in place as I had hoped, and I thanked God for the large black velvet rose Momma had insisted on stuffing between my bosoms. It saved me from full exposure.

Dorothy took one of my gloved hands into hers, and I noticed a very strange movement. She wore long white kid gloves, but her hands and fingers were bare. The empty fingers of the gloves she was wearing hung from the rest of the glove on the side of her hands. As she spoke, four hands danced around her face. Two hands were obviously hers, sporting nails manicured with bright red polish. But there were two other sets of white kid fingers fluttering along around them. Since other women at the party had the same arrangement, I decided it must have been the proper way to wear evening gloves. No one else in the room wore black gloves. They all wore long white kid gloves. I felt like Bette Davis in Jezebel. Later I was to learn that women of wealth wore those white kid gloves only once. After that, they either gave them away to the Salvation Army, or threw them out, because cleaning made them look used and no longer new, a contradiction that belied the definition of "old money."

Still holding me by the hand, Dorothy maneuvered me into position for introductions to the many smiling, hazy faces. Jimmy hung over me and seemed proud, if vaguely uncomfortable, cracking his knuckles and introducing me to the rest of his family and to the other guests. Except for Richard Rodgers, who gave me a hug and planted a big kiss on my mouth, all the rest either pecked me above the ear or shook my hand. I could sense that Richard Rodgers did not like Jimmy, and the feeling was vibrantly mutual.

Many men commented how pretty I was and clapped Jimmy on the shoulder, winking and saying what a lucky man he was and lingering too long over the cabbage rose at my cleavage. An older woman reeled over to us and, while pumping my hand vigorously, wished us luck.

"Ellie Reinheimer, Howard's wife," Dorothy hissed through clenched teeth. Disapproval flitted across her features as she passed the wife of Oscar's lawyer down the receiving line.

I was struck by Susan, a former starlet, Jimmy's half-sister and Dorothy's daughter. She was a few years older than I, but she was so at ease in her surroundings that I truly envied her. Hiding her own beauty, she came to Dorothy's silver anniversary party dressed as the mother of the bride, with her hair powdered gray and tied back in a bun. Her dress was also a gray color and very matronly. The outfit on her daughter made Dorothy edgy. It seemed that Susan was some-what unpredictable. Her get-up that night got her a lot of mileage. She kept looking at the elevator doors, and I realized that she was waiting for Hank -- her husband Henry Fonda, who was starring in Mr. Roberts -- to arrive after his show. When he finally entered, she ran over to him, and they both laughed as he surveyed her.

I met Henry Fonda that night. It was such a strange feeling to look into the face of a man with whom I had shared so many emo-tions in so many darkened theaters of my youth. He looked older than his pictures, and his blue eyes had a piercing quality to them.

Jimmy wandered over to the buffet while I found us a place to sit. I divested myself of my wayward belongings, straightened out my dress and hitched it back up. He returned carrying two plates piled high with chicken and salad. When we had finished our dinner, Oscar came over smiling benevolently and asked me to dance. After some unfortunate encounters with patrons of the Copacabana, physical contact with an unknown man always made me uneasy. Oscar was not only a strange man, but my future father-in-law and a man of great stature. Many eyes were watching us, which made me feel even more uncomfortable.

Back in Jamaica, when I still attended high school, we danced ev-ery weekend at Paul DeMatteo's house. We called ourselves the Cher-okee Music Makers after Tex Benecke's record. While Paul's mother played cards with the neighborhood women upstairs, keeping a wary eye on us, we danced in his basement. I was considered a good dancer, but it was easier dancing with guys who were my own age and not considered all that important. Older men held me too tightly, and our knees bumped. Poppa always said he couldn't dance with me because I held my legs too close together and didn't allow for him to step through them.

Oscar put his arm around me, took my damp, now glove-free hand into his, and we started bumping our way across the floor. He was holding me too close, and he danced just enough off the beat that I had to concentrate on his movements and not on the music. It was kind of a cerebral off-beat dancing. We kept bumping knees. As we swung around, one of us would invariably step on the hem of my dress, and we'd stumble. As I jacked it up, I felt Oscar's fingers feeling the stays, which were holding up the bodice of my dress.

"My, oh my, I didn't know they put stays in dresses anymore," he said, genuinely impressed.

"The world would be a better place if they still did!"

God, what was that all about? Why did I say that? What did it mean? I wanted to be bright and make a statement about femininity and prettiness, and it came out like something inane. "The world would be a better place if women wore stays?" If they were Victorian? What was I talking about? I didn't mean that. Whether he heard me or not, I'll never know, for he made no comment and continued to concentrate on dancing just off the beat. When the number came to an end, he steered me back to the table, and we sat down. I was perspiring all over.

The next man to dance with me was one of Oscar's cronies named Milton Cohen. Having been informed that I was Polish, he asked the band to play a polka. Thank God, he could dance! Milton was a head shorter than I, but he was full of life and had no problem following the beat of the polka music. We bounced around the empty floor, the only ones to brave the frenzy of the dance. I wished those proper theater folk could have seen me when I danced the polkas, obereks and mazurkas at the Polish Hall, downtown on St. Mark's Place. The music made the blood race through my veins.

91

At that moment, there was nothing more exciting than to give my-self over to the dance.

After Milton brought me back to the table, Jimmy and I limped across the floor. He hated to dance and would have gladly passed on it, but he felt it was the proper thing to do. We bumped knees as he pushed and yanked me around the dance floor. There was no joy in him at all; he just didn't respond to the music. I vowed to teach him, to share with him my love for dancing.

People began to drift out, and we, too, said our good-byes. Jimmy again shook hands with the men and did the goose-pecking with the women. This time I felt closer to him, since we had done it together. He had finally shared me with his family, and I was grateful.

I realized that most of the women wore subdued colors. My flaming taffeta stood out like a sore thumb. I vowed to tone myself down in the future. We ended the evening in Hamburger Heaven on Madison Avenue where, in my state of heightened agitation, I spilled a bottle of ketchup on my burnt-orange dress. Blood and fire: It was not a good omen.

Later in the week, I asked Jimmy if anyone had made any comments about me. I was curious about the impression I had made. He recalled only that Hank Fonda had made a remark.

"What did he say?"

"He said he thought you had a roving eye," Jimmy informed me, and he laughed.

After the heat of exposure receded from my face, I wondered what did he see? Did I look as if I were checking out the men at the party? Could my curiosity and need to know be translated into a "roving eye"? Was my desperate desire to size up a situation and find my safe place in it a subtle signal to men? Was the fear behind that search some kind of a turn-on?

We set the day of our marriage for June seventh. I felt in tune with seven and thought it was my lucky number, for I was born on December the seventh, a neat half-year away. That our marriage date fell on Dorothy's birthday seemed to be a double bonus.

Chapter 8

My future husband was somewhat iconoclastic. He was in a better social position than I. He knew the rules and also knew which ones he could break without paying too high a price. He felt that an engagement ring was "gauche," so we didn't have one. He also felt that a wedding was too much fuss and bother. We would be married at City Hall in the judge's chambers. It sounded simple and chic.

Not having a wedding relieved me of the pressure of dealing with my father, who in most social situations wound up getting drunk. While singing dirty Polish ditties, he would reel around the room, squinting through his glasses, looking for a pretty woman to pinch or pat on the behind. There were times when he would fall asleep in some corner on the floor or end up draped over the edge of a table. When he subsided into his drunken dreams, his snoring and snorting lent a cacophonous accompaniment to even a relatively loud orchestra. At those times, both Momma and I would grow rigid with embarrassment. Jimmy's decision not to have a wedding stilled my fears and lifted the awesome responsibility of familial shame from my shoulders.

The two people who were the most appalled by our plans not to have a large wedding were Dorothy and Momma. Dorothy had misgivings about its appropriateness and felt that her friends would not understand. There was also the factor of the innumerable weddings that she had attended and all the presents that she had bought over the years. We were not giving her an opportunity to allow people to reciprocate, and she felt thrown off balance. The religious difference didn't bother her too much. Her concerns were not from a spiritual point of view as much as from a more practical social level. We were shirking a social responsibility. It was not proper not to have a wedding. Since we were to be married on June seventh, on her birthday, she felt partially pacified. In her heart of hearts, along with her reservations about me, she felt we were doing the wrong thing.

Momma's feelings ran more to her fears that the neighbors might think I was pregnant. She was concerned that there could be no other reason for not having a church wedding and getting married so quickly. Anyway, what did the judge's chambers have to do with getting married? A wedding happened in church, not at City Hall. She didn't think it was exactly a shot-gun wedding, but going off alone within a few weeks to be married left her asking questions to which she received no answers.

After spending a great deal of money on my sister's wedding, she was willing to go into debt to offer me "a nice spread," as they called those brawling affairs in those days. I knew she had very little money and the wedding would come out of the few dollars she managed to squirrel away, without my father's knowledge, from her paycheck every payday. It was not until many years later that I realized that history had repeated itself in a new generation. Momma had also married outside of the church because Poppa had a former wife. Divorced parishioners were denied the sacrament of marriage. In the eyes of the church, their subsequent mates lived with them in sin.

In the late Twenties, in a Catholic country like Poland, not to have a church wedding was unheard of. Momma was branded an adulteress, a sinner, and we in turn were bastards. That may have been the reason she followed Poppa out of Warsaw into the armpit of Poland, into Minsk-Mazowiecki, to get away from pointed fingers and malicious gossip. The posed pictures in our family album documenting those years show us sullen and her face filled with despair, aged beyond her years.

I not only rejected a church wedding, but any wedding at all. How much of our history we both wanted to leave behind us will forever be a moot question. I will never know how she felt about her decision. I do know how much I hurt her when I left not only a wedding but also a church wedding out of my life.

Poppa could have cared less whether or not I had a wedding. He whittled his days away making swings and birdhouses for my nieces, taking time out to stagger up and down the cellar stairs to sneak surreptitious slugs from the bottle of rotgut he called his "homemade vodka."

Oscar, like my father, didn't seem to care either. Both men lived in their own worlds, in which their children seemed only to intrude.

My future family found me rough-cut. P.J. Wilhousky, conductor of the All-City Chorus, had called me "a diamond in the rough." They weren't as generous as Wilhousky in their assessment of me, though. He had been able to see the diamond underneath all that roughness. All they wanted to do was to cover me over with a patina of acceptability. Dorothy was already busy polishing my edges. I rationalized that it was better at this point in our lives to keep the families apart.

By the time I decided to marry, I had listened to enough sermons in church when I was a child and, as I grew older, enough programs from the Ethical Cultural Society on Sunday mornings on the radio to have made a decision. Catholicism never took root in me. Christ's sacrifice left me with a tender sadness for Him, but with never any understanding of why He had to die for my sins. At that time, I hadn't committed any sins bad enough to require anyone to sacrifice himself on the cross for me. Original sin went right by me. Placing that burden on a baby seemed unfair. I had no choice about being baptized, but when communion and confirmation came along, I argued and went through with the ceremonies more for Momma's sake than for my own. I knew that if I ever had children, they would go to the Ethical Culture School and I would not lock them into either Judaism or Christianity. They could make their own choices. Give me a child until he or she is six, and that

95

child will be mine forever. The dogma of the Jesuits sat uncomfortably on my shoulders.

I had always been suspicious of the church due to the fact that there were no women at or near the top of the hierarchy. Men ran the show, while the women, who were called nuns, dressed in their black habits, scurried around sweeping floors and doing all the menial work. Women who weren't nuns were considered to be the cause of all the problems on Earth. It never made any sense to me. Men started the wars, not women. Like Poppa, they were the ones who seemed to be angry most of the time. Yet women were the evil ones, the temptresses, the adulteresses, the witches who preyed upon men and dragged them down to eternal damnation and even worse, sex. The "roving eye" remark Hank Fonda made bothered me. Virtue seemed to have been based on virginity, not on goodness. It was painfully one-sided. The game of restrictions existed only for women. The men could do pretty much what they wanted. Their behavior wasn't restricted. Authorities winked at male peccadillos and stoned the women. It seemed to be a given. There was nothing anyone could do about it. They created a male God who sanctified their behavior. Lesser men in long dresses, called cassocks, vestments, robes, wearing all kinds of head gear, carried out those restrictions. They forced virginity on single women. When the women became brides, they forced uninterrupted motherhood on them.

In a country church in England I once visited, there was an inscription on one of the dark stone walls:

"MARY BENTON DIED AT THE AGE OF
THIRTY-NINE, AFTER GIVING BIRTH TO
FORTY SONS AND FIVE DAUGHTERS"

It stopped me dead in my tracks! After I reread the chiseled markings on the wall, I had to do some fast arithmetic to make sure it was possible. It could be true only if poor Mary Benton started menstruating at nine and all of the babies were premature, or if she had several sets of twins. What awesome barbarism! Yet she was honored for her contribution to the church and to God. She got an honorable mention, an inscription on the wall after she died at the age of thirty-nine, having her forty-sixth child. The painful reality of all of those orphaned children and of her husband mounting her again before she had time to heal made my own body constrict in pain.

What kind of God was it that allowed such cruelty? The church itself shattered my faith in divinity, at least in divinity as a loving, kind father figure. Momma had been the one who had been kind to me. Where was the Mother in the Trinity? Why was she left out? I was beginning to get an itchy sensation that the whole thrust of Western religion and, therefore, Western civilization, was to keep women in line. I vowed not to burden my children with the faith of the fathers. Human values based on what was best in human experience would be a guide for my children. Oscar and I agreed on that. Jimmy didn't care. The Ethical Culture Society became a future possibility.

Momma bought us linens and made us matching robes. She marveled at how much material she had to use to cover Jimmy's six- foot, five-inch frame. The Hammerstein gift was much more elaborate. Oscar gave us a choice. We could either have a convertible car or a trip to Europe. Although my Chevy was in better shape that Jimmy's Austin, it needed some work, so we opted for a new car. The only one my tall future husband could fold his long legs into was a Sunbeam Alpine. Oscar presented us with the keys the day before we were married.

Amid presents and good wishes, I left Can-Can and all the friends I had made there. Gwen Verdon took up a collection from the company and brought us a beautiful silver dinner bell, to summon our future maids, she said. Jimmy, who had been the assistant stage manager next door to Can-Can, took a two-week vacation from his show, Me and Juliet.

On the seventh of June, we packed our shiny new silver blue car, wired some flowers to Dorothy for her birthday, and headed downtown to be married by Judge Markowitz. He was a close friend of Howard Reinheimer, the family lawyer, and seemed delighted to perform the ceremony. Just as our mutual vows were exchanged in his dark, oak-paneled office, the bells in the church steeple across the square from the City Hall began to toll out eleven o'clock. The judge, solemn in his long black robes, informed us that it was a good omen. He assured us that we would have a happy life together. Jimmy and I glowed at each other. "Mazel Tov," Judge Markowitz had said.

Buddy, Jimmy's partner, accompanied by Cappy, his current girl-friend and future wife, acted as Jimmy's best man. As I repeated the vows, the ceremony assumed a strange feeling of unreality to me. Some part of me hung suspended, apart from it all, removed from the process of what was happening. One moment I was single and free; the next moment, after the intoning of a few words, as if by magic, a new name had been grafted onto me. I was no longer me. I was some-one else, a married woman, a wife belonging to the tall skinny man next to me, who must have felt just as strange as I did, although he didn't say anything.

Part of the vows embarrassed me. It brought back the days of my communion and confirmation. I felt silly playing those roles and go-ing through those games, but it seemed to be a necessity to belong. As a child, I had reluctantly taken the vows to become part of the Catho-lic Church. Here I had taken them to become an accepted member of society, a married woman. Inside of my deep self, I knew I would never belong to anyone. On the outside, I had to play the game. I was twenty-four, old enough to be married, old enough to be part of the mainstream of society, not forever straddling its fences. As an old Pol-ish saying goes, "Slowo sie zeklo" (the word was said), and I was mar-ried. Buddy and Cappy threw fistfuls of rice after us as we ran down the massive stone stairs of City Hall.

Chapter 9

After the ceremony, we folded ourselves into the fresh leather smell of our shiny new Sunbeam Alpine and headed for Florida and the Keys. The southernmost tip of Florida, Key West, was our ultimate destination. Skindiving had become Jimmy's passion. We planned to do some of it in the coral reefs off the coast of Florida. One of our stops was to be at Uncle Arthur's, my father-in-law's paternal uncle and the only one left of that older Hammerstein generation.

Jimmy, ever the optimistic chance taker, hadn't plotted out our honeymoon trip. As a result, we got lost in the swamps of New Jersey, in the vast stretches of the Meadowlands, under the Pulaski Skyway. The day was overcast. Having no sun to orient us, we headed west instead of south. We crisscrossed the swamps back and forth, through the garbage strewn backwaters of my youth -- Jersey City, Union City and Bayonne -- until many hours later we found the right road and finally headed south.

Night closed in around us as we sped past billboards and neon signs. The lengthening dark spaces bordering the highway flashed by with no lights breaking the monotony of the farmlands of southern New Jersey. Eventually we reached the outskirts of Washington, D.C. As the night traffic whizzed past us, our car sputtered, jerked a few times and came to a standstill. A great deal of grinding and clicking with the ignition key left it dead. After a dozen "shits" and a few more dozen "fucks" from Jimmy, we had to have it towed to a service station.

We spent the first night of our honeymoon in a motel reminiscent of the squalid brownstones that flanked Ray's Diner, in which we had met six months before.

The next morning, after some adjustments, the car was ready. We were both testy from lack of sleep and from mounting tension. Jimmy stared ahead without wanting to talk, brushing aside my cheerful efforts at understanding and humor. I wouldn't have been able to discuss what was happening intelligently anyway, and I didn't really know what to say. A flaccid penis of the night before, the first night of our honeymoon, was not part of my experience with men. All I had ever known, as far back as I could remember, were men poking me with their erections, either while dancing or necking. I developed a vague curve in my spine from arching away from that insistent bulge. More recently, I had to face the problem as part and parcel of getting work on Broadway. Humor didn't help much either. Comforting and assuring my new husband that it was opening-night jitters -- ha! ha! -- didn't seem to make him feel any better.

So he took it out on the car and rammed it into first gear, leaving a trail of rubber. With each change of gear, he almost stripped the transmission, until he got it up to the top RPMs. We did eighty, passing everyone else on the road. After a relatively uneventful trip through Virginia, the car burped its way into a filling station in North Carolina, leaving a trail of blue smoke behind us. Again we spent the night in a no less tacky local motel.

Our second evening out on the road proved to be more successful. At least he got his erection back. We made love and finally had a good night's sleep, leaving at dawn and eating breakfast in a truck stop. At this point, both of our digestive systems ceased to function. Tired and headachey, we argued about the way he was gunning the car. The new engine of our new automobile hadn't even been broken in. Forcing it past fifty played havoc with the motor. Questioning his wisdom and his lack of concern for our new vehicle led to one of the first rages I ever saw my new husband fly into. He sputtered, spittle flying from the corners of his mouth, as he gunned the car, his knuckles turning

CINDERELLA ❧ AFTER THE BALL OR, JUST KEEP GOING

white on the steering wheel. Ugly, mean words poured out of him. I was a drag; he knew what he was doing. How dare I question him?

When someone attacked me, I usually clammed up, not knowing what to say, as the rage and pain spread through my body. We drove along in silence, my hurt turning to rigid indignation. Not knowing how to express my feelings without making things worse, I grew more and more stiff until my back went into a spasm. We ended that night in a hospital with a doctor testing me for polio. No polio was found, but I remember lying rigid on that cold stainless steel table, filled with rage and fear, with all those bright lights shining down on me.

The silent man to whom I had pledged myself could be very cruel. He didn't want to discuss anything and told me it was none of my business when I asked him how he felt. It was rage, not polio, that caused the rigidity in my body. The emergency room doctor gave me a shot of a muscle relaxant. We stopped at a local bar and grill and had a drink.

It was still raining as we sped through Georgia. The air outside was damp and heavy. Tall trees arched above the roads and hid the sky from view. As we flew through the night, insects by the thousands left their lives upon our windshield. We had to stop in the pouring rain to wipe them off, since the wipers couldn't handle the load. Cars whizzed past, covering us with sheets of water.

The new day found us having another breakfast of eggs and grits. With undigested food in our distended stomachs, we burped our way in and out of beat-up, weathered gas stations. Unshaven Southern car mechanics, in their baggy overalls, called their buddies to take a look at the belching sports car that the Yankees were pushing in and out of their filling stations.

Granted unfairly, I was blaming my new husband for everything that went wrong: for our distended stomachs that wouldn't digest our food, for the sweltering muggy rainy heat, for the stuffy moisture-laden motel rooms, for the burping defective car, for the neon sign outside the window that kept us up all night. He responded by coming down with an attack of bronchial asthma, a condition I was to learn he had had ever since he was a small child, when he spent his younger years alone on The Farm in Bucks County, having only the golden retrievers with whom to commiserate.

His labored gasping for air sent us to another hospital, this time in an ambulance. He choked, as if he were on the verge of death. I was panic-stricken as the ambulance sped us through another glistening rainy night, past dilapidated clapboard houses and deserted filling stations. This time, it was he who was wheeled into the emergency room and laid out on a shiny steel table. The doctor administered adrenalin and placed an oxygen mask over his face. Soon we were able to leave not only the hospital, but also Georgia. Since we were both past any possibility of sleep, we got into the car and headed south, passing the WELCOME TO FLORIDA sign on the Georgia-Florida border.

I had been brought up to believe that men solved problems, at least mechanical problems. I was beginning to learn that it wasn't universally true. Just because my father and most of the Polish men of my youth could fix almost anything, it wasn't true of the men I met out in the world, in the garment center, or in the theater. Jimmy's beautiful hands had no sense of relation to the world around him. They joked in the family that Jimmy took after his father, who could only hold a pencil and write lyrics.

On the trip south, he kept pushing his luck, as well as the car, to the limit. During another rainstorm, this time in West Palm Beach, we ran out of gas. I sat in the soggy Sunbeam Alpine in stony silence until he finally flagged down a passing car and came back some time later with a can of gasoline. We sputtered to a rather elegant and clean gas station -- in that playground of the very rich -- and were on our way again.

The newly filled gas tank got us to Uncle Arthur's house. He turned out to be an elderly gray-haired gentleman, given to paunchiness. One of the first things my new Uncle Arthur told me, as he took us through his home filled with memorabilia of theatrical days gone by, was that he was on female hormone therapy for his eye problems. He had grown rounder as a result of the injections. He had also developed breasts, which he proudly patted as he spoke.

"For the first time in my life, sailors whistle at me on the beach and try to pick me up." He winked at me as he shared his newly found attractiveness.

Uncle Arthur lived alone in Palm Beach, surrounded by the ubiquitous green and yellow floral prints favored by the local decorators. He was one of the seven children of Oscar Hammerstein I, and at eighty-one, he was the only remaining offspring of that generation. Like the "Old Man," as he called his father (they all seemed to give that name to their fathers), he, too, was an inventor.

Oscar Hammerstein I had a series of cigar-making machine patents to his credit. He also had been the original Hammerstein theatrical entrepreneur when, at the age of fifty, he went temporarily bankrupt. Arthur proudly followed in his father's footsteps, producing thirty-one shows on Broadway, which included Rose-Marie, Naughty Marietta, The Firefly, and High Jinks, before he, too, went bankrupt in 1930.

"It was during the Great Depression; everyone did it. Everyone went bankrupt," he declared proudly, expanding his budding chest.

Uncle Arthur seemed rougher than the rest of the family, closer to the gutter, not as genteel as his nephew Oscar II. He would have found the "royalty" who peppered Dorothy's parties ripe for some of his practical jokes. Delighted with human companionship, he painted a panoramic view of celebrity-filled accomplishment and, with bold strokes on a large canvas, regaled us with stories of the family.

His father, Oscar I, Jimmy's great-grandfather, born in 1848, came to this country when he was a teenager, in 1863. He was the eldest of five children. In 1868, he married Rose Blau, the only woman he ever truly loved. She died in 1876, right after the birth of her fifth child at the age of twenty-five and left Arthur and his three brothers orphaned. Their first son had died in infancy.

So many of the Hammerstein men lost their mothers at a crucial time in their lives. Oscar II, my new father-in-law, lost his mother when he was fifteen years old. He worked out his feelings of grief by pasting sports figures in a scrapbook. His grief and loss recurred later in his life when he found out that his first wife had been unfaithful to him. He went to the LeRoy Hospital on Madison Avenue in New York and had a nervous collapse, pasting pictures of baseball players in a scrapbook, murmuring their names, until he again recovered.

The original Old Man had given his son, Uncle Arthur, his first job at sixteen as a bricklayer in an apartment house in Harlem, called the Kaiser Wilhelm, following in the footsteps of his own father, who was in construction back in Stettin, Pomerania. Harlem in the 1880s was relatively deserted, and Oscar I decided to speculate in real estate. He followed the logic that to get people uptown into his apartment houses, he had to create some entertainment for them. In 1889, he built the Harlem Opera House, which later became the famed Apollo Theater, up there in "the sticks" above Central Park, accelerating the expansion northward for New York City and in the process fueling his lifelong obsession with opera, which lasted until his death in 1919.

Uncle Arthur worked as a laborer doing plastering at the Olympia Theater and then for the Manhattan Opera House. His father built the theater on Forty-Fourth Street, eventually the site of Macy's Department Store. It opened to its first production in 1892. At that time, the Old Man was beginning to give the staid Metropolitan Opera, which catered to the social set, a run for its money. He brought over Nellie Melba, John McCormack, Luisa Tetrazzini and many others.

Never without his top hat, cigar, Prince Albert coat and striped trousers, the original Old Man was a spunky and cantankerous curmudgeon, a five-foot, five- inch Napoleonic dictator, courting publicity whenever and wherever he could find it, using up as much space in the newspapers as Teddy Roosevelt, sometimes even more. At one period in his life, he had as many as forty law suits going on at one time. He let the lawyers handle his cases, rarely getting directly involved in litigation, concentrating instead on opera and publicity. Before he died in 1919, he had built thirteen theaters and laid the ground work to the area that became New York's theatrical center and Broadway.

Along with the plastering, bricklaying and construction, Uncle Arthur became his father's "lieutenant general" and shared in running the growing real estate, theatrical and operatic empire. His brother William, my father-in-law's father, who was very proper and subdued, took care of the daily details and subsequently ran the Hammerstein Victoria Theater. With its animal and freak acts, it provided the money that kept the flamboyant Oscar I active in the building and production of grand opera. Oscar I caused such a problem for the "old guard" and their Metropolitan Opera that they brought him out for $1,250,000. They also prohibited him from producing opera in New York for ten years.

The broad strokes, which appeared on Uncle Arthur's canvas as he filled me in and bored Jimmy, revealed a different side of the family. Something alive and vibrant existed in the personality of the original Oscar I. I wondered what had happened to the family along the way that made it subsequently so stiff and so uncomfortable.

While the storm outside furiously whipped the palm trees, depositing tattered fronds all over our new Sunbeam Alpine, Uncle Arthur pushed mounds of papers, pictures and articles around the large table in the dining room. He was working on a biography of the Old Man with Vincent Sheehan. With apparent devotion and still prodigious memory, he fingered every scrap, every picture, explaining where it fit in the life of his father, a man so unlike his son William, Arthur's brother, and so much at odds with his grandson Oscar II, who not only found him embarrassing but unnerving. Where the original Old Man sought publicity with a vengeance, his son William shrank from it, as did his grandson Ockie, who bowed only to the pressures of publicity that his success had imposed upon him. I was realizing that Jimmy would shrink from it even more. The threat of "bad form" and failure in his father's eyes had tempered his need for theatrical notoriety.

Arthur's present relationships seemed vague. He had a wife, somewhere up North, named Dorothy Dalton, and a daughter named Elaine who had been a movie actress. He continued speaking deep into the night. His voice grew raspy. We became more and more sleepy. Jimmy had heard most of it before. As the night progressed, he yawned and grew more and more embarrassed, not only by his great-grandfather, but also by his uncle. To keep awake, he paced furiously in front of the windows, cracking his knuckles, impatiently waiting for the weather to break so we could get out of there and do some skindiving.

My family went back to my mother's mother. My only memory of my grandmother was of a small round face peeping out from under mounds of feather comforters and pillows. She spent most of her life in bed. The rest of our history in Poland had been wiped out by the Germans from the west, the Russians from the east, the Swedes from the north, the Asian hordes from the steppes of Asia and anyone else who wanted to get from one end of Europe to the other. Poland had always been at the crossroads of Europe and was always attractive to traveling, marauding predators. Much of its history disappeared with each wave of enemy soldiers as they swept across the land, burning and looting. It's no wonder the only heros of Poland were the fighters. There were few others left behind. A whole country was caught incessantly in the trap of geography.

Uncle Arthur, undaunted by the lateness of the hour, pored over his pictures with a magnifying glass and chomped on his Havana cigar, a cigar probably rolled by one of the machines descended from his father's original invention. He spoke of beautiful showgirls and having known Jeannette MacDonald. (I adored her, and I had not yet become aware that it wasn't chic to find her talent admirable). He discovered Mae West and was at the very center of the theatrical activity of his day. He recounted the story that when Mae West met his nephew, Oscar II, she thought that he was too classy to be in the theater and advised him to go back to law.

"My Old Man knew how to spend money and enjoy life. He was generous and gave it away, not like your Old Man!"

He squinted at Jimmy, who, arrested in his yawn, looked startled. "Your Old Man is tight, much too tight. He doesn't know how to spend his money. He just sits on it. He's not well- invested, and he doesn't get good counsel! Howard's still his lawyer?"

Jimmy looked uncomfortable as I interjected, "He bought us a car . . . I mean, he gave us the Sunbeam Alpine for our wedding present."

I moved my head in the direction of the window, where the silver-blue bomb was parked outside, pelted by rain and covered with tattered brown palm fronds. Uncle Arthur's eyes flew wide open.

"He did? Well, what do you know! He must like you!"

Uncle Arthur's statement implied a great deal. Didn't Ockie like his own son? He let him drive around in that old beat-up Austin. I found it difficult to believe. I don't know why I found it so hard to believe. I didn't much like my own father, and he didn't like me.

"You know," Uncle Arthur continued, wagging his finger at Jimmy, "I gave that skinny father of yours his first job! I promised my brother Willy that I'd keep him out of the theater, but Oscar kept insisting, the most persistent bastard I ever knew, so I made him an assistant stage manager in <u>You're in Love</u>. That was the beginning. Gave him twenty dollars a week. Who would have thought? Look where it got him! Does the stuffy old bastard have a girlfriend yet?" He shook with laughter as his newly formed breasts bounced up and down on his chest. It was as much as Jimmy, who didn't want to hear any of it, could bear.

"Listen, Uncle Arthur, Dad is neither tight or stuffy! Just because he's not on page one or in the gossip columns doesn't mean he's stuffy! I think he and mother have a marriage made in heaven; you know that!" he blurted out in a barely controlled sputter.

Arthur spread his hands apart and waved his cigar. "Marriage made in heaven, ha! Well, why not? Your grandfather Willie and his wife Allie had a marriage that was like a big love affair. It might have lasted all the way to heaven. Who knows? Well, I've had four marriages. Made in heaven? I don't know."

"Listen, Uncle Arthur!" Jimmy stepped up beside me as if to present a united front. "We want to have the same kind of marriage that Mumsie and Dad have. I want us to be the first marriage in the family that doesn't end up in splitsville. I want to hit it big by thirty, have a marriage that's made in heaven and lasts forever!"

He looked down at me, and both of us smiled. I wanted that, too.

"Just because Mumsie and Dad's marriage lasted this long doesn't mean that he has to run around!" Jimmy uttered the last phrase with obvious distaste. Uncle Arthur finally caught the drift of Jimmy's discomfort and backed off.

"You're a good son. Humor me; I'm a dying old man." It stopped Jimmy in his tracks. "Anyway, I'm not looking to insult you, or him. But Ockie, you know. . ." He looked over at me, "Reggie, his brother, gave him that name, because he couldn't pronounce Oscar. Ockie was already at Columbia studying law. Have you met Reggie?"

I nodded, recalling the tall man with the cherry nose, weaving his way in and out of the living room furniture at The Farm.

"His mother, my sister-in-law, Allie, shortchanged him. Called him the clown. She adored Ockie, though. He was a genius. But to her, Reggie was always the clown. Both lived up to her expectations. Strange."

He paused. "You know, I got that skinny bastard Ockie a job in a law office. He had to stay away from the family business for at least a year, but he was terrible as a lawyer. Got lost somewhere in Jersey serving somebody with a subpoena, had to call the cops to find him. So after a year, I gave him a job in the theater for twenty dollars a week. Twenty dollars,, would you believe it? He became a better assistant stage manager than a process server. <u>You're in Love</u> was his first job with me and then <u>Show Boat</u>; that made up for everything. Great success. Still, he was always a bit stiff."

He raised his hands to still Jimmy's defense. "But a poet like me... You know I wrote 'Because of You.'" He pulled out the sheet music and pointed to his name emblazoned across the title page. It was time to leave. Arthur was repeating himself.

He died the next year, in 1955, before the biography of his Old Man was published in 1956. The book caused a bit of a furor, for it presented the original Old Man, Oscar I, as a bit of a scoundrel, lacking in the dignity that the family had acquired.

In the naivete of my youth, I wondered how could anyone who was so rich be so tight. Poppa was stingy, but he had no money, and that was his excuse. But among the Hammersteins, there were millions that could be shared, yet Uncle Arthur, who obviously knew him well, called Oscar stingy and stuffy. When questioned about it, which wasn't often, Oscar insisted that he denied his children any part of his wealth as a matter of principle. I felt vaguely uncomfortable with Jimmy's insistence that principles were more important than feelings for family.

When I was in <u>Top Banana</u>, once during a conversation with our director, Jack Donohue, we covered similar ground. The two polarities that we dealt with were talent and kindness rather than principles and feelings. The essence was similar, even if the words were different. In those days, I was caught up with art as God and talent as the way to divinity. The gay boys and I were discussing the subject on the back stairs of the Winter Garden Theater. Smug in our righteousness, we all concurred that talent was the highest human attribute. Jack Donohue disagreed violently with us. He felt that talent was fine, a bonus, but kindness was really what defined greatness in a human being. He was a few years older than we were, and we felt him to be a bit sappy. Time brought me closer to his way of thinking. Talent was the icing on the cake. Kindness was the real substance.

I began to see that what Oscar felt for his children wasn't much different from the way my father felt. Both men were apparently ungenerous. Poppa didn't share anything because he was greedy and thought that sharing his meager wealth with his children was a waste of time. Oscar felt the same way, but he hid behind something more subtle than greed. He hid behind principle.

With Arthur's revelations, another side to my new father-in-law began to surface. In spite of the present he gave us, I began to understand the bind in which my new husband had been caught. I was allowed to think that Poppa was stingy and mean. How could you allow yourself to feel that way about a man who was not only your father, but Oscar Hammerstein II, one of the most powerful men in the theater?

I felt that the present of the car was a token of Oscar's generosity to us. Later I found out that Murray Jacobs, Rodgers and Hammerstein's business manager, who worked in the theater district, saw Jimmy's patched-up Austin. It was he who prevailed upon Oscar to buy us a new automobile. He appealed to Oscar's sense of appropriateness by pointing out how strange it looked for his son to be riding around town in such a beat-up vehicle. The marriage gave Oscar an opportunity to be generous without making it look as if he had abandoned his principles.

Present or no present, Arthur still insisted that Oscar was tight. I wondered what else I would find out if I stayed around and listened to Jimmy's great uncle. I was not given much of a chance. Early the next morning, not even waiting for breakfast, and much to the old man's disappointment, Jimmy whisked me away.

We started south and soon cleared the mainland. The sky opened up, and the sun came out, sending shafts of brilliance down upon the soggy world. The beauty of the Florida Keys released the joy in us, and we laughed as I pointed to a sign rising out of a dune that said "Waterski" and mentioned to Jimmy how delighted I was to find Polish people that far south. Then we looked again and exploded with laughter. "Water Ski," it said. There were no Polish people here, after all.

As Jimmy drove and took out whatever furies were still possessing him on the car, I began to see him in a new light. There were nooks and crannies in him about which I could only guess. One of them was that for some reason his father had to remain god-like in his mind. Oscar could not be blemished by human imperfections. I was still awed by his talent and success and was barely scratching the surface of the family history, but I began to realize that Oscar was no more than human. He might have set himself up as invincible, Buddha-like in his calm demeanor, but he had other human failings, and one of them seemed to be that he was less than generous with his children. It differed sharply with his public image. He was very generous with his many philanthropies, sharing his largesse with foundations and other needy organizations. I was starting to discover that he was stingy, distant and often insensitive toward his own children.

As I grew older, I came to realize that the older generation has few illusions about the younger generation. The older generation has already been there. Youth may infuriate and perplex us, but we have lost our illusions about it. We were once young and remember that chaotic, highly pitched and tormented state. It seemed that way with Uncle Arthur. He knew his nephew Oscar and admired his success and productivity. As a member of the older generation, he seemed to have few illusions about him. It might have been Arthur's perception of Oscar's self-righteousness and stuffiness that seemed to rankle him, or the quality of a trial lawyer carefully dissecting each word. Something in Oscar set him apart from the foibles of humanity, and it irritated the octogenarian.

It was a similar quality I caught in my new father-in-law when I drew a picture of him later at The Farm. He resented the drawing, reproaching me for making him look like a banker. He was right. The drawing reflected the qualities of a businessman, not of a poet. We both understood that poets had a different quality. He was aware of the difference and wore ascots around his neck to further the poetic image. I had caught the underpinning, that which had been there before the poet surfaced. I caught the quality of the lawyer who became a lyricist, the banker who became the writer.

111

Chapter 10

The next stop on our honeymoon was a skindiving academy. Not a plain skindiving school, but an "academy," housed in a Quonset hut, sheltered just off the ocean by a large sand dune, with skindiving gear stacked up against its shiny metal walls. Framing the periphery of the beach was an outdoor practice swimming cove for beginners.

I needed to practice, having always been an indifferent swimmer. Actually, I never wanted to get my hair wet, and I swam like a turtle, with my head arched above the water. We spent the first day in the outdoor pool becoming familiar with the scuba gear: faceplates, tanks, hoses, weights, flippers and depth meters, to prepare us for the trip to the coral reef, out in the distance. Jimmy waved a spear gun around, cocking its shaft and shooting it into the sand.

With all the equipment weighing my body down, I could barely move on shore, but once I got into the water, I floated free, suspended over the swaying seaweed. After watching Jacques Cousteau's TV series, "The Silent World," I had become enchanted with his undersea photography, never realizing someday I would have the opportunity to experience that silent reality for myself.

The hours I spent in that protected outdoor cove were some of the best times I had during the whole honeymoon. The boulders lining the edges of the pool created a feeling of security, while keeping the space free of large waves and marine predators. I swam round and round between the immense rocks, listening to the soft popping noises made by the shrimp. Small, almost tame multicolored fish brushed my body and peered with apparent curiosity into my faceplate. The filigree fans of burgundy- colored seaweed swayed below me, gently floating on an unseen current of water. I hung above it all, suspended in an enchanted space. Memories of almost forgotten dreams surfaced in me, of watching the Earth from some great height. It was the closest I ever came to the enchanted days of my youth in Poland. As a child experiences the wondrous joy of a new reality, I was also experiencing a new world, and the joy followed.

On our trip to the reef, we included an inflated inner tube with a net attached to it to hold the fish Jimmy would spear. He brought along an extra set of spear guns with their ugly rigid shafts and still more ugly thick rubber bands that danced around the gun stem like the fingers of Dorothy's white kid gloves had danced around her hands at the anniversary ball.

In the distance, the waves broke on the surface of the coral reef, edging the horizon with a thin line of white lace. We putted out in our little boat, the droning motor breaking the silence of the open sea. It was not unlike what I had done with Poppa a hundred times before in Poland on the lake behind Minsk-Mazowiecki, and then years later in Oyster Bay on Long Island. There, too, we would bob up and down in the water, like the bobbins Poppa threw out with the fish lines. They danced around our boat waiting to hook all the fish in the area. In those days, my sister and I sat squirming on our hard wooden seats, pleading with Poppa to take us back to land so we could pee. He would hand us a tin can and laugh at us, as his gold teeth sparkled in the sun. Eventually, we had to face the trip home, but never before it turned dark. Then there'd be a confrontation with the cursing dock-yard owner and Poppa arguing over the deposit for the boat. Favoring our smarting sunburns, we'd head for home, with Poppa driving twenty miles per hour in the middle of the road.

We never ate the flounder he caught, but our rose bushes grew lush from the mounds of fish we buried under them. The neighborhood cats, attracted by the smell, kept us up most nights after our fishing excursions, scratching around in the garden and calling to their friends to join them in the feast. Sometimes Poppa threw the fish back into the lake or bay, saving himself the bother of burying them under the rose bushes and fighting with the cats. The irony was that none of us really liked fish. Poland was, to all intents and purposes, an inland country, acquiring Gdynia and Gdansk only after World War I. Pomerania may have come from an old Polish word pomorze, which meant "by the sea," but Poland lost title to it many years before. It seemed ironic that my new husband's family had part of its roots in the old Polish soil of Pomorze (Pomerania), before it became German.

In Poland or in Oyster Bay on Long Island, we stayed always within sight of land and were secure in the knowledge that we could somehow get back. We knew the general direction in which we had to swim if a problem arose and we had to fend for ourselves. In the Florida Keys, although we had the guide with us, we were alone in a small rowboat in the middle of the Gulf Stream, out of sight of land, bobbing fiercely on the breaking waves. The edges of the breakers might have looked like white lace in the distance. But breaking around us, they became formidable. As the waves tossed us about, the equipment rolled around in the bottom of the boat. We clung to its sides, keeping our legs and feet up and out of the way. As the angles of the waves changed on the side of our boat, some patches grew smooth and dark, for a quick moment exposing a great depth, not reflecting the light of the sky. I could see the current under us sweeping the seaweed swiftly by, suspending us over the rushing chasm below. Through shifting waves, I could barely see the tops of coral trees down in the murky depths. Broken pieces of seaweed sped by under the boat.

A "caution!" light went on in my head, which I ignored. As Jimmy plopped backward into the water off the side of the boat beside me, almost swamping it, I too, prepared to make the journey into the depths below. Our guide helped to put me together with all the scuba gear, plus some extra weights so that I wouldn't have to fight so hard to get under the surface. Muttering a silent "Hail Mary" and noting that no shark fins sliced the surface of water in our vicinity, I, too, flipped over backward into the open ocean. The guide followed closely behind me.

After the initial shock of the cold water, I sank deep into the silence of the Gulf Stream. My teeth clamped around the mouthpiece, and I dragged air into my lungs. As I plummeted down, the shadow of the boat against the sky above me grew smaller and smaller, becoming like a toy, bobbing high above on top of the waves. The swift current carried me away as the weights plunged me deeper into the muffled silence. There seemed to be no bottom as I sank downward, nothing to break my descent. The volume of water pressed against my chest, making it difficult to breathe. I felt as if I were being buried alive. My faceplate leaked and filled with water. It began to fill my nose, and I began to gasp. All I wanted to do was to rip everything off and pop back up to the surface. The equipment made it impossible. I was a leaden, sinking weight. My jaws ached as I clamped down on the mouthpiece. Choking on the salt water that was filling my faceplate, I pulled the air and the burning water into my lungs. My rapid descent alerted the guide, who plunged down after me. After taking a look at my stricken face behind the sloshing salt water, he grabbed me by the hand. With a few strong, sharp strokes of his flippers, he brought me back up to the surface.

In those few moments after the initial burning, choking horror, I had become one with the water. A stillness descended over me. Pictures swam before my eyes: visions of Mamma bent over the ironing board in Jamaica, Long Island; scenes of Poppa with clippers in his hands, cutting white roses in the back of the house. In that moment, right after the panic subsided, I wanted to be left alone, wanted to sink back into the arms of a comforting stillness that had begun to spread through me. As my body plummeted downward and was being swept away by the current, some other part of me also drifted. I no longer struggled, allowing myself to be carried along into a new unforeseen and uncharted journey. The darkness gave way to an inner light. An internal illumination glowed brighter within me.

A sharp tug on my arm, almost wrenching it out of my shoulder socket, brought me back to realty. The guide hauled me over the rough wooden edge of the boat, scratching my thighs, but getting me out of the water. With one hand, he yanked off my faceplate, sending the salty water spilling around me. With the other, he undid the weights around my waist and sent them flying over the side of the boat. They sank, cleaving the water and catching a glint of sunlight as they plummeted out of sight.

The pain of my bloody scraped legs brought me completely back, choking and sputtering. I began to shake in that hot, moisture-laden Gulf Stream air. My teeth began to rattle. The guide wrapped me in his shirt and covered my legs with his dungarees. I was embarrassed that I had failed him, that I had not risen to the occasion. I had behaved like a wimpy, helpless woman. He looked me over.

"You all right?" I nodded. "Had too many weights on, almost sank you," he added cryptically. I stopped berating myself, stopped doing an internal <u>mea culpa</u> and wanted to scream at him, <u>Whose fault was that? I put myself in your hands, and you almost drowned me, you jerk!</u>

"You look all right," he added as he looked me over. He was not a man of many words. I nodded, not wanting to blame him, not wanting to reproach him, or to incur his anger in any way. After all, he had saved my life. Out there in that tiny boat, I felt completely at his mercy.

"I think I've gotten chilled." I apologized, blaming the rattling of my teeth on physical weakness rather than for want of courage. "You go back in." I smiled cheerfully at him. He folded into the water, spitting into his faceplate to keep it from fogging up, and disappeared beneath the waves. I followed his air bubbles to a spot in the distance, where another set of bubbles belonging to Jimmy was breaking the surface of the water.

Panic-stricken and shaking, the front of my legs scraped and bleeding, my throat and lungs burning from the salt water, I began to realize how close I had come to dying. My life may not have flashed before me, but the scenes were forming for the movie to take place, right there under the boat, in which I was bobbing. There was no fear during the experience, only a deep, silent, dark peace. The fear grew in me with the realization of how close I had stumbled to the ultimate brink.

As the boat continued to sway on the waves, the shaking was replaced by nausea and an overwhelming desire to get out of there. A longing bordering on obsession swelled in me to replant my feet on the solid ground of Mother Earth. Nothing could get me back into that water again.

Jimmy surfaced next to the boat, with a thrashing bright green moray eel on the end of his spear. Blood from the wounded animal ran down his arm and into the water around him. He tried to push the squirming hissing creature into the net that hung suspended from the inner tube by the side of the boat. The stricken snake-like fish, thrashing wildly, sank its teeth deep into the rubber of the inner tube. A whistling sound escaped from the puncture as the tube relaxed into the water. I heard a "shit" and then a few "fucks" from my husband as he flung the speared and thrashing eel into the boat. I clamored away from the struggling fish as Jimmy proceeded to whack it with an oar. The barbs on the arrow shaft wouldn't release it, so he pummeled it to death. Finally, it stopped thrashing around. Jimmy unscrewed the head of the arrow, sliding the dead eel off the gun shaft. It lay bleeding on the bottom of the boat, bright green and still, its mouth open. Even in death, the three rows of teeth inside the contorted mouth seemed poised for attack.

From time to time, Jimmy and the guide surfaced at the side of the boat, sputtering and spitting into their faceplates, flicking off their spears dozens and dozens of multicolored fish, whose spectacular brilliance left their bodies along with their last gasp. No other fish being unceremoniously shoved off their spear shafts could match the sinuous splendor of the moray eel. Not to miss even one denizen of the deep, which unfortunately swam through his field of vision, my new husband taped a pair of old eyeglasses into his faceplate.

The bottom of the boat became alive with squirming, shuddering, dying fish. I pulled my feet as far away from them as I could and wondered. When they died, did the image of their lives unravel before them as the spear violated the envelope of their skins? Did a silent comforting darkness surround them? Was an inner light turned on to guide them through a silent comforting corridor? Why not? If some of it could happen to me, why not to them? The spark of life once burned as brightly in their bodies as it still glowed in mine. We were all forged from the same fire, cut from the same fabric of the sun. Walt Whitman was right; we were all part of that one great soul. As each fish shuddered its last gasp and lay still, a glaze formed over its eyes. I bid them adieu, bid them a pleasant passage to the light, and thanked the blazing sun above me that I was still alive.

The next day, Jimmy and the guide went out again. Their enthusiasm wasn't infectious enough to induce me to join them. I chose to stay behind on the beach. My scraped legs had scabbed over, and I didn't want to open the scratches in the biting salt water or to attract any sharks with the blood. I enjoyed the sun that had begun to shine again. While collecting shells and pieces of coral on the littered beach, I waited for the two piscatorial hunters to come home. They returned at twilight with another load of thrashing, dying, speared fish on the bottom of the boat. After getting acknowledged for their skills by the local fishermen, they again dumped the dying and dead mass over the side of the boat into the arms of the waiting ocean.

Uncle Arthur told us about a wonderful out-of-the-way French restaurant not too far from him, on one of the Keys. With a flush of sunburn surfacing on our shoulders, we went there that night. When the owners heard that we were on our honeymoon, they sent over a split of champagne and sang us some French songs. My new husband loosened up and had a good time. We shared a wonderful evening filled with laughter and good cheer and spent a warm, loving night together.

The next morning, the rain again followed us as we headed farther down south. We spent the next few days in a motel room, part of the time getting on each other's nerves. Television had not as yet invaded the outer perimeters of the country. There was nothing to listen to on the radio except hillbilly music. It hadn't yet become respectable enough to earn the title of "Country and Western." There was no <u>New York Times</u> to read, no crossword puzzles to fill in. All we had was a cramped motel room, the rain, the humidity and the diminishing promise that the sun would shine one day.

When I lived at home, Momma made me pay rent. Part of the unspoken agreement between us was that she continued to do my laundry. During my honeymoon, the moment of truth had arrived. I finally had to wash the accumulated mound of dirty clothes. My doing this chore was a given, an unvoiced agreement coming along with the marriage vows. I bundled all our clothes and schlepped them through the rain to the local laundromat. In the laundry bag, I included not only my cotton shirts and underwear, but also Jimmy's cashmere socks and cashmere sweater. After they went through the washer and dryer, they emerged small enough to fit a midget. Not only had they shrunk, but they also had become as hard as a board, and a terrible raw animal stench filled the room as I tried to stretch them out. I was so humiliated that I wanted to cry. My new husband laughed. He could have cared less. Clothes were not one of his priorities.

Then finally we awoke one morning to find the sun bright and shiny above the sparkling sea, and we headed out to do some sightseeing. Key West can be a bit of a disappointment. There is a rather humble and polluted public beach, an Army base, Ernest Hemingway's house and a fort. We joined some tourists for a sightseeing trip to the reef. While gingerly picking my way across a shallow coral bed, I stepped on a sea urchin, a living pincushion of bony spines that left their sharp barbs in my foot. Limping back with my foot burning, I spent the night with one leg hung over the side of the bed, soaking in a bowl of vinegar. The local wisdom had it that it would help to melt the sharp slivers in my foot.

Jimmy, on the other hand, burned his shoulders. The sun had not been out long enough for him to get a gradual tan. His partially

Scottish skin -- on his mother's side -- turned beet red. Between the Noxema on his shoulders and the bowl of vinegar beside the bed, the smell in the musty, damp motel room was overwhelming.

It got so I feared the coming of each new day. What disaster would befall us next? We stayed on, determined to persevere and to do some deep-sea fishing the next day. Jimmy caught a marlin, and the boat captain again clubbed the creature to death on the bottom of the boat, setting the pilot fish, which had been attached to the large gray marlin, scrambling. I scooped them off the deck and sent them to find another marlin to guide through the depths of the open ocean. Same thing happened with a grouper, a "Jewfish," the locals called it, explaining it was because it had a large curved nose. The grouper was immense. It took two men to drag the dying fish over the side of the boat. When they finally heaved it on board, they caught Jimmy's leg underneath it. He was badly scraped by the fish's sharp spiny fins. I spent part of the night daubing his legs with hydrogen peroxide.

The next day, we decided to head for home. The hell with it; enough was enough! Once we made the decision to leave, we shot out of there like greased lightning. Who called it a honeymoon, anyway? There was little sweetness in it. It seemed more like a time of discomfort and growing insecurity, a terrible time of small humiliations and big embarrassments, of unexpressed fears and long painful silences.

The car made it back with no breakdowns. It really didn't want to be on the honeymoon with us, so it, too, was eager to get home. We made it back in record time, not stopping to rest or to sleep. We drove in shifts, chewed gum, drank coffee and played hinkey-pinkey, a game of rhymed syllables, until we got back to the familiar congestion of New York City.

Not knowing how to face family and friends, we holed up in the apartment and lay low for a few days. How could we have explained to them why we had barreled back? Our early return might have intimated things had gone wrong on our honeymoon.

120

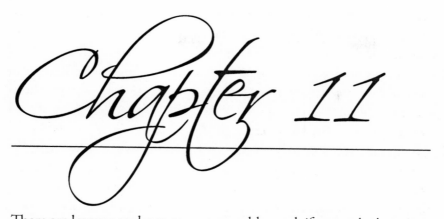

Chapter 11

There are lessons we learn as we grow older and, if we are lucky, wiser. There are laws that become discernible, laws that lie silent beneath the surface of everyday reality. If we discover those laws and begin to hear them, if we learn to listen to that inner voice telling us when we have broken those implicit rules, then we can live a life that is balanced, based on truth, based on things working. When the inner voice becomes stilled or we tune it out with various reasons or justifications because we don't really want to hear it, then we bounce from chaos to chaos, never alighting long enough in peace to make our home there. The lesson that accidents, chance, or fate try to teach us when chaos hits us is that we are out of sync, out of tune, discordant with the road of our destiny. We are off our path, out of rhythm or cadence, We wobble along, de-cadent or decadent, out of step, out of balance, at odds with ourselves.

One of my philosophers had wisely said, "Ride the horse in the direction it is going." It seemed like a deceptively simple statement. One of our major challenges in life is to find the direction in which the horse is going. It is easier said than done. We are given clues when we stray off the path. Some of those clues include accidents, others chaos, and the ultimate ones manifest themselves in disease. When these discords fill our lives with repeated bouts of dislocation, we are being warned that the horse we are riding is not moving in the same direction. The horse we are riding is dragging us. We are not bouncing gaily on its back, but are holding on to its tail for dear life. Some of us are even digging our heels in against the pull of our destiny and fight our way all the way to the grave. There are some other philosophers who have defined that futile gesture as being noble. The truth is that the horse is going to go where it needs to go, no matter how hard we fight it.

The things that have been right for me have always made themselves easily available to me. I don't know exactly what makes that decision. Perhaps it's some deeper level within me, my guides; perhaps some would call it that omnipresent, unmovable mover. I have a sense that it's something, somewhere, beyond my apparently conscious level of sensing or perceiving, that rises to fulfill my needs and desires. All I know is, if the thing is right for me, it literally falls into my lap.

If I were going to school and left my pen home, I would find a pen on the sidewalk along my route. If I needed change for the bus or for the cafeteria in school, I would often find coins in the gutter at the bus stop. Books I needed literally appeared on the library shelves right under my nose. Fallen magazines opened to pages exposing articles I had to read.

When things were not right for me, I could spend weeks researching them, trying hard to track down leads that led to dead ends, often experiencing upsets through frustration and disappointment. My stubbornness, will, or ego often pushed me to prove something by pursuing it past the point of its self- revelation.

There is a truism in the Protestant ethic extolling great effort. You have to work hard for what you get. I find that is not true. If you have to work hard for something, then it is not right for it to be. You are not on the right road, not on the right track. You are not riding the horse in the direction in which it is going. So many efforts of Western civilization are a symptom of that misalignment, that misdirection. What is right for us settles into our lives like a familiar companion. The gears mesh. No reasons are needed for it to be there, no explanations, no justifications. It is a law that we have not as yet formulated as a law, because we in the Western world do not deal with the implicit. The whole thrust of our civilization is to define and then to redefine the explicit. We are at the point in time where only external verifiable data is considered as a candidate for the title of law. The other levels that are ever with us and clamor to be recognized at the walls of our inattention, we call chance, accident or fancy. That is not the whole truth. Explicit data deals only with half of it, only the explicit, external part. That is where the philosophers I studied at Hunter College failed me. I felt that they never dealt with the really intangible, the really unknown parts of our being. The implicit laws are as constant as the explicit. The truth may be that we have lost the clues to that inner world that seems to exist only through dreams, myths, legends, superstitions, parables, old wives tales, intuition, feelings and hunches.

Had I known then that great effort produces only a great deal of action, throws up a great deal of dust and obscures the truth, I would have known that no matter how hard I tried to fit into a new redefined self, the old real me would rebel and begin to sabotage my life. The great effort to keep myself going was only a symptom of the fact that the road that I was taking was not a natural and easy path for me to travel.

At one point when I finally began to write this book, I found it difficult to stay with it. Other things became more compelling, more demanding of my attention. It was much easier to build a deck, mulch the garden, go for a ride, have lunch with friends. In the process of building the deck and lining the hole under it with scrap iron, I tipped a cast iron radiator across my ankle and broke the instep. That didn't stop me. I continued to hobble around, calling it a sprain. Then the universe upped the ante, and I dropped a full sheet of one-half-inch plywood across the same instep, this time breaking my big toe in the process. That put me out of commission altogether. I couldn't even hobble around.

The physical universe forced me to sit down and write. The universe gave me a clear signal that I had to write the book. It might be called an accident or a coincidence. Why not look at it in the bigger picture? I was being given guidance. I was being told what to do. Because I didn't listen, I was forced to sit down and write. The explanation of coincidence is too pat, too easy. When we don't listen to small nudges, we get big ones. We even get catastrophes when we turn off the inner voice. A catastrophe makes us sit up and notice. It's a different way of looking at things. Nothing in nature is lost; it is all recycled. Therefore, accidents and coincidences are only recycled, more intense forms of warning. It is saying, "You're off the path, you're out of step, you're not riding the horse in the direction it's going." Therefore, every upset can be recycled into a lesson, into an early warning sign before the universe ups the ante and gets our attention through a catastrophe.

Had I known then about this subtle but ever-present reality that exists on another level, I would have listened to what the car we were given by my new in-laws was trying to tell me, what it was trying to tell the both of us. The car didn't get through to me, so the honeymoon itself made a valiant effort. Had I been listening to that nagging inner voice, I would have gotten out, bag and baggage, fled back to New York, uncoiled from the pretzel I was becoming trying to fit in, and continued with my life alone, to face an altogether different destiny. Maybe that's not the way it works either. If I didn't listen, then I wasn't meant to hear. That argument opens other unending ramifications.

Like my father-in-law, I was a cockeyed optimist, and I was going to make things work. I was going to barrel through, and it would all be all right. The blessings that then surrounded my life I had taken for granted. It was only when they stopped manifesting themselves that I realized how blessed I had been and how much I had lost. Those inherent, internal, implicit laws had not become as clear to me then as they did later on. I turned my life over to my new husband and began to look to him to take control of the wheel for our future together.

Chapter 12

I had always wanted to live in a garden apartment on the West Side or in Greenwich Village, but that was beyond our means. While we were gone on our honeymoon, Dorothy lost no time finding us a second-floor apartment on Sixty-Seventh Street and Madison Avenue. She knew the broker and got us a six-month deal we could not refuse. It had only one problem. Facing the street, it reverberated with noise of the buses on Madison Avenue. I already slept with earplugs and an eye mask. In our new apartment, I had to keep the windows shut to keep the noise out. The whole place shook as the buses accelerated up the hill, shifting their gears and gunning their motors, right under our rattling windows.

After our honeymoon, we spent much more time with Jimmy's family. They seemed grateful that the marriage had brought their son back to them. I thought that it pleased them, for that's the way I would have felt at the time. Later in life, I was to realize that grown children are a mixed blessing.

Presents began arriving, mostly from Oscar's associates, who were also their social friends. Dorothy and Richard Rodgers gave us a silver Queen Anne place setting for six, with the initial "H" etched neatly into the pistol handles. The forks had three straight prongs, and the set contained extra soup spoons that I had already learned were to be used for dessert. The "H" on the pistol handles filled me with a sense of unreality. My initials had always been "BMR" (Barbara Maria

Redzisz), and now "H" was etched into the handles. Who was that new person, I wondered, as "H" and "BHR" appeared on the stuff of my life? We were quickly accumulating presents worth a great deal of money. Silver serving spoons arrived along with crystal decanters and many beautifully wrapped boxes of silver frames, frames from Tiffany's, Jensen's and Winston's. Momma made us a set of cafe curtains that covered the bottom half of all the rattling windows in the apartment, giving us privacy.

I returned to school in the fall, cramming my subjects into the last remaining year in order to finish by the following June. At home I had become a housewife. I had to learn how to cook, and after a few months, with much trial and error, became quite good at it.

"Dad," as Oscar asked me to call him after Jimmy and I were married, and Richard Rodgers, who became "Dick," were in the midst of preparing <u>Pipe Dream</u>. Judy Tyler, who landed the part of the new leading lady, had a big loud chest voice. She coached with her husband, Colin Romoff. Big chest voices were in demand at that time, so I, with my reedy top soprano, also went to him for coaching.

Colin was an amazing confluence of talents. He was a brilliant musician, transposing at sight and playing by ear. When he accompanied people at auditions, he became a one-man band, humming from the side of his mouth like a trumpet, banging out rhythms on the top of the piano and tapping the floor with his feet. When the spirit moved him, he got up from the piano and kept the song going with one hand, while rat-tat-tatting the rhythm out with the other. It got so that producers would watch Colin instead of the auditioners who were trying to land the job.

At that time and during my marriage, I found it difficult to have an orgasm during intercourse. The fact that I couldn't "come" with my husband gave me a great deal of anguish. There was an implication in the then-current psychological literature that women who didn't "pop off" easily when stimulated by a penis were somehow less than female. "Frigid" was the word of the day. I tried everything: positions, liquor, even fantasy. Along the way, the concept of "frigidity" got redefined. At first, you were "frigid" if a penis didn't make you "come." Then you were "frigid" if you couldn't "come" with the help of a finger or tongue. Then you were "frigid" if you couldn't make yourself "come" while masturbating.

The first person I ever heard talking openly about sex and masturbation was Florence Baum when I was in <u>Top Banana</u>. She was going through her angst earlier than I was to go through mine. One day while sullenly staring at herself in the dressing-room mirror, she announced to no one in particular that she hated herself so much that she couldn't even make herself "come." At that time, I found her announcement brazen and embarrassing. It took me many years of trial and error to get anywhere near her openness and honesty.

Sometimes during intercourse, the contact was made, and I felt myself rising to the pleasure, but the wrong movement or a minor change in rhythm brought the whole thing to a halt. I would give up, disappointed and frustrated at the failure. Jimmy often stayed with me past the point where anything could happen. His endurance only made me physically sore. At times, I faked an orgasm, thrashing around just to have him "come" and get it over with. Often during our lovemaking, we were like two pieces of wood in the night trying to catch fire by the frantic rubbing of our bodies.

Not once during our entire marriage did we reach orgasm together. God knows we tried. The thought nagged at both of us that our marriage bed wasn't complete because we couldn't "come" together.

I later learned that some people fit better than others. It is the clitoris that needs to be stimulated, whether by the penis or by the tongue or by rubbing up against a tree. I think human beings became upright when the great apes freed their hands to diddle with their private parts as they sped along in the tall grass. Otherwise, why would their paws end at that forbidden area? It's the clitoris that pops off even when the penis is in a woman. It gathers the vagina into itself, and the vagina spasms. Sometimes even the anus and the uterus spasm. It all takes place because the clitoris is engaged and rubbed into a frenzy.

Whatever else happened in bed wasn't written or talked about, any more than the part played by male ignorance. We deferred to the men in our lives, looking up to them to share with us their wisdom and superior knowledge. Sexual information was still generally withheld from us, but men behaved as if they knew, as if those secrets had been made available to them. Many marriages must have foundered on the shoals of that ignorance with the pain of disappointment it brought to many young, equally ignorant, brides.

Along with worrying about the quality of my orgasms, I was having trouble with my middle voice. The top notes were fine and clear. The bottom notes were strong. When I sang in the middle, when I tried to push the deeper lower voice up past the break into the higher register, I began to sound very breathy and raspy. Along the way, periodically I began to lose my voice.

The low booming chest voice was the voice that was prized in those days. Most of the pacesetters in the musical theater were homosexual males who liked women to be more like a man in many ways, one of which, was to sound like one. It was most acceptable in those days to sound like Ethel Merman or Dolores Gray, loud and deep. Gay men also set the trend in fashion by designing clothes for boyish women. The ideal woman was expected to be tall, flat-chested, slim-hipped, and thin, like a pubescent boy. Pubescent boys became the ideal of femininity. The door came completely off the closet in the Eighties when one designer used young, tall, thin, flat-chested, slim-hipped boys to model his haute couture.

The truth was out. In the meantime, the image had stuck, and many young women died from anorexia and bulimia, trying to mirror the image of female perfection spawned in the minds of homosexual men. Older, more voluptuous women were completely discarded as being unacceptable, and curves became declasse.

Since I was into doing the right thing, I plunged into making my voice sound like a man's. Some teachers had me screaming in closets, a la Wilhelm Reich and his orgone box, breathing with books on my stomach, singing with a small hoe-like instrument pulling my tongue forward, clutching at my throat trying to keep my elusive Adam's apple from moving up, or putting my hands behind my head with the thumbs on my chin, forcing my mouth to open, to push the sound out with as much force and volume as possible.

I could always make the necessary bellow during the lesson, but the day after the lesson left me hoarse and breathy. Up to that point, I had a passable soprano, which got me into Top Banana and Two's Company. But just before I married Jimmy, at the recommendation of Arthur Lewis, who put me in Can-Can in order to make me available for the late and unlamented Sweet Thursday, I went to work on my voice with Herbie Greene. He had me do the octave jump, which took me from the bottom of my voice to the top in a kind of glottal bellow not unlike a yodel.

It was "in" then to study with Herbie Greene. Rosalind Russell, Sydney Chaplin, Judy Holiday, all relied on his expertise. To get ahead on Broadway in those days, you had to have a singing teacher for the voice and a coach for the music. Colin Romoff filled in as a coach. Herbie Greene became my voice teacher. Like lemmings, following each other into the abyss over the side of a cliff, all of us followed the singing teacher and coach trail. It was ironic that at one gala, celebrity-filled festive dinner at one of the hotel ballrooms, while I was sitting at a table down front close to the dais with my new in-laws, awards were given out for a variety of musical accomplishments. Herbie Greene received one for the contributions he made to singers on Broadway. The person presenting the award to him was a hoarse Sydney Chaplin, followed by a rasping Rosalind Russell.

After bellowing in his studio on Fifty-Seventh Street and Seventh Avenue, I was beginning to have recurrent troubles with my voice. It seemed that I really needed help, at least more help than Herbie could give me. Everyone was into analysis in those days. They, in turn, analyzed everyone else who came in contact with them. Sharing your problems with a psychiatrist was the universal panacea. Herbie was being "shrunk" and was a true believer. One day, I was bellowing from the bottom octave to the top. The center came out fuzzy.

129

Herbie, sitting on the piano bench with one leg tucked under him, gave me a word of advice. "You seem to have a problem with the middle voice, and that means your problem is probably sexual. You seem to fear the middle, to give yourself to the middle." He then paused and measured his words. "Sex also happens in the middle."

I couldn't dispute that. Since I wasn't having vaginal orgasms, I thought that he had guessed my shameful secret. In an effort to correct my wanting sexuality, along with my raspy voice, I went into therapy. Years later, a similar madness entered my life, but at that time it was self-perpetrated.

After I had gotten my divorce, I dated a tall, handsome neurotic named Howard. After I bought the house in Rockland County, New York, which at that time was considered to be "in the sticks," we'd go to the country on the weekends to do some work. I'd feed Howard, and we'd make love. Howard would then go to sleep while I went out and did heavy labor, digging up the garden, spreading cow manure, and generally doing what needed to be done. When Howard woke up, I'd feed him, and again we'd make love. He would go back to sleep. I would return to work.

One weekend, after the leaves had fallen, I noticed that a large branch had to be removed from a tree because it was growing too close to the house. Howard took a long aluminum ladder out from behind the garage. He placed it on the branch just inside the cut he had to make with the saw, making sure he wouldn't saw the branch out from under himself. We had planned it very carefully, placing the edge of the ladder at precisely the right spot, to no avail. When the cut was made, the branch rose up out of reach of the shorter ladder, sending Howard and the ladder crashing down to the ground. No one told us that the weight of the branch held the ladder in place. As the sawed-off branch fell, he and the ladder hovered in the air for a split second. Then he crashed down after it. He hit the ground all in one piece and then bounced up and down two times. Bong, bong, he went. My breath caught in my chest, but I wanted to scream with laughter. Howard sat dazed, rubbing his back. I know it wasn't kind, or even funny, but

I never knew that a person could bounce like a ball, but Howard did. I helped him up, checking to see if any bones had been broken, made him a hot toddy, and put him to bed. He got up the next day feeling better, though a bit sore, but none the worse for wear.

We almost forgot the incident until a few nights later, when Howard wet the bed. We had been into a lot of mutual analysis, trying to figure out why we fought so much. To explain his bed-wetting, I distilled some of the psychiatric claptrap that was being disseminated and deduced that he wanted to revert to a more infantile dependent level, return to the womb, have his diapers changed, etc. I was getting a lot of explanations about things in those days.

When Howard wet the bed again, I sent him to see my analyst. The analyst was wiser than I thought, suggesting a physical check-up. We found out that Howard had a kidney infection, most probably precipitated by his fall from the tree. The doctor prescribed antibiotics, and Howard got better. His wetting the bed did not have a psychological origin. It had to do with the physical problem of falling out of a tree, going bong, bong, and hurting his kidney.

The beginning of my voice problems had a similar origin. I was having trouble singing because I was trying to get my chest voice too high up in the top register, not because it was tied up with my sexuality, the "middle" notwithstanding. At the time, there was no room for practical observations like the fact that my voice was being pushed past its limit and Howard hurt his kidneys by falling out of the tree. The obvious physical "fact" had no room in the realm of the accepted psychiatric "theory."

Chapter 13

Oscar had encouraged me to sing for him and for Richard Rodgers who, as I grew to know him, became known more familiarly as "Dick." The understudy in the renamed <u>Pipe Dreams</u> was still not yet cast, nor were the roles of all the prostitutes. The anticipation of singing for Rodgers and Hammerstein created a panic inside me that I could barely control. The fear of discovery on a variety of levels seemed imminent. I had chosen a very strange place where I was going to hide my fears, and that was on the exposed mountain top of the stage.

Fear of performing was a given. Separating myself from the group to stand alone, isolated and vulnerable was only one of the furies that pursued me. As a singer, I had some others. It wasn't always that way, but as I entrenched myself in the theater, realizing more and more how much panic I carried within me when I sang, I still proceeded as if possessed, as if the plunge forward into my own panic was beyond the control of my will.

When I was younger and by myself, joyful feelings flooded my body when I sang, or even hummed tunes. Creating sounds was not only one of my greatest passions, but it filled me with such pleasure that I had to make a concentrated effort in order to move through the goose pimples that erupted all over my skin when I sang. Always in danger of choking off the music from the loss of breath, I had to reach deep down into my body and hook into the large muscles to keep the sound moving.

Often as I sang and my body tingled, a feeling of lightheadedness emptied out my brain. When I opened my mouth and filled my body with the vibration of sound, it felt as if I had sent a coil of my inner spirit out upon the air around me. There were times when I felt as if I and the air around me vibrated as one unit. To send music out upon that gift of air seemed like the greatest of blessings. It was that joy and passion that I wanted to share with others, to move in them the feelings that the sound-carrying breath moved in me.

In the early days of my youth when I still searched for truth, it never occurred to me that the response that I would flush out of the emotional bushes when I sang would turn out to be the then dreaded beast of sexuality. I was hoping for it to be perhaps on a higher plane, perhaps more spiritual in nature. I was hoping that it would be something dealing with "truth and beauty, beauty and truth," as Keats and the Romantic poets would have had us believe.

As I sang at more auditions, many of which often led to performances, I became aware, in those hypocritically rigid days at the Fifties, that my singing was creating not only a sexual response in men, but it was also creating situations that I didn't know exactly how to handle.

I realized that if I were to continue to sing, then I had to learn to walk a very fine if double line, one that made a lovely, good-girl, ladylike sound that would get me jobs, while I kept under wraps the passion, goose pimples and almost boundless joy with which singing filled me.

As I look back on it, the double life began when I was still a very little girl back in Poland. Somewhere back then, very early in my young life, I looked around me at the way that people acted and said to myself, "They are all lying and acting as if they were crazy. For me not to be punished and become the subject of ridicule, I, too, would have to lie and learn to act crazy."

Since I felt deeply and saw reality from a different point of view, undoubtedly from my love of Nature or my left-handedness, I thought that I must either be odd or very different. The part of me that was true and sane had to go underground; otherwise I would be discovered and severely punished. I didn't know then what the difference was. But I was aware that what I saw and felt seemed to be at odds with what others around me perceived. I was derided as being a changeling, a foundling, a god-damned princess left by some Gypsies, a child blown in on the north wind of a fairy tale. So, as a very small girl, I embarked on a journey of subterfuge that created an almost irreconcilable duality in my being.

The need for that duality existed not only in the Poland of my early youth, but followed me across the ocean to America. When we landed in Hoboken, New Jersey, in 1938, we encountered social extremes based not so much on perceived wealth -- the United States was considered to be a classless society, and the truth had not yet been exposed by the unrelenting glare of television -- but, more to the point, on the more simplistic definitions of good and evil.

Movies set the stage. Cowboy heroes wore white hats and rode white horses. Cowboy villains wore black hats and rode black horses. Women were either virgins or whores, pure or sullied, good girls or harlots.

On the level of social acceptability, after you learned the language, you were either savvy or ignorant. To be ignorant implied stupidity. At that time, for a child, being stupid was probably a greater sin than being poor. There was no in-between, no gray area. The bridge defining reality was not based on the inclusive "and." The bridge defining reality collapsed under the exclusive weight of "or."

My philosopher friend, with his admonition to ride the horse in the direction it was going, created not only a directional duality within me, bouncing backward on the galloping steed, but with our assimilation in the new culture of America, I internalized, in a very personal way, the good and evil of the American cowboy frontier, doing them one better.

I began to ride two horses, both of them backward. One horse, on my left, was as white and brilliant as the summer sun at noon, sailing across the sparkling sky. The other horse, on my right, was black, like

134

the midnight sun of despair, lost to the light of day, cold and wintry, coursing through the murky chambers of the night. My panic rode them both, holding onto their tails for dear life.

The two horses thrashed ahead in tandem, dragging me along. One, above ground, the white stallion for all the world to see, was open, smiling optimistic, positive, warm, filled with the light of acquiescence. The other, the black horse, galloped under ground, hidden, dark, cold, wary, filled with rage and the fear of discovery.

The duality, like a rising Spring tide, forever warmed by the relentless sun of rationalization, seeped into other areas of my life. As much as I rejected the Christian dichotomy of body and soul, I impaled myself on my own definition of good and evil, as that which was or was not socially acceptable. To be accepted, you not only had to be "good," but you also had to "know." It didn't matter what it was that you had to "know." It had more to do with the fact that at any moment you shouldn't give yourself away and expose yourself as not knowing and appear to be stupid. So knowledge became essential.

Since you couldn't know everything, then you had to act as if you knew. To that end, I became aware that an education was a great asset and a hedge against admonitions of stupidity. It was probably one of the main reasons why I worked so diligently to get my B.A. degree and then my subsequent M.A.

Facts would become my friends. Facts, as the tenants of my mind, would silence the needs of my heart. They would form a wall between me and the danger of discovery. Facts would become the bridge between the two polar horses of my life. They would become the woven girdle that would yoke together the two galloping giants of my being.

It might have originally been a good idea, but it wasn't all that easy to make it work. As I galloped along, pulled by the gravity of my life, straddling the two images of power that I had created, the white one on the left, above board, the black one on the right, below, the chasm between them widened and grew, until I, riding them both backward on the wings of my panic, was almost torn apart.

As a young child and as a budding performer, I cradled the duality within me as my only means of survival. I not only had to hide the passionate pleasure evoked in me by singing, which would have defined me as a wanton and not as a "good" girl, but I also had to hide another damaging secret which would have branded me as stupid. That other potential brand on my forehead was my inability to read music. It wasn't that I didn't try. The gears just never meshed. I couldn't make the jump from the concentrated line-by-line effort to the automatic rote that didn't need conscious thought to make it work. The same problem surfaced when I tried to learn to type. I could never make the leap from the conscious control of each finger to the unthinking, automatic movement of my fingers across the keys.

The fact that I had a good ear, and that there were not too many good jobs available in the evening, saved me from altogether abandoning a singing career in the theater. After hearing the melody of a song once or twice, I could usually repeat it verbatim. Listening and watching very closely became my way of life, a wariness to size up any and all situations, find my place in them and try to feel safe.

Chapter 14

In New York City, as part of our educational experience, we had a musical organization called the All-City Chorus. At the beginning of the fall term, all of the high school glee club teachers from the five boroughs comprising New York City selected their top singers to audition. Since it was a great honor to be part of the All-City Chorus, the chosen few, joined by the All-City Orchestra, blessed with talent and courage, got to sing at the yearly concert in the cavernous auditorium of the Brooklyn Technical High School in the Borough of Brooklyn.

Before we could perform at the yearly concert, we had to audition at Julia Richman High School on the East Side of New York City for a conductor who was called, with awe and wonder, Peter John Wilhousky. With a name like that, I hoped he was at least partly Polish. To be selected for the All-City Chorus was not only a great honor for the chosen specific performer, but bestowed great prestige upon the performer's high school glee club teacher. We had to learn a song that Mr. Wilhousky picked out for us to sing. It was called "Just a Song at Twilight." I practiced it until it filled all the empty spaces in my brain.

After I had gotten into the All-City Chorus and had gotten to know Mr. Wilhousky, I asked him why he made us sing that particular song. It seemed such a sad song for a bunch of teenagers to plow their way through. He told me that it had all the pitfalls that a singer could confront in a piece of music. It made it easier for him, as he put it, to separate the wheat from the chaff at the auditions.

On the day of my first All-City Chorus audition, we sang and repeated that same song. Hundreds of us made the effort and either got through all or parts of it. Sopranos, altos, tenors and bassos not only plowed, but chopped their way through the lament.

The Friday night before the big moment, my mother starched and ironed my white blouse, forever advising me that instead of wasting my time with music, I should take stenography and typing. She didn't know that learning to type was no less of a problem for me than learning to read music.

Then on a Saturday morning with the lengthening shadows of the fall term in the air, we all converged on Julia Richman High School. We came in all shapes, sizes and colors, boys and girls, some shy, some boisterous, all hoping to become part of something bigger, something that was taking place inside of that looming brick building in the East Sixties that housed the mythic Wilhousky and the All-City Chorus auditions.

Friends from former semesters greeted each other and filled themselves in on what they were presently doing and how they had spent their summers. I envied them for their sophistication and their apparent ease. All those strange faces scared me, especially the boys. I hadn't spent much time around boys because Washington Irving High School was a girl's school. The boys' noise and fast movements frightened me and made me even more shy.

We filed into the auditorium, boys on one side and girls on the other, waiting for the legendary figure of P.J. Wilhousky to make his appearance. He was known for his great talent as a musician and for his demanding perfectionism and discipline as a conductor. The kids who had worked with him the semester before, spoke of him with apparent awe tinged with fear, shooting glances in the direction of the door on the side of the auditorium from which he would momentarily appear. While we waited, there was furtive conversation to keep the anxiety from surfacing, great anticipation and excitement, the mulling of words of the audition song, feigned nonchalance and restrained jubilation. My heart began to pound, not only in my ears and throat, but in my whole body. Could I pull it off? Could I get into the Chorus without giving myself away?

I sang wonderfully well hidden in the group, as long as I could sing top soprano, which usually carried the recognizable melody. There were times I was asked to sing second soprano (there seemed always to be a shortage of second sopranos) because I seemed to be so capable in the lead line. At those times, I would wedge myself between two second sopranos and fake the notes until I learned them. At the moment of truth, which was usually the performance, no matter where I sat, I always reverted to the melody line at the top. At those times, our glee club teacher, Mrs. Greene, would scowl and with her chubby right hand try to pull more sound out of the second sopranos, wondering where the power went. With her left hand, she'd be pumping up and down, trying to dampen the sound bellowing forth from the top sopranos, of which I was an exuberant and enthusiastic part.

My only problem became apparent when the words were different; then I had to fake the second soprano part and slide triumphantly into the top sopranos as soon as I was able. For me, singing in the glee club was not only a matter of knowing my part. For me, it was a matter of strategy and careful planning. As a general rule, my unbridled enjoyment of singing got me through unscathed on the outside, while I shook on the inside, always wondering when I would be caught faking.

My reverie was broken by a loud bang from the outside as the large auditorium doors of Julia Richman High School were shut and we were all sealed inside the large hall. Latecomers were locked out. Excuses were rejected. Then a much smaller door on the side of the stage was opened, and onto the stage walked the mythic conductor, P.J. Wilhousky. He was tall, imposing, quite slim for his age, with straight grey hair, which was slicked back, covering a nicely shaped head. Over his upper lip, he wore a thin grey mustache, which sprouted neatly under his pinched but slightly bumped nose.

Patrician in aspect, I thought. The word came back to me from a lesson I learned the week before in history class. His tan set off the whiteness of his hair to a great advantage. I couldn't help thinking what a wonderful looking old man he was. To a sixteen- year-old, a man in his forties, and one with gray hair, pushed the limits of survival. He carried his own music portfolio. A pretty young girl carried his coat in after him.

Mr. Wilhousky paused before he sat down on a bench at the piano, turned out front and bowed his head to the pulsating auditorium, as an ovation shook the roof off the old high school building and sent the resident pigeons soaring toward the East River. The pretty young girl who followed him across the stage sat behind him and busied herself by draping his coat on one chair and positioning his portfolio on another.

Without looking down, Mr. Wilhousky's hands sank on to the piano keys and brought forth chords that seemed recognizable to the students who had been in the chorus the year before. Then as he looked down at his fingers, the former members of the chorus, who were scattered among us novices throughout the great hall, started to sing a song that was totally unfamiliar to me.

"Madame Jeannette, when the sun goes down..." A great tapestry of closely woven sound filled the auditorium. My skin exploded with goose pimples.

"Sits at her window in the rush of the town..." The sound built and spread out as the maestro looked down at his hands and carefully pushed the keys on the piano. It vibrated through all our bodies. Some of the girls around me were trying to hold back their tears.

"Waiting for someone each close of the day, someone who fell at St. Pierre, they say..." Then the top soprano and tenor voices broke through and sang a line that blended back into the main sound: "Madame Jeannette, she will wait there, I know..." He lifted one hand, the fingertips of the other still lingering on the piano keys, turned to the singing group, and with his eyes closed, led them.

"Till her eyes have grown dim and her hair's white as snow..."

140

With the raised hand moving almost imperceptibly, he guided them from word to word, gently punctuating each sound.

"Wait there and watch there, till one of these days..." The whole singing group became a single organism poised to react to his slightest gesture.

"They take her to slumber, in Pere Lachaise, in Pere Lachaise..." With barely a movement, as the last note hung in the air, he folded the sound upon itself. The song had come to the end. He raised his head, as if from a vision, opened his eyes and looked out into the auditorium as the assemblage exploded. By now, even some of us new people were openly crying.

I had never heard "Madame Jeannette" sung before. The memory of the sound still held the hair upright on my body. I had never heard anything sung with such compressed intensity and emotion. The stricken longing in the song produced an echo in my aching heart. I shared and rode a wave of deep feeling that swept over all of us. With every cell in my body, I wanted to be a part of that music, to share the kind of joy that music awakened in me. I prayed that Mr. Wilhousky would pick me and trembled that my accent wouldn't return, as it did when I became nervous. I feared that I would not be chosen, or I would forget the words, or screech on the high notes. In a spirit of desperate hope, taking deep breaths to still my pounding heart, I resolved to do the best I could, as I instructed my knees to stop shaking.

As we sank back into our wooden auditorium seats and quieted down, P.J. Wilhousky turned his handsome tanned face to the very young and very pretty girl with him and said something. They both laughed, he louder than she. He then took out a pipe and deliberately lit it, motioning to the monitors who were waiting off stage. Cards were passed out and instructions given. We were directed to sit in sections, according to our voices and to fill out our cards.

The auditorium became a cacophony of unstructured sound and of banging wooden seats as everybody scrambled to the places to which they had become assigned. I found the sopranos down in front on the left-hand side of the auditorium. With trembling hands, I filled out the blank spaces of my card.

How could I ever make it? I loved to sing, but I couldn't begin to even learn to read music. My voice didn't thrill me too much either, especially its highest notes, which sometimes sounded a bit screechy. Why did I come? What obsessed me? What made me think that I could make it into the All-City Chorus and be accepted by Peter John Wilhousky? The lyrics of the audition song began to career through my brain, scrambling the words and obscuring the meaning.

Just a tong at twilight. No, no, no! "Just a song of twilight..."

When the sights are low. "When the lights are low, when the lights are low..."

And the sinking shadows. "Twinkling shadows, twinkling shadows..."

Slowly come and go. "Softly, softly, softly come and go."

Dear God, I'll never remember the words. A buzzing was filling my ears with a great roaring sound. I could barely remember the melody. The people in the first row were moving in a single file up onto the stage, positioning themselves to audition by the piano, carefully passing their cards to the monitors, giving up their last attachment to security. The monitors, in turn, gave the cards to the maestro, who read the contents, looked up at the mostly terrified and twitchy singers and, striking the introductory chords, took them through the first few bars of "Just a Song at Twilight." Well, at least we didn't have to sing "Madame Jeannette," I thought, with newfound hope and relief. Dozens of tenors sang first. Some faced up-stage, and you couldn't hear them at all. Mr. Wilhousky waved them on. They disappeared into the crowd and out into the outside fall air. Now and then, a beautiful tenor voice filled the hall, and the maestro allowed the young hopeful to sing the song through to the end. The cards of the chosen ones were squared off, carefully placed on one pile on the left, the rejects were thrown on another, and the possible alternates grew higher on the third pile.

I settled down to listen, to concentrate on the words and the music as the contestants filed by. Some of them were as panic-stricken as I. Others seemed to take it all very casually. They read and did their homework as they waited their turn. I prayed, returning to a habit that I had picked up in my youth.

HAIL MARY FULL OF GRACE,
THE LORD IS WITH THEE.

"Just a song at twilight, when the lights are low..."

BLESSED ART THOU AMONG US WOMEN.

"And the twinkling shadows softly come and go."

AND BLESSED IS THE SEED...

The sopranos were now filing onto the stage, moving over, one at a time, slamming the wooden seats up and down in the process. I bumped along with them, caught in the movement. Again a part of me wanted to bolt out the back door, but it was too late. Then I, too, stood, handing my card to the maestro and peering into the face of Peter John Wilhousky, who looked at my card, then at me, then again at my card and asked, "What kind of name is Redzisz? Hungarian?"

He decided to have a smoke at that moment and relit his pipe, which didn't look as if it had gone out.

"Oh, no, I'm Polish," I blurted out.

I knew I was too loud and too vehement in my reply. I couldn't take it back, so I cringed inwardly.

He smiled at me. "I didn't mean to insult you. You look Hungarian."

"No, I'm Polish. I thought you might be Polish, too. Your name. Wilhousky, sounds Polish."

"No, my background is Russian."

He mimicked my slight but apparent accent as he laughed. I should have known better. Most Polish-sounding names ending with "y" were either Jewish or Russian. As he smiled, I saw his discolored yellowing teeth, which were like my father's, who also smoked. He put the pipe down and looked at me as his very clear blue eyes twinkled.

143

"Are you afraid to audition?"

My eyes grew wider, and I nodded my head. The rest of me became rigid as the black horse of my panic flicked its tail in my face.

"You don't have to be afraid. I'll help you."

He struck a chord, and as I started to sing, he sang softly along with me. As I looked at him, apparently willing to help me, I gathered some courage and a great deal of heat. He looked me full in the face, took my card, and snapped it down on the squared off accepted pile on the left-hand side of the piano.

People were looking at me; a silence had settled over the immediate group. Two monitors exchanged knowing glances. P.J. rarely sang with people, and here I was accepted, while sopranos with apparently better voices, but not as good looking as I, were not. Part of me felt like a fraud as a feeling of shame crept over me and the black horse whinnied. Another part of me brushed it off, thinking of how proud Mrs. Greene, my glee club teacher, would be, and what points I was scoring for myself at Washington Irving High School.

After the audition, I burst out of Julia Richman and flew through the crisp fall air with the leaves turning red and golden on the trees, wheeling my way home like the soaring pigeons, except that I flew underground and soared on the BMT subway.

The following week, back at Washington Irving High School, Mrs. Greene announced my victory to the glee club. The school paper wrote me up and pointed out that I was the only student from Washington Irving High School to make the All-City Chorus. I was sixteen years old, in my sophomore year, and on top of the world.

Rehearsals began the following Saturday at Julia Richman High School, the same place where we all had auditioned. The looming building seemed less imposing after we had become part of a chosen group. A sense of purpose united us. Hundreds remained, culled from thousands that had come to audition. We shared a confidence and a camaraderie that I had never experienced before. As we filed in, this time sopranos and tenors down front on opposite sides of the auditorium and the altos and basses behind them, the ubiquitous monitors passed out sheet music, which they carried into the hall in large cardboard boxes. I gathered up my newly acquired treasure of classical music and waited for our conductor.

Mr. Wilhousky entered briskly down the center aisle of the auditorium with much less fanfare. With the beginning of rehearsals, the piano was relocated to the lower orchestra level, to assist the singers. This time, he carried his own music case and cashmere coat. I wondered where the pretty young girl had gone to. With deliberate precision and with every eye in the auditorium riveted to his every gesture, he neatly folded his coat and placed it over the back of the chair. Then he took out his music, carefully arranged it on the piano, turned to us, all poised and waiting, and welcomed us to the All-City Chorus. We all beamed at our good fortune and listened as he explained the program and procedures. The concert would be around Christmas. We would be performing with the All-City Orchestra, which had gone through the same process of auditions and was now rehearsing somewhere in another building in a different borough.

I was not familiar with classical music, and most of it was strange to me. All I had known were the words of the popular songs of the day that I had learned from the multicolored song sheets that we bought at the grocery store. My musical heritage consisted of sad Polish folk songs I had learned as a child from young cavalry officers, the Ulani, as they groomed their horses and I, a little girl, stood listening with my nose pressed against the bars of cavalry barracks outside Minsk-Mazowiecki.

The All-City Chorus was not as free-wheeling as my high school glee club. It was a very disciplined group. Most of the singers could read music, and many of them hoped that the Chorus would be their first stop on a journey that included the possibility of a professional career. I was coasting on the prestige and possibility of a new experience that it gave me. Having gotten into the chorus was only the beginning. I had to learn my part, and I did. My old friend, the top soprano, with its usually predictable melody line, came to my aid. After the first rehearsal, I took the music back with me to my high school. Once the classes were over, I plunked out my own part on the piano and learned it, often in the cool darkening music rooms of that blessed place, my Washington Irving High School.

During a break in the first rehearsal, while I was tentatively getting acquainted with some of the other singers, one of the monitors came over and asked me to go backstage.

"Mr. Wilhousky wants to talk to you," he informed me causally.

I started to shake and wanted to bury myself in the anonymity of the group. I was sure that Peter John Wilhousky realized what a mistake he had made and was throwing me out of the chorus. I decided not to accept my fate graciously. I would argue, plead with him, tell him it wasn't fair, explain to him that he was ruining my life. How would I ever be able to face Mrs. Greene, my family, and my friends? They would never understand why I had gotten chucked out and would think I was somehow no good, maybe even stupid. *HAIL MARY FULL OF GRACE* . . . Please let me sing in the Chorus. Please don't let him throw me out.

Mr. Wilhousky was drinking a cup of tea and puffing on his pipe in the first dressing room the off the side of the stage. I ducked under a light, tripped over some ropes and stumbled into his lair.

"Still afraid?" He squinted at me through the smoke that curled up from his pipe, and his blue eyes twinkled.

"Oh, no," I lied. "Just clumsy. Ha, Ha!" I felt like an idiot. Why doesn't he get it over with? Why is he humiliating me?

"Were you born in this country?" He looked straight at me.

"No." Damn the accent. "I was born in Poland, in Warsaw," I emphasized, hoping he recognized the intra-ethnic wisdom that superior Poles came from Warsaw. The distinction was lost on him.

"What do they call you at home, Miss Redzisz?" Why is he asking me all those questions? Why doesn't he just get it over with and throw me out? But why not humor him?

"Well, generally Basia. When my father wants something, he calls me Basiunia. When he yells at me, he calls me Baska. My mother just calls me Basia, but my sister, who doesn't like me very much, calls me

Basioryzda." I was a bit long-winded, I thought, but I couldn't stop talking.

"All that, ha?" he remarked looking at the card. "It says Barbara here."

"I know, but I don't like Barbara." I made a face as he shifted his pipe and chuckled.

"If you had a choice, what would you call yourself?"

"Cecelia," I answered earnestly.

"Cecelia?" He burst out laughing. "You don't look like a Cecelia to me, not even a Cissy." I turned beet red. He laughed again.

"I like Cecelia." I defended myself. I knew there was a reason, but for the life of me I couldn't think of it.

"Did you know that Cecilia is the patron saint of singers?" I shook my head, embarrassed to be caught off guard again. That was what I had tried to remember.

"What do your teachers call you?"

"Barbara," I conceded.

"Is that your given name?"

"I was christened after St. Barbara. I was born on December seventh. The closest saint they could find in Poland to December seventh was St. Barbara, whose birthday fell on December fourth."

"December seventh?" His white eyebrows arched up. "Pearl Harbor baby, hah?"

He again squinted at me through the smoke of his pipe. I felt like a mouse, and he was playing with me. Since the Japanese attacked Pearl Harbor on my birthday, I always felt vaguely responsible for the Second World War.

I hated the name Barbara; it sounded like "barbarian." I pictured natives jumping up and down in the bushes. It was bad enough that most Americans felt that we didn't wear shoes in Poland, as they shouted at us and pronounced their American words very carefully in the misguided notion that we were either deaf or dumb. Being called Barbara, after the barbarians, was the last straw. I decided to try a new tack.

147

"Mr. Wilhousky, I want you to know how grateful I am that you picked me to be in the Chorus. It's one of the most wonderful things that has ever happened to me in my life, and even though I don't read music, I'll learn my part and do the best I can."

"You don't read music?"

His eyebrows shot up again. I had given myself away.

"Barbara. I'll call you Barbara. I like Barbara" He accented the I. "My secretary is no longer with me, and I need someone to do some work."

Relief flooded through me. I wasn't being chucked out, after all. In fact, oh, my God, he's asking me to be his secretary. Momma was right again, I should have taken stenography and typing.

"But I can't take steno or even type. What happened to your secretary?"

I recalled the pretty girl following him across the stage. For a moment, the laugh lines on his face seemed to stiffen and grow deeper, as he explained, "She wasn't..." he searched for a word and having apparently found it, finished his thought, "devoted enough. You won't have to type. I need someone to help me with the Chorus recordkeeping in Brooklyn."

He must have noted a trace of alarm on my face, because he went on smiling as he settled back in his chair and added, "I admire loyalty and hard work. Do you think you would have time to help me, Barbara?"

My chest almost burst open with relief and joy. Help him? My God, of course, I'll be able to help him. I nodded. Wait until I tell Mrs. Greene that I'm Mr. Wilhousky's secretary. "I could come anytime after three. That's when my classes end."

"Come next Monday to 110 Livingston Street in Brooklyn. I'll have some work for you."

After carefully twisting the lead to the exact length on his gold pencil, he wrote the address on a little piece of paper and handed it to me. As if by magic, the monitor appeared at the door.

"Sal," my new employer nodded to the tall black-haired, pimply-faced tenor, "Barbara is going to be my new secretary. She'll take Louise's place."

Sal looked surprised, as if he didn't know that Louise had left. He shook my outstretched hand and, with ill-disguised discomfort, mumbled something about welcoming me on board. I floated out of the dressing room. I was the Maestro's secretary, and I didn't even have to type or take steno.

Since Momma had never heard about the All-City Chorus, telling her I was Mr. Wilhousky's secretary didn't impress her very much. She wondered what kind of secretary I would make without being able to type and to take steno. She again urged me to take it as an elective.

I pushed to the back of my mind whatever questions were rat-tat-tapping for my attention regarding Mr. Wilhousky's reason for choosing me to be his secretary, rationalizing instead that he had seen that I was in some way special and that he had appreciated the fact. I liked the feeling.

"You're a diamond in the rough," he said to me a few weeks later as I was filing the Chorus cards at the Board of Education office at 110 Livingston Street in downtown Brooklyn. "You could do with some polishing."

Maestro or not, I didn't like hearing it from him. If I were so special, then why did I need all that polishing? Being his secretary wasn't all fun and games. He seemed to want to play creator of perfection, a Svengali to my Trilby, I was later to read about. But at the time I chafed when he pointed out that my cuffs were soiled, not understanding that as an art major I painted and used pastels during the day. I bit my tongue. After all, being his secretary gave me status, and I liked the feeling of importance. One day, after part of the rehearsals had gone by, he offered me singing lessons.

"You've been working very hard for me." He buffed his manicured nails with his thumb. "I'd like to give you some singing lessons. Would you like that?"

Would I? By now I was getting sucked into the excitement of performing and becoming a real singer on a real stage somewhere. I had no money to study, and the offer was like a dream come true. Possibilities that had been rattling around in my brain could start to become a reality. I couldn't refuse him. Part of me was grateful for the status he had given me as his secretary. Another part of me resented him for constantly correcting me. There were things about him I didn't like either, but I didn't have the freedom to point them out to him. The offer of singing lessons stilled my growing resentments.

Wilhousky, which we all secretly called him, had a studio in Carnegie Hall that he shared with another singing teacher. It was in that studio that he scheduled my Wednesday lessons. I had heard of Carnegie Hall, but had never been there. In fact, the only time I went that far uptown was to the Radio City Music Hall to see the Christmas show. The only other time was to audition at Julia Richman High School. Uptown Manhattan was no-man's land for me. But, on the following Wednesday, with my cuffs clean, since I had carried an extra blouse in my school bag, I took the creaking old elevator in the ancient soot-covered concert hall up to the top floor. The building was filled with young students. Being among the dancers in their leotards and the singers with their music portfolios filled me with a renewed yearning to be part of this new life.

On one of the top floors in Carnegie Hall, I entered Wilhousky's dusky domain, which had walls that were covered with enormous medieval tapestries. Towering stained glass windows filtered in blue light, creating a mood of twilight in the vaulted room. I had seen windows like that before only in church. Fringed cloths were draped on the shiny black piano. Others covered two old carved and balding couches. There was a tall Chinese screen in one corner. Behind the screen was a tiny gas stove and a barely visible wide bed, which was also covered with another large fringed paisley throw. I didn't much like the fact that it was dark and gloomy in the studio and that a bed was hidden behind a screen in the corner.

Once I was inside on Wilhousky's home ground, his attitude toward me changed. He started to tell me the story of his life, impressing me with his membership at some country club and the trophies he'd won in golf and music. He rambled about problems with his wife and of some girlfriend who didn't understand him. I didn't want to know that he had a girlfriend and that he was still married. The morality of my early youth was still with me. He spoke about his former secretary, about her not being cooperative and loyal enough. I wondered if she had been the girlfriend. Then he began to tell me what he saw in me and how beautiful I was. I listened, not knowing how to react to what he was telling me, all the while becoming more and more uncomfortable. What could I do? The whole thing was becoming very complicated. I did the best a sixteen-year-old could do. About his problems with his wife, I looked compassionate. Regarding his girlfriend and her lack of understanding, I looked commiserating. Toward his former secretary, I was beginning to feel some sympathy.

As he gave me strange incomprehensible French songs to learn, he laid out the future that he was beginning to envision for me. He saw me as a European <u>chanteuse</u>. I had to learn French. I never sang in French. I never even heard it spoken, except for an occasional phrase at the movies, so I bought records and learned the songs phonetically from them. Edith Piaf became my favorite. It wasn't easy to find some of the music, because he gave me songs which weren't exactly on the hit parade, like "<u>C'est un Jour</u>" and "Nature's Love for Psyche." I spent hours at Patelsons, on West Fifty-Sixth Street behind Carnegie Hall, tracking down each new piece. Not only did I not understand the words of the songs in French, but I didn't even understand some of them when I read the English text. After a series of what seemed to me eminently uneventful lessons, he decided that I was going to be another Hildegarde and I had to learn "Darling, <u>Je Vous Aime Beaucoup</u>." With the very limited Polish Catholic background of a sixteen-year-old virgin, I stumbled through all those lost-love laments while he accompanied me on the piano.

"You have unusual beauty. Your eyes are set far apart. You have eyebrows that don't have to be plucked; they are naturally arched. When you listen, you tilt your head to the side, which is very appealing in a woman," he proclaimed.

151

Or in a dog, I thought. What I really wanted to do was to sing sad Polish folk songs, which opened my heart and gave me goose pimples. Polish folk songs weren't "in," he told me, and my suggestion was lacking in "cosmopolitan sophistication." So there I was, chopping my way through Massenet's "Elegy" in Polish- accented French. In spite of myself, I began to get caught up in his vision of my future.

"You carry yourself well. You stand up very straight, like a queen. Strange for someone of your background," he mused out loud, something he did about almost anything that came into his head.

Why was it strange because of my background? What was wrong with my background? Memories of "greenhorn" and "Polack" flashed through my mind, as images of the humiliation we experienced in our first years in America came flooding back to me. I was beginning to feel more and more uncomfortable with him, but I also felt trapped. If I resigned from being his secretary, then I probably couldn't remain in the chorus, and I would lose the singing lessons. Both had become an important part of my life.

It was at this time, about one year into my lessons, that a series of events came to a head and, in an unforeseen way, resolved the situation between us. My lessons with him were generally banal. He told me to be patient, that it took time. How he stood them, with my making little apparent progress, I'll never know. As for me, in order to remain his secretary, in spite of his constant corrections and his efforts to polish the Polish diamond in the rough, I managed to look forward to them. Dreams of becoming a singer were crystallizing in my head. My future was starting to take form.

It was a very hot and a very muggy September day in New York. Wilhousky was taking me through a vocal exercise in his dark and stuffy studio. I was working on "Darling, Je Vous Aime Beaucoup" and dreaded when we would have to leave the pure simplicity of MA-ME-MI-MO-MU to chop my way through the song with my tormented French. As the humming sound of the exercise carried me higher and higher, a kind of connection established itself between my chest and my head. All of a sudden, my voice took off, and my body began to vibrate. The hum in my head filled the air around me. As I soared above high C, a wave of goose pimples swept over my body. There was no screech at the top, only a largeness that kept spreading out. As the sound poured out of me, I wasn't sure if it was happening inside or outside me. The room itself had become alive with sound. Dear God! Is this what real singing is all about? Why didn't someone tell me? These were heavy-duty goose pimples. I've been piddling through with my squeaky soprano, only to find this awesome sound inside. Mr. Wilhousky sitting at the piano was looking up at me with wonder. As my singing stopped, the room settled down, and the shimmering in the air subsided.

His excited voice broke the silence. "I knew it was there; I knew it! When I first saw you, I knew it was there." He looked at me. "I wonder if you'll be able to deal with it."

I felt a bit put down. Deal with what? What was he talking about? All I knew was that I made a series of sounds that filled me with such joy that my body could barely contain it. I was afraid that he might think it had something to do with sex and try to grab me. In a flash, that's exactly what happened. He staggered up from the piano bench, flung his arm around my shoulder so that his hand flopped into my blouse, cupped my breast and squeezed my nipple. I tried to twist away from him, but he pulled me over, and we both toppled onto one of the balding, paisley-covered couches, in the process knocking over the Chinese screen that hid the bed from view.

My emotions were in a chaotic frenzy. Part of me was ecstatic from the singing. Another part of me was flushed with embarrassment that my nipples were still hard from the sound I had just made. Was it "dirty" that I had just felt all that joy? At the same time, I was panic-stricken thinking that the singing had awakened some kind of sexual madness in him. Why did he grab me and pull me down on top of him? The sound was mine. It had nothing to do with him. I didn't want him. He was my teacher and, I had come to hope, my friend. How dare he touch my body? I felt betrayed, violated and shamed as a rage swept over me.

As I fumbled to free myself from his frantic embrace, his face under me flushed crimson, and his breath came in fast gasps. He kept clutching at parts of my body. I couldn't quite place the smell that came from him as I pushed away at his busy hands. It had something to do with plums. My eyes caught sight of a bottle of brandy, with a picture of the purple fruit on it, standing on the wobbly little table next to the couch.

As I struggled to free myself, I tried to cover the awkwardness of the situation by saying that my father made plum brandy, too, and it had a nice smell. Wilhousky blearily focused on me as if I were crazy. I finally wrenched myself free from him and then backed away, stumbling over the furniture, gathering up my belongings, leaving the "Darling, Je Vous Aime Beaucoup" sheet music on the piano for the next secretary to learn. I bolted out of the studio, past the ballet dancers, down the many flights of stairs, and hurried toward Central Park West and the Independent Subway, which would take me back home to Jamaica, Long Island, all the while shaking with rage and humiliation, with the black horse galloping through a dark and treacherous night.

There was no one I could talk to. Momma wouldn't understand. She would only tell me that I shouldn't have gone to a man's apartment, even if he called it a studio. She would continue that I had brought it on myself, that nice girls didn't do that. I tried to understand what happened. I was sixteen, and I knew I was pretty. People told me that. But I had been pretty for the entire year before, and he hadn't grabbed me. What did I do? Was it the singing? Was it the sound I had made? Were the joy that I felt and the goose pimples something "sexual"? I flinched at that word. He made me feel unclean. I also felt a sense of loss, of having been betrayed. I respected him. He was old enough to be my father. I never felt that I wanted to nuzzle up against him and share the feeling that necking with some of the boys my own age stirred in me.

What was I going to do? At the next rehearsal of the Chorus, we both acted as if nothing had happened. He was pleasant, with the laugh lines growing stiff around his mouth, as he avoided my eyes. I filled up with heat and rage every time I looked at him. He had tried to rape me. He fell from being revered in my eyes to being vilified. I felt trapped, with no apparent way of escape. I tried keeping to the circle of friends I made for myself in the Chorus, while he chided me whenever I came close enough to hear.

"You must feel there's safety in numbers," he observed. "It's a shame that you can't rise past your narrow provincialism and see yourself as I see you." he casually advised me through his yellow teeth as his eyes grew more and more icy in their blue crispness.

I stared at him in silence. What I really wanted to do was to scream at him, "You old fart, you big pig. You betrayed me, gave me importance, work, status, and then you turned on me. I'm jail bait, San Quentin quail, and you're no Erroll Flynn, or even Charlie Chaplin. I'm only sixteen, and you abused me, took advantage of me. I still don't know what happened. Did my singing cause that reaction in you? Will it do that in others?" But I said nothing as the white horse took over and I smiled pleasantly hoping to get through the concert without any further confrontations.

As I filed the Chorus cards at 110 Livington Street in Brooklyn, he continued to muse out loud, "It's a pity. You could go far. You have the gift."

One Saturday morning, a few weeks later, we were rehearsing Handel's <u>Messiah</u>. He was touchy and displeased with the singing of the top sopranos, so he stopped the proceedings. One by one, he had each girl stand up and sing.

"<u>...for the Lord, God omnipotent, reigneth, Hallelujah...</u>"

The tessitura lies very high at that spot. One by one, he had the sopranos screech through the phrase. I was sitting in my usual seat in the last row of the top soprano section, ready to do his bidding. As my turn approached, I became more panic-stricken, fearing, on the one hand, that I wouldn't be able to sing and, on the other, that the same sound I had made in his studio might come out again. What effect would it have on the singers around me, especially the guys? Would they think I was a loose, wanton woman, capable of creating unbridled sexuality in them? I was almost deaf from the shame-filled, galloping panic that roared in my ears. My breath came quickly, and I trembled as I clutched the music with sweaty hands. By now, the singers in my row were in states not as acute as my own, but bordering on a greater or lesser panic, as they screeched through the "Hallelujah." Some did very well; others stumbled. He had them repeat the phrase until they did it correctly. One of the sopranos, after he badgered her to repeat the phase over and over, became hoarse in the middle of a word and in tears stopped singing altogether. He finally left her alone.

The soprano next to me finished, and I looked up for my turn, my execution. Wilhousky called the name of the girl on the other side of me and passed over me without letting me sing. On top of everything going on inside of me, I felt a flush of profound humiliation. A silence expanded in my brain, causing it almost to explode as it pushed the roaring sound underground.

The way he did it, having each singer sing methodically, one by one, until he got to me, made me realize that he had planned it. He had gotten even with me. He had humiliated me in front of the whole group. Had I sung and failed, I would have only sung and failed. By not giving me the opportunity to sing, he erased me. In the moment that he took to pass over me, he denied my existence as part of the Chorus. There was no way to confront him. He could always spread out his hands and hide behind compassion as he sucked on his pipe while fixing me with his cold and deadly stare.

"But I knew how frightened you were of singing in front of the group." There was no way I could answer him. We both knew what had happened and what had precipitated his subtle vengeance.

My friends at the Chorus wondered at the change in my relationship with the Maestro, but I never discussed it with them. The concert came and went. The following semester when the new auditions came along, Mrs. Greene pushed me forward as her trump card, to try anew for a place beside the great Maestro. She got a chance to attend the concert the year before because I represented our high school. I refused to try out again. Without a Washington Irving High School student in the All-City Chorus, she was denied the opportunity to attend another concert.

She pressed me, flushing red with suppressed disappointment and anger. I finally reluctantly told her what had happened. She listened, all the while growing more and more flustered. I thought that she might become apoplectic as she tried to restrain her rising rage.

She finally sputtered out, "Could you have misunderstood?"

"No!" I replied adamantly.

"How can you be so sure?"

"He pulled me down on the couch and grabbed my bre . . ." I couldn't say it.

"You must be mistaken. The Maestro wouldn't do that. I've never heard of anything so scandalous. You're a dirty-minded girl to accuse the Maestro of such a vile thing," she raged on.

"I didn't accuse him of anything. Mrs. Greene, you wanted to know, so I told you what happened. And it did happen!"

I felt like crying. I wasn't dirty-minded, but somehow I knew I had created something in Wilhousky for which I felt vaguely responsible. What it was, I wasn't sure. Whatever it was, it wasn't good. For when I subsequently felt that same response from other men, I feared for my safety. I felt threatened, dirty, and at the mercy of something that was dark, uncontrollable and extremely dangerous.

Years later, after learning how to sing without giving away the passion in me and sabotaging my voice in the process, I often wondered whether the seeds of my subsequent hoarseness and my recurrent voicelessness were sown in that dark and dungeon-like studio in Carnegie Hall with the illustrious Peter John Wilhousky. It took me many years to find my own true voice again.

Chapter 15

Peter John Wilhousky may not have been on the same level of musical celebrity as my father-in-law, Oscar Hammerstein II, but on the scale of relative values, when I was still a young teenager, he filled a similar niche. Seven years later, with Wilhousky and many other singing teachers behind me, some who also wanted me to have them "cream in their jeans," as they put it, when I sang, with a corroding patina on my confidence, I prepared to sing for Dick and Oscar. The musical <u>Kismet</u> was the smash hit of the season. Every soprano in the world used "This Is My Beloved" as her audition song. I joined their ranks.

Auditioning is like birth and death. You do it totally alone. As you wait mumbling in the wings of a strange theater, you are only one of a series of singers tucked away on the edges of the stage, surrounded by ropes, switches and props from some other show, some other reality. You listen to the singer auditioning ahead of you. On this level, auditioning for a Broadway show, the performers are all professional and good. You wonder if you'll rise to the standards they have set. Then a "thank you" cuts through the darkness beyond the footlights. More often than not, you emerge out onto the empty stage, with only the bare light bulb shining down on you. Its glare casts long shadows on your stricken face, making it tense and much older than it was before you entered the theater. To lessen that cruel exposure, you stand just upstage of it.

Out there in the dark sit a group of people, usually men, who decide your fate, who hire you, who make it possible for you to pay your rent, to study, to live your life. If they decide to hire you on the spot, and that is rare, you sail home on the wings of your success. If they take their time, not knowing quite what they want, or as yet not finding exactly the right person for the part, or they want to audition you again in a hotel room, then you hang suspended, like the person in the song I was about to sing from <u>Kismet</u>.

I walked forward out into that darkened, cavernous theater, with only a bare bulb hanging from the ceiling just above the stage. Having given my music to the piano player, who sat under the stage, in the pit, very far from me, I also gave up something familiar to hold onto. Somewhere out front, I heard the voice of my father-in-law encouraging me to go on, not to be frightened. He must have seen the stark panic in my face. I barely heard the opening chords of the song, which by then I could have recited in my sleep.

We started out in the same key. I heard the pitch. The voice was clear. I had once sung a whole song, a half tone off. It wasn't easy to do, but once I started, I didn't dare change. The producers out front loved it, laughed a lot, told me they never heard the song sound more atonic, more Stravinsky, and mentioned other modern, obscure composers. I had gotten the job in spite of my ultramodern rendition. They liked my determination. At least that pitfall wasn't going to stop me this time.

As I continued to sing, the panic I had held at bay welled up. The roaring in my ears almost overwhelmed me. My knees turned to jelly. My heart was beating so loudly that it almost drowned out the sound of the piano. The breath stayed high and shallow, not hooking down into the deep recesses of my body to give me support. Planted like a tree on the stage, not able to move, not able to raise my arms, I barreled along, opening my mouth and making sounds through the sheer force of my will. Gasping for air, as I had done beneath the water in the Gulf Stream, desperately listening for the chords that were my only friends, and the only signposts along the way, I continued to sing.

Through most of the number, I had kept control over myself, keeping the voice flowing, loud enough, on pitch, in rhythm. The passion stayed locked deep inside me. Hank Fonda had already informed them that I had a "roving eye." I had to be careful, or they would consider me a "loose" woman.

But once the music started in me, it created a life of its own. The sound rising on the breath of air vibrated the ecstasy. As I lifted my voice into the last phrase, into the home stretch, my skin tingled. As the pleasure filled me, I no longer felt the panic and gave myself to the sound thundering through me. It was as if I stood under a waterfall of light. A cascade of stars poured down upon my skin and awakened the joy. The moment it passed, I stood there aware that I had given myself away. Pulling myself together, I bowed my head. The audition was over. I made no major goofs. I sang the song. It wasn't one composed by Richard Rodgers, which I would have had to sing letter-perfect. So I was safe on that score. I might not have been right to play Suzie. I hoped I could do the understudy job and at least get into the chorus as one of the prostitutes. The sound subsided around me.

Oscar's voice cut through the darkness. "Thank you, Basia."

I picked up my music, and before I hit the stage door, another soprano had begun to sing her audition. I had sung for Richard Rodgers and Oscar Hammerstein II! I had sung for Dick and Dad! I had sung for my father-in-law! This couldn't be happening to me, but it was.

I stepped out of the dark gloom of the theater, into the bright light of day. Although I had been inside in the dark cavern for less than an hour, it had felt as if I had been there for an eternity. Time had stopped. I felt the same way as when I was a child in Jersey City or Bayonne, at the Cameo or the Bijou, sitting inside those Art Deco movie theaters for hours, sometimes from eleven in the morning until six at night, watching the double features, the shorts, the coming attractions, Movietone News, the cartoons, the local advertisements, and the races. The movie houses were filled with kids screaming and yelling as they ran up and down the aisles, dragging in their wake the smell of urine that flowed down behind them and dried in puddles at

160

the foot of the stage. The daylight outside would hit us like an alien reality as we blinked our way out of the gloom of the theater after the last THE END. Its yellowish glare had a sense of other-worldliness about it. It always seemed, at least for a short space of time, as if the reality had been on the screen in the bluish white glow of the darkened theater. It was with the same sense of unreality that I walked after my audition through the crowds along Broadway. Could anyone see what had happened to me? Didn't it show in my face?

When I arrived home, the apartment was empty. Jimmy was with Buddy, probably playing squash or tennis somewhere. I sat by the phone hoping for it to ring, hoping that the R H office, or even Oscar would call me, fearing the call might come while I was gone. As I sat waiting, the doubts grew in me like a physical mass, spreading pain in my body, spreading doubts in my mind. Maybe Dad wants to spare me, doesn't want to hurt me. Strange to call that imposing man "Dad." It must be a difficult situation for him, having to deal professionally with the wife of his son.

That night, Jimmy, flushed from a day at the squash court, and I had dinner with the family. Going there was very easy. We just walked down Madison Avenue from our new apartment on Sixty-Seventh Street to their townhouse on Sixty-Third. Living so close in the same neighborhood, we had become part of their community. Chris and Billy were going to join us for dinner. I had met both of them before at their silver wedding anniversary ball and my coming-out party, when I became Cinderella at the ball. Billy was Oscar's son by his first marriage, and I realized that Dorothy would probably be extra tense. She didn't much care for Oscar's former family.

Chris, Billy's wife, was very pretty, although she toned herself down and drank to get through many of the social situations. She had been a singer and never let on how wise, intelligent and sensitive she was. Keeping a low profile was her way of surviving. I often wondered what she had been like before she had married Billy. She, too, had high cheekbones, blonde hair and dancing eyes. What made her distinctive was her deep throaty laughter. She chuckled a great deal, finding humor in situations that others were too tense to notice. She had two blonde daughters, which Billy had adopted, from a former marriage, and a daughter named Diana, who was Oscar's only grand-child. Diney was the heiress to the throne. I realized that Jimmy's marriage put me in the position of challenging that status. If I had a son, it would throw the whole neat picture out of kilter.

We arrived early for dinner. Jimmy disappeared to make some phone calls. Dorothy had not as yet emerged from her lemon-col-ored bedroom. Oscar walked into the parlor bearing two vodkas. I had stopped having port before dinner, realizing it was not the proper thing to do.

After the audition, in my own apartment, the trembling had subsided. But now confronted with my father-in-law once again, I began to shake. Sitting on the edge of one of the bow-legged chairs, I clutched the drink between my knees to steady it, wait-ing for the verdict.

No verdict came. Oscar told me what had become obvious. I wasn't right to understudy Suzie. We both knew that, although in some corner of my being, I had hoped that the possibility existed. He carefully explained, as he sank into the satin couch and sipped his vodka, that Dick had different ideas concerning the casting of the prostitutes. I had a lovely voice with a very individual quality. I shouldn't be so frightened when I auditioned. But he understood, since almost everyone seemed to have the same problem. He did feel I had a future in the theater. I breathed a sigh of relief.

"You look wonderful on the stage. The stage gives some people status and adds to their quality. Like a camera loves some people and makes them stars in the movies. You know, like Marilyn Mon-roe. The camera absolutely loves her. The stage also adds some-thing. You look very glamorous up there. You have a big face, high cheekbones and wide-set eyes. You also carry yourself well. I think that's why Dick thought it might be too much for a prostitute. You have an imposing quality."

I might have an imposing quality and a big face, my voice may have been fine, but I still didn't get the job. Somehow I didn't believe him. Was it my singing? Doubts again surfaced in me as I listened and he continued.

"Something exciting came out of you at the end of that song. Were you aware of it?" He smiled at me. Oh God! Here it comes, all that containment in vain. I had blown my cover. All I could do was nod.

"Yes."

"You should allow it to surface more often. It's very good! What came out of you at the end of the song, you should get into the rest of your performance. It's what we all look for. It's the magic in the theater. It's the feeling of excitement that singing and some performers awaken in people. Gertrude Lawrence had it, you know. She died a few years ago; she was Dorothy's great friend. They came over together with Beatrice Lillie in Andre Charlot's Revue. Her voice didn't have your individual sound. She wasn't always on pitch, but she had a quality. 'You only see the light of the stars when the sun goes down.' Her lights came up when the house lights went down. It's like a star coming out! Gertie had that quality. You need more experience, but it's there." He stopped and sipped his vodka.

I had stopped breathing as I listened to him. Now I relaxed. Not only was I not bad, but he was paying me a compliment. I wasn't a wanton, dirty creature allowing my voice to lead men into frenzied, rampant sexuality. What I had was exciting, what was considered best in the theater. The joy rising in me when I sang, and which I feared might expose my passions, was where the magic came from. I could have wept with relief. I didn't have to work on it, to get it into the rest of my performance. It was already there, very close to the surface, every time I sang. All I had to do was to get out of the way and let it flow, let the black horse of my ecstasy out of the corral and into the light of day. He said I had a quality similar to Gertrude Lawrence. Gertrude Lawrence! I couldn't believe it. I knew she had been in King and I and was a close friend of the family. Her death in 1952 still hung heavy in the air when they mentioned her name. Then why wasn't I right for a part as one of the prostitutes? I was wondering whether to put him on the spot and ask him, when his next question turned the tables on me and shifted the direction of the conversation.

"How will you manage marriage and a career? Will Jimmy let you?"

"I'm sure Jimmy won't mind." My heart, which had opened

with the tone of the conversation, now closed down and started to accelerate with anger. I resented his implication that I needed Jimmy's permission to have a career. "Will Jimmy let you?" stuck in my craw. I bit my tongue. After all, I was speaking to the man who wrote "My Lord and Master," the man who believed a woman's place was to follow her "Lord and Master" around and help him to get his act together.

I contained myself as I asked, "You don't think a woman should have a career?"

By now, I knew that Dorothy had given up her decorating business because Oscar disapproved of it. It was at the time that his Hollywood career had been on hold: his nine years of creative drought, as he called it. He based his decision on the fact that her career made her tense. The truth seemed more closely allied with the fact that her success was a discomfort to him.

"If both of you have to go out of town, Jimmy may want you to be with him. Dorothy always came with me."

I knew Dorothy had mixed feelings about that. It gave her an edge against Dorothy Rodgers, who stayed back in New York when Dick went out of town. I was beginning to see that being Oscar's wife had some drawbacks. Dorothy had to follow him out of town. Having nothing to do with the show, she had to spend long boring days in the elegant hotels of Boston, New Haven or Philadelphia. She hated hanging around, but put it to good use, feeling pacified that she was doing her "duty." She did most of her Christmas shopping and letter writing at those times. I found that most of the women around these men shopped a great deal, did a lot of needlepoint and filled in many crossword puzzles. I was already on the way myself, learning to do needlepoint.

Looking at Oscar, who was giving me fatherly-in-law advice, I wanted to add, "Of course I'll be with him. Who would get his laundry together?" But I refrained. Actually, Jimmy and I never had discussed what we would do after we were married. It was understood by both of us that I would continue my career. My husband seemed to have no problems with that issue.

"Jimmy seems to have no problem with that at all," I continued. "There may be times I may want him to go out of town with me!"

I smiled, changing the equation a bit. "I understand there are tennis courts in Philadelphia and even in Boston."

Oscar laughed and wagged his finger. "It doesn't work that way, tennis courts or not!" he chuckled, but with the next statement, an edge crept into his voice.

"A woman's place is, behind, I mean, beside her husband." He corrected the slip he made, very quickly. "A wife's place is beside her husband." He repeated. "To help him fulfill his destiny."

He nodded his closely cropped head a few times, as if agreeing with himself. As he sipped his vodka and surveyed me, the heat rose in me again. I still held my drink clasped tightly between my knees, and the inside of my patellas had grown numb from the ice cubes. Fulfill his destiny! I'm not going to stop him from fulfilling his destiny! What about my destiny? If I had magic on the stage when I auditioned, then maybe he should help me to fulfill mine! Do I have to hide my light under a bushel, just so his could shine? Other than his being a good tennis player with an excellent serve, I hadn't as yet become aware of the destiny I was supposed to assist him with. I was willing to do that, but not by burying my own life under his. Listening at night to the plans he and Buddy hatched during the day at the various athletic clubs where they played squash and tennis left me wondering where his destiny would manifest itself. I didn't want to cross Oscar in any way, so I refrained from further explanations.

At that moment, the buzzer downstairs announced that Billy and Chris had arrived. With their arrival, Dorothy and Jimmy converged in the living room. Oscar and I had just been through what Jimmy had called a "Lord Chesterfield talk." With the rest of the family now present, I knew the talk was over.

They had heard about my audition and wondered how I had done. Oscar repeated what he had told me, leaving out the advice he gave me about following my husband around. Whatever the truth might have been concerning my employment, he pushed it over on Dick, saying that his partner didn't feel I was right for one of the prostitutes. I didn't get the job.

"Don't feel badly. Dick doesn't like any of the female members of the family in any of their shows!" Billy interjected and laughed. Chris chuckled.

"Why?" I wanted to know, not yet realizing the ramifications of his statement.

"Dad doesn't feel too comfortable with it either!" he added.

Oscar squirmed. Jimmy cracked his knuckles. Dorothy fingered her neck and twisted her pearls. Chris again chuckled. I could feel the tension solidifying around me. A universal raw nerve had been plucked.

Oscar cut through the tension. "It's not that I'm uncomfortable, but Dick writes the music and casts most of the singers!"

Billy laughed out loud. My father-in-law scowled and left the room to get more drinks. Having had his say, he felt the subject was closed. With Oscar out of the room, we shifted around in our down-filled satin taupe-colored couches as Chris told us a story of when she herself had auditioned for Richard Rodgers. It happened not too many years before, just a short time before she and Billy were to announce their engagement. (It seems that the Hammerstein boys liked to keep their engagements a secret). Dick had originally hired her for one of their shows. The first evening out of town, Jerry Whyte, the general manager of the show, came up with a bouquet of flowers and a note asking Chris to join Dick in his suite after the day's rehearsal. I knew that situation well, and I also knew that there was no delicate way to say no if you wanted to keep the job, at least when you were still in the chorus. After removing all of her make-up and making herself as plain as possible, she dutifully followed Jerry Whyte to Dick's suite. Her pale Scandinavian beauty, make-up or not, must have been compelling. Dick met them at the door of his hotel room in his bathrobe. Room service had delivered a beautifully prepared dinner for two, with the mandatory steak, medium-rare, and chilled champagne. (Shades of the Copa and Jack Entratter!) She felt she had to stay for dinner. During dessert, she told him about Billy and how she was to become Oscar's new daughter-in-law. It must have been one of your average awkward moments. She continued that he was very nice about it and didn't force himself on her in any way. The tone of the encounter changed, and they chatted cordially about the show. From that moment on, he was very cool toward her.

Soon, another blonde ingenue in the show refocused his attention. He had a blonde ingenue in every show. It was one of the closed secrets in the theater, the "shared narrative." as it came to be known later. Everyone knew about it, but the information never made it into the media or gossip columns. A kind of gentlemen's agreement, a secret kept by the old-boy network kept those facts confined within the theatrical community. They never made it out into the general public.

So it was with Dick. His out-of-town life was an open secret to all of us. That may have been the reason he didn't want any of the women in Oscar's family in the show. It would have shrunk his stable of ingenues. After listening to Chris's story, I felt somewhat mollified, realizing that my getting the job had little to do with my talent, or lack of it. It had to do with internal politics.

The two collaborators, Oscar and Dick, not unlike Gilbert and Sullivan, seemed to have a very civil, very specific relationship. Little apparent affection passed between them. Oscar didn't want to rock the boat with family members, female or male. He wanted to keep the peace. Years later, George Abbott told me that he had to write a letter of recommendation for Jimmy, who had worked for him as assistant stage manager, before Oscar, Jimmy's own father, would hire him. On our late and unlamented honeymoon, Uncle Arthur made the family seem like one large theatrical mill, where all could find a niche. That was not true. In subsequent years, I found work in other shows. I never worked for Rodgers and Hammerstein during or after my marriage.

My next audition was for <u>Pajama Game</u>, and I made the chorus replacement with no trouble. My new status as Jimmy's wife warranted an article in the Sunday magazine section of the local newspaper. The headline of the piece read, "HOW <u>NOT</u> TO GET AHEAD IN THE BUSINESS, MARRY THE BOSS' SON." I didn't know then how prophetic that statement would turn out to be in my life. <u>Pajama Game</u> was a safe bet. It was an established show on Broadway. I didn't have to go out of town and leave Jimmy. I could disappear in the chorus and also continue going to school.

Chapter 16

People's attitudes toward me had changed. I was no longer one of the girls, one of the chorus gypsies. By marrying Jimmy, I had set myself apart. People who had been my friends asked me why I still wanted to work and implied that I took jobs away from other more needy performers. No one really believed me when I tried to explain to them that we needed the money, that we lived off the salary my husband made as an assistant stage manager and I made as a singer.

In the Fifties, there was a circulating group of singers and dancers that worked most of the Broadway shows. When one show closed or went on the road, they auditioned and got into another. The musical directors and choreographers knew them to be professionals, with theatrical savvy. I had begun to flow with that circular current of employment. <u>Pajama Game</u> was my fourth show on Broadway. By getting into it, I began to join that creative tide, which swept from one production to another. Being in the chorus was a good way to begin life as a performer and to learn the business. As a budding performer, you made a salary and got on-the-job training.

There was one pitfall, though: Once producers put you into the narrow niche of chorus work, it was very difficult to break out. They saw you as a dependable underpinning of sound and movement, which framed the production and often not much more. Leads and supporting roles not infrequently went to much less experienced, much less talented new faces, while chorus members chafed and clawed their way for the few lines they were called upon to deliver, for which they were paid a few extra dollars. Sometime understudies made it out of the chorus because either the star or one of the principals got sick and couldn't go on. Shirley McLaine emerged out of the chorus of <u>Pajama Game</u> that way a few months before I joined its ranks.

I was never an ingenue and, even less, a soubrette, even though with the help of Herbie Greene I had tried, albeit with disastrous consequences, to push my chest voice high up into my head. My quality was that of a leading lady. Ingenue and soubrette in the musical comedy of the Fifties broke down into the virgin and whore classification of women that was afloat in the larger population at the time. The ingenue played the virgin; the soubrette played the whore.

As the virgin, the ingenue possessed a very specific package of qualities and behaviors. She was usually pretty, young, slim, blonde (although not always), innocent and usually possessed a high, lyric voice. Her movements were restrained, and her legs were always crossed. The high lyric voice of the ingenue expressed a life not yet attached to the body, a life of the girlish imagination, centered around romance, a life of dreaming and idealistic immaturity. These aspects were considered to be good and pure, the stock and trade of innocence, of the tender bud straining to burst into flower and then into fruit, through the singular path of righteousness, i.e., marriage. The ingenue hoped and constantly moaned in song about her soon to be perfect future, based upon the love of the man on whom she had set her sights. There was a quality in the ingenue of an incipient younger sister. She usually was quite boring, in most cases lacking even a borderline vestige of humor, settling for a marginal life of her own. Without the mirror of a good man in whom she could discern her own reflection, she had no reason for being. Pure, unblemished love defined her, as did the gargantuan mental blinkers she wore about life and reality. She skipped around the stage a lot, and not infrequently one of her hands fluttered up to her face to hide real or imagined shame. Her costumes were usually light in color and frilly, made of lots of material that hid her body from view. She embodied and immortalized the concept of "younger flesh."

170

The soubrette, with underlying intimations of whoredom, could be all the things that the ingenue could not. She was often cast as older, bawdier, darker (but not always), more robust than slim, with large bosoms that she could shake at the audience. She was usually freewheeling and driven by her lust to make, as it were, the first move with men.

If the voice of the ingenue came out of her head and was called a head voice, with a high, lyrical and exciting quality related to the mind, then the voice of the soubrette came out of the chest and was called a chest voice, low, sexy and exciting to the body. She was allowed to have a risque sense of humor and was often the butt of sexual jokes. Hers were qualities that would have been unheard of in the ingenue. The soubrette could never be considered as part of the family; she would always have to be an outsider, perhaps the wanton daughter of a drifter. She herself could even be some kind of a transient, a performer in a circus or a passing minstrel show, always from the wrong side of the tracks. The ingenue may have skipped her way around the stage, but the soubrette moved more slowly, more deliberately as she slinked her way across the boards leaving a trail of musk in her wake.

There was a third category of female performer that was beginning to surface in those heady days of the musical comedy theater in the Fifties, and that was the leading lady. The leading lady transcended the polarities that typified the ingenue and the soubrette. She began to personify a new woman possessed of both mind and body (and even a spirit). She could have a life of her own, with the recognition of love and romance as part of it. Leading ladies began to fuse the fragmented opposites of ingenues and soubrettes into a more complete and complex whole. The role of Anna in <u>The King and I</u>, with Gertrude Lawrence, as neither an ingenue or a soubrette but as the leading lady, emerged as the ideal for the third category. The list expanded to include Mary Martin, Julie Andrews, and Barbara Cook. They may have begun as ingenues, but they emerged as larger types than the narrow constraints of ingenues dictated and moved into the wider and more encompassing roles of leading ladies.

There was an unfortunate byproduct of the ingenue-soubrette dichotomy before the category of leading lady evolved. Many of the ingenues, as they became older and could no longer portray the youthful innocence demanded of them, tried to move into the ranks of the soubrettes vocally by forcing their voices into the lower register and by raising their low chest sound higher into their heads. That vocal calisthenic became a cottage industry for many of the singing teachers of the day and resulted in the loss of many singing careers due to hoarseness. I myself touched the hem of that particular madness.

I was never part of the ingenue-soubrette dichotomy. I looked like neither, having been called an "old soul" from as far back as I could remember. An "old-soul" quality could not play an ingenue. It might play a soubrette, but then it had to have a low chest voice. I filled neither category. My only recourse was to play leading ladies. There was only one problem: I was a relative unknown. Since leading ladies often carried the show, my chances of being cast for the leading role were slim.

The fact that Arthur Lewis, of Feuer and Martin, took a chance on me for Sweet Thursday, in which I was to play Suzie, a prostitute with a leading-lady quality, seemed to have been a momentary fluke, which, with the sale to R.H. and renaming into Pipe Dream, ended my hope in that direction. Richard Rodgers of R.H. pushed Suzie back into the niche of a soubrette, an out and out prostitute.

George Abbott once advised me to get a job as an understudy to a leading lady and pray that the star got sick. Hanging around in the wings wishing for the leading lady to become ill seemed like a thankless job. When I was preparing to star in Sweet Thursday, it seemed like a step in the right direction. Having lost it, I put my ambitions on hold and got a job in Pajama Game, in another chorus, in a show in town.

Pajama Game was one of the two shows in which I performed that was like an extended family. The other was Fiorello. Hal Prince and Bobby Griffith were two of the producers of Pajama Game. Before his death, Bobby Griffith's decency and kindness permeated his

172

productions. After his death, Hal Prince carried on with the tradition. As a result of the warm feelings backstage, our theatrical lives were filled with festivity. We celebrated our birthdays with cakes, our baby showers with presents, our anniversaries with mutual congratulations. There was good will and much laughter in those two productions. The pace was set by the management.

Chapter 17

After an article appeared in the Sunday supplement of the New York <u>Daily Mirror</u> that Jimmy and I had married, more presents arrived, mostly from friends of the Hammersteins' who hadn't heard of our marriage until then. By this time, I knew enough that thank-yous expressed by a phone call were "barbaric," as Dorothy would say. Only handwritten notes would do. I went to Woolworth's and bought myself some snazzy but simple stationery with the chic name of "Fifth Avenue" on the box.

Writing had always been difficult for me, not only because English was my second language but because I had been born left-handed. In Poland, my left-handedness branded me as a <u>manka</u>, a daughter of the devil. My deficit had to be corrected. Both my parents, and subsequently my teachers, tied my small left hand in a sock and wouldn't let it see the light of day until I had learned to force a pencil across the page with my right hand.

With the memory of that lateral pull still alive, I carefully wrote some stilted notes of gratitude. Wanting to be as civilized as the rest of the family and not a barbarian, I sent them all out into the world, secure in the knowledge that I had done the right thing. About a month later, I answered a knock on the door and stood with newly awakened expectation as the delivery man deposited boxes from Tiffany on our foyer floor. I thought we were getting more presents and eagerly tore open the packages. At first, the blue and grey stationery came as a bit of a surprise. Next came a box with "BHR" on some of the sheets of paper. A crest with my initials graced another. They appeared in all shapes and sizes: business paper in two categories, with and without crests, some without envelopes, social notes, thank-you notes, calling cards and some whose use I couldn't determine and had never seen before. On one of the boxes, I found a taped note from Dorothy informing me:

> *Dear Boschia,*
>   *I thought you could use these. I saw Ellie Reinheimer on the street the other day, and she told me your stationery was a bit tacky.*
>
>   *Love, Mother*

Surprise turned to humiliation and then to rage. Tears stung my eyes. My simple "Fifth Avenue" notes had not been untacky enough. I had to get a truckload of stationery from Tiffany's to get the point. With shaking hands, I called Jimmy at the club. He assured me that all his mother wanted to do was to help. Didn't I know she meant well? Didn't he tell me that? I found it difficult to believe that she meant well, that her gesture was a token of good will.

And who called my stationery tacky, Ellie Reinheimer, wife of Howard Reinheimer, the family lawyer? I recalled the small dark lady with plastered-down bangs, a la Anita Loos, reeling around at the anniversary ball. As I gathered, she had become a pacesetter as far as stationery was concerned. Not daring to reproach Dorothy and to sound ungrateful, I called her and thanked her for her generous present. She repeated the story again of her meeting with Ellie and how she thought my stationery was a bit tacky.

By the time that she had sent me her latest barrage, she, who as a color-conscious interior decorator should have known better. She knew that I was an artist and loved earth colors. There was nothing blue or grey in my life, although levels in me were moving in that direction. I wondered why she chose them for me. "Because they are the safest colors, dear," she later informed me when I casually asked her. That's how I learned that blue and grey were socially safe. Had I been asked, I would have opted for beige or parchment, but obviously that would not have been safe enough.

The stationery wasn't enough. We had little money to spend on our new apartment. Jimmy had a lot of Danish modern furniture. I was beginning to assemble a collection of eclectic pieces. Even after pooling our belongings, our new apartment looked somewhat empty. Dorothy proceeded to fill in the blanks with what she felt we needed. It was a difficult situation for me. I had some very definite ideas about the home I wanted to create for Jimmy and myself. Dorothy feared that my taste might not be proper enough, so she dragged me through the furniture wholesalers, lamp discount centers and showrooms, vetoing what interested me and buying things she felt we should have. During one such foray, while picking out wall sconces of antique brass for Steve Sondheim, she delegated me to the clearance counter and to cheaper fare. I once again felt like Cinderella after the ball.

Dorothy thought we needed a pumpkin-colored room, which is what she called the orange creation we came to live with, accented with elephant gray draperies and carpet. Stuff kept arriving. We had to keep smiling with gratitude. Jimmy would have preferred not to take anything from his parents. Oscar may have made her give up her decorating business, so she stilled the need in herself by not only redecorating her own home every year but by extending the service to family and friends. We became her latest project as she filled our lives with objects.

I may not have liked her colors, but the quality of the things she bestowed upon us was fantastic. Some of her gifts were so good that they never wore out. Thirty years later, the bed sheets with their blue embroidered borders still graced the beds of my nieces. When years later I visited Poland, the towels hanging in my aunt's house were still recognizable and intact. Panels of the original draperies, redyed and recut, still hung in the homes of my relatives and friends.

I guess I shouldn't have been so fussy, but I wanted my own style and my own taste in my own home. Our apartment became a version of Dorothy's, but on a smaller, less extravagant scale. Once we allowed her to fill our lives with objects, the floodgates had been opened. She must have thought that the more she gave us, the less I would be able to express myself, and therefore it would preclude me from creating a "tacky" atmosphere.

Jimmy kept assuring me that she meant well, while tripping over new stuff he hardly even noticed. I had misgivings and felt uncomfortable in all that pumpkin and elephant grey. I longed to surround myself with shades of pale olive green and smoky lavender, or peach, or even burnt russet. I hated insipid pale blue, orange and elephant grey. So, not to seem ungrateful, I bit my tongue, occasionally complained to Jimmy, and chafed.

With time, her comments became more pointed. When she came to tea, she not only brought a tin of Earl Gray breakfast tea but also some furniture polish and a bottle of starch with which to stiffen the already stiff Swiss tambour organdy curtains. It seemed like a never ending put-down, but Jimmy kept insisting that she was only trying to help me. It was after she sent me a jar of silver polish after a friendly dinner at our new home that I found it difficult to forgive her and steeled myself against her gestures of generosity.

It happened after we had settled in and had Dorothy and Oscar over for dinner. I carefully prepared the roast and the vegetables, even making a fresh apple pie. The day before, I had starched the curtains, polished the silver and the furniture, vacuumed, cleaned, dusted, and even embroidered pumpkin colored dots over the red berries on the couch upholstery so that everything would match and be perfect. The day after our dinner, which was very pleasant, before Jimmy and I had even finished breakfast, Arnie, the Hammersteins' chauffeur, arrived at the door, bringing me a jar of silver polish. My arms fell at my sides with hopelessness.

There was no way to please her. Doubts galloped and chased each other like wild black horses across the field of my mind. Was it because I was a Polish immigrant from the wrong side of the tracks?

Could it be that I exhibited so few social graces? Did she put me in the category of the Polish maids at the farm and felt it her duty to teach me the way things were done, as she probably once taught them? Could it be that I was a singer and had been a showgirl? But she herself had been a showgirl. I had put myself through college and recently finished my degree in philosophy. Didn't that matter for anything? Could it be that she preferred that Jimmy had married Buffie or Muffie, or any one of the other debutantes?

I cried, confused, angry, doubting my own worth, wondering if maybe Jimmy was right; maybe she was trying to help me. Something inside of me said, no. What I felt was valid. I felt as if I had become some kind of a scapegoat in her life. Jimmy's sister Susan had warned me about Mumsie and her Naval inspections. I thought she had exaggerated. It wasn't until Dorothy traced her white kid- gloved finger along the molding in my apartment that I believed Susan. In spite of it all, Jimmy kept assuring me, "Look how wonderful Mumsie is. She can't do enough for you."

The perception that he lived his life behind a set of self- imposed blinkers began to solidify in me. His myopia included not only his father but also extended to his mother.

During the run of <u>Pajama Game</u>, I became pregnant and stayed with the show until I could no longer wear the costumes. Not breaking with tradition, when I left, the company gave me a baby shower. and amid many wishes of <u>"merde"</u> and "good luck," I left a family of friends.

During the pregnancy, we spent a great deal of time with Dorothy and less and less time with Oscar. He was at rehearsals with <u>Pipe Dream</u> or at meetings at the Fund for the Republic, ASCAP (where he was a board member) or the Theater Guild. We ate our dinners in the blue dining room, which was still splendid, but not as frightening as the first night when I had received my social baptism there.

The new life that I had entered was not of a piece, as I had naively thought. There were imperceptible seams there. The longer I was married, the more I realized how wide and deep those seams were. Seam does not only mean two pieces of cloth sewn together, like a marriage joins two people together. It also means a tracing of that which is not apparent on the surface: a seam, a tracing in the earth of minerals, of iron or gold, of limestone or sand, or even uranium. It lies deep, ready to be mined, to be brought to the surface, to be exposed to the light of day. Those seams also lie buried in human configurations. They may lie dormant for many years, many generations, until enough energy in the form of a traumatic explosion blasts them out of the psychological rock. It takes a great deal of pain for that blast to take place. When the rubble of the explosion is exposed to the light of day, to the light of truth, then a certain kind of healing can take place. My mother didn't like us to cover our cuts and bruises; she felt that sunshine had a healing power that was greater than the healing power of bandages. What I and those around me in the Hammerstein family needed was that kind of explosion, that kind of rending asunder, that kind of exposure, so that some healing could take place, but that wasn't to be. It all had to remain unsaid, hidden from view, seams hidden, boiling and festering, in the deep caverns of the psyche.

Even though I wasn't to be in <u>Pipe Dream</u>, word trickled back to us that the production was in trouble. I sat in on some of the rehearsals. From the other side of the footlights, it became apparent that things weren't working very well. The original part of "Doc" in <u>Cannery Row</u> had been written with Henry Fonda in mind. Unfortunately, although studying for a whole year, Hank could never sing well enough, so he lost out. He would have given the part a brooding inevitability that the boyish Bill Johnson, with his nice musical comedy voice, never projected. John Steinbeck later wrote a letter to Hank:

<u>You will remember...that when I was writing</u> Sweet Thursday <u>I had you always in mind as the prototype of Doc, and I think that one of my sharp bitternesses is that due to circumstances beyond our control you did not play it when it finally came up. I think it might have been a different story if you had.</u>

The letter found its way to Oscar, and he broke it down for us over dinner one night, pointing out flaws in the syntax and the misuse of popular jargon. "Personality-wise" and "otherwise" created knowing laughter around that elegant table.

Helen Traubel, playing the part of a former social worker, was miscast as the madam in Pipe Dream, even though Reggie thought her casting in the part to be a good idea. As an opera star, she kept posturing on the musical comedy stage as she had done in grand opera, going out of character to take her bows and playing the part with a broad wink at the audience, letting them in on the secret that she knew that the part she was playing wasn't her own off-stage persona. Her voice, which had given her a magnificently successful career in opera, was wobbly and out of sync with the demands of musical comedy.

Oscar and Dick had a reputation in the theater as the creators of family entertainment: clean, wholesome musical comedies that didn't deal with the seedier aspects of life. They couldn't face making Suzie an out-and-out hooker, even though Dick was pushing the character in the soubrette direction. They had her dolled up in slick, pasted-down hairdos with Peter Pan collars, which belied the part that John Steinbeck had written. What he wanted to present, in the original novel, was a storm-tossed waif, unsure of herself and not very happy with her life.

It was at this point, during the second month of the production of Pipe Dream, that Richard Rodgers entered the hospital to have part of his jaw removed due to cancer. He survived the surgery, but lost much of his vitality and turned to drink. Oscar carried on with the show relatively alone. He couldn't face the fact that it was a story about prostitutes. The prostitutes had to be enchanted with their lives. They had to have the hearts of ingenues. The madam only wanted to school the girls in the social graces and turn them out into society as proper wives. None of the seedy reality of prostitutes percolated out past the footlights. It was all light, fluffy and gay, and it didn't work. Oscar had a very naive side to him. He never truly believed, becoming astonished, when Jimmy told him that the male homosexuals of the theater had adopted his song "Keep It Gay" as their national anthem. What Noel Coward did with "You're the Top," they did to "Keep It Gay," adding verses to his opus that would have made my father-in-law blush.

Steinbeck objected and tried to make himself heard. He wrote letters to Oscar, whom he deeply respected. The letters were at first apologetic, couched with deference, backing out the door; all the while, he spelled out his reservations about the direction the show was taking. As time progressed, his letters grew more and more strident and more despairing. He watched and paced in the back of the theater as the action on the stage refused to catch fire.

As is the case with many writers, Steinbeck had trouble expressing himself orally. It was difficult to say why or how. The words were there, and he put them together in the proper sequence, but you couldn't easily understand what he said. The sounds he made came out muffled and unintelligible. I remember one party at my in-laws, where he wedged me up against the fireplace and kept me captive with his size as much as his presence. For one-half hour he regaled me with stories, making faces, laughing, nodding sagely at me, hrrumphing, mumbling ohs and ahs, while I, in desperation, tried to catch a word here and there, to get a drift of what he was saying. He seemed so intent and earnest that I persevered in trying to understand him. I grew stiff with attention, nodding and agreeing with him, asking general obvious pertinent questions, for he took them as encouragement and would launch into new volleys of mumbles, hrrumps, ohs and ahs, while I literally jumped at each word that came out with some clarity so I could continue the uneven exchange.

He obviously wrote better than he spoke, but his writing didn't translate well to the stage and sagged woefully in Pipe Dream. I watched the posturing whitewashed prostitutes, and they looked more like a group of students at a girls' dormitory than a gaggle of fallen women. There was none of the sleaziness of the later film, "McCabe and Mrs. Miller," none of the despair and degradation, just a lot of good clean fun. Prostitutes or not, Oscar wanted nice family entertainment.

As I watched the rehearsals, he must have felt my sense of loss and disappointment at not being part of the show, for he named one of the hookers after me. When the show programs were printed, he brought one home and left it casually on the vestibule table. There, written for posterity to take notice, was "Basha," played by Signy. I wouldn't have minded if it had said "Basha" played by Basia. He had done that before with other members of the family. For Dorothy, he wrote a song called "Let Me Be Like the Girl on the Prow" because he saw her like that: courageous and regal, facing the waves of the ocean on the prow of the ship, as she plied the high seas from Australia. He dedicated the "Soliloquy" in Carousel to his son Billy and named the character of Billy Bigelow after him. I joined the list, if not in song, then as an honorable mention, as one of the prostitutes.

The show opened out of town to very mixed reviews. Some critics found it "RH negative," but Rodgers and Hammerstein had pulled magic out of their hats before and brought in hits that were in trouble during the tryouts. The whole theatrical community waited to see what they would do. There was gossip about the show, about the going-on, about the opening night party at which Oscar danced with one of the prostitutes while Dorothy watched, the despair openly spreading across her face.

The gossip would stop when I joined the group. I wasn't part of it anymore because I was one of the family. No one shared the slivers of human vulnerability with me until years later, when I was no longer married to Jimmy. It seemed that everyone knew that Oscar had a dalliance with one of the girls who had played one of the prostitutes in Pipe Dream. After I got the divorce, people couldn't tell me enough about it. They repeated it with glee, marveling at my ignorance and disbelief.

If it were true that Oscar had fallen off that finely honed razor's edge of fidelity, then I might have better understood Dorothy's barely controlled resentment toward me. I would have realized that it was like the father beating the mother, the mother abusing the child, the child kicking the dog and the dog biting the cat. In our case, it didn't go that far down. The mother didn't have a child to abuse -- all her children had flown the coop -- so she abused the next possible person in line. My timing had been bad. I stepped into Dorothy's life at a time she needed a scapegoat. She couldn't scream at Oscar; that would have caused the finely wrought seam not only to surface but to rupture, so she deflected her rage to me and battered me with her frustrations.

I had no one to abuse, so I abused myself. With my doubts growing, my adequacy shaken, my supreme optimism uprooted, I became adrift in a sea of criticism. What she couldn't do to Oscar's young paramour, she did to me. Her new competition was young; I was young. She was pretty; I was pretty, She was blonde; I was blonde. She had been a showgirl; I had been a showgirl. She had large boobs... That was the only difference.

The two males in her life echoed each other. Her son married me. Her husband, hankering after "younger flesh," fell in love with a prostitute in Pipe Dream. It might have been that our chemistry was bad and that we just didn't click. But her unrelenting barrage against me could only be explained within the context of something bigger than the fact that I was from the wrong side of the tracks and her son had chosen to marry me. After all, she wasn't that involved with Jimmy's life. The larger context is the only way I can explain her unrelenting cruelty to me at that time.

The next show Oscar and Dick put on after Pipe Dream was a musical version of Cinderella, which was made for television. The night of the premiere, the family met at the Oak Room of the Plaza to wait for the reviews. The Oak Room had always been a tradition with them. Amid all that paneled and hushed splendor, they waited to hear what the critics had to say about the show.

I had risen another notch. Starting at Ray's Diner, I had my first rite of passage at Downey's Restaurant. Subsequent opening nights found me at Sardi's, which was the best place of all to wait for the reviews, with everyone stopping by, shaking hands and sharing best wishes. The Oak Room at the Plaza was posh and subdued, fraught with wealth, but with none of the real fevered excitement of an opening night at Sardi's. We all sat around an enormous round table that gleamed with crystal and silver. Peering over gorgeous cascades of flowers (heavy with trailing orchids), we chomped on little square wedges of toast covered with caviar and sipped our champagne.

The maitre d', who was familiar with the family, had prepared the table to accommodate the whole Rodgers and Hammerstein clan. Shining, expectant faces surrounded the table, with subdued talk and veiled concern. It was the first time I had seen Dick Rodgers since my audition and since his operation, where they had removed part of his neck and jaw. He seemed deeply self-conscious about his appearance. Smiling lopsidedly at me across the wide expanse of table, he called to me, telling me that I reminded him of Eva Gabor.

"Are you related to her? Are you one of the Gabors? No one said anything to me about that! I know them!"

He looked around, wondering why he hadn't been told. I wondered if I looked like a Gabor to him at the audition.

"Oh, no, no, no. I'm not related to them."

I wanted to put him at ease and to clear the air. Some of the people around the table were listening to our conversation.

"You should capitalize on that look. It's not bad."

His eyes widened as he assured me and turned his good unscarred profile in my direction.

"Do you plan to stay in the theater?" I nodded, "It might get you work. They can't sing! You could be a Gabor with a voice! Not a bad idea!"

It might have been a great idea, but it didn't get me a job in one of his shows. He continued, "What you need to complete the picture is a Hungarian accent. Can you do a Hungarian accent?"

"I no can do Hungarian, but I try Polish accent. You like to hear Polish accent?"

We both laughed, as did some of the people sitting around the table. I smiled over to Jimmy, who looked vaguely uncomfortable. Oscar had drifted by the table to get some caviar and hadn't missed my Polish Gabor imitation.

That night after we got home, flushed with the dazzle of the evening and aglow from the champagne, I was abruptly brought up sharp by my husband, who laced into me with the accusation that I had humiliated the whole family by putting on a "cheap show." Dad had been shocked, and all of the other dinner guests had been stunned. I couldn't believe it. I had seen no one looking stunned. They all laughed. We had a moment of fun. It felt as if they were laughing with me, not at me. Fun was hard to come by at those gatherings. I tried to explain that all I said were two sentences with a Polish accent. What could be so terrible about that? But he was enraged. He repeated that Dad had been stunned. I couldn't believe that Oscar objected to my feeble attempt at humor. Worse of all, that he spoke to Jimmy about it.

I felt betrayed and slowly began to understand some of the panic in Dorothy's face and the silent self-effacement of Chris. Hammerstein wives, like children, were to be seen and not heard. The next time the family met, I swallowed my pride and kept as silent as the other women in the family. Silence grew in me as my new vehicle for acceptability and my new heritage. Part of me shrank as I gave birth to a smaller me, who flung her emerging new self into the open arms of her new family of the living dead.

With the growing silence in me, backing up as rage into my throat, I continued in therapy. It was partly because Herbie thought I should work on my center, on my voice or on my sexuality that I continued. It was also that I wanted to get rid of a growing despair that was becoming a more apparent part of my life and was filling its empty corners. Marriage had not brought me happiness, acceptance or a sense of belonging. It made me feel safer from humiliating encounters with men, but that was not enough. On the contrary, marriage to Jimmy, instead of providing protection, just emphasized my sense of periphery. In spite of being part of the central ferment of his father's life, he always lived on the periphery himself. Now I, who had wanted so much to belong to the center, had unwittingly joined him on its edges.

As a couple, we became part of the inclusive theatrical circle, sitting at select tables at glittering affairs held at the major ballrooms in the more elegant hotels in New York City. There was something happening almost every week: fundraisings, commemorations, awards, the Emmy presentations, the Theater Guild, etc. Most of them I had never heard of before. We usually joined Oscar and Dorothy at the family table. There were times when an oversized limousine picked all of us up, transporting us regally through the city traffic to have the hotel door opened by an elegant doorman in a stunning outfit. We'd glide toward the elevators and to our table down front by the dais. Stars, politicians, writers, and nobility stopped by the table to exchange a few words with Oscar, laugh a short loud laugh and be on their way, with Oscar guiding their eager hands away like brides' mothers or politicians do at reception lines.

It was a life of glitter, movement, noise and a great deal of champagne, filet mignon, which usually tasted like cardboard, and speeches that were mostly reverential. At these dinners, the men threw mutual bouquets at each other in the form of awards. A similar crowd went to all the functions. They were not the people I knew when I had worked on the stage, but mostly the ones behind the scenes who made the whole thing work, made its financial and social wheels spin, the movers and shakers of the theater. Some of my prettier young girl-friends made it in on the arm of a successful older man. Generally, it was a mature crowd.

Mostly the men glorified each other with awards. You say nice things about me, and I'll say nice things about you. Give me an award or a plaque in this ballroom, and I'll give you one at the next gathering. From these dinners I learned how wonderful all the men were. All had great humanitarian instincts, were loving devoted husbands and generous fathers. They glowed with self-importance, changing the world for the better. I sat looking up at the stage, at the dais, at all those appreciative faces and wondered about their relationships with their wives and their children. Did all the women orbiting around them have that stricken look that had become Dorothy's trademark? Had some of them become as silent as Chris and I?

After I became pregnant, I'll never forget one event that had a different effect on me. It was so impressive and dealt with acknowledgments of such worth on such a monumental scale that it had to be held at the Madison Square Garden. During the course of the noisy evening, a party led by Tyrone Power paraded across the stage. Whatever else he might have been, he was to me the epitome of male beauty, filling my impassioned youth with his brilliant white teeth and dark arched brows. He, and others who looked like him, were the subjects of my veneration. Their faces fused into the faces of men that I subsequently fell in love with.

The beloved star of my youth led a party of three men in tuxedos, tall and straight like elongated penguins, accompanied by three of the most beautiful women I had ever seen, wearing Scarlett O'Hara gowns in muted shades of rose madder, gowns that billowed in waves round them. All three had capes matching their dresses, capes that swept the floor, as they circled around the gorgeous men. The lights in Madison Square Garden caught and enhanced their satins, their diamonds, their hair and their riveting beauty.

That's the way it was supposed to be, I wanted to yell out. It was supposed to be beautiful, sparkling, filled with vibrant, muted color. I felt it still existed somewhere, that dream of beauty. If it still existed for me, how could I find it, where could I look for it? I watched the spectacle of beauty with growing dismay outside of me, as the life taking root inside of me grew larger and I grew heavier with child, still thinking my now silent thoughts, still dreaming my now silent dreams.

The pregnancy helped me to get through the days. I became calmer, less sensitive of criticism, more content. Jimmy became gentler to me, grateful that I was having his baby, and through that commitment, cementing our lives together. It was to be his love child he often remarked, and he prided himself for knowing the exact moment it had been conceived.

One day at The Farm, with the family around the dinner table and before anyone knew that I had a "bun in the oven," as Jimmy put it, Oscar made a five-hundred-dollar bet with us that we wouldn't have a baby for at least a year. Jimmy jumped at the chance to beat him. Oscar raised his brows and asked how could we be so sure. As I patted my still flat stomach, I confided that I had some inside information. We all laughed, but only my husband and I shared our new secret and we felt conspiratorial.

Oscar then casually added, "I'll add one hundred dollars to that if it's a boy."

I flinched, as did Billy, who had given his father, a daughter, Diana, whom he insinuated into every situation and into every conversation. Diney or not, he failed Oscar again, and the throne was still vacant, waiting for a male heir. My flinching had wider ramifications. I resented the second-class position held by women. Because we in Poland depended totally on Poppa for our economic survival, he ruled us with a dictatorial hand. Here in this chic, money-filled elegance, I thought it would be different. It was not so. The putdowns of women were sometimes more subtle, but they were always there. The ways in which men trivialized their wives, mothers, sisters and daughters seemed to be universal and constant. When the women were around, they discussed general topics that could easily be picked up in the magazines of the day and to which women had access. When the men retired to the study, that's when the real talking began, where the real deals were made. That's where I wanted to be, not discussing Ahmpeer furniture and Mambooshay clothes with women, but the real stuff of life, which seemed to be monopolized by men.

Years later, when I did the Milliken industrial show, I had a few dates with Frank Kingsley, who ran the musical productions for the Milliken Corporation. Before he picked me up on our first date, he gave me a few books to read.

"Why are you giving me these books for?" I asked him, somewhat taken aback.

"We'll have something to talk about," he assured me.

I felt like Scheherazade, on the verge of a thousand and one nights. The implication that I needed to read books to be able to converse with him was laughable. Because I was pretty, blonde, in the theater, and a woman, I had to be dumb. On our second date, after reading all the male biographies he had given me, I gave him some books to read so that he could converse with me. As he sat in the banquette at the Colony, he couldn't believe that he had to do some homework to date me again. He held the pile of anthropological studies gingerly under his arm.

That old painful furrow of female inadequacy was being deeply plowed by my new family. Perfectly bright, intelligent women became cute and dumb around the men. Those who didn't want to seem vapid remained silent, like Chris. It griped me no end. I insinuated myself into the male conversations when they clustered in groups talking about business or politics away from the women. I learned very quickly as the groups I joined dissolved, only to rearrange themselves without me, that I was to be seen and not heard. When I was still single, I was humored and allowed to share male conversations, but after I had married and was growing with child, my opinions no longer mattered. They had shrunk with my sexual availability.

"What does a pretty girl like you want to study philosophy for?" my father-in-law had asked me on our second meeting. I should have taken note. It seemed that in public women were only necessary as decorations; the prettier, younger, and more decorative, the better. They were also like chickens and other nest builders, creating a context, a frame from which men could gaze at the world and fulfill their destinies. The implicit other function that women provided and that were less ambiguous was sex and the bearing of male children. Only males carry the male chromosome that create sons. It's a toss with loaded dice and a fixed game that blames women for not having boy children. Women who bear a succession of daughters have an uneasy sense of failure dropped on them by the ephemeral "they" who make the rules.

Considering his inability to communicate and his lack of need for affection, I began to wonder if Jimmy had married me because my seemingly sturdy Polish frame promised constant and recurring motherhood. "Good peasant stock," he'd say as he patted me on the head from his great height. He often told me that he loved me, but his ardent courting died down after we married. Within a few months, I felt we were like an old married couple. For all of his youth -- he was twenty-eight months younger than I -- he seemed like the oldest man that I had ever known. Passion slipped by us and was not part of our predictable sexuality. After a few feeble attempts at trying to talk to him, trying to get him to understand that we weren't spending enough time together, weren't really getting to know each other, were passing each other like ships in the night, going our appointed rounds, not getting any closer, he impatiently brushed me off with, "We spend more time together than the average American couple."

For a split second, I wondered if that were true. Then I wondered where he got the statistic and how he figured us into the equation. It was an area he didn't want to discuss, so we didn't discuss it. A kind of objective offhand involvement seemed to be enough for him. No matter how I tried to open him up, the trunk lid remained shut. He became in the context of my life not only my husband but also an emotional stranger.

Chapter 18

The Farm served as our second home on weekends. The pictures in the silver frames projected a life at The Farm that no longer existed. During and after the Second World War, Jimmy, his cousin Jennifer and Steve Sondheim had all lived there with other children. There were no children there anymore. The Farm was a place of elegant, well-manicured, chic silence.

On one of our many weekends there, in my exuberance, I threw my arms around my husband, while he stood there like a stick. He didn't seem to mind too much my display of affection when we were alone, but in front of his parents, although unspoken, it was verboten. He pushed me away. While they exchanged glances, he laughed his embarrassed laugh. I was filled with confused humiliation. I should have known better. We had been sitting on the veranda of the big white house, with its tall graceful columns casting deep shadows against the sparkling white walls.

It was a lovely summer evening. They had been playing tennis all day. I was enjoying my new pregnancy. Sitting, looking at him, his sharp blue eyes lost in the deep tan of his face, his teeth picking up the light in the deepening dusk as he spoke, his white tennis togs gleaming even whiter against the white house, I felt such a rush of tenderness toward him that I leaped up and threw my arms around his waist. Without missing a beat in the conversation he was having with his parents, he gently but firmly slid out from under them and folded himself into a rocker. He could have softened the rejection by sitting on one of the wicker couches and pulling me down next to him, but he didn't. He sat alone.

I stumbled off the porch and crunched my way across the freshly raked gravel of the driveway. They continued to discuss sets of tennis and games they had lined up for the next day as if nothing had happened. Their voices receded behind me: Dorothy's Australian twang, Oscar's borderline New Yorkese, and Jimmy's sputtering exclamations. I passed the spreading wisteria, like an enormous bubbling fountain of white flowers on the front lawn. The moon hung low on the horizon, large and full, surrounded by a halo. Poppa would have predicted rain for the next day. He would have proclaimed it a certainty, if smoke from the chimney hugged the ground, and if the chickens went to sleep late. There was a stillness in the deepening twilight. I must check the chickens in their pens before I go in tonight to see if they are still pecking and clucking around, to see if it will rain tomorrow. I spoke half aloud to myself, trying to change the painful subject in my mind.

There was nowhere to go. Where could I run to? Tomorrow, if the chickens went to bed early and the sun shone, the family would either play tennis or croquet. If the chickens went to bed late and it rained, they were never at a loss. Bridge, Scrabble, crossword puzzles, double crostics and chess filled their days. I wanted to talk to someone. I hated games.

There was so much I wanted to share with them about the beauty around them that they seemed to take for granted and seemed to exist only for them to reorganize: about the mushrooms that would sprout underneath the dark fragrant pines after the first fall rains, about the small brook gurgling below in the distance, which was being destroyed by the Black Angus, about the meadows filled with waves of bobbing flowers. They would have laughed at me and called me an incurable romantic or, worse yet, overly emotional, which was to them a major no-no. My throat ached with unspoken words, and my heart wanted to burst with unexpressed feelings.

192

I shuddered, realizing it had grown damp and chilly. Reluctantly, I knew I had to return to the house where people played games day and night, where no children laughed, where no music played, where books had to be cut open to be read, where smiling faces existed only in dozens of silver-framed photographs on shiny table tops. Partially because Oscar was always potentially creating, a reverential hush filled the house. Even when he wasn't creating, a silence-filled homage to his profession had became a habit that had to be respected.

As the dew appeared on the lawn and seeped through my shoes, I wondered what I had gotten myself into. Why was I bringing a child into this world? How would he survive? I had already assumed it would be a boy. He would learn to stand up when an older woman entered the room, would learn to peck the area above her cheekbone, would send impeccable thank-you notes on blue and grey stationery, would navigate table silver like a yacht at a regatta, would push the chair under the knees of his dinner partners, would refrain from eating until his hostess lifted her soup spoon to her mouth. Dozens of other imperative graces would brand him as knowledgeable and therefore acceptable.

Where would the affection come from? Would Oscar be a better grandfather to his grandson, or would he tease him across that shiny battleground of the dinner table and, with neat razor strokes, undermine him, as he undermined his own sons? Would he invent another Sammy Goldstein to humiliate my unborn baby, as he humiliated his son Jimmy? Would Jimmy be a better father? With all my heart, I hoped so. He seemed to want a family so badly.

My life at home had been very different. We even fought differently. There was nothing subtle about the blows we inflicted upon each other. We used battering rams as we raged, taking our often visible lumps. There was an open, clean hate about it. Among the Hammersteins, everything was in such good taste that even the blows were subtle. You never quite knew, in your confusion after the blow had landed, whether you had been wounded or not. It was like a thin razor cut. The blood didn't show immediately. It oozed out after the cut had been made, after you left the scene, after the moment had passed. Because it wasn't out in the open and clean, it festered and formed seams of psychological pus in the form of raging resentments.

Most of life among my new family seemed to be lived through some kind of remote control. Feelings weren't expressed. Joy could be shared only through suppressed laughter, not too loud, for that would have been in bad taste. "Sentimental" existed on the same level as "gauche" and precluded any feelings of exuberance. "Maudlin" was not only a venal sin, but also a cardinal infraction. Grief was not to be shared or dealt with. It, too, had to be suppressed and experienced alone, as Oscar had done at the death of his mother.

Human emotions made him uncomfortable. He was not only embarrassed by his grandfather Oscar the first's flamboyance and extravagance, which had been inherited by Uncle Arthur, but apparently any show of human weakness also disturbed him. Once, when he was still a young man, Oscar II was walking with his grandmother, Janet Nimmo, who had emphysema. When she sat down on a stoop to catch her breath, he felt "dreadfully ashamed." He didn't like what people thought of the situation. She showed too much human weakness.

Oscar I, the original Old Man, showed little affection for his children, His son Willie, father of Oscar II, was stiff and proper, and cold to his children. Oscar II was not only distant with his children, but he also treated them with indifferent cruelty. I wondered how my husband would behave in his new role as father.

Unseen hands puffed up the pillows as soon as the occupants left the chairs. Unseen hands emptied out ashtrays as soon as the last swirl of smoke settled in the ashes. Unseen hands cared for the children to keep the adults from being bothered with them and to maintain the pristine order and silence. Only Honey Bun, the golden-colored little dog, felt no restraint, as she yapped around people's ankles, unashamedly begging to be petted and held.

As they played their endless games, when they did speak, through tiptoeing whispering servants, it was about a vague kind of liberalism that expressed itself with a kind of general objective benevolence toward people. Still, Oscar was the first to admit that he crossed the street when confronted by a cripple or a blind person.

The words that came out of him through his lyrics began to amaze me. How could such a dichotomy exist within one person? How could he be so distant and removed from his own offspring and still write "Dites Moi," "Getting to Know You," "My Favorite Things" and all the other songs he wrote for and about children? Their actual presence made him uncomfortable. Later on, I would see that he literally raised his arms and shoulders up and away, whenever my son, his own grandson, got too close to him. It was the story of Dr. Jekyll and Mr. Hyde all over again, but not as extreme. Even Poppa changed as he got older, giving my nieces (his grand-daughters) some of the love and care he denied his own children. Oscar seemed to have an intellectual appreciation of the younger set, often listening in on their phone conversations to catch the flow of their words to use in his lyrics, but he seemed to lack any emotional connection to them.

My young husband -- and I call him young, because after we were divorced, he blamed the break-up of the marriage on the fact that I was an older woman -- seemed like a lot of young American males I knew both before and after him. He evolved with a strange kind of detachment, as if the mind had no connection to his heart or his sense of compassion. It was as if he weren't aware that what he said had any impact on the people around him.

After we were married, I became aware of the stream of foul language that flowed from him almost nonstop. In time I could look at it as a joke. Back in those days, I never even allowed myself a "damn." He never used foul language around his parents, but he glorified in calling me a "cunt," "my cunt" and ultimately "my fucking cunt." My initial discomfort gave way to despair because my requests for him to stop had no effect.

He generally reacted with one of two emotions, either sexuality or anger. His sexuality was a constant, having nothing to do with affection. His anger had to do with being questioned. Any question sent him into paroxysms of rage. It was then that he sputtered out "fucking cunt," "nagging cunt," "fucking drag" and whatever other profanity was <u>au courant</u>.

Jimmy did have an awesome need to succeed and show his Old Man that he was OK. What he didn't seem to notice was that his Old Man could have cared less. All he wanted Jimmy to do was to keep a low enough profile so that the family name didn't make the papers. It seems that the only time Jimmy got any attention was when he got into trouble. Then the Old Man dragged in his lawyers and accountants to bail his son out of debt. He kept Jimmy in his will and part of the trust fund only by a hair's breath, but he left him no cash, pointing out that he gave him enough money while he was still alive.

My poor husband tried to please his father by trying his hand at the production of plays. He should have been a tennis pro. It was one of the things he was good at and loved to do. As a producer, he had to work too hard keeping all of the myriad details in his mind, and that wasn't his style. I urged him, if he were going to stay in the theater, to become a director. After we parted, he gained some distinction in that field.

Jimmy seemed at sea in his despair to beat the Old Man. There was a quality in him that males have when they are part of a subculture or a minority in a country. If one of their own cannot become top dog or leader, they often self-destruct. In Ireland, they do it through violence and liquor. In Poland, they do it through insurrection, defiance and liquor. In the United States, the blacks do it through drugs and liquor, and the Indians do it through liquor. Jimmy couldn't become top dog in the lineup that featured his father, so he self-destructed by being reckless and then ultimately, years after we parted, by dabbling in drugs. The process seemed the same.

Years later, before the divorce, when both Oscar and I despaired at Jimmy's growing reckless behavior, Oscar confided in me that he thought both of his sons put together might have made one good man. Jimmy's recklessness and Billy's caution might have balanced themselves out to create one full person.

The two current women in the family were also like the opposite poles of the spectrum. Chris and Dorothy: one laid back and waiting, the other wound up as tightly as a spring ready to pop. Dorothy asked me to call her Mother. I couldn't call her Momma, for that was already taken, and calling her Dorothy seemed disrespectful, given my European background. In Poland, you didn't call grown-up people by their first names. An older man was called Pan Soandso, and an older woman was called Pani Soandso. Momma's friends called her Pani Yoozia; Poppa was either Pan Redzisz or Pan Andrzej. Calling my motherin-law Pani Dorothy sounded silly, so reluctantly I called her Mother.

It wasn't until many years later, after I had left the family, that I understood why she was so highly pitched, but at the time I was married to her son, I trembled at the violence and anger in her. She, too, never allowed her emotions to come out into the open. "Bad form," she would call it. It churned in her. Small dribs and drabs of it found their way out. Diseases and ailments were like waves of devouring ants upon her body. Medical specialists, referred by Ben Kean or Harold Hyman, the family doctors, relieved her symptoms with drugs, only to be replaced by other specialists who relieved her new symptoms with still newer drugs.

Her nose suffered; she lost her sense of smell. Her throat suffered; she was hoarse, and she wasn't even a singer. Her feet suffered; her arches were falling, and she wasn't even a dancer. Her back suffered. She couldn't sleep. Her hair was falling out. Her nails were brittle. Her body put on weight. Her chin and bosoms sagged. Veins came out on her legs, liver spots on her hands. The whole process of aging overwhelmed her, and she couldn't come to terms with it.

There was no apparent way to come to terms with it, if her husband told her son that someday he would want "younger flesh." She knew that her flesh was no longer young, and the fear grew stark in her face.

To a stranger, she was a handsome, imperious woman, leonine in aspect, with a red hairdo, aquiline in profile, straight, tall and trim, seemingly in control, but her eyes, her poor eyes, could only betray the hidden terrors within. She, too, seemed to be waiting, but not with the quiet surrender that Chris had evolved for herself. She seemed to be waiting to make some terrible mistake for which she was to be punished. Little did she realize that her mistake was to grow old and that twenty-five years of a marriage "made in heaven" would not save her from the ravages of old age and from the opportunities that a powerful man in the theater faced every day of his life.

Oscar had grown important through his talent and good professional choices. "I never made a decisional mistake," he once told me, echoing a statement made by his grandfather many years before. "A man never makes a mistake. He does the best he can, at the time," Oscar the first had told his son Arthur. That attitude of certainty, of "right" thought and action, seemed to permeate the Hammerstein men. Neither Dorothy or Oscar could go much further. He was the most powerful producer and lyricist in the theater. She had British blue blood pulsing through her veins, resulting from her Illegitimate descent from Edward the Sixth, King of England. It didn't seem to be enough for either of them.

He wanted to be acclaimed as Poet Laureate of the United States. Had he been born in Britain, he would have probably been knighted. Being a citizen of the United States precluded that honor. They both felt vaguely uncomfortable around plain show folk, who they felt were of a different class, so they entertained only stars. Closer friends were some of Oscar's old cronies from college, Dorothy's British royalty and very rich businessmen. The businessmen served a double function, not only as dinner party companions but also as backers for Oscar's shows.

Oscar was a wonderful speaker. His New Yorkese accent was backed up by a muffled deference that added to his charm. He seemed to be adored by the general public, who interpreted his personality through his beautiful, romantic lyrics. We all fell in and out of love to the accompaniment of his songs. Autograph seekers clamored around him, especially after he appeared on Edward R. Murrow's, "Person to Person" television show. With a bemused, benevolent tolerance, he good-naturally signed all slips of paper that were extended to him.

The only desire in Jimmy's life, other than the fantasy life he had about fishing, tennis and passing everyone on the road, was to hit it big so that the Old Man would think that he was wonderful. After we married, I tried to find out what he was doing with his friend and partner, Buddy, all day. I soon discovered that Jimmy and Buddy were working on a long-playing record of memorable sports events they planned to call "The Greatest Moments in Sports." Both he and Buddy dug up miles of recorded farewell speeches, blunders, play-by-play narrations, everything they could find in the sports world, everything that was funny or in some way important.

When they finally put the master tape together, Jimmy played it for me. It happened on the same night I was going to tell him that I had seen a doctor and that we were having a baby. I wanted to hear what they had been working on along the way as they were splicing the material together, but he wanted to surprise me with the finished product. I listened to the tape as he and Buddy paced up and down the room, bumping into each other and making comments about the quality of the sound and the cuts they had chosen. It was an enormous undertaking they had imposed upon themselves. They did a wonderful job. I wasn't much into sports, but I was moved by Babe Ruth with his farewell speech and laughed along with the two producers at Harry Wismer's classic foul-up. My skin crept with terror at the description of the falling <u>Hindenburg</u>. I was amazed and impressed and told them both about it, congratulating them on their apparent success. Then I asked my husband, as a matter of course, if he had signed releases for all the voices he had used on the record. At my inquiry, he grew apoplectic.

"You're a fucking drag, a God damned cunt! You put a damper on all the stuff I try to do! It's none of your fucking business whether I got releases from the performers! All I asked you is whether you liked it, not for your business advice!" he sputtered as spittle flew from his mouth. I shrank back as if he had struck me. Buddy backed out of the apartment. My husband continued to scream at me like a person de-

ranged, as the saliva went flying. The phone rang. He stopped to answer it and spoke to someone as if nothing had happened, exchanged
pleasantries, and in a few minutes seemed to quiet down.

In utter disbelief, I retreated to our bedroom. After listening to
the record, I had planned to tell him we were going to have a baby. Not
wanting to take the wind out of his sails, I waited until we finished
listening to the record he and Buddy had created, never realizing that
my relatively innocent question would throw him into such a fury. So
after his outburst, symbolically like a chimpanzee, offering my rump
in pacification, I told him the good news. It seemed to erase my inquiry into his business affairs, and he turned to me, saying, "Preggers
hah! Groovy! I always wanted to make it with a pregnant woman!"

Columbia Records at that time was handling most of the Rodgers
and Hammerstein material, and it produced Jimmy's record. It was
an instant success and earned a gold platter. There had been nothing
on the market before that which dealt with memorable moments in
sports. Before he and Buddy saw any income from it, the sports per-
sonalities whose voices he had used and from whom he hadn't sought
releases sued him. Harry Wismer felt they ruined his career by exposing his boo-boo to the whole world. Columbia Records settled with
the litigants, and the partners never collected a cent. The record is still
making money.

Chapter 19

My husband seemed always to be tired. If not cracking his knuckles, he was always yawning and stretching. It amazed me that he had so much energy when it came to playing tennis and squash. When Buddy wasn't around or he didn't have a game lined up, not unlike my father, he slept through the days and watched sports on television at night. From <u>Me and Juliet</u>, he went into <u>Damn Yankeees</u>. One of the things he had to do in the show was to teach the incoming replacements how to juggle baseballs. When he wasn't cracking his knuckles, his hands were busy throwing things up in the air. It left him with a bad habit. Apples, oranges and nuts all became candidates for a toss through the air when he was around. He also had frequent attacks of bronchial asthma. I tried to help him with a diet of health foods, but he consistently rejected them.

"Why not?" I would try to convince him. "When a cow or a horse gets sick, they change its feed to a better, natural diet. How are we different from animals?"

But in those days, it wasn't popular to claim that we were in any way like animals. We were made in the image of God, and anyone who didn't believe that was called a Communist. The word heresy had gone out of style, but Commie was in, and it covered most of the same ground that heresy had in the past.

Vitamin therapy wasn't used until thirty years later, and diet as a healing agent didn't become popular until twenty more years after that. Nutrition may have been denied and ignored by the medical establishment, but it was avidly explored by stage performers who had to do eight shows a week and relied on their health. As they were interviewed on the talk shows, they disseminated the good word of health foods through the newly emerging medium of television. In my gut, I knew we are not only what we eat, but breathe and drink. To go against the medical establishment branded all of us early nutritional flag wavers, as members of the lunatic fringe. My new husband laughed at my earnest explanations concerning good health and patted my head, denying any validity to good nutrition. He wouldn't take vitamins or change most of his eating habits, as he continued to smoke, coughing his way through the nights, keeping both of us awake.

We settled into a very predictable pattern. Every night after the theater, we'd watch the "Late, Late Show" from our enormous extra-long double bed. I would fix him a snack on a wooden board with slices of very smelly cheese, salami and, for my sake, some cucumbers and tomatoes. He'd have that with a glass of beer. The salami had to be accompanied by a big dollop of Bahamian mustard. It all had to be laid out on neat squares of Triscuit crackers. After he downed most of the stuff on the board, grinding it into small pieces with his teeth, he would burp and fart his way through the night, stopping only to accent the concert with his coughing. Sometimes when the weather was very damp or he was under some other strain, he would wake up gasping for air and drag on the inhalator, which he kept by the side of our bed. With his bronchial condition, the nicotine in the tobacco, the mold in the cheese, the yeast in the beer, the spices in the mustard and the nitrates in the meat were probably bad for him. I tiptoed around him with my nutritional life, wedging squares of fruits and vegetables in between the slices of cheese and salami.

When we lived in Poland, just before the Second World War, there were few processed foods. I was raised on natural produce that we grew in our own garden, some of which we stored in our cold cellar for the winter. I remember helping Momma and some of the local women in the village to shred barrels of cabbage, adding handfuls of salt and placing a firm apple on top of each barrel, before weighing it all down with a wooden lid, covered by a large stone. This mixture would slowly start to ferment and to smell. As the pungent aroma filled the house, we knew we were on our way to sauerkraut. There was no refrigeration for us in those days in Poland. Everything had to be preserved, dried, pickled or smoked.

As the summers spread their bounty before us, the smell of cooking raspberries and strawberries filled the house. The crowded berries wedged together in the caramelized sugar became immortalized in their sweetness. Before they cooled, we ladled the sweet-smelling preserves into jars and sealed them for the winter. The rings of mushrooms we picked every fall, which both Momma and Poppa dried and threaded like enormous brown wreaths, hung in the workroom next to the house.

My youth was spent eating health foods, with their rich earthy aromas. In this country, only the faddists were able to indulge themselves. J. I. Rodale wrote about the dangers of pasteurized cows milk and refined wheat. Carlton Fredericks, on his daily radio program on WOR, vilified the white flour and white sugar lobby, until they conspired to get him off the air. Gaylord Hauser pushed nutrition as the next Nirvana. The medical establishment ignored the obvious and prescribed drugs instead of dealing with the fundamentals. I was one of the voices crying in the wilderness at that time, finding comfort only at the Salad Bowl on Seventh Avenue and Fifty-Third Street, where I could munch on bowls of greens, shredded carrots, raisins and raw beets. Along with their organic, life-enhancing nature, we left behind in Poland the intense flavor of foods. Everything in the United States tasted bland. To compensate for the lack of flavor, foods were doctored up with sugar and salt, paving the way for problems with obesity and possible high blood pressure in the future.

Jimmy's asthma might have been helped by natural foods, but he resisted any change in his diet and continued to suffer bronchial attacks. The only time I had an asthma attack was when I was about eighteen years old and worked as a model after school at the garment center. One Saturday night, I dragged my girlfriend Amy to a dance in downtown Manhattan at the Ukrainian Hall. I loved to polka. Although the politics of the Ukraine and Poland were at odds and the Ukrainians were considered by the Poles to have been worse than the Nazis during the Second World War, their music was close enough to be jubilantly shared and enjoyed.

At the dance, I met a man named Mike Slifka. He was a photographer and a pretty good dancer. He was in his late thirties, had thin, streaked blondish hair that covered his relatively large head, and a wide, deeply lined Slavic face. He stood at the edge of the dance floor with cameras dangling around his neck, and as people whirled by him, he snapped their pictures. After taking a few pictures of me, he handed me his card. I noted that his name Slifka, which meant "small plum" in Polish. (This seemed to be a strange coincidence, considering the bottle of plum brandy I remembered sitting next to Wilhouskys' balding couch). We danced a few dances. That was it. With the dance over, Amy and I toodled our way back to Jamaica, Long Island, on the Independent E subway train.

I had been looking for a photographer in those early days because the modeling bug had bitten me, and good pictures were the first step in modeling. I called Mike Slifka and made an appointment. He had a store with a photography studio in the back, downtown in the Ukrainian section in New York City, not too far from the Ukrainian Hall.

He perched me on a stool, clicked the camera, played Ukrainian music on the record player and offered me some vodka. I barely sipped it, leaving most of it untouched. There were no moral judgments connected with my decision; alcohol gave me a headache, so I stayed away from it.

A few weeks later, we met again to go over the proofs and to choose the best of the pictures for the portfolio I was planning to put together. As we bent over my photos, with my eager smiling face looking back up at us from the pictures, he proposed to me. It seems I had passed some kind of a test he had set up for his prospective wifetobe. The criteria became immediately apparent. I didn't hop into bed with him on the first date, which meant I was a good, clean girl. I didn't drink, which was also a plus, and I was intelligent enough to run his store out front while he ran the photography studio in the back. In the two weeks it had taken him to develop my pictures, he had put our whole future together. What to do? I didn't find him attractive. He seemed nice enough, but I wasn't thinking of marriage. I was still in high school. He, at thirty-eight, seemed like an old man to me, shades of another Wilhousky.

As gently as I could and feeling grossly uncomfortable about the whole situation, I tried to explain to him that I had to finish high school. I also wanted to go to college. He informed me that I didn't need college to run his photography store, that I already had enough smarts for that. Then, when I ventured that my mother wouldn't want me to marry so young, he insisted that he wanted to meet her and to plead his case personally. I couldn't get away from his obsessive courting.

The following Sunday, he came to dinner. As I looked at his deeply lined craggy, almost Mongol face, I felt him to be more Momma's contemporary than mine. He charmed her, kissed her hand, brought her flowers, discussed politics with Poppa, brought me a necklace of amber beads, and ardently pressed me for an answer. Poppa thought he was a prince, someone he could play pinochle with, and felt I had made a good catch. Momma liked him, but she wasn't all that sure I should get married at eighteen, especially to a man who was twenty years older. She felt the thirteen-year age difference between her and Poppa was too much. I had no intention at all of marrying Mike Slifka.

Along with my modeling responsibilities after school at FiermanKolmer, I also worked the switchboard, relieving the regular operator. Every time Mike called, I disguised my voice and told him I was unavailable. He should have gotten the message, but he didn't. I sent the necklace back to him and tried to soften the blow by telling him what a nice, attractive and successful man he was to have his own business, explaining again that I wanted to finish college and have a career in modeling, which would leave me no time to marry him and mind his store. Therefore, I couldn't be his wife.

He kept hounding me. Somehow he found the place where I worked, and one day he burst through the showroom doors like someone possessed, tracked me into the models' change room, calling me a whore who led him on, accused the other models of being prostitutes, informed my boss, Max Kolmer, that he was a pimp, and screamed out that my mother was a madam who ran a house of ill repute in Jamaica, Long Island. He raged and ranted like a crazy person, until three salesmen grabbed him under the arms and threw him out, bolting the double entrance doors behind him. He banged on the locked doors until he finally got tired and left. We remained shaking within. Before he was shoved out of the door, he called the assembled salesmen dirty Jews and said since I was giving them "some," why couldn't he have "some," too? I was immobilized by humiliation, fearing that some of my co-workers might think that what he said was true. Eventually, it all quieted down. We even laughed about the commotion he had caused. I learned that the other models all had experienced incidents more or less akin to mine, with some of their stories varying only in the details.

My boss, Mr. Kolmer, gave me some good advice. "Honey, never take any presents from men you don't plan to go to bed with," he said, chomping on his cigar. "Taking presents leads men on."

"But I gave the necklace back," I assured him, as the heat of humiliation flashed through me.

"That doesn't matter. The guy felt he could make it with you. You led him on." The conversation embarrassed me, and I felt he was wrong, but a part of me wondered if he was right, that maybe I had led him on. Was I really at fault over what happened? The memory of Wilhousky breathing down at me, smelling of plum brandy, came vividly back to me. With him, as with Mike, I felt that I had given no reason to hope. With others, I told stories and developed charm to delay their inevitable lunge at me. Mike had couched his primary

206

interest in a proposal of marriage. Other men used sexual pressure as a matter of course with dating or getting a job. They felt it their right to get "some" just for buying dinner.

Right after the incident in the showroom, I started to gasp for air and couldn't catch my breath. Mr. Kolmer, after giving me his counsel, sent me home. My breathing grew more and more shallow as I rode home on the subway. A vise seemed to grip the center of my body and moved upward to choke my throat. The more I thought about what happened, the more upset I became. By the time I got to Jamaica, I was gasping for air. There was no Q40 bus at the stop, so I grabbed a cab, never having done that before in my life. Cabs were too expensive. My sister was already home from school, and she paid the driver. Engulfed by intermittent blackness and gasping for air, I barely made my way up the stairs, as she called the doctor. By the time he came, I was lying on my bed almost in a coma. After a shot of adrenalin, my heart flew into a flurry of activity and brought me back to full consciousness.

"You've had an asthma attack," the doctor informed me, as he busied himself over his bag. "Have you had asthma since childhood?"

"I've never had asthma," I replied. He didn't believe me, and judging from the way he looked at me, I realized he thought I was lying. Then I told him what had precipitated my attack and the rage that filled me. He gave me a bemused look.

"There's no proven connection between asthma and emotional trauma," he carefully explained. Asshole, I felt like informing him. Even then I knew that my emotions found an outlet through my body. It was no use to argue. He had restored my breathing, and I was grateful for that. The arrogance of doctors had always amazed me. They felt they had the corner on knowledge dealing with sickness and disease, and that emotions and nutrition played no part in it.

It was at this time that I met Frank Ertola, a cop who lived just south of us in Ozone Park. I told Frank the story, and it just so happened that he worked downtown in the same precinct in which Mike had his photography store. I can still picture Frank and his partner, dressed in their dark blue uniforms, nonchalantly swinging their night sticks as they walked into Slifka's store. Waving their sticks like wands in front of his nose, they advised him to leave me alone, or else. In those days, especially to first- and second-generation im- migrants, a nod from the police kept people in line. They still had memories from the old country of gendarmes knocking on their doors and of people disappearing in the middle of the night. I never heard from Mike Slifka again, until my husband decided that his next project was going to be a sports film containing a segment about blind golfers.

After Oscar bailed his son out of the record fiasco, Jimmy and Buddy embarked on a sports trilogy. The first clip was about Jessie Owens, who won the Olympics in Germany and put Hitler in a rage that a colored man could best the "Master Race." It was relatively easy to assemble; we used existing footage, which I helped to edit.

The second short was more difficult. It had to do with blind golf- ers. At that time, not too much film existed on them. The whole short had to be shot at a tournament. We would have to follow one of the blind golfers in the contest as he was led through his paces by a guide acting like a human seeingeye dog, who relayed to him what strokes were appropriate, the lay of the golf course, the distance to the pin, any traps the blind player had to avoid, and so on. It was a noble un- dertaking, for blindness had not stopped these golfers from making a valiant effort to be part of the game. With the baby in my stomach growing larger, I looked forward to being out in the country for the weekend, away from the tensions of the family; that is, until I found out the name of the photographer they had hired was Mike Slifka, one of the tormentors from my past.

My first reaction was to stay home, but Jimmy wouldn't hear of it. I begged him to get someone else. He patiently explained that my feelings were irrational. What happened almost eight years before had no bearing on the present. Mike Slifka was a good photographer. He had probably forgotten all about me, besides which he was cheap.

As the breath caught in my chest, I feared I was going to relive the asthma attack that my earlier rage had precipitated.

What I refused to do eight years before, I got to do eight years later. Pregnant and reluctant, I carried photographic equipment up and down the fairways behind Mike Slifka. When he met me, he first looked at my distended stomach, then at Jimmy. He didn't say anything. I didn't say anything, either. In my silence, I was storing up rage against my husband.

Charlie Boswell, the blind golfer whom Jimmy and Buddy had chosen to feature in the film and whom we followed for three days, lost the tournament. He blamed it on my husband and the relentless whir of the cameras that followed him from hole to hole. We shot three days of film on a man who not only lost but, worse of all, had not signed a release. After losing the meet, he was reluctant to sign the waiver. Had he won, there would have been no reluctance on his part to have us use the film. A release would not have been necessary. But having lost the tournament, he didn't want his failure publicized. We had shot thousands of feet of film that would be worthless. I couldn't believe it was happening again. Remembering the apoplectic explosion from my husband when I questioned him about releases for the record he had produced, I refrained from inquiring into his business affairs again.

After the tournament, our beaten champion sat staring into sightless space, while Jimmy and Buddy ran around wondering what to do. They were told they couldn't use the film, that they were responsible for the man losing and that they themselves would lose the thousands of dollars it cost them to put the weekend together. Buddy ran to the club manager with whom he had the original agreement. After a long discussion, the club manager leaned on Charlie and convinced him to sign the release.

I'll never forget that afternoon. The beaten golfer sat there, tears in his sightless eyes, smiling a mirthless smile, the little black mole on the side of his lip twitching, as they poked the pen into his hand and then held the paper for him to write his name. I turned away as Jimmy yanked the release from his trembling hand. Mike Slifka stood under a tree, endlessly smoking his cigarettes. He looked at me, not saying a word, but the look on his face betrayed him. It seemed to imply, "He may be a Hammerstein, but you would have done better with me."

The trip back home was tense and silent. Jimmy and Buddy had gotten the footage. At the last moment, they had also gotten the release. I was in the sixth month of pregnancy, and that night, as on every other night, we had sex. I must have been tired, resentful, or just generally tense, for to get over my growing belly, Jimmy had to yank me over. As he jerked my leg, I felt a sharp stab of pain at the base of my spine that radiated out to the left side of my body. It happened just that fast. I yelped like a dog that had been hurt. The next day, I called the doctor. He told me to come in for Xrays. I refused to have an Xray taken during my pregnancy, feeling it was dangerous to the fetus.

After the incident, there was a dull ache at the base of my spine pulsing out to my left hip. For the rest of the pregnancy I had to wear an orthopedic corset. The corset consisted mainly of stays, with the stomach cut out in the front. It was laced up the back. As the summer grew hotter and the bulge that proceeded me grew larger, I grew more and more uncomfortable. The stiff stays held my body rigid, allowing my growing stomach to float freely before me. I recalled the conversation I had with Oscar at the ball, that the world would be a better place if women wore stays or were more feminine, or whatever that meant. There I was, the ultimate manifestation of femininity. Was the world any better because of it? No, I thought, only more overpopulated. One of the few things that my father-in-law and I shared was the use of a corset to protect our backs. He was also wearing a brace at the time, because he suffered from a bad back. Both of us hobbled around that steamy, hot summer and favored our aching bodies.

Chapter 20

The last few months of pregnancy gave me a great deal of trouble. Along with the corset chafing my body in the heat, I developed toxemia. The baby was so large that I wondered if I were having twins. But, no, the doctor heard only one heartbeat. We packed a bag and were ready to fly to the hospital at a moment's notice. It was also at this time that we moved to the West Side. With the coming of the baby, we needed a larger apartment. A two-bedroom "pad" on the West Side cost us less than the one-room apartment on the East Side. Years later, I learned that a suicide preceded us to our new apartment. A woman tenant had jumped out of the fifth-floor window to her death. Had I known, I would have felt that it was a bad omen.

During my pregnancy, I introduced Jimmy to my old friend Stanley Prager, from <u>Two's Company</u> and <u>Pajama Game</u>, and they teamed up to do some writing. Based on how happy Jimmy and I seemed to be, Stanley proposed to Georgianne Johnson. They got married. We all became friends. I joined the circle of successful young married couples in the theater. We went to parties where Mel Brooks and Carl Reiner honed their dialogues, later becoming the raw material for the record, "The 2,000-Year-Old Man." Phil Reed did brilliant turns with Mel about Aguilar, the Mexican movie idol. Many of those parties attended by a whole crowd of our theatrical contemporaries were held at the homes of either Neva Patterson or Mary Rodgers.

Jimmy had grown up with Steve Sondheim, who called Dorothy his surrogate mother, and he was always around with some new game he invented and actually pulled out of his trunk. Steve was there, along with Leonard Bernstein, with whom he had just finished <u>West Side Story</u>. Hal Prince, Betty Comden, Adolph Green and Arthur Laurents were also part of the crowd. Jerry Robbins would drop in, and we recalled the madness we shared in <u>Two's Company</u> and discussed Bette Davis' health. Her jaw operation, which was diagnosed as osteomyelitis, closed that particular show. Malicious gossip along the Rialto said that she was afraid to carry a stage production. It wasn't so. I saw her in the hospital, her face immobilized by bandages, and remembered her pain.

I usually sat quietly and watched those gatherings. My growing stomach made me uncomfortable. I enjoyed the laughter, but I found so much of the humor, although excruciatingly funny, filled with cruelty, archness and elitism. They were people for whom the only values seemed to be talent, youth, beauty and, last but not least, chicness. There was little kindness, and even less apparent loyalty. Everyone was fair game for the quick jab. The gatherings were filled with a great deal of backbiting, high-pitched laughter and swishiness, which wasn't to hit the general public for about fifteen more years. Susan Sontag defined it as "camp" and added the word to our general lexicon. Before then, "campy" was a word that belonged only to the theater.

Some of the bisexual men were more beautiful than the women. Within the sheltering arms of the theatrical community, most were openly gay. Many were married and had children, for they straddled both sexes. They had social respectability with a wife and family, and kept their young, beautiful, slim-hipped boys on the side. I often wondered how the women fared in those marriages. Years later, George Abbott an avowed heterosexual, explained to me that marriage comes in many forms, and all it takes to survive in it is kindness and tact. He was speaking from the detached wisdom of his seventyseven years. I hadn't gotten there yet and still swayed to the rhythm of my emotions. For me, logic had little to do with passion.

Jimmy's half-sister Susan was the only woman I knew at the time who could hold her own in that apparently clever group. She had developed their kind of humor and screeched with them at their parties. We all laughed as she told the story that she wanted a baby so badly that when her temperature was just right, she would call Hank (Henry Fonda), no matter where he was, even when he was doing a matinee in <u>Mr. Roberts</u>. During the break between shows, he'd rush home, they'd have sex, and she would stand on her head so that the semen would flow in the right direction. They never had a child together, even with all those gymnastics, but adopted a little girl whom they called Amy. They, too, went through a divorce.

When Susan later remarried, she had a son by Mendy Wager. She was Hank's wife at the time when Jane and Peter were barely teenagers. I remember those thin, attractive, highstrung, upper- crust, blond children visiting with friends during the holidays, spreading their suitcases, clothes and tennis racquets all over the meticulous furniture of their step-mother's apartment, across from the street from the Planetarium in New York City. Susan recalled that in her own youth she hated a governess for making her roll some hair ribbons and neatly stack them in her bureau drawers. She tried to complain to her Mumsie, but Dorothy didn't understand.

Hank was much older than my half-sister-in-law and even more remote than my father and Oscar. Susan, too, went into therapy trying to make her life work. I'll never forget the day she joined us on one of our skindiving forays, bringing an elegant hamper of cheese, pears and white wine. No paper cups and paper napkins for her. She lugged real glasses for the wine and a linen tablecloth along with cloth napkins, all embroidered with her initials, on and off the row boat.

Hank didn't want her to leave him behind, but he wouldn't join us. When we returned to their brownstone later that night, he staged a memorable welcome home for her. The front door of their house opened to the foyer, through which, to the left, you could see the kitchen. In the center of the kitchen ceiling was a spotlight. It was dark when we finally got home, tired and covered with sand. As we opened the door, there in the dark kitchen, with only a spotlight above him, sat Hank, clutching his daughter Amy to his breast. He wanted to establish his desolation and to show Susan how she had deserted the two waifs. He had wrapped his legs, one around the other, which he did wherever he sat, but it was difficult to do on the high stool he had chosen for the scene. As a result, he teetered back and forth, as he waited for us to walk in and find him. Susan broke down with laughter. The next moment, the staged scenario filled her with guilt. She knew what he was doing, but she never left him alone again and never went skindiving with us, either.

Then on one hot September night in 1954, a cramp doubled me over, and my water broke. We sped across town to Doctors' Hospital, where after sixteen hours of labor, on September 13, I gave birth to my son Andy. Images flash back to me from that night. I remember coming out of the anesthesia, with blinding lights all around me. One of the masked faces with a female voice was telling me to bear down. My legs would fly forward as I straightened them out, in my drugged stupor forgetting the natural childbirth training classes.

She yelled, "No, no, no! Don't straighten out your legs! Bear down!" They would fly out before me, as I stretched them out again.

"You have nice legs, but you don't listen. Bear down!"

I tried to squat, but realized that my arms were strapped down to the sides of the delivery table and I couldn't move. I struggled to get up, to squat, to bear down, but I was flat on my back, with the straps holding me firmly in place. At one point, my legs had also been strapped down. Finally, after sixteen hours of labor, they performed an episiotomy, which they euphemistically call an incision, and pulled my son out with forceps.

No wonder they call it labor. I never worked so hard and so unrelentingly in my life. Back in my room, after they took the baby from me, before I even had a chance to see him, the nurse who had been yelling for me to bear down, patted me on my arm, which was now turning black and blue from the straps, and informed me that I had a healthy baby boy weighing seven pounds and eleven ounces.

Relieved, I slipped back into the darkness. I had given Jimmy a boy, which was the first successful production he could present to his father. One of the best things I remembered before I sank into a deep sleep was that my stomach was flat and I could see the bulge my feet made under the blanket at the foot of the bed. I didn't feel all that empty, for they packed my uterine cavity with miles and miles of gauze. The stitches on the incision they made to enlarge the opening for my son's large head was throbbing, my back ached, but I was relieved, jubilant that it was all over. Before I fell asleep, between the loud crashing of the service elevator doors just outside of my hospital room, I thought, Pippa just passed by ... "God's in His heaven, and all's right with the world."

The first thing the next morning, they brought my new baby to me. With enormous blue eyes, he looked up at me as I looked back down at him. There in my arms was a new person probably wondering who I was, looking at me with a piercing quality in those sharp eyes. The current psychological wisdom was that a baby was a blank clean slate, an empty blackboard, waiting to be written upon. No way! The person looking up at me did so with a clarity and perception often missing from the eyes of adults. I smiled down at him, as he squirmed in my awkward arms, and thought, "We're stuck with each other, you and I. We'll have to make the best of it." He looked as if he were thinking the same thing. I removed the blanket that covered his head and saw for the first time the wounds the forceps made on his poor bald pate.

"They'll heal," the nurse assured me.

"But his head is crooked." I looked at the marks indicating the direction in which the forceps must have pulled. The head slanted that way.

"Don't worry. The bones are soft; they'll round out. In a few days, he'll be as good as new," she said.

I wanted to yell at her, "But he is new. How much newer could he be?"

Something in me tugged at the pain he, too, must have gone through. How much we two had experienced together, even if both of us had been drugged into just this side of oblivion.

A story came back to me, told by Florence Baum, when we both worked in Top Banana and she had a daughter with Mel Brooks. When Mel came to the hospital and saw his daughter's head on practically sideways like my son's, he remarked, "Don't worry, dear. Mommie will knit you a nice cap to cover your head."

Well, my son could also have used a nice knitted cap to cover the wounds of his birth. As I slipped back into the fog caused by the drugs, my mind drifted. I wondered if Florence ever knitted that cap. She wasn't the type to knit and crochet. Momma was more the type. Maybe Florence would lend me the cap, only for a few weeks, only until my sons head healed. I made a groggy note to call and ask her.

Much to the dismay of the whole staff, including my doctor, I insisted on nursing my new baby. They kept informing me that nursing was unnatural, unsanitary and, they should have added, not very nice. I persisted and guided the nipple to my son's lips, and the fluid seeped out. He rolled the nipple around in his mouth and shared with me the pleasure that completed its circuit through both of our bodies. Each time he suckled, I could feel a tug, a spasm in my uterus and knew it was healing, going back to normal. I wondered why doctors dissuaded mothers from breast feeding. Why did they want to put a wedge between mother and baby? Why did that equation upset them so much?

We were both rudely interrupted as the nurse scooped my son out of my arms, away from the nipple, and carried him screaming to his lonely bassinet, away from the warmth, the smell, and the comfort of my body. How terrible, I thought as the weakness engulfed me. How barbaric, to put babies into those small lonely boxlike coffins, those early intimations of death, lying there all alone, helpless, screaming by themselves, and hearing the screams of others. How frightened they must feel. But I sank out of my own sight into the miasma of drugs.

The next morning was like a carnival. I had become a star, shining in the firmament of my new motherhood. Again, as if by magic, "slowo

216

sie zeklo," (the word was said), my small, noisy corner room next to the crashing doors of the freight elevator was neatly exchanged for a suite with a sunny river view. Flowers filled the tables. Everyone called. Momma was delighted, selfeffacing, begging my pardon for calling, and wondering how we were, delighted that it was a boy, and telling me that Jimmy had called her right after the birth. She felt proud but saddened, telling me that Poppa almost cried when he was told that he had a grandson.

"How is Poppa?" I inquired.

"Not good." She spoke in English, as if my new status demanded the change, as if others were eavesdropping on the phone.

"He very sick. He go to St. Albans Veteran's Hospital for operation soon, maybe next week."

Poppa was having prostate trouble. The pasty yellowgray color intensified in his face as the sickness grew in him. Momma kept in check the fear that was gripping her. "We come to see you? Poppa, too?"

"Of course, anytime! Today?" I wanted to reassure her. She hadn't fully forgiven me for not having a wedding, but having a baby had reestablished our old bond between us. I was now a woman, her daughter still, but a woman. I had become a different person. She felt a bit uncomfortable about coming to the hospital and running into the Hammersteins. She had invited them to her house in Farmingdale for dinner. They politely finessed every invitation extended to them and never made it. Momma was a great cook and needed an area in which she could impress them. She needed something to equalize their wealth. They never invited her or Poppa to dinner at their home. Whether they were rich or not didn't make that much difference to Momma.

She shook her head as she said, "Right is right. They should invite us. You married now two years. They should ask us!"

She was right; they should have. I realized that my family wasn't important enough for them to have made that gesture. All those manners, all that stilted etiquette, had nothing to do with kindness and consideration. Still, Momma was curious to meet them. She rarely heard of them in the Polish circles in which she traveled. Since English was still difficult for her, she didn't read the American newspapers. Oscar's fame escaped her. Our simple life style left her wondering. She saw little of the money in our lives. Pumpkin-colored rooms and elephant-grey couches had little appeal for her. She liked bright colors and floral patterns. Thinking the taste strange and keeping it to herself, she was willing to accept it if it made me happy. A baby boy was her new grandson. We already had twin girls from my sister. This was the first boy in the family, and she was excited.

"We come this afternoon. You need anything?"

"No, Momma, thank you. I'll see you soon!" We hung up just as Jimmy, having gone home, showered and shaved, bounded back.

"Old Oscar Hammerstein III looks great! His head is a bit crooked, but they tell me it's gonna be OK. How ya feel?"

"Still tired and achy. Oscar <u>Andrew</u> Hammerstein III. Don't leave Andy out!" I wanted to get part of my family in there, too. Poppa's Polish name was Andrzej, I knew it would please him to have it wedged in there, so I called my son Andy. The name of Oscar had skipped a generation, and my son stood in line to inherit it. Ockie had an uncomfortable ring to it. Kids in school would laugh at him with a name like "Ockie." I knew how cruel kids could be. I still couldn't believe it. My son! Oscar Andrew Hammerstein III! That tiny person in there with so large a name. Would he also inherit the talent? Not only the name but the talent seemed to skip one generation. I wondered if the talent would again follow the name. My family said he looked like me. Momma glowed and told me that Andy reminded her of me when I was a baby.

"He smiling all the time, like you. Your sister born angry, but you smile all the time! Andrzejek like that, too. He smile! Is good!"

Jimmy's family said he looked like him. We had made them all happy. In a strange way, Jimmy and I looked a bit alike. We both had high, wide foreheads and high cheekbones. My small pointed chin looked better on a woman. His receding one didn't matter too much on a man. Pictures of Jimmy and early pictures of my father resembled each other.

Calls flooded the hospital switchboard. Nancy Merritt, my dear friend from Hunter College, wished me well. The cast of Pajama Game sent flowers. The cast of Damn Yankees, organized by Gwen Verdon, whom I had known from Can-Can, sent a large bouquet. Jean Stapleton also took up a collection. A few days later, a silver frame arrived with all the information on it concerning Andy: his date of birth, the time, his weight, height, mother's name, father's name, etc. The silver-frame disease was catching; it was infiltrating the rest of the theater.

Billy, Jimmy's older half-brother, was the first Hammerstein to call. "Does my mother hate you!" he enthusiastically informed me. I had given Oscar a grandson. All that Billy could manage was a granddaughter. His mother therefore hated me for having succeeded where her son had failed. I had never met her and saw only pictures of her in Billy's house. She was a small, pretty, double-chinned woman called Mike (after Myra), with breasts the size mine were now, enormous.

When Billy was much younger, he had a conversation with Tex McCreary and Jinx Falkenburg, who were writing an article about him. He explained the family tree to them.

"Oscar I had seven children, one of which was William (Willie), who had two sons, one of which was Oscar II, who had three children, one of whom was me, William (Billy)." Tex inquired further.

"If you ever have a son, what would you name him?"

Billy answered without hesitation, "Oscar III." He felt it would fall upon his shoulders to carry on the male line and tradition. Now Jimmy and I had usurped him. The name was taken. He had failed his father again. Even his mother couldn't forgive him.

Mary Rodgers, Dick's daughter, called to say, "How clever of you, my dear! You really did the wise thing having a boy!"

It was a statement I was to hear throughout the following days. It seems I had outdone myself by having a boy child. I was set. Again, presents poured in. This time, I was ready for them. I even learned where to write on those little note papers: first page, third page, then second and fourth. That was the order. Once you grasped it, you were set for life.

Oscar and Dorothy stopped by that afternoon. They explained that the relocation to a room with a river view had been at their request. My father-in-law brought a check with him for Jimmy for winning the bet, and an extra hundred for me, for having a boy. He discreetly slipped Jimmy a bonus, to cover his business debts. After a few pleasantries, he left to look at his new grandson, and came back nodding his head, as if in agreement with himself.

"Jimmy looked like an angry Jew when he was born! The baby looks like him, but not angry." He laughed and seemed pleased.

Dorothy brought me a beautiful bed jacket and a bed tray, so I would be able to have breakfast in bed more comfortably. Who was going to serve me? I wondered. They had taken care of that also by arranging for me to have a mother's helper who would be there for the baby, at least for the first few weeks. All I had to do was to heal. There were few problems that their money could not solve. I had wondered how I was going to get around. How I was going to care for Andy? My body still throbbed with pain, but it was all taken care of. I was grateful to them for the money, the gifts and for the room overlooking the river, wondering if I would still be by the noisy, busy elevator shaft if I had given birth to a girl.

Chapter 21

Before I went back to work, I joined Jimmy on a trip to England to be with him as he codirected a London production of <u>Damn Yankees</u>. Andy was tiny, not yet six months old, and I didn't want to leave him. Jimmy insisted that I be at his side, just as Dorothy had been at his father's side. Reluctantly, I left my baby son with Dorothy and Oscar and went abroad. A longing for my new child stayed with me during the whole trip. It filled me with an intensity of feeling I never thought I was capable of. My body missed my baby.

When I talked to Jimmy about it, he felt I was being foolish. Mother love was not instinctual, he informed me. He reminded me I had never before exhibited any predisposition along these lines. He was right, of course, but all of me, my arms and my heart, missed my son.

In time, I had to give up all the other feelings I had and concentrate on my relationship with my husband. He even returned to my bed long before the time I would have allowed him, had I felt that I had the choice. But if I "held out," as he put it, he might have turned to another woman for his sex. Same with going to London; I had to give up my child temporarily to follow him.

"Mumsie and Dads will take care of him. The baby sitter can live with them while we're away," he assured me. Our mother's helper fell right in with their plans. She was enchanted to touch the hem of theatrical royalty. I followed Jimmy to London. After agonizing if I would have to make the choice between my husband or my child, I wondered what I would do, having already made the choice, which betrayed my responsibility to my son.

Dorothy lent me her seal fur coat, which weighed a ton, and bought me an evening dress so I would pass inspection with her friends in England. We visited them all, including Lady Duckham, and stayed at the Claridge, one of the most beautiful hotels in London, which had a fancy bathroom. I had never seen a bidet before. Leaning over the bowl, I sprayed my face and hair with a jet of water, much to the hilarity of Jerry Whyte and my husband. Jerry was the London representative of Rodgers and Hammerstein. He was spreading the Rodgers and Hammerstein empire around the world, producing The King and I and South Pacific for them abroad.

We filled Jerry in on the gossip from back home. He, in turn, filled us in on the news from England. It seems that he had organized the prostitutes in London to report to him for theatrical favors. In return, they gave him invaluable political, stock market and inside business information. He was a very funny man and good company, even if at the time I thought him disreputable. Prostitutes! My word! I had a lot to learn.

It seems the rain followed us everywhere, not only on our honeymoon but also in Europe. After the London opening, we sailed over to the Riviera and spent a few days vacationing on the cuff, some kind of a writeoff from part of the European Hammerstein empire. They had to leave the money they made overseas in order to avoid paying United States taxes on it. We benefitted from those loopholes.

The best times I remember were the Italian Alps, as we wove our way higher and higher into the snowy peaks. The villages looked like Monopoly pieces way down there in the valley at the bottom of the mountain. We'd lunch on fruit, cheese, French bread and white wine, which was a mild version of what we drank back in the States and which, in Europe, never gave me a headache. After a second honeymoon on Cap Ferrat, again in the rain, we returned to the United States.

I'll never forget the look my son Andy gave me after I dashed up the elegant, softly carpeted stairs. It seemed to say, "Who are you?

Why are you taking me away from this nice colored lady who has been taking care of me?" He started to yell, trying to push me away, to get back into the arms of the maid. I called him by a Polish diminutive name I had used when I played with him, which meant "my little piece of gold."

"Zlotko, Zlotko, it's me, your mommie!" My heart was broken. My son had forgotten me. Upon hearing my voice, some buried memory returned, and he looked more closely at me and touched my face, gurgling and blowing a bubble, as I crushed him against me.

The money Jimmy made on <u>Damn Yankees</u> in London carried us for a few months. He then formed a partnership with Barbara Wolfson to produce <u>Blue Denim</u>. I went to work at the City Center for a season of musicals. The mother's helper returned to live with us, and we needed my income to pay for her salary. Jimmy's opening of <u>Blue Denim</u> and one of my performances fell on the same night. I did my show and arrived at his theater at curtain time. Oscar and Dorothy were already there. I could see the look of displeasure on Oscar's face. I had not been there with his son to share his opening night with him. He didn't understand that it wasn't in the furtherance of my own career. Our financial problems forced me to audition for the City Center and for another job in the chorus.

As we grew short of funds, I began spending my own money. Jimmy never asked me if I needed anything. He just assumed that the bills somehow got paid. They did, and very early in the marriage I became penniless. Savings that I had squirreled away when I was single, ten dollars at a time over a period of eight years, were gone. The major part of Jimmy's salary went to pay off his business debts. What was left over covered our rent and some of the rest of our needs.

When Jimmy's projects flopped, Oscar came to his son's aid with I.O.U.s and his "Lord Chesterfield" lectures about responsibility. The furthest thing from my mind when I married my husband was that we would have money problems. We might have all the other things to deal with like sex, family and careers. I never thought money would become our number one and constant irritant. We were surrounded by wealth, by people with enormous sums of money. There were times we had to worry whether we had enough for gas to get to The Farm on weekends. New clothes became a luxury, except when Jimmy embarrassed Dorothy by showing up for an opening in an old suit. She sent him to Brooks Brothers and outfitted him from head to toe.

After the birth of Andy and the resumption of our lives and careers, Jimmy and I saw less and less of each other. Blue Denim closed without recouping enough money to repay the investors. I felt a loneliness settling in around me.

I later laughed as I told my friends that my husband had membranes under his armpits, like bats or frogs do, that prevented him from lifting his arms and putting them around me. Why not? Some people have the remnants of vestigial tails at the end of their coccyx. I also knew a man who had an extra set of nipples, under the regular two on his breast. He eventually had them removed by plastic surgery. Amazing how those dormant mutations have a way of re-emerging and shaking our faith in our own divinity, in the idea we're made in the image of God. God with an extra set of nipples, or even a tail? My word! But membranes under his arms? After Jimmy bought a new skindiving suit, which cost him a lot of money, I asked him about our unpaid bills.

He turned on me in a rage. "You're a nagging cunt. You never had it so good!" Wrong! I never had it so bad! Before, I had freedom. Now I was trapped. We passed each other like robots, making small talk. I called both Andy and him my two Zlodkos. The term of endearment had become a hollow gesture.

What amazed me the most, judging from his desire to have a family, was the thought that Jimmy would be a wonderful father, giving his children the love he himself seemed to have missed. That was not to be true. After the first blush of fatherhood and the attention he received for having produced a boy, Jimmy ignored the baby completely. It was as if he, too, like his father, was waiting for Andy to grow up so he could play tennis or chess with him. He was following in the footsteps of a long-established Hammerstein tradition where the males ignored their children.

Oscar often remarked, "A child is not interesting until he is at least seven years old and can play chess." Consequently, he had nothing to do with his own children until they learned how to push chess pieces across the board. I could imagine Jimmy as a young boy, his skinny legs dangling under the table, desperately trying to learn the game so his father would pay some attention to him. By the time he did, it was too late. The damage had been done. The focus of that young life would be to get the approval of the father. Many years before, Jimmy wrote off his mother as being inconsequential. Pleasing women seemed unimportant, at most irrelevant. The wives suffered, as did eventually the mothers. I inherited that legacy in a new generation with my own son as he, too, clamored for his father's attention. Could you call it heredity or environment? It seemed so deeply imbedded in the male psyche of the Hammersteins that I opted for heredity, a chip off the old block, flakes off a larger stone.

Oscar I, the original Old Man, after he lost his wife Rose and remarried, lived at the Victoria Theater in New York City and rarely saw his own family. Meeting his grandson and namesake, Oscar II, when the boy was seven, he called him a "kind of a grandson". His own son Willie called him "my shadow of a father" and shunned publicity to distance himself from his flamboyant Old Man. Kindly Uncle Reggie fathered a daughter during a night of reconciliation with a soon-to-be former wife. Regina Hammerstein surfaced many years later. She not only looked like Reggie but could have been her cousin Diney's sister, they looked so much alike. All that her newfound family feared was that she might make some claims against the estate. I wondered how my own son would fare. Jimmy never bought him any toys and barely looked into the crib when he came home from the club. He felt that I fussed with him too much. We never could agree on what was enough and what was too much.

"You'll make a faggot outta him, a momma's boy!" Jimmy would taunt me.

I wanted to retort with, "Either that, or you'll make a robot of him like the rest of your family!" The current psychiatric "wisdom" was that mothers created faggots. Momism ran rampant throughout the culture, throwing the redefined bundle of guilt again on the shoulders of the mothers. Forever on the mothers. Too much affection produced sissies. But what was too much affection? How could you give too much affection to a helpless creature like a baby? Along with "penis envy," Freud resuscitated the Oedipus complex as a topic for discussion. If you loved a baby boy too much, he would either be a faggot or become sexually fixated on you. There seemed to be no way out. Abandoning him, as Jimmy had been abandoned, produced an inability for closeness, for affection, for intimacy. I was beginning to see that motherhood was a bind, a no-win situation.

With the therapy I recently resumed, I could no longer deny my growing rage. It wasn't too hard to spot. I'd go to the analyst, cry and scream for fifty minutes, then come back the following week and cry and scream for fifty minutes more. This went on for many months. It became apparent even to the Pollyanna in me that I was stifling to death and had created my own entombment. There wasn't enough fresh air around me to support my life. I didn't ask for inspiration, just survival. Even survival was being denied me.

Then somehow I began to feel a breeze. Somewhere in my psyche I had left a back door open. My pent-up rage and frustration were pushing it open wider. The cool draft of freedom turned me in the direction of escape, in the direction where a tiny light glowed in the distance. I would keep trying, but some core of me wanted to blast those seams of futility out into the fresh air into the sunshine to let them heal.

Nothing seemed to change outwardly in our marriage. My husband kept telling me he loved me. I kept telling him I loved him. We went on like everyone else around us, except that I had begun to hate him. The amazing thing is that my hate changed nothing in the relationship between us. I realized how surface it all had been. Were all relationships so devoid of emotional content? Did they all exist on a level of surface ritual, passing like ships in the night only stopping to go bang, bang in bed?

Was the rage I carried in me the same as Dorothy carried in her? Was her marriage as basically empty as mine? Reflected in my own mirror, I was beginning to see eyes, although not blue and watery like hers, but eyes that reflected a growing bewildered sadness.

I was not yet thirty and had apparently gotten it all. I was the Cinderella after the ball, after she had married the prince. Was this all there was? Where had the passions of my youth gone to? Where was the joy, the wonder? After months on the couch of raging and ranting, one analyst told me I needed a hobby to take my mind off my problems. I dumped him. Another told me I needed to talk dirty to him and offered his hand to accompany my frustrated sexual demands as he slid beside me on the couch. One put me into group therapy. In the group, I had to play games so my identity wouldn't be exposed and I wouldn't spill the Hammerstein beans. Nothing worked. I cried by myself wondering how I was to deal with the rage and the pain that had become an actual physical aching in the center of my body and seemed to be making my voice more and more hoarse, endangering my professional career as a singer.

Poppa hadn't been much different with Momma. As I looked at pictures of her back in Poland, when she had been about my age, just before my sister was born, I could see the same look of stark raging despair. The look on her face echoed the feelings I was beginning to harbor. Do most women go through this? Do they hide it better? Is that what caused some of my girlfriends to bury themselves in the bottle? It was a time before women discussed their lives. You were some kind of a failure if things didn't go swimmingly with your husband. The front was enough. A good front fooled everyone, and no one knew how desperate you were. Most women danced around the lives of their husbands or lovers, never hearing the beat of their own drums.

Most men ignored their children; that was a given. I had hoped it would be different with Jimmy. All men stayed little boys and played games until they died. No one told me that, but it became obvious during my marriage. I had become not so much my husband's mommie,

227

for his Mumsie was never really a mommie, but a kind of gofer with whom he could have sex. I was the one who took care of all our physical needs. I shopped for food, meat, clothes, everything. I took care of all the things he either broke or that fell apart through rough use. I did the laundry at the local laundromat. I gathered up his clothing every week and schlepped them to the cleaners. I paid the bills every month and wrote letters to the utilities when they made billing mistakes. I made sure that there was gas in the car and that the car was serviced, not trusting it to him, for we found ourselves stranded by the road more than once. I tipped the doormen, made dentist and doctors appointments, had the windows washed, hung the curtains and draperies and even tacked down the rugs. I knitted argyle socks for him, made him a cashmere vest to match a coat Dorothy bought him at Brooks Brothers, shined his shoes, changed the sheets, shined all the brass and silver, waxed the furniture, vacuumed the floor and made two meals every day, breakfast and dinner, plus an after theater snack.

The babysitter took care of Andy, wheeling him to Central Park every day. After she spent a few weeks with the Hammersteins while we were in Europe, she proclaimed one day, while sprawled on the kitchen chair as I swept around her, that she liked steaks and lamb chops, thick ones. I wished her well and gave her an opportunity to find them somewhere else. We were into chicken and hamburgers and had steak only when we got it from Mary, the Polish maid at The Farm. Mary was kind and knew our plight, so when we visited, she would pack us a cardboard box of beef that the farmer butchered for the family every year. She had to be surreptitious about it, for she knew "The Master" would not totally approve. Oscar's generosity, not unlike my father's, was greater to those outside of the family.

As a child, I had developed a rage against my father. There was nothing I could do about it. Momma said it was terrible to hate him and God would punish me. I was a bad girl. All little girls loved their fathers. I wondered why I was so bad and why my mind raged with excuses and justifications against him. Whenever he could, even before I was twelve, he called me a "scurva" (whore), making fun of me, calling the freckles on my shoulders a disease, which I covered with long sleeves way into my twenties. He said my legs were thick and ugly. I later became a Copa girl, having gotten the job because my legs were one of my great assets. To him, my voice trembled like a "barani ogon," which meant "shook like a ram's tail." I grew up thinking I was an ugly duckling. To this day, I'm amazed when people find me attractive. It got to the point that I used to have a dream about Poppa. The dream left me shaking with rage and tears of frustration. In it I would dismember him, cut him into small bloody pieces, then methodically with my heels, I would grind each piece back into the body of Mother Earth.

The first time I had that dream about Jimmy, I realized I had to get out of the marriage. The urge to run was tempered by fear. It was one of the two dormant and deep fears that dogged my life. One was that of raising my child alone without a husband. The other was to die povertystricken. Both had been Momma's, and both of them I had made my own.

Momma had reason to be panic-stricken about raising us alone. She had forced Poppa to bring us with him to the United States. He wanted to leave us behind in Poland. She came here, to this new world, with no family, no friends, unfamiliar with the language, alone with two small children and Poppa. It's no wonder she was panic-stricken. She feared he would desert us. Going on welfare was a shame she would not have been able to face. I, who spoke the language and had educated myself and knew my way around, in my soul of souls, had the same fears. A panic about raising my family alone and facing a penniless old age loomed large before me.

When I was rehearsing with <u>Top Banana</u>, Phil Silvers wanted us to have an authentic feel for the burlesque sketch at the end of the third act. He took the whole company across the river to see Minsky's Burlesque, back to one of our first homes in the United States, in Jersey City, New Jersey.

Minsky's was a ramshackle burlesque house that had seen better days. Peeling gilt paint exposed stained walls. The wooden seats were hard, and their splintered edges caught our clothes as we squeezed between them. We laughed as the performers did their turns, and all our comics joined them on the stage. We had old pros with us like Joey ("It feels so nice out: I think I'll leave it out") Faye, Herbie Faye, Jack Albertson and, of course, Phil himself. They all joined together on the stage for one of their bits.

"We are the girls of the chorus; this is our opening night." Turn the leg out at the hip. Lots of laughter. The place was turned upside down for us, until the local showgirls came out. I'll never forget them, older women wearing too much makeup, their thighs puckered with fat (which was later to be called cellulite) shaking their blubber across the stage in fluffy pink costumes bulging at the seams, not quite hiding their dark curly pubic hair. How we all laughed at them. They went through their paces, flashing their behinds at us in the cancan, while the entire theater rocked with derisive glee. I looked at them and wondered. They probably had the same dreams I did. What strange twists of fate brought them to this stage, wobbling around in skimpy costumes and making ludicrous fun of themselves? It seemed so far removed from me, young, beautiful, talented, with my life before me. Yet that scene always haunted me. Those puckered thighs wobbling up and down on that burlesque stage never left me.

Chapter 22

Periodically in our lives, there seem to times when for no apparent reason things somehow bunch together, and then they blast apart. Sometimes a cluster of chaos and tragedy happens to one person. Sometimes it stretches out over a period of time, and just as you recover from one disaster, another strikes you. Then there are times when a group of people is brought together, either willy-nilly or through some grand indifferent design, to experience a tragedy, a catastrophe, a sharing in some kind of disintegration.

When it happens all at once, like a terminal illness or the death of a loved one, the churning energies come together and explode, cascading over the top like a volcano, leaving in their wake the singular petrification of destruction and grief. All we can do then is try to pull our lives together, clutching at the remaining straws, trying to weave them into a new and coherent pattern. Many of the straws disappear, like the fragments of dreams, gone forever beyond the reach of our fingertips, leaving holes in the design we have called our lives.

Often the events creep up on us slowly. The explosion is in slow motion, moving out from the center like the expanding universe, spreading out over a period of a few years. Sometimes the spread continues for a lifetime. As the pieces of our lives fly slowly apart and we cling to our sanity, trying to survive the disintegration, a whole new game is being reassembled. Cruelly, we are left out of the planning stages. All we experience is the result, manifested in pain, tragedy, and loss. There are times when, like Job, we reel from a single blow. Before there is a chance to recover, another blow downs us. Life becomes a recurrent series of mishaps. We fall lower and lower into what seems to be a deep dark well. We work our way up trying to find footholds on the slippery cold rocks. Just as we begin to see the light above and a cool breeze refreshes us, something, some great invisible hand, pushes us down again. We start the desperate climb back up, each time with less hope, each time with more anguish and desperate effort.

Sometimes a group of people are brought together to share an event, as if the fates were conserving energy. The catastrophe occurs through an air crash or the sinking of a ship or an act of terrorism. Lives are assembled, blasted apart, and the individuals are left to pick up the pieces alone.

It took me many years of hacking through my recurrent despair to get an inkling, an understanding, of what happened not only to me but to all of us at that time, in the period of just over two years, the span of time that I was coincidentally older than my husband. We seemed to be part of a larger spin, of some greater vortex, careening through time: my subsequent miscarried baby, Jimmy, Dorothy, Oscar, Reggie, Momma and Poppa. Recurrent bouts of optimism and the responsibility of raising my son kept me going. To leave him orphaned at the mercy of the Hammersteins was a burden I couldn't inflict upon him and could not take into the void with me. So I kept scratching my way upward, clutching at the slippery sides of the well, grasping for the light far up above me, always beyond my reach.

With the loss of the role of Suzie in <u>Sweet Thursday</u>, the downward roll curved its way into my life. All the blessings and luck that I had taken for granted began to leave me. Nothing I did seemed to make any difference. As some larger positive force stopped working for me, I kept on dealing with piddly dislocations, trying to hold it all together, trying to make the habits of my life work, trying to make my marriage with Jimmy work, as we were all trying to make them work, as Dorothy was trying to make hers work with Oscar, and Momma was trying to make hers work with Poppa. We all seemed to be moving in a similar direction. Our tightly knit, closely patterned lives were unraveling and wobbling like drunken tops before coming to rest. We were all reaching the end of a particular spin, of a particular vortex, careening out of control, bumping into walls, then shuddering and finally falling, belly up.

Had the women on the burlesque stage at Minky's given up too soon? That couldn't be, for they were still trying; they were still going strong. Did the double-edged sword of wish-fulfillment work for them also? Was that stage in Jersey City all that was left for them? I shuddered and counted my current, if rocky, blessings.

Andy and Basia Hammerstein

Jimmy Hammerstein and Oscar Andrew Hammerstein III

At the Copa

Copa Girl — Basia Regis, 1950

Chapter 23

In the pursuance of my young dreams to have both passion and wisdom in my life, I trudged on with the goal of a college degree on the one hand and a career in singing on the other. The double-edged sword of wish-fulfillment blessed me with whatever tentatively quickened my heart. Both areas opened up for me with unforeseen consequences. In retrospect, it is difficult to say which had been more important to me at that time, the passion or the wisdom. But they worked in tandem, like the two galloping horses that, on another level, dragged me backward through the wake of my life.

To continue with my schooling and to fill my mind with much-needed information in order not to appear stupid, I needed to work. My employment career began at sixteen as soon as I was able to get a Social Security card. I applied for the job of a "soda jerk" at a Whalen Drugstore in Flushing, Long Island, and brought home two hundred and ten dollars that first summer. During the rest of the year, I attended Washington Irving High School.

My life in high school was a time of great joy and achievement. By the time that I graduated, I had become leader of Arista, (the honor society), was vice-president of the senior class, ran for and was elected to the Governing Council, was sent as a delegate to the Manhattan Governing Council to be elected as secretary. During a UNESCO Forum at the United Nations, I represented Washington Irving High School. I wrote for the high school newspaper and drew pictures for the art magazine. Even after I left the All-City Chorus, I was elected to the presidency of the Glee Club. In my senior year, I won a second prize in a city-wide essay contest, sponsored by the Advertising Club of New York, dealing with the future of advertising. Upon graduating, I received a variety of awards: The Alexander Medal for excellence in art from the School Art League, the Gold medal from the School Athletic League, and a Merit award from the Bank of Savings for having accrued the most credits in service to my school since it opened.

It was a heady time for me, and my confidence grew in proportion to my success. I could walk down the halls and be greeted by dozens of fellow students. Everyone knew me. My face graced the bulletin boards. My Polish-accented English could be heard at most weekly assemblies announcing upcoming events, welcoming honored guests and passing out awards to other students.

In Washington Irving High School, surrounded only by other girls, I had reached the pinnacle of accomplishment and power. There was little else that remained for me to pursue and to attain. So it came as a bit of shock when Lily Fernandez, my home room classmate, became a John Robert Powers model. It seems that Oleg Cassini spotted her on Fifth Avenue, and because she reminded him of his wife, Gene Tierney, he introduced her to some of his friends and launched her on a career in modeling.

My competitive spirit rose to the challenge. I, too, decided to become a model. A part of me had been awakened to the possibility of a singing career by P.J. Wilhousky, although I put that ambition on hold after I left the All-City Chorus. Still, modeling might, in some way, take me in the direction of show business. It all seemed all of a piece out there somewhere, as I rode the rumbling noisy subways and dreamed.

I couldn't wait around on Fifth Avenue hoping to be spotted by Oleg Cassini, so I did the next best thing. The New York Daily Mirror had an extensive section of classified ads. I searched through "Models Wanted" and realized that in order to find my next job, I had to head in the direction of the garment center. What I didn't know at that time, right after the Second World War, was that models came in a variety of categories. One group contained the photographers models, beloved by the camera, whose beautiful faces smiled back at us from our newspapers and magazines. Their employment was iffy and temperamental. Another category contained the showroom models, who worked nine to five, in the houses around Seventh Avenue. They held steady positions for many years and could plan their lives with some degree of predictability. Still another group of models did the fashion shows. They were elegant, tall, skinny women, who wore clothes on their great bodies as if they hung from the branches of long-stemmed elm trees.

There was another category of models that was not advertised in the Daily Mirror. It dealt with borderline pornography. Photographers often exchanged proper pictures that could be used in the legitimate areas of modeling for sleazy sets that they sold to girly magazines. Saxie Holtsworth ran a modeling agency on Broadway that specialized in funneling young girls, often fresh from the sticks, into a life of borderline and often out-and-out pornography. The pictures they posed for use in girly magazines, often in order to pay their rent, followed many of them into their marriages and into more substantial careers. Much money changed hands to get back those early risqué and often disreputable pictures. Many photographers grew rich from the side occupation of blackmail.

Since I needed a career that not only enhanced my status in school but came with a steady and predictable salary, I opted for the garment center. One day after school, with my Daily Mirror want ad section rolled neatly in the spine of my notebook, I took the subway uptown to the Thirty-Fourth Street station on the Seventh Avenue subway. Then I walked uptown a few more blocks into the center of the garment industry.

One of the Daily Mirror ads stated that showroom models, size 10, were needed in a coat and suit house at 500 Seventh Avenue. As I stood in front of the building directory in the cavernous foyer, unraveling my rolled-up want ads and trying to find a corresponding name on the glassed-in panel on the wall, one of the elevator operators padded across the shiny marble floor toward me.

"You looking for a showroom job?" He looked me over, stopping only at my bobby socks, as he inquired.

"I guess so. I want to be a model," I answered, not too sure what I was getting into, as I checked my neatly rolled socks.

"Then ask me." He stood up very straight and smiled. His double row of brass buttons shone in the lights. "I'm the guy who runs the elevators. I'm a starter. They tell us when they need girls. Hop in; I'll take you." He crashed the massive elevator doors shut behind us. My heart began to race as I got off on the fifth floor.

"Good luck," the starter shouted to me, as the elevator doors again crashed shut behind me. In front of me in the foyer over a large open double door that led to a showroom surrounded by banquettes hung a sign that said Fierman and Kolmer Co. A tall blonde model in a black satin, slip-like dress, came over to me.

"You looking for a job?" She looked me over without making any comment about how I was dressed, passing over the sloppy-joe sweater and the bobby socks.

"I want to be a model. The man on the elevator, the starter, said you had a job?" I blurted out. As we stood in the foyer of Fierman and Kolmer, a short dark man in his late forties who looked like a tanned Al Jolson came out from a side office, chomping on an unlit cigar. He spied me, and as he moved into the foyer, he positioned the cigar in such a way in his jutting jaw that it pointed to the ceiling. With the cigar like a lance before him, he smiled and looked me over as he spoke to the blonde model.

"She want a job?" he inquired of the other woman in the foyer as he threw his head in my direction. "How old is she?" They both looked over to me.

"I'm eighteen," I lied, feeling left out of the conversation between them.

"You wanna be a model." He rolled the dead cigar from one side of his mouth to the other. I nodded. "You work as a model before?" He lifted his eyebrows. I shook my head. He kept staring at me as his button brown eyes narrowed and he kept smiling. "Shirley," he said as

240

he turned to the blonde model, "tell her to get a girdle and some stockings." I flushed a beet red. "She's got to get rid of the bobby socks and the loafers. Teach her how to walk. She looks like a perfect size ten." They both looked me over and nodded in agreement. "This is Shirley. What's your name?" He leaned over in my direction as the waft of cigar smoke seeped through me.

"Barbara Redzisz. I'm still going to school. Can I come after school? I can be here by three." He threw back his slick black- haired head and laughed as his false white teeth not only clanked dully in his mouth but rearranged the dancing cigar.

"You got nerve." He laughed again. Shirley looked completely taken aback. "Why not? Summer's coming. Can you work full time then?"

"Yes."

"Good, Barbara. I'm Max Kolmer, of Fierman and Kolmer." He pointed to the sign over the showroom door. "This is Shirley, my head model and showroom girl! She'll teach you the ropes."

Max Kolmer, with his almost year-round tan and slicked-down black hair and busy cigar, became my dear friend. He took me under his wing and often gave me good advice. In the beginning, he let me work whatever hours I could squeeze in after school. Then, the following summer, he gave me the opportunity to work full time. I made three hundred and fifty-five dollars that first year, which was one hundred and forty-five dollars more than I had made the summer before at Whalen Drugstore as a soda jerk. My dreams were coming true.

That first year, I learned not only how to walk like a model, tall and straight, like a tree, so that no creases showed on the coats and suits that I paraded before the buyers, but during slack times, I learned how to work the switchboard. In time, Max Kolmer gave me the opportunity not only to model and to work the switchboard but to do some designing, to go to uptown fashion shows and rip off the more exclusive designs, drawing them surreptitiously in the bathrooms after each set. Because Momma had taught me how to sew, over the years, he also paid me to oversee one of his clothing factories in Long

Island City. Back in Washington Irving, I flaunted the career move I had made, as I had flaunted my stint with the All-City Chorus. Not only could I call myself a model, but, more important, I was making some money.

At Fierman and Kolmer, I made a whole new set of friends. Most of them, at the time, were older than I. One of my closest buddies was Charlotte Hudzik, whom we called Shatzie. She was not only Polish, which created a bit of a bond between us, but was also an unusual beauty, with features that could have landed her jobs as a photographer's model. She had aspirations in that direction. One day, with the Daily Mirror spread out on the dressing table before her, she looked over to me. I was putting on my makeup and covering some of the pimples that occasionally erupted on my still quite young face.

"There's an ad in the paper." She pointed to the newspaper and conspiratorially looked around. The showroom was at the moment waiting for the inevitable influx of buyers. "They're looking for show-girls at the Copacabana, I want to try. Come with me?" Her finely angled face assumed a look of pleading, "I'm afraid to go alone. Come on. All we need is shorts and high heels."

I looked at her. Why not? I would be eighteen in six months. The year had passed quickly. Anyway, I was curious to see what the Copacabana looked like, way uptown off Fifth Avenue in the East Sixties, even farther uptown than Carnegie Hall.

The following Tuesday after work, we splurged and took a cab to the Copa. As we walked east from Fifth Avenue where the cab had left us, I could see other tall, young and pretty girls with their trademark--the large round, patent leather hat box--scurrying in the same direction.

The Copacabana canopy under the Hotel Fourteen sign was very impressive, extending all the way across the sidewalk to the edge of the curb. We entered a darkened lobby in which hung the stale odors of liquor and cigarette smoke. We left our hat boxes with one of the bus boys and got on a line of hopefuls that disappeared into an even darker cavern below. From the center of the cavern, lights defined the audition area. The whole process moved very quickly. Six girls were asked to walk onto the brightly lit, newly polished dance floor. Columns decorated to look like palm trees flanked its sides. On a slight rise in front of the dance floor, back of a railing around a very large wooden table, barely seen because of the overhead lights, sat a very large man. His name was Jack Entratter. He directed the proceedings not only with his voice but with a small flashlight that glowed and danced like a dull cigarette in the darkness that surrounded him. He had the contestants stand there and pose. Then with a flick of his wrist and a vocal command, he had them turn around. The last request was to sashay, a kind of simple dance step, right-left-right and then repeat left-right-left. When in doubt, sashay, Doug Coudy, our Copa choreographer, would later tell us when we mixed up or forgot the routines. When they finished sashaying, the flashlight- wielding impresario excused the dancers with a curt "thank you" as other men who drifted in and out of the darkness stopped at his bare table, exchanged a few comments about the girls in the line and, as often as not, laughed.

Our turn came. Shatzie and I, with our knees shaking, walked majestically onto the dance floor. Our showroom training showed. We stopped between the towering, palm-shrouded columns, blinking at the bright spots in the ceiling that temporarily blinded us. We went through out paces. I felt like a piece of meat on display. But friendship was friendship. Shatzie needed my support, and I was curious. Jack Entratter's voice proceeded his massive bulk as it emerged out of the shadows.

He leaned across the railing and addressed me. "What's your name?" I looked around at Shatzie, wondering if he had made a mistake. "You," he jabbed his flashlight at me, "what's your name."
"Basia Regis" I gave him the name that I felt might be appropriate for the chanteuse I was going to become. "Basia" was a diminutive of Barbara and would stamp me as being Polish. "Regis" had a nice ring to it and was an Americanization of Redzisz.

"Basha Regis, that sounds like a stripper. Are you a stripper?" I blushed scarlet, perspiration formed on my upper lip, and I shook my head. "Step forward. We need a girl for the summer show. Basha Regis, would you like to work for us?"

He waved the other girls that stood in the line with me, including Shatzie, off the shiny dance floor and into the murky sides of the night club.

I realized I had been hired as a dancer, at seventy-five dollars a week, which was a princely salary. It seemed I fit the parameters of perfection that had been set by a former Copa girl, Olga San Juan: an oval face more heart-shaped than round, slightly slanted large eyes with a good body that could move. Her face, with a Carmen Miranda head dress and turban, appeared on all the posters and on the front of the bandstand in the night club.

In June, I began my career as a Copa girl, doing three shows a night and having every other Monday night off. Facing Shatzie, with whom I had come and to whom I was to have given moral support, was the most difficult part of having gotten the job at the Copacabana.

When I took the new job, Max Kolmer had misgivings about my new career, but chomping on his cigar, he wished me well and even brought the whole compliment of showroom models to cheer me on in my opening night. At the end of the summer, after a series of ugly confrontations with Jack Entratter, when he eventually wedged me up against the wall, crushed me with his six-foot, eight-inch frame and came all over my legs, I left the Copa. Since I couldn't continue as a Copa girl, having burned my bridges with the behemoth impresario by throwing up all over him after he came on my legs, I set my sights on a Broadway show.

The double-edged sword of wish-fulfillment was about to cleave its way into my life again. Again, an ad in the classified section of a newspaper came to my aid. It announced that there was an open call for singers in the chorus of a new Broadway musical called Top Banana, which was to star Phil Silvers. The Copa may have been my first job in show business, but it didn't feel like the direction in which I eventually hoped to travel. A job in a Broadway show might fit the bill on a variety of levels and finally set me on the right track.

In the early 1950s, it was almost impossible to get into a Broadway show without being a member of Actors Equity. On the other hand, it was impossible to get into Actors Equity without being in a show. It was a double bind. To give an opportunity for non-union members, Equity had to provide open "cattle calls," as they were known, at the end of the Equity auditions. Every young and old hopeful came to those cattle calls. Sometimes the long lines waiting to audition snaked around more than a block. Since most of the shows were cast in the summer, many of us eager optimists sweltered in the heat and became drenched during many a late-day thunderstorm.

The ironic part was that the open calls were held because they were mandatory, not because the producers needed more performers. By the time the open calls were scheduled, at the end of all the union auditions, most, if not all, of the principal parts, and even the chorus parts, had been cast. It was a mandate that occasionally landed a job to a non-union member and undermined the reality, created by the other unions, that Broadway was a closed union shop.

On a hot and muggy day in the summer of 1951, I stood at the heavy metal stage door of the Winter Garden Theater. The line before me disappeared quickly behind it as the line behind me grew longer. Like at the All-City Chorus auditions, the contestants who turned out for open calls were all shapes and sizes, all colors and ages. Hope was the catalyst, not the reality of the employment situation. The participants waiting to audition moved forward to the heavy stage door, tense with anticipation. They were pushed aside by those who were on the way out, slack with disappointment. The metal door clanked back and forth, as ever-new contestants filed in.

A line of ten singers was asked to stand on the vacant stage in the enormous and almost empty theater. Gloomy light bulbs hung bare over the waiting contenders as I joined their ranks. The girl just behind me, being number eleven, was asked to remain outside of the clanking metal door. After the noise and the clamor of the traffic outside, it was relatively silent inside that dark and musty theater. The silence was broken by a voice from the back of the theater, a voice that ordered all of us to move upstage so that the shadows, which fell from the overhead lights, could be kinder to our faces.

Again, I was asked to step forward, while the other nine girls were dismissed. I began to shake. Singing in a chorus, even in a Broadway show, seemed like a safe enough place to further my theatrical career. But I dreaded auditioning alone upon that exposed stage, to those male voices that came out of the darkness in front.

I unrolled my music, having gotten in the habit of rolling up newspapers and often loose pieces of paper to fit them into the spine of my notebooks, and handed it to the pianist in the pit. The dancing figures of Jeanne Crain and Dan Dailey on the pink cover of the sheet music flashed before me as he flicked open my audition song and hit the first few chords of "You Were Meant for Me." a slightly insipid song I had learned by myself, without the assistance of a coach or teacher.

With my passable, not yet trained for the theater soprano, and with the passions of singing and the accompanying goose pimples held firmly in check, I was given an opportunity to get through the first fifteen bars.

"You were meant for me, I was meant for you,
Nature patterned you and when she was done,
You are all the sweet things rolled up in one"

As I lingered on the last note of the line ready to plunge into "You're like a plaintive melody," all hell broke loose. Out of the gloom of the darkened theater, a gray-haired man with a thin mustache not unlike Wilhousky's ran down the aisle toward the stage, waving his arms and yelling.

"Hire her, hire her. Who is she?" More restrained voices, farther back in the vastness of the empty dark theater, hissed and with loud whispers declared, "We have our six singers. We don't need another one, Jack."

"Hire her. I don't care. She can be Phil's straight man. I want her in the show."

246

Other voices joined the give and take, and men with their arms filled with scripts and music darted up and down the aisle, adding to the commotion. I stood alone on the stage as Jack Donohue ran down the aisle, jumped up on the stage, very sprightly for an older man, and began to pump my hand.

"Welcome on board." He held on to my hand as he guided me off the stage and into the wings. He kept on talking, without waiting for me to answer. "Have you ever done a show before? I don't recognize your face? What's your name?"

In 1951, in the month of July, another Jack had given me a job. This time it was Jack Donohue, the director of <u>Top Banana</u>, who got in line as my potential benefactor. I was hired for ninety dollars a week, which was better than my salary at the garment center or even the Copa, and was signed to a white contract. People in the chorus were hired on pink contracts, but at that time the distinction was lost on me. Very quickly, it became very clear to me that a chasm existed between the principal players, who were signed to white contracts, and the chorus members, who were signed to pink contracts. The chasm was not only financial, and that was considerate, but also social. A caste-like class distinction existed between the two groups based on the color of the contracts and the jobs they represented.

Because I had been hired on a white contract in the part of AS CAST, I had the status of a principal player, but not exactly. In actuality, I was placed in the chorus as the seventh member of that group and was given extra work as Phil's straight lady, for which I would not have to be paid extra. I again realized very quickly that the extra work that had been given to me would have gone to the other girls in the singing chorus, for which they would have gotten some extra pay. By hiring me, the producers not only got an extra chorus member but an extra body who could deliver some straight lines to Phil and not exact extra enumeration.

Whatever Jack Donohue saw in me, it moved him in the direction of obsession. Throughout the subsequent rehearsals, he stalked me. I had to create and recreate myriad excuses to get away from him.

He fell into the same category as Wilhousky, Slifka and Entratter: an older man who, because of the position of power and employment that he held, tried to force himself on me. I grew rigid with resentment against him as I had done before against the others.

When I shared breaks with the other chorus gypsies, he would appear and hang around, making me and some of the other chorus members uncomfortable. As a director, he was basically a very patient and kind man. He didn't seem to have the same streak of cruelty that Wilhousky possessed. But his sexual insistence made my life a living hell in my first Broadway show. Once we moved out of town, he stalked the hallways of the hotels in which we stayed, waiting for me, hiding in doorways as I recharted the routes to my room every night, using not only the elevators but dark winding stairwells to avoid him.

Because he would turn up whereever I seemed to be, it became the gossip of the day that I was his girlfriend. It was also widely speculated that I had gotten into the show because of it. There was no way to counter the allegations, so I worried, fretted and waited until the show would open back in New York and he would go back to Los Angeles.

Then the focus of the gossip shifted. An item appeared in one of the columns that Phil Silvers was squiring me around town. That was also untrue and had been cooked up by our publicity agent. That unfortunate item caused the dancer whom he was actually seeing to attempt suicide. It was hushed up, but the incident led to one of the few really personal conversations I had with Phil.

He asked me into his dressing room before one of our out-of-town tryouts. He confided in me that the only reason that he had not jumped on my bones was because I was Jack's girl, dancer girl friend or not. Then he went on to inform me about his marriage to a Miss America and told me that he was really Romeo locked in a comic's body. His soul didn't fit the package that had been given him at birth. I was getting used to having men tell me their life stories, so I didn't even try to explain my relationship, or lack of it, with Jack Donohue. I was grateful that, real or not, it kept Phil Silvers at bay. As he finished the conversation in his dressing room, he reached over and, with the tips of his fingers, squeezed my breast.

"Orange," he said, looking as if he hoped that it had been closer to grapefruit or even watermelon. I was getting used to the impotent rage that filled me when men behaved in this way toward me. I backed out of his dressing room and talked to myself as the black horse of my indignation grew and galloped in frenzied circles.

Since I had been hired not only as the seventh chorus member but Phil's straight lady, I had to learn what to do. Near the end of <u>Top Banana</u> was a long burlesque number in which Phil, dressed up as a clown, was the master of ceremonies. In it I had two important roles to play. One was that of a magician's assistant; the other was that of a Gypsy fortune-teller.

As the magician's assistant, I stood center stage, in a long tight green satin dress, wearing a large pink satin turban on my head. As Phil spun around downstage of me, in his baggy green pants and his huge floppy green beret, wagging a rubber cigar at the audience, a flower made of pink ostrich feathers began to grow from between my breasts. (Maybe that piqued his curiosity, which he had expressed in the dressing room). The tall pink column of feather flowers emerged on cue and almost covered my face.

Phil, cavorting downstage with the audience, feigned ignorance as they began to titter with a realization of what was happening upstage with me. Then, again on cue, he looked upstage, saw the flower growing out from between my breasts, did a series of takes, rolled his eyes, flapped his cigar, and got a big laugh as the house came down. To create the illusion, I had to learn to pull a wire that held the flowers in place between my breasts with my thumb behind my back, out of sight of the audience. The wire caused the flowers to rise slowly, as if growing out of my chest. Since it was all pantomime and needed no words or singing, I did fine, always getting the pre-planned laugh.

My other great moment occurred during the same burlesque sketch, when I had to cross the stage in a red Gypsy costume full of sequins, shiny baubles and jingling bells. Boots covered my shaking feet, and a red bandanna rakishly clung to the side of my head. As I sashayed across the stage, Phil, still in his floppy green clown costume, did a double take, spun in place, flapped his rubber cigar at me and inquired, "What a lovely young lady. (Pause) And what do you do, my lovely young lady?" He danced around me, never stopping, his legs bending, his arms flying, his cigar flapping in my face.

"I'm a Gypsy fortune-teller," I answered, with as much power as my voice could muster.

"A Gypsy fortune-teller, ha," he exclaimed, as his headlight- sized glasses framed his bobbing face.

"Yes, would you like <u>your palm read?</u>" I asked him consistently all during our rehearsals. He then flung his palm upward in front of me, and I, from a Dixie cup filled with red paint hidden in the folds of my skirt, with a dainty paint brush painted his palm red. My apparent duplicity and his total surprise always brought the house down. Always, that is, except during opening night in Boston. I had never really delivered lines on a large professional stage before. My time came, as I mumbled my lines in the wings...

"...like <u>your palm read.</u>"

HAIL MARY FULL OF GRACE

"...like <u>your palm read.</u>"

My big moment arrived with the crash of laughter from the sketch before. I started across the stage with all the stuff of my costume clanging around me. The beating of my heart deafened me to such a degree that I could barely hear the cues that Phil was throwing in my direction. As I got to the center of the stage, he came to a sudden halt just before me and inquired, repeating the same few lines that we had rehearsed, "And what do you do, my lovely young lady?"

"I'm a Gypsy fortune-teller." So far. so good. My voice came back to me as from an echo chamber.

"A Gypsy fortune-teller, ha." He repeated the line we had rehearsed a dozen times before, setting up the cue for me to answer.

I blurted out, "Yes, would you like to <u>have your fortune told?</u> It stopped him dead in his tracks. He spun around to face me. His clown outfit fell in folds around him and became momentarily still. His eyes grew as large as the buttons on his clown suit.

"How do you plan to do that?" was his next inquiry, as he dove to save the skit. With a wave of heat joining the panicked ringing in my ears, I realized that something had gone wrong and I had been the cause of it.

Grasping for the familiarity of the over-rehearsed line, I blurted out, "Would you like <u>your palm read?</u>" And I brushed the red paint over his extended open hand. It all went by so quickly that no one seemed to notice, and the laughter exploded following the predictable look of stunned surprise on his bewildered clown face. For me, in that moment, it was as if time had stood still, as if I were swimming slowly through a sea of molasses, as if the embarrassment would never end. I wanted to pack my suitcase, go back to New York, leave the theater, and hide my head in shame.

That evening after the show, after the last curtain had gone down, as we sat around the empty darkened stage devoid of props, with the scenery tucked high above us in the rafters, exhausted and exhilarated from the chaos of opening night, Phil came up to me and said, "Listen, schmuck, things like that happen. Just keep going. Never stop. Just keep going. It wasn't all that bad. We got the laugh," he assured me. "But remember, just keep going."

It was good advice on a variety of levels, advice I turned to, as it became a phrase that chased the hamster on the wheel of my mind. Just keep going, it kept repeating, as the hamster and I both raced in ever narrowing circles.

Top Banana — Magician's Assistant

Top Banana — Phil Silvers, Herbie Faye and Joey Faye

Top Banana — Phil Silvers and Jack Albertson

Two's Company — Bette Cavis Show

Basia

Chapter 24

Jimmy went on the road with the minishow of <u>Damn Yankees</u> to play the casinos in Las Vegas. I had to stay behind with Andy and with my growing new pregnancy. Our long angry silences had been broken only by fights over money. When he left for the road, it was as if a stone had been dropped into the ocean. He vanished without a trace. The world that had been a troubled "we" ceased to exist.

Walking through the empty rooms of the apartment, I felt relieved, no longer driven to do his errands and to be at his beck and call. In time, he sent me an occasional letter with a check, and one that said "I love you," written in faint pencil on the inside flap, which I noticed only after I looked closely at the envelope. The distance that hung between us when we were together now was real. We were separated by actual space and time. The days grew into weeks. The weeks grew into months. A panic spread itself through me. I knew I would have to go it alone. The thought made me rigid with fear.

With Jimmy gone, I spent much time away from the family. Oscar didn't seem to feel very well. He complained of stomach cramps. Dorothy looked more frightened than ever. They called me, wondering how Jimmy was. He hadn't communicated with them, either. I told them I didn't know. They were embarrassed for me. Oscar got on the extension and advised me, "Maybe you should have gone with him, dear." He repeated his constant refrain.

"But, Dad, who's going to take care of the baby?"

"Couldn't you get a girl? You had a girl before," Dorothy suggested.

"We can't afford to do that."

Since Oscar was covering Jimmy's debts, they should have known better. Dorothy seemed to be oblivious to the fact that we had money problems. After Andy was born, they paid for the mother's helper, but the novelty had worn off.

"We'll see if Morrie Jacobs [their business manager] can track him down and see how he is," Oscar consoled me.

"Would you ask him to send me some money?" I flinched, knowing how gauche they thought my request must have been. "I need to pay some bills and get some food."

"Didn't Mary pack you some beef from The Farm?" Oscar inquired. I realized then he knew all along that we were getting CARE packages from the Polish maids.

"That's been gone a long time," I assured him, as the heat of embarrassment rose in me. I had been caught. Caught at what? At sharing their slaughtered beef? It shouldn't have made that much difference, but it did. I knew it did.

I often wondered if Dorothy's despair was rooted in the fear that she might fail in making Oscar's life as perfect as he demanded it to be. That seemed only a part of it. He left little notes in rhyme under her pillow, to let her know when she had failed him. It's no wonder she had insomnia. For her, going to bed must have been fraught with peril.

There was a regimen at The Farm that was followed every day that Oscar was in residence as Lord of the Manor. Three characters took part in the play that was acted out each and every morning. The feature player was Oscar, supported by Mary, the Polish maid, and Peter Moens, who was Oscar's Norwegian masseur and who, with his son Walter, ran The Farm. The scenario of the play never changed, and the cues never varied. As long as each person went through his or her appointed rounds, things ran smoothly, and peace was maintained. No little notes in impeccable lyrical verse from Oscar graced Dorothy's bed chamber.

When things were out of sync, or when one of the players missed their cue or overslept, or when the Polish maids eventually left, there was hell to pay. Oscar roared around the elegant, silent house, sullen and as mean as a hungry predator. The teddy-bear quality of his public image was replaced by the roaring, tearing rage of an ogre unleashed.

When the regimen at The Farm worked, it had the choreographed precision of a Balanchine ballet. Oscar got up every morning at six o'clock and went to the bathroom. When he finished using the john and as the flushed water rushed down through the pipes to the septic tank on its way underground, it passed by the maid's room. This was Mary's signal to get up and hurry to the kitchen to squeeze a large glass of fresh orange juice and to pick up the morning paper. She left the fresh squeezed orange juice and the morning paper, along with a fresh rose, on a silver tray near the landing.

When Mary turned on the kitchen light to begin her day and to squeeze the orange juice, Peter Moens in his farmhouse across the field, seeing the light go on in the main house, picked up his cue. He gathered the heated towels and headed for the pool cabana. Oscar stopped at the landing, drank his juice, glanced at the headlines and went to the pool in back of the house to take his daily swim. As he got out of the water, if the weather was chilly, the warm towels were wrapped around him. He then stretched out for his hour-long massage. During warm weather, he luxuriated on a chaise lounge and soaked in the rays of the early morning sun.

As he was being massaged, Mary was scurrying around the kitchen preparing his breakfast: steaming coffee in a silver pot, crisp bacon, scrambled eggs, medium, not too soft and not too hard, with a touch of Bahamian mustard. At the breakfast table, a crystal vase held another flower. Honey sat in the center of another silver tray in an enormous crystal bee with movable silver wings.

During the winter, when the water was too cold for a swim, Oscar walked around the fields, often leaving single tracks across the crisp white snow. After he checked the paper, he neatly folded it under his arm and lumbered upstairs to the john next to his study where he finished reading it, while throwing handfuls of licorice candy into his mouth.

My mother called the bathroom our corner of sighs. To Oscar, it was his room of inspiration, which probably meant the same thing, since inspiration in its most ancient form meant the incorporation of air. Once Oscar disappeared upstairs into his inner sanctum and then his study, he rarely emerged, except on weekends to play tennis or to have one of his meals.

Then one day it all came apart at the seams. The movement outward, the movement of disintegration that had been put into play into all of our lives a few years before and that initially emerged out of Pipe Dream, caught the maids peripherally in its spin. Their leaving was an extended continuation of the process. Together, Mary and Josephine, the Polish sister, ran the elegant home. They grew too old to putter up and down those beautifully carpeted stairs, so they left.

Dorothy hired a butler and a series of maids. None knew the exact choreography of the orange juice and the massage. Mistakes were made. Cues were not picked up. A flushed john did not alert the new help to the squeezed perfection of the orange juice. Breakfast, with eggs just right, was not waiting at the exact moment that it was supposed to emerge upon the highly polished mahogany table. The silver started to look a bit tarnished. The sparkling crystal sparkled less brilliantly. The place was falling apart. Oscar raged around The Farm slamming doors and avoiding human contact, acting as if everyone were in a conspiracy to undermine his breakfast ritual and his comfort. Hushed voices came from the master bedroom. Muffled reproaches announced his displeasure. Dorothy would emerge puffy-eyed and red-nosed. She'd re-alert the butler and give fresh instructions to the new maids. But help wasn't the way it was used to be, as they say, and not everyone was a Polish maid. Not everyone knew how to create a life of perfection for Oscar so he could write his lyrics.

Dorothy no longer wanted to go to The Farm. Little poems began to appear with deadening regularity under her pillow. She developed, and never completely lost, the look of a person about to disappear under quicksand. More silver polish and starch appeared with Arnie at my door. She even complained that Chris, Billy's wife, hung her laundry on the line outside her farm house, a mile away across the field, only to aggravate her.

One year, we spent Christmas Eve at The Farm. All the gifts that came to the house in town were carted westward to Bucks County. The presents were placed in a growing mountain of multi-colored boxes around the sparkling, towering Christmas tree. An avalanche of gifts transformed the living room into a warehouse of beautifully wrapped packages. Hundreds of presents arrived from around the world, presents that had to be noted, appraised and for which little blue and gray thank-you notes had to be sent.

We were all there. Andy, barely a toddler, was busy inspecting the premises, bending over to smell the flowers, which were cradled in evergreen branches and filled all the corners of the room. Occasionally, he tumbled over headfirst into the arrangements. I had to watch him every moment, for he had no reservations about sending not only the flowers, but also all those impeccably framed pictures, crashing down on the floor around him.

Oscar wasn't too happy about all the changes occurring around him. Not only was it rocky for him with the new help, noiselessly but awkwardly plying their trade, but having a small child around the house made him uncomfortable. On Christmas Eve, we sat around the tree and opened packages. It was like a well-oiled assembly line. One person opened the presents; another saved the cards, noting a small description of the article. With a pencil sticking out of her red hair, Dorothy made a list. There were those that were kept; others were put on piles for future redistribution to friends and family, as birthday's or anniversaries dictated. She never forgot a person's birthday or anniversary, or a holiday, in her life. That is, except where Jimmy and I were concerned. We were married on her

261

birthday, June seventh. It never ceased to amaze me that she not only forgot our first anniversary but also all the subsequent ones that followed.

One Christmas, I was a recipient of one of those recycled gifts. With excitement, I fell on my present and tore open a large, beautifully wrapped box. Inside was an overnight case, all shiny and black, with a mirror and an insert for jewelry. I raised it up to savor the rich leather smell and discovered "DH" inscribed on the side, under the handle. My new initials were "BH." How could that be? I checked the name on the card. I hadn't made a mistake. The present was for me. As I looked up, I realized that Dorothy had noticed it, too, for she grew immediately flustered.

"How could the luggage man make such a mistake??" Her fingers flew to her neck. "I'll have him retool it." She grabbed the case from my hands and shoved it behind her, as she continued to disembowel the mountain of presents spread out before her. It was difficult to believe, in spite of the distribution going on around me, that she had given me another hand-me-down, going as far as overlooking the initials someone else had imprinted on the case for her. With the list of presents growing ever longer every year, it must have been difficult for her not to have made an occasional slip-up.

One holiday after <u>Pipe Dream</u> had opened, Oscar bought Dorothy a beautiful gift of diamonds. Her hands trembled as she opened the velvet box lined in white satin, on which spread a sparkling sprig of diamond flowers, which could have been worn either as a pin or a necklace. Dorothy didn't seem to know what to do with the present. After trying a variety of possibilities, above the ear, on top of her red hair, on her shoulder, she finally hung the shimmering flowers around her neck and fingered the skin above it, drawing attention to the fact that her "turkey neck" didn't do justice to the diamonds, while making some kind of muffled comment about men who bought their wives expensive jewelry. Ha! Ha!

When you become famous and people want to please you, they find out what you collect. Then every subsequent Christmas, you receive an addition to that collection. It seems that many people who knew Dorothy were aware that she collected Loestoft china. Examples of their generosity graced the majestic breakfront in town. Every Christmas, packages were opened to a chorus of ohs and ahs, as the delicate pink and white lotus china was unwrapped and set very carefully aside to bring back to New York City. After Oscar's death, Dorothy gave the entire collection, which had filled the breakfront on the first-floor landing in the townhouse, to the Sydney Museum in Australia.

Dorothy Rodgers and Dorothy Hammerstein were immensely competitive, and they vied to give each other the more impressive present. Both were talented, gifted women, with unlimited funds to fuel their competitiveness. They outdid themselves in a frenzy of uniqueness. Right after the holidays, both women would start looking for the perfect gift to give to their counterpart in the following year. It had to be original, tasteful, chic, expensive, but not obviously so. It would never do to seem to be <u>nouveau riche</u>.

One year, Dorothy Rodgers won hands down! She had one of those Loestoft china plate patterns woven into a rug. The rug arrived just before Christmas and was placed under the settee on the second-floor landing in front of the breakfront that housed the growing collection of plates. Soft pale-green scallops formed the outer perimeter of the rug. It grew lighter toward the center as it turned a delicate pink. Fully unfurled in the center of the foyer, it floated like an enormous water lily on a sea of highly waxed, black and white tiles. Mumsie never got over that.

Dorothy Rodgers had wonderful taste, which was also eminently pragmatic. She invented the Johnny Mop. As a result of that invention, she was one of the pioneers of the disposable society. Years later, she designed a house in Connecticut where the water pipes were painted different colors. If there was a break in the plumbing system, you could track the appropriate pipe to the right bathroom and not have to rip out the walls to find the leak. The central hallway of their palatial home had a series of strategically placed skylights. As the sun passed overhead, it lit and relit the interior of the house, giving it movement and light. Staying home in New York City and not having to follow her husband out of town honed Dorothy Rodgers' many talents.

The fierce rivalry that existed between the two women belied their many similarities. Existing as appendages to the men who gave them status, they survived in somewhat different ways. Dorothy Hammerstein opted for wifehood. Dorothy Rodgers was more her own person.

The presents coming from Josh and Nedda Logan were always the most interesting, because they had moveable parts. The honey bee with the hinged silver wings on the breakfront tray at The Farm came from them. Even their Christmas cards, as you opened them, turned, spun and twisted right off the page, right out of the envelope.

One momentous Christmas, as Andy toddled around the mounds of presents and got on the nerves of most of the elders who were not used to having a baby around, while I ran frantically after him trying to keep him out of trouble, Luther, the black poodle, who in the dark looked like a monster on our first visit to The Farm, was sleeping in one of the corners behind a vase of flowers and Christmas tree branches. My son tipped over to get a better whiff of one of the roses and stuck his nose into Luther's mouth, at which point Luther bit him. Andy yelped. Luther barked. I jumped in to protect my screaming baby. Oscar jumped in to protect Luther. Dorothy, flushed out of her list-making, wasn't quite sure what had happened. Blood appeared under Andy's nose. Luther had bitten people before. I had voiced my concern. No one paid any attention. With my son heaving deep sobs in my arms, I took a stronger stand.

"You should do something about Luther, or you'll have a lawsuit on your hands."

"Don't be stupid, Bawrsha," Dorothy spat out at me.

"Don't call my wife stupid, Mother!" Jimmy sputtered at her.

"Are you planning to sue me?" Oscar the lawyer yelled over to me. His eyebrows disappeared into the furrows of his forehead.

I blurted back at him, "I know he's bitten other people! He's dangerous!"

Andy was screaming more from the commotion than from the pain. All he had gotten was a little nick. We were yelling over him, as Oscar defended his dog.

"Luther is not dangerous!" He cradled the black poodle in his arms, apparently more concerned with the poodle than with his own grandson. He then disappeared up the stairs to his study, dragging the struggling dog behind him. We all remained in the living room, shaken. The explosion had been so violent and so unexpected that it left everyone vaguely disoriented. We busied ourselves leaving the room, gathering up the remnants of decorum to dress for dinner and to act as if nothing had happened.

Dinner came and went. The incident was never brought up again until a few months later when Andy stuck his nose into the mouth of Billy's golden retriever and the whole thing repeated itself. Billy was so upset that his guilt was harder to deal with than his father's rage.

In an interview about Oscar for the <u>Daily News</u> on September 23, 1980, Mary Martin was quoted as saying, "He [Oscar] truly loved people. He also had a terrible temper. I didn't see it but once, just a little bit, but Dorothy said it could be violent. But it would take an awful lot to make him that cross."

When Oscar was interviewed by others, he claimed to be temperamental only about his craft, his art, and the lyrics he wrote. He was probably as passionate about his craft as he was about his needs. I saw him in action only at home, when his creature comforts were compromised, or when Luther, the black poodle, came under censure, and then his rage was awesome.

Chapter 25

Christmas in Poland was very different for us. Perhaps memory dulls the undercurrents of tension. It's the wonder of it all that stayed with me. Decembers in Poland were, and probably still are, colder than the Decembers in and around New York City. There was always more snow. Part of the holidays were spent sleigh-riding and ice-skating. I remember walking back from the frozen, glistening lake with my skates slung over my shoulder, my toes numb in my boots. At home, the fire in the stove thawed out my lifeless feet, releasing the excruciating pain with the pulsating flow of warm blood.

Momma usually stayed home and cooked. We entered the warm kitchen, stamping the snow off our boots, as rich, pungent smells filled the house. On Christmas Eve, we had a lenten meal, no meat, just pickled herring that Momma had put up for the winter. There were times we shared a fresh carp, filled with bones, which Poppa caught through a hole he chopped in the ice of the frozen lake. We waited the whole day before Christmas for the first star to appear in the eastern sky, running to the frosted double-paned windows, before the sun had set, to make sure it was not yet shining. The appearance of the twinkling white diamond in the brilliant blue cold of winter meant we could end our fast and sit down to eat.

Momma cooked a traditional Christmas Eve dinner for us, featuring a clear red beet barszcz. Into the barszcz she ladled cooked white potatoes, which turned pink as the dark liquid penetrated them. We carefully sliced the potatoes in half to see how deeply the soup had stained them, marveling that the center almost always remained white and firm. Other platters covering our festive table were laden with stuffed pierogi. Some contained mushrooms and sauerkraut; others were filled with pot cheese. There was a babka and a compot of dried fruit. Powdered favorki, surrounding large glasses of steaming tea, completed the meal.

In the evenings during the preceding year, Poppa, with his glasses perched above his nose, sat making little ornaments for the Christmas tree. Some he fashioned out of straw and beads. They spun like Chinese pagodas when we hung them from the evergreen boughs. (Josh Logan, with his directorial love of movement, would have loved them.) Others were tiny castles carved out of wood, which he meticulously decorated with brilliant colors, wetting the fine pointed brush in his mouth, before he dipped it into the paint. We cut round discs out of tissue paper and notched the edges. They formed round balls after we bunched them up. Wreaths of cookies and candy were threaded and hung among tiny red crab apples on the branches. If the borders between countries were open, oranges arrived from Italy and Spain, bringing exotic foreign fruit from far away lands. The oranges had little red flecks in them, like droplets of blood. We knew that the future and the coming spring would bring a crucifixion of the Christ Child at Easter, the Child we were so joyously welcoming. To this day, the smell of peeled fresh oranges evokes in me the memories of Christmas in Poland.

I remember only the good things about those days. The painful memories that came later seemed to have taken place in a whole different life, as if they had happened to another person. Gone were the fears that accompanied the holidays, like the time my sister pulled the Christmas tree on top of herself and almost burned the house down, for we used real candles on those tinder dry evergreens. Gone were the memories of the fights we always stirred up whenever we had to meet around the dining table.

After I married, the bony Christmas perch reeking of the lake bottom was replaced by caviar. The rest of the meal was like any other meal. There was no wonder. It had no special meaning. We didn't hang around the frosted windows with growing anticipation to spy the first star in the heavens. There was no trudging through the snow to go to midnight Mass, to rejoice in the music, as Poppa rejoiced in the politics that were thinly disguised within the nativity play. We no longer crunched our way back home through the glistening snow, with the night air so cold that the little shutters in our noses closed and refused to open until we were home again.

Christmas in the United States had lost its meaning. Year by year, it became more eroded, as Momma tried to keep the tradition alive in the face of our growing indifference. I still felt a tender affection for Christ and His suffering. I could never figure out what His suffering had to do with the church and Christianity. In Poland, Christmas was a time of myth. It was a time that stirred levels that were implied, a movement of feelings having roots in deeper needs, in a deeper reality. It churned up a memory of joy and pleasure, filling us with an enrichment that would last until the next festivity, the next holiday. It wasn't like that in the United States, in our new home. The holidays had the same form. The same characters acted out the parts, but the content was gone. We went to church. We ate. We exchanged presents. We no longer sang Christmas carols; they came over the radio and sang at us. Having become a parent myself, I went through the same motions for the sake of my child, so he could go through the same motions for the sake of his children, and so on and so on.

When intermarriage occurs, as it does more and more in this country, old-time customs seem to become more diluted. Few of the fundamental stirrings remain. Homage is paid to the ritual, to the exchange of presents. The inner reality, the inner content of joy, is left out. Traditions that had been hallowed became hollow. Some called it commercialization, but it was something else that had been lost, a belief in a subtle implicit, rather than explicit, reality.

In my life, I experienced a double loss. The emptiness that replaced the bitter-sweet joy of Christmas surfaced not only in my marriage, but it also solidified around my new family. I hadn't as yet realized that I had been caught up in the vortex of a larger loss, a larger unraveling, an unraveling that the holidays could not erase.

Chapter 26

Four years into my silent marriage, I sat with my two-year-old son on my lap, with another life growing in me, and I tried to talk to my in-laws about the fact that my husband didn't need to talk to me. They already knew about the problems we were having from our phone conversation. As I sat at home agonizing over my husband's extended silence after he left for Las Vegas, I wondered what I could say without betraying my marriage bed, "fouling my own nest," as Momma would have called it. Sitting in their lush living room, I steadied myself for the conversation. The phone rang somewhere in another part of the townhouse. Dorothy swept out of the room, on the way catching her reflection in the gilt mirror and fingering the pearls around her neck.

Andy and I were left alone with Oscar. My father-in-law looked vaguely uncomfortable and shifted his body in the sofa. Some of the confrontations with his children, with the new servants, the mediocre success of <u>Pipe Dream</u>, Dick's operation and the emerging problems with <u>Flower Drum Song</u>, his most recent musical, were difficult for him. I sat there with Andy squirming in my lap, wondering where to start, as Oscar swished the white wine in his glass and expressed an ancient observation almost to himself.

"I always felt that both of my sons put together would have made one good man."

That was that. He took a sip of his wine. What do I do now? I wondered. No wonder both of his sons had problems.

"Does he keep in touch with you at all?" He looked up over his drink and took the both of us in.

"Not really, I mean, he sends me a check now and then." With "I Love You" written in pencil on the flap, I wanted to add. The conversation went off on a tangent of finances.

"Well, he has a lot of debts. I've helped him out, you know!"

I nodded my head with the memory of the growing stack of I.O.U.s in the desk drawer. The resentment that his son had imposed on his generosity showed in Oscar's face.

"He's a lot like his great grandfather: reckless, with little respect for money. Went bankrupt, you know. So did Uncle Arthur. I wonder if he'll follow in their footsteps. I hate to contribute to that recklessness. Billy is too cautious, more like my father. Put them both together..." His voice trailed off. He looked back over at me. "You should be with him." The endless litany.

I felt trapped by frustration. How could I leave? I worked nights in <u>Music Man</u>, had a small baby, a new pregnancy, and little money. I hoped he would offer us a loan, maybe some more stock certificates or interest in the trust funds he was always setting up for strangers. No offer came. Uncle Arthur had been right. In spite of the reluctant loans and accumulating I.O.U.s, Oscar was basically cheap. As I sat there, with my proverbial hat in my hand, no offer of help came. He looked levelly at me, and the blue eyes did not twinkle.

"You know, you always seemed to have a problem fitting in. You should have learned how to play tennis, bridge and chess. It might have helped."

"I was taking tennis lessons when I got pregnant with Andy." I defended myself. "I had to stop. The doctor advised it." I added, trying to validate myself with professional opinion.

"Yes, but there was still chess and bridge. You never joined us when we played."

I couldn't explain to him that I studied Goren and played dummy hands with Jimmy, trying to grasp the intricacies of the game, but it never took root in me. I grew to hate it and dreaded the nightly lessons. Competitive games made me feel uncomfortable. I was not a happy loser, and I didn't like to make resentful enemies by winning. So I didn't play.

Oscar interrupted my thoughts. "I'll talk to him. You know, when Jimmy was about sixteen, I took him for a walk at The Farm and asked him what he planned to do with his life. He told me it was none of my business. That skinny jerk walking next to me told me it was none of my business! Can you believe that?"

I guessed that not all of the Lord Chesterfield talks had been successful.

"I'll talk to him, but I don't know that it'll do any good."

He shrugged his shoulders, as if the matter were out of his hands. It surprised me to learn that Jimmy told his own father that it was none of his business what he did. I wasn't the only one he refused to share his life with. It should have made me feel better. Somehow it only added to my sense of helplessness. I realized there would be no help from the family. Finding his behavior reprehensible, they would hide behind their principles. They couldn't add to his recklessness. It sounded reasonable. There seemed to be no understanding of the fact that I was still their daughter-in-law, working in another chorus, pregnant with another baby and needing money for the child I held on my lap, their grandchild and Oscar's namesake.

Jimmy finally came home from the road. Oscar had spoken to him. The enraged silence that greeted me at his return made me realize he would never forgive me for letting his father know that we had problems. It was more important to present a happy face than to have a happy life. He joined the production staff of Flower Drum Song. We started to work our way out of debt.

One night, after our shows, we had dinner with Larry Blyden, who was negotiating with Rodgers and Hammerstein to replace Larry Storch. Flower Drum Song was in trouble, and there were many cast changes. Larry was impressing Jimmy with how much money he was asking from Rodgers and Hammerstein and how enraged they were. He seemed to be the only one around who could do the part. They finally relented, paid him, and never fully forgave him for taking such a strong financial stand. Jimmy, on the other hand, was impressing Larry with his six thousand dollar investment in the show. My ears picked up. The rent wasn't paid; I was ducking behind the pillars in the lobby to avoid the landlord. He was investing six thousand dollars in a show? I couldn't wait to get out of the restaurant to ask him about it. The conversation that started in the street led to a confrontation when we got home.

"Where did you get the six thousand dollars?" I asked, daring to face his wrath by asking him a direct question.

"It's none of your fucking business!" At least he put me in the same category as his father.

"Where were you all day?" I insisted, wondering if one of his projects had come through and had brought in a six-thousand-dollar advance.

"At the office." He looked away, searching for something to juggle.

"I called the office. They told me you were home! People kept calling all day! Where did you get all that money?"

"Did you take the messages?"

"Yes, but that's not the point! Where were you? Playing tennis at the Boulevard Gardens?"

"Yeah, so what? You're a fucking nag! You're making me lie to you. I've never lied to you before!"

"Jimmy, your brother called. He was at some kind of a conference where you were supposed to meet him. He called about a dozen times. Were you with Buddy?"

"Look, its no crime for a guy to take an afternoon off once in a while and get in some ten-ten. Get off my ass!"

"Jimmy, I'm tired of asking for help from your father! He resents it, and I don't like it much, either! I'm tired of being a poor relative because you blow our money on some scheme or other. I'm tired of being alone, of working in my condition, and tired of waiting dinner for you. We're having another baby, and all you seem to care about is playing tennis and squash with Buddy. You haven't been in the office for days, or weeks, for that matter. Where were you?"

"It's none of your fucking business what I do with my time. You never had it so good, so what're you complaining about? Stay away from my Old Man. Don't sucker up to him! And get rid of that kid you're carrying, I don't want another anchor around my neck. I don't want it!"

He turned and slammed out of the bedroom. I followed him, enraged.

"You don't want the baby? Maybe you don't want the marriage, either? Maybe you want a divorce?"

"You said it, you fucking cunt. I didn't! What you need is a good beating!" He lunged at me, sputtering as he tore off my nightgown. Methodically, he proceeded to slap me on the face. Then he made a fist and punched me on the head. Grabbing me by my hair, he kept me at arms' length and slapped me, as I struggled to free myself. I couldn't land any blows on him, for his arms were too long and he held me too far away. His body was out of reach. I flailed at him, as he kept punching and slapping me.

"I didn't get married to be questioned to death. You're a fucking cunt who needs to be put in her place! It's none of your Goddamned business what I do."

I started to scream. He let me fall against the cold tiles of the bathroom. Andy had awakened in his crib and was also screaming. I went over to still him as Jimmy got into bed, turned his back to me and pulled the blanket over his head. I wanted to kill him, not only for the last outrage of the beating but also for the vile, abusive language. There was a large black radio on my side of the bed, a solid, heavy square thing that technology had not yet miniaturized. With the strength of my rage, I flung it at him. The radio caught him with a thwack! broadside, as it splintered on the side of his head. He banged his ear and shook his head, as if the ringing had awakened him. I feared he would begin hitting me again and dove back into the bathroom, which had the only lock in the apartment. I needn't have bothered. It was over.

Another historical pattern seemed to be repeating itself in the Hammerstein family. When Oscar I was sixty-eight in 1915, he married a beautiful young woman named Emma Swift (because she reminded him of his first wife Rose, he later told his son Arthur, who related the story to us). He and Emma had a tumultuous relationship. Although his death certificate stated that he died in 1919 from diabetes, the story that made the rounds attributed it to the fact that one night, while he slept, Emma poured a bucket of cold water on him. He jumped out of bed, barely dressed himself, and finished the night on a bench at the railroad station. Soon after that incident, he died at Lenox Hill Hospital. The family always blamed Emma for his death. The Old Man had never been sick in his life and had been expected to live forever. Even though it was the end of July, they said he caught a chill. Emma did him in.

After my most recent confrontation with Jimmy, in spite of the time that had passed, I empathized with Emma. Her four years with the original Old Man equaled my four years with the most recent young Old Man. Enough was enough! At the funeral for Oscar I, John McCormack sang "The Lost Chord." It should have been called "The Last Straw." Some woman may write that song yet and launch her husband on a voyage to the happy hunting grounds with it.

The next morning, Jimmy got up, dressed and, without a word, left early. I took a look at myself in the mirror. The skin around my eye had turned a purple blue. My jaw ached. Dark spots were emerging on my arms and shoulders. A red palm print still throbbed across my back. God! The shame of it. I wanted to call Momma to ask her how she dealt with Poppa when he abused her. Why didn't she leave him? I knew she would tell me to stay, as she added, "They're all the same."

Anyway, Poppa was dying of cancer. He was still at home, slowly dragging his bones around from chair to bed, then back to the chair again. His suitcase was packed, ready to accompany him to the Veterans' Hospital. All his life, he threatened to leave us when we didn't behave and to spend his days in the halcyon halls of the soldier's last stop. He was now ready to go, not necessarily out of choice and not looking forward to sitting on the long veranda, whittling or reading. He was waiting to go there to die. What faced him was not old cronies recounting exploits from the "Great War" but the certainty of pain and the inevitable end.

Momma was desperate, unreachable, frightened almost into immobility. I couldn't burden her with any more problems, so I called Dorothy at the townhouse. I wanted her to see me, for her to see what her son had been capable of doing. Billy answered the phone, which seemed strange, for he didn't live with them, and both of them came over. When I opened the door, she stared at me with utter disbelief.

"I can't believe he'd do that. I mean, Ockie never hit me. I've punched him on the arm occasionally, but he never hit me. Where did he learn to do that? Certainly not from us."

The only observation Billy could make was "What did you do to provoke him? What did you do to get him so mad?"

I was learning the male way of thinking: Blame the victim. Most abused people are women, children and the old. Since most abusers are males, then blame the victims for their abuses. Never blame the abusers. Take them off the hook. I would have gladly hurled the radio at him, but it lay in shattered pieces in the waste basket next to the bed.

"I asked him some questions, that's all, just some questions. We're broke, and he's investing a lot of money in the new show. I just wanted to know where it was coming from."

Dorothy glanced over to Billy, and both of them looked quickly away. I knew something was going on, something of which I was no longer a part. Was that why Billy was so desperate to get in touch with Jimmy the day before? It never occurred to me at that time that there was a continuation of the unraveling of a larger spin, a larger play of destiny at that moment. All I saw was the disintegration of my marriage and the part that lack of funds played in it.

"I'll send Arnie for his things." Dorothy offered, as she and Billy pecked their way out of the foyer. My rage carried me through the packing, as I cleaned out Jimmy's drawers. There wasn't all that much to pack, since he had again lost most of his clothes along the way. Cartons from the grocery store stuffed with his belongings filled the foyer, as I cleaned the house with a vengeance. <u>Out! out! damned spot, the blight of my life, out! out!</u> I mumbled as I packed.

Later in the day, Arnie, their chauffeur, arrived and shamefacedly ferried the packed boxes and suitcases to the family home. I felt a sense of exhilaration after I cleaned the house and got rid of him, but I feared the moment when the rage would subside and I would be left to face my life alone. That night with much make-up around my black eye, I sang and danced in <u>Music Man</u>.

The day after my beating, I learned that Oscar had gone into the hospital for a gall bladder operation. Billy was being "the man of the family." That's why he had come over with Dorothy. They were concerned about Oscar, his father, her husband, whispering together, united by a common bond of fear. The situation with me was becoming a problem, too. Although they were fed up with Jimmy's behavior, I could feel their discomfort around me, his possibly soon-to-be former wife.

In those subsequent days, all I did was cry and mope around the apartment. I did the show at night, while a babysitter came to stay with Andy. His care took up most of my days. Then I became aware that something was wrong with the pregnancy. I began to spot. I knew and feared the symptoms. At first, there was just a small brown stain; then more and more appeared. I went to the doctor, and he told me to quit work and to stay off my feet. It was good advice, but who would pay the bills and take care of my son?

I was becoming disoriented, filled with despair, awakening around four in the morning, not being able to sleep. I couldn't think straight about anything. A word would attach itself to me, pull up the fear and grief from the area around my heart. It would spin round and round in my brain. The black stallion of my raging brain changed into a luckless hamster that ran in the cage of my mind. It never appeared to be out of breath, and yet it never let me rest. It raced madly on, dragging me behind. There were times I felt as if my mind were attached to my body only through the anguish. I acted in spurts out of a careening chaos that carried me along down a circular if slippery slope. There was no escaping, no way of outrunning the avalanche that had caught up with me and absorbed me in its downward plunge. The black stallion resurfaced, replaced the hamster, drew ahead of my fading white horse, as the joy in me grew fainter and fainter, eventually falling back and disappearing altogether. For the first time in my life since I could remember, I became frightened of being alone, alone on the edge of that enormous double bed like the storm-tossed boat of the Ancient Mariner.

> "Water, water, every where,
> And all the boards did shrink;
> Water, water, every where,
> Nor any drop to drink."

Pieces of poetry, snatches of song, ran round and round in my head. Noises in the apartment kept me awake. I had dead bolts put on the doors. Staring into the blackness of my bedroom, I imagined shapes that I thought I had left behind in my childhood. Things loomed near me. Bears lurked in corners, ready to leap at me. As I lay in my bed, I felt there was someone in the hall. With the lights out, I felt the terror close in. I kept the light burning all night. Andy was also restless, as he coughed and cried. He seemed to sense my despair. His bright inquiring eyes looked over at me. Whenever I could, I smiled over to him and rocked him to sleep or placed him on the double bed with me. In the mornings, he would wander around the apartment looking under the dust ruffles and behind the draperies.

"Da, Da?" he'd ask the empty corners. "No Da Da?" He'd look at me, trying to get an answer, trying to find out where his father had gone. My heart ached for him. How would all this pain and chaos affect him?

Chapter 27

One night, while waiting to go on in the "Picklelittle" number in <u>Music Man</u>, I collapsed in the wings. The spotting had become heavier. I was growing anemic from the loss of blood, feeling as if I were poisoned. The poison was not only affecting my mind but eroding my body. After he left, Jimmy had sent me fifty dollars the first week, seventy-five the second, and nothing after that. Dorothy kept in touch, inquiring about Andy, assuring me that they would see to it that Jimmy took care of us.

It was on a hot July day that I went to see my gynecologist again. I was in the sixth month of the pregnancy. The fetus was small. I hadn't gained any weight. My stomach was still flat. After poking around through my spread legs, my doctor informed me that the fetus was probably dead. The heartbeat hadn't been audible for the preceding six weeks, but he hoped for the best, rationalizing that it may have become muffled behind some large organ in my body. With the heavy spotting, he was almost sure that the life within me had died. What to do? I wondered. The baby may have been dead for six weeks? Why hadn't he told me?

A spark of hope glimmered in me. Being alone wasn't all that great. Jimmy was staying with his parents, up in one of the bedrooms on the third floor in a bed much too short for him. Maybe we could try again. Maybe we could make it. Maybe the separation made a difference to him, too. I dialed their number. Dorothy answered the phone.

"Mother, I'm at the doctor's office. The baby is dead inside me."

"You poor thing, come on over. It really has all descended on you, hasn't it? Poor Bawrsha."

She sounded softer, actually concerned. I took the bus to their townhouse on Sixty-Third Street. How different it was to go up those carpeted stairs again. I was no longer afraid of them, of whether they would find me acceptable. What I now trembled over was my physical disintegration and my uncertain future.

Jimmy came down the stairs to greet me. We embraced awkwardly, both of us somehow relieved that the separation was over. He went upstairs and packed his suitcases. Dorothy must have outfitted him, for he came down the stairs with more clothes than he had when he left. Arnie, the chauffeur, never meeting my eyes, drove us across town and helped Jimmy to get his things back into the apartment.

After a few days together, I realized that nothing had changed, and my hopes started to wane. We again passed each other like strangers, but I resolved to make a greater effort at fitting in. Oscar said I should learn tennis, bridge and chess. I couldn't take tennis lessons, so I tried to learn bridge and chess. It was even more difficult than before. Nothing stayed in my racing brain.

It became apparent to me that I had to do something with the dead fetus. The doctor wouldn't take it from me. He was only ninety-eighty percent certain that it was dead, and he didn't want to take the two percent chance that it wasn't. I felt that the dead tissue within me was trying to kill me. One night while Jimmy slept, I got a bucket of soapy water and started to wash down the walls. I didn't have the courage to throw myself down the stairs or to use a pruning hook or a coat hanger. Five hours later, just as the paleness of dawn softened the dark corners of the apartment, after I had gone through the kitchen, both bathrooms, foyer and the livingroom, I doubled over. As the water sac broke, I realized that I was aborting the dead fetus.

The ambulance rushed us over to the emergency room to the same hospital in which Andy had been born. My doctor was already there. A large red stain had spread out under me and became strangely warm and comforting. It became almost as comforting as the darkness that enveloped me. Hands lifted me up and slid me onto a cold steel table. Footsteps accompanied me as I was rolled down some corridors. A sweet feeling of peace spread through me, like a long awaited friend. It was welcome and blessed. Through the darkness that claimed me, I thanked it for having found a place in my body and for stopping the hamster on the wheel of my mind and for reigning in the black stallion still galloping on the wings of my rage. Little silver paisley tadpoles danced an ecstacy-filled ballet in my head behind my closed eyes, as I sunk deeper into a warm darkness.

Then it all suddenly changed. Faces peered down at me, faces covered with blue masks. They strapped my wrists down as I began to throw up. Something was being jabbed into my immobilized arm. I tried to free myself, to run from the torture chamber that the cold steel table had become. There was no way to get out of there. The straps held me down. My vomit gagged me as I convulsed. The memory of the Gulf Stream flashed before me, flooding me with choking despair. Then the shuddering seized me, my knees shook, and my whole body trembled. I couldn't keep my teeth still. The chattering noise they made sounded like hailstones on a metal roof. My whole body, with nothing to cover its nakedness, jerked around the steel table as the chills seized me. Enormous goose pimples crept from my legs up to the base of my neck, making my hair rise.

"Please, please, no more. Take it off. I'm c-c-cold, I'm c-c-cold. Please c-c-c-c-c-over me," I heard my voice pleading, as if from a distance.

Though the darkness and the pain, I heard my doctor yelling,

"It's the blood! Take it away; take it off!"

They pulled the tape off my arm and undid the straps. I continued to shudder. The movement was carrying me off the table on which I lay like a bare piece of meat. Through the pain, with the room jerking wildly around me, I saw my husband. I didn't know he had been there. He sat so silently in the corner. Relief and warmth flooded me, tempered by humiliation at my bare exposed bleeding body.

281

I called out to him, "Jimmy, c-c-c-c-cover me. I'm c-c-c-c-cold. H-h-h-hold me. I'm c-c-c-c-cold."

He sat there without moving, as I almost shuddered myself off the table. The lights reflected squares off his glasses, and for a moment, I caught the dark dots of his eyes. He stared at me as if I were a specimen in a jar, in a test tube, objectively watching me from his silent corner. As I stared back at him, trying to keep him focused, he receded into the far distance and became very small. Someone finally threw a blanket over me, covering my tormented cold body. With the blue masked faces peering down at me again, I slipped back from the present horror into the former comforting blackness.

My body spasmed far into the night as I lay alone in my hospital bed. Shadows floated into my room, rustled something around my arm and floated out. Finally, I lay warm and still in that state between sleep and waking, cocooned by the blankets that had been tucked in around me. Time floated by. Later that afternoon as twilight brushed the room with lavender, a dream-like state filtered me back into semi-awareness. The moon rose and hung over the river. It wasn't a perfect disc. It was more like a Van Gogh orb of swirling light. It transformed the sky into a dome of golden lava. As it touched the surface of the East River below, it broke into a million splinters of crystal. The black sky behind the moon was deep, eternal and smooth, smoother than death itself. Down below, little toy boats, specks on the surface of the river, passed from the blackness into the shimmering reflected stillness of the water, then back into the darkness, trailing behind them the broken V of a wake.

One moment, the panorama outside of my hospital window was like a flat painting shimmering in the distance; the next moment, I was part of it, and the colors throbbed in and around me. My eyes gave up trying to focus. I flew out of the open window into the warm night air, leaving my hospital bed, the glittering city and my pain-filled life behind. I sped toward the stars. Their light touched me with the gentle caress of butterfly wings. I sailed past them with the same freedom as I flew in my dreams when I was a little girl, surveying the Earth, enchanted by its emerald splendor. Now I seemed to be hurtling toward a dark empty object, darker than the inky void of the sky. There were no stars, no velvety moth wings, only an empty mass of cold solid darkness. I felt the air in my nostrils penetrating my body, rushing swiftly by, as I hurtled through that endless empty dark space.

Much later that night, after the clatter of the hospital corridor had died down, I lay fully awake, alone in my empty room. The moon was gone from the dark and quiet sky. The "Pearl-Wick Hamper" sign flashed on and off across the river in Queens. I looked around my bed. Although alone in the room, I knew that Jimmy had been there. He sat and watched in the operating room as I almost shuddered my way off the table. My body spasmed again. It brought back the memory of the terrible cold, the chattering of my teeth, and of my asking for him to hold me and to cover me. I turned my face away, not only from the pain but from the humiliation. The memory of those cold steel eyes sliced like a razor through me. He wasn't going to change, and neither was I. There was a deeper problem between us, deeper than sex, deeper than money. We were complete strangers. I didn't know the person who sat staring at me in that operating room, staring at me without making an effort to help me.

During the horrors of that night, I heard death howling in the distance. Its call almost claimed me, and its sound echoed in my mind as it seduced me back into that time before dawn when the hour of the wolf gathers up its victims and its grayness creates a passage. I felt that a few hours before I barely escaped from the clutches of eternity, and my husband didn't even raise a hand or lift his membraned arm to help me.

The sound of approaching footsteps echoed in the empty hospital corridor. My doctor looked in through the open door and whispered, "You're up. How do you feel?"

"Tired. What are you doing here in the middle of the night?" My voice sounded distant.

"Delivering a baby. They all seem to want to be born before dawn."

He looked out of the window, out into the pink tinted eastern sky, then turned around. After appraising me, he said, "We almost lost you." He patted my arm. "You hemorrhaged and went into shock. You look all right now, somewhat pinker." Stepping back, he surveyed me again.

"I remember being on my way out, hurtling through space, to that empty dark void in the sky."

"Well, I guess it wasn't your time." He took my pulse. "Don't worry. You'll have other children."

I somehow knew that I wouldn't, that Andy would be my only child. I tortured myself with the next question. "What was it, a boy or a girl?"

He assessed me again before he answered. "I really couldn't tell. It reverted back to tissue."

"Why did it die?" The belt of pain was clutching me around the middle. "What caused it to die?" I insisted asking.

"It just parted from the placenta and ceased being nourished. It's relatively rare, but it happens," he answered me matter-of-factly.

"But why? I had such an easy pregnancy with Andy."

"It might have been an imperfect fetus, or it might have aborted of its own accord. You seem to have been very upset. Maybe you're run down. Perhaps your body isn't up to having a baby."

I looked at him and wondered: If being upset causes a miscarriage, then most of the women in the world would be miscarrying. There must be some other reason. Obviously, he didn't have an answer, at least not a medical answer.

"I wonder if it could have known what I was going through. I wonder if it felt my anguish," I pushed on.

"You're lucky that you miscarried. You could have carried it to full term. That can happen."

I shuddered at the thought of carrying a dead fetus for three more months, and I thought better of telling him about my washing the walls.

"Things aren't going well with you, are they?" His voice grew quiet, gentle.

"No, not too well."

"I saw your husband here last night. He's the tall, silent type, isn't he?"

"You noticed!" We both chuckled. "Did he come near me last night? I wasn't here the whole time."

He looked sharply at me and then avoided my eyes, as he changed the conversation. "I understand that your father-in-law is here, upstairs." He pointed to the ceiling.

"He's had a gall-bladder operation. I think he's O.K. We expect him home soon." Inclusion in the "we" gave me small comfort, but it established me as still being part of the family.

"You sure you couldn't tell what it was, a boy or a little girl? I wanted a little girl so much. There was nothing there at all, nothing recognizable?"

"Don't torture yourself. It was tissue, dead tissue. That's why it gave you so much trouble. You should feel better now. In a few weeks, you'll feel as good as new." He patted me on the head, like a patriarch of old. "Are you in pain now?"

"Yes, my whole body aches as if I'd been beaten or stretched out on the rack."

He gave me another shot, and I slipped back into a heavy sleep. The clatter of breakfast trays in the corridor outside of my room woke me up. I was still groggy from the shot. They again packed my vaginal cavity with gauze to stop the bleeding. I dreaded when they would have to pull it out. It felt like a disemboweling when they unraveled the gauze from within my vagina. It came out inch by inch, stained and resistant, sticking to the walls of my tormented orifice, as if reluctant to leave its new found, moist and warm home. A few days later, I clutched the railing at the sides of my hospital bed and gritted my teeth as the nurse tugging it out into a bloody steel pan assured me that it didn't hurt.

My pubic hair was gone, shaven along with my identity. I had no memory of anyone scraping away at my short hairs, making me bald, naked like an adolescent schoolgirl. Hair makes us women. How I looked forward to that small furry patch when I was a little girl. I wondered why they called it a "snatch." May Muth, in <u>Two's Company</u>,

285

called the hair piece that covered a bald "snatch" a "merkin." I could use a "merkin" now to cover my poor bald, shaven "snatch." Hairlessness makes us little girls, helpless, dependent frightened little girls like sheared Samson, all the bald nuns, Marines and the wives of Hassidim. Loss of hair makes us all dependent and weak, lacking in identity, possible of manipulation. My poor bald, red mercurochromed Venus mound. How I hated when they did that. I've always felt it had more to do with power than with hygiene. Again, the "T" of the white gladiator's diaper holding it all together cradled my stomach. My arms ached, turning black and blue from the straps of the night before. My poor body: All that work and no baby.

A drop of clear fluid dripped from the nipples as I patted my swollen breasts. Oh, my God! I have milk and no one to give it to. I couldn't stop the tears. The waste. I wanted to get away from my body, from the pain, from the wasted fluid that was flowing from my breasts. I wanted to slip back into the empty black void of my earlier sleep. The dull ache in my womb made the here and now a senseless reality. Please, please! Let me go! Let me check out! Let me return to that comforting darkness.

But life was up. The machine of life, of segmented perpetual motion, urged itself on to fulfill its own needs. I wondered if crying could cause a miscarriage, could cause my baby not to want to be born. Was it more than just a blind growing? Did it have a will to live? Did it have a will to die? At almost six months, it must have had some human characteristics, but it was dead for six weeks. So it really died at four and a half months. According to the Japanese, that was old enough to have a soul, which they claim entered at four months. How did they know? The Catholics lay a greater guilt trip on women. The soul entered at conception, so you got stuck with the guilt from the very beginning. I wondered when it did enter, that spark we call life. My poor nameless fetus was almost half-way there, a great deal of head, small grub-like body, not unlike a salamander, reminiscent of a chick or a tadpole, so like all the other creatures. Still there are some who deny evolution. Where did that spark go? Where did it emerge from at the moment of its first glow, its first lightning? Would it hover around me and become apparent to psychics as they read my life in the future.

"There's a little girl around you," they would say, "the loving spirit of a little girl."

I would always try to hold back the tears and know the sense of loss that began the night before would always be with me. My desire to have a little girl would never be fulfilled. Only her spark would hover around me, visible only to those in whom the passage through the merged polarities of extremes, creating a gray area, was still open.

I wonder if I'll ever be able to love another man again. I didn't want anyone to touch my body. I went back to Jimmy's bed too soon after Andy was born. The memory of that return sent the episiotomy throbbing on the edge of my vagina. It won't happen again. Then I'll probably lose him. All we seemed to have was sex. Now even that had become impossible. The memory of his eyes staring at me from across the hospital room chilled my blood. As my mind raced on, I floated in and out of focus.

Somewhere out there in the hospital corridor, cushioned as if from some great distance, I heard women speaking in Spanish. Their sound resonated in my mind. "La vida es sueno, la vida es sueno." No, not a dream, a nightmare. "Donde esta mi nino?" Where? I don't know. "No se?" Gone, dead? Why are they speaking in Spanish? Maybe they can bring the baby in; maybe it's hidden among the others in the baby room. Maybe the women can help me? "Por favor, ayuda me, el nino es un muchacho, or una muchacha?" I rambled inside of my mind in my high school Spanish, trying to make contact. Boy or girl? Please let me know. "Nada, nunca, nada, no esta aqui." Only tissue, dead tissue, dead cells. No baby. No one to drink the milk in my breasts. Mamusiu, where are you? Where are you? I need you. Don't leave me. Gdzie sie zchowala Mamusiu; czego zchowala Mamusiu? (Where have you hidden Mamusiu; why have you hidden Mamusiu?) I've lost my baby, my little girl. I feel sick; the smell is making me sick. Mr. Clean is here. Bald head, bald Venus mound, the eunuch is here with his ammonia, clean the house, wash the wall, lose the baby. It's dead anyway. The fetus is probably dead, reverted to tissue. Lose it, force it out. Out! Out! damn clot. Why did it die? Oh, God, why did it die? Everything hurts; my head hurts. I hate that terrible smell. My teeth are sticking together. I need some water. My arms hurt; they're so heavy I can hardly lift them. The water's so cool. Oh. God, I'm going to throw up.

As I started to drink the clear cold liquid, a spasm doubled me over, and I threw up, wetting the blanket before me. The inside of my mouth felt cooler and cleaner. My head throbbed from vomiting. I closed my eyes and eased my legs over the side of the bed. Then I sat up. Through the blackness, the sudden surge of heat and a whirl of dancing sparks, I sensed I was lying on something cool and hard. Drops of sweat trickled down my face. I looked up into metal circles that held a mattress over them and realized I had fainted and lay on the floor, by the side of the bed. I lay there, the only cool place in the room, until the swirling sparks receded into the distance.

The buzzing of a thousand locusts quieted down as I worked myself up the side of the bed, and then into the bed itself. My hands were clammy and trembled on the sheet as I lay there. Warmth came slowly back into my body, and the rivulets of sweat ceased to trickle their way down my face and between my swollen breasts. The only warmth I felt before I fell was the gush of blood in my womb. Through all the gauze that filled my body like a stuffed turkey, I wondered how much damage I had done to myself by trying to get up and out of bed.

I dreaded the reality of eventual human contact. If only they would all leave me alone, the efficient nurses, the detached waitresses, the family, the ever-present family waiting in the wings. I just wanted to enjoy the luxury of my fatigue. Even now, in my sorry state, I felt guilty about not working. I wondered if or when I could go back to Music Man. Will I be able to sing again? I made a raspy sound. No response came from my body. My flabby stomach muscles needed work, so I took a deep breath. There was a dull ache under them, the ache of emptiness. My tiredness seemed strange. I was almost as exhausted as when Andy was born, but I hadn't gone through labor, just a miscarriage. The transfusion and shock must have taken their toll. I felt wrung out, like a limp rag, heavy on the sheets.

My thoughts drifted to my son, back in the apartment with Jimmy taking care of him. Maybe I could have more children with someone else. I doubted it. I would never remarry. Andy would be an only child. There would be no more children with Jimmy. They say that love is the other side of hate. They're wrong. Love is the other side of fear. The fear rose in my throat. How I fear to leave him. I should have gotten out right after that disastrous honeymoon. In spite of what it was trying to tell me, I stuck around, and there I was in this pickle. I married him, and in that marriage I made a bargain, not to that transparent God, the "idea" made manifest in the heavens, not to the black-robed muttering judge who married us, but to myself. I had closed the doors on who I was, on my youth, on the single optimistic person I had been, gave up my unpronounceable name, became the "we" that "we" never solidified into. They say you can't miss what you've never had. I never had a happy marriage, but I missed it. I knew that I missed something better than the life I had with my husband. Still, the fear spurred the hamster on the wheel into hope, yanking at the white stallion to catch up, to emerge, and to stay above in the sunlight.

Maybe we'll be able to work it out. Maybe we'll be able to talk to each other, heal the wounds that fester as unspoken words between us. Maybe we can still have a marriage. What's a marriage, anyway? A series of adjustments, they say, a series of compromises. I don't really know how to be married. It seems to be a settling for less, when more was promised, the disillusionment of dreams, the shattering of hopes.

First things first. I've got to get myself together, wash my face, brush my teeth, comb my hair. Be a good, clean little girl. Very carefully this time, with much less bravado, I eased my legs over the side of the bed. There was a weakness in them and a throbbing in my knees. I walked myself, hand over hand, across the bed, along the pale green wall to the bathroom. Then I carefully sat on the cool seat of the john and stared down at the floor. Neat white tiles, fitted expertly together, stared back at me. No cracked linoleum here. No stories to read on the floor between my feet, as I had done in the myriad bathrooms of my youth. There were glorious tales to be followed along the cracks in those linoleum floors. Faces emerged and disappeared. Large noses and cavernous foreheads surfaced only to blend into profiles of animals, trees and flowers. Stories chased each other across those floors, repeating the never-ending panorama of knights on horseback, dragons flaming from mountainous caves, birds sifting through the clouds. A crack in the floor, a break in the linoleum added a new element, a rift, a valley, a chasm for the knight to vault, for the dragon to surmount, the bird to skim through. Nothing existed in the pristine perfection of the white tiles under my feet, nothing but the cool precision of tiny white squares.

The water felt good on my face. I hadn't the strength to brush my teeth. I could barely hold the toothbrush. Trembling, I crept back to bed and worked my way under the covers. The overnight case sat under the bed; my head had barely missed it when I hit the floor. With one hand, I searched for it and pulled it up on the bed beside me. My fingers caressed its smooth cool blackness, broken only by the rough grooves. The scars were there from the time Jimmy threw his skindiving gear on top of it as it sat in the trunk of the car. I tried to mend it with black shoe polish, but the gouged-out scratches broke the smooth shiny surface. Nothing could really mend them. Would I mend from the wounds of the marriage? Would I be able to fix myself as I fixed all the things my husband broke? The "BH" on the side in gold letters looked a bit crumbly, and the imprint of the "D" under the "B" stood out in bold relief. The past always under the present. The past always reappearing, reemerging, forcing us to look at it, the ever-present past.

I clicked open the top of my night case and saw my sad looking face in the mirror. I've aged a great deal since I married that young sportsman. The mass of dubious heritage that came along with him had put bags under my eyes and wrinkles across my brow. I covered

290

my matted hair with a black turban and gained instant glamour. Then came the mascara. If I didn't want to see the world through slits, I'd better stop crying. With my hoop earring back in my ears, part of my identity returned. I replaced my wedding band. The swollen finger resisted it as I tried to work it back on. Maybe it's some kind of omen, I thought. My body is rejecting the wedding band as it rejected the baby. Maybe like the honeymoon, and the car, it's trying to tell me something. Jimmy still wore his wedding ring. I wondered how long that would last. It's such a symbolic gesture to keep wearing it, such an even greater gesture to remove it. Some say the ring finger is connected to the heart. Others say it's a shackle, a cuff, not unlike what a slave wears when it's in bondage. Through most of history, only women were expected to wear it. Now, some men chose to do so.

I placed a bit of eye shadow on my lids to tone down the redness and swelling. Dorothy, blinking her bald eye lids, insisted that mascara worn during the day was <u>gauche</u>. Today, I needed all the help I could get, <u>gauche</u> or not, so I piled on the mascara and the eye shadow. Then some lipstick, and I was all set to face the world. Feeling better with my face heightened in color, my mind took off. The face, a presentable offering to the world, a gift. To present the face is to offer a gift, so it should be as presentable as possible. To face the world with my face. My mind was beginning to do its number. I tried to still the hamster who was preparing for its daily workout. At that moment, my doctor made his appearance and stopped the internal racket in my brain. He looked a bit tired.

"Don't you ever go home?" I smiled when I saw him coming through the door.

"Babies don't take time out, you know. My, you look better!"

"It's the make-up." I flapped my newly darkened lashes at him.

"I saw your mother-in-law coming into the building. She's not here?" He looked around the room.

"She wouldn't come here just to see me. She's probably with Dad."

"Oh, yes, the gall bladder operation. She looked a bit desperate to me. Is she all right? Is he all right?"

"I think he's all right. That's what I hear. The operation was a success, but as for Mother, well, she always has something wrong with her. Either her sense of smell is gone, or she has bumps on her chest, or her voice gets hoarse. I thing she's just probably worried about Dad."

"Psychosomatic?" he ventured.

"I hate that word. I don't know if it's psychosomatic, but she does seem to have a series of recurrent problems. She always looks to me as if she's coming up for the third time."

"You don't much like her, do you?" He wagged his finger at me.

"Does it show?"

"Only when you bare your teeth." We both laughed. The laughter felt almost unnatural to me. It hurt my stomach. "Beautiful woman. She must have been stunning when she was young." He pulled a chair closer to the bed. We were getting gossipy.

"Stunning enough to have been a showgirl," I added.

"A showgirl? The illustrious Mrs. Hammerstein, a showgirl?"

"You betcha. She doesn't discuss it much, but she was a show-girl in <u>Charlot's Revue of 1924</u> with Beatrice Lillie and Gertrude Lawrence."

"You've met them?" His eyebrows shot up.

"Just Bea Lillie. Gertie Lawrence died before I married Jimmy. They were part of the celebrity trail that moved from town to The Farm."

"Sounds impressive to me."

"Like everything else, it looks better from the outside."

"Aren't you part of that flow?" I loomed larger in his eyes.

"Just barely, and that's only because I'm her daughter-in-law. She wouldn't have anything to do with me if I hadn't married my son. I mean, <u>her</u> son. Ooops, Freudian slip." We both laughed out loud.

"You look to me like you belong, more than belong." He looked me over, and I blushed, remembering my naked vulnerability of the night before.

"She doesn't think so. She never felt right about her son having married me. To her, I've always been the Polish immigrant from the wrong side of the tracks. She's always put me in the same social category as the Polish maids and looks down her aquiline nose on all of us. The pox on her!"

"How's her marriage to Oscar? They look truly devoted to each other. I mean, I don't know, but I saw the Edward R. Murrow interview on Person to Person, and they looked like they were happy together."

"I guess it's all right. Jimmy keeps telling me that their marriage was 'made in heaven,' and he wanted us to be like them. They're old folks, and I don't want to be old folks. I don't know. Jimmy seems to be the oldest young man I ever knew. Anyway, all I feel when I'm around them is a great deal of tension. She reminds me of a fennek."

"What's a fennek, an Italian vegetable?" he asked.

"No, that's finoccio. A fennek is a tiny fox-like animal with big ears that lives in Africa and shakes all the time. I think the word finicky comes from it, or the other way around." He looked levelly at me before we both burst out laughing.

"You made that up."

"Just the part about finicky, but she does look scared all the time."

"Does he run around?" The picture of dignified Oscar running around made me laugh again.

"I don't know. There are rumors, but there are a lot of rumors about everybody."

As yet I didn't know about his stint with one of the girls in Pipe Dream. The family was the last to know. You had to get on the outside of it to see what really went on in the inside. Like Spinosa's great beast.

"They seem to be devoted to each other, yet something's very wrong. I feel it."

"Well, then maybe you should have some compassion for her. It's difficult to live with that kind of tension."

"You know she claims to have royal descent from Edward the Sixth of England, through one of his mistresses. She giggles and covers her lips every time she reveals that shameful secret."

293

We both chuckled that time. I didn't want to be left alone to think, so, like Scheherazade, I entertained my doctor with stories.

"Illegitimate descent is hard to prove." He nodded sagely.

"Or disprove."

"Is royalty important to her?" he inquired, in borderline disbelief.

"Very. They entertain Sir Percy and Lady Jean all the time, plus Lady Duckham and a host of favorites. It doesn't stop Sir Percy from pinching women on the behind like my father does, but he's excused because he's royalty."

"Why should that make any difference to you? It's their problem. If you were to believe the archivists, we are a nation of mostly aristocrats and nobility. The minute former immigrants make enough money, they seem to look for royal ancestry back in the old country. Everyone lived in a castle, and there were no peasants, didn't you know?" He raised his pinkie in a gesture of holding a very elegant cup of tea.

"Oh, I don't know; you may be right. Even my father claimed to have royal blood coursing through his veins as he snapped his suspenders and wiggled the toothpick sticking out from between his gold teeth. He claimed we lost the old family manor and lands in the last partition of Poland way back in 1795. I always felt rather foolish about it. I mean, I always knew I was a princess, but Poppa." We laughed conspiratorially. The doctor had met my father when he came to the hospital, some time before, when Andy was born. "If there is any royalty in my family, it would come from my mother. She's the gentle one and bears a striking resemblance to the Dowager Queen Mother of England. Feature for feature, they could be sisters."

"What does Oscar think of all this royalty? I've heard him speak, and he seems to be a liberal and a great philanthropist."

I bit my tongue. They were still my family. Anecdotes were all right, but intimate revelations still required discretion.

"Well, the story I heard was that there was a family on the Rhine called Hammerstein, and when Dad became famous, they got in touch with him to find out if they were related. They had a castle and everything. I don't think they came up with a common ancestor, but they sent him knockwurst and Liebfraumilch every Christmas since then."

"It might have been all that knockwurst that did him in." He glanced at the ceiling, the floor above where Oscar was recuperating. We were having too good a time discussing the family, and I felt appropriately wicked. I was allowing myself some fun at their expense, something I wouldn't have considered even a few weeks before. It seemed irreverent, with Oscar in the hospital and Dorothy worried about him. As we spoke, I realized I was already beginning to distance myself from them.

"How are you and your husband? How's Jimmy doing?"

"You were here last night; you saw," I was embarrassed to admit.

"Yes, but appearances can be deceiving."

"He never came near me, did he? I almost shuddered myself off that metal table, didn't I?"

He shrugged his shoulders. "Some men are more demonstrative than others."

"Demonstrative? I could have landed on the floor. I begged him to cover me, to hold me. I was so cold that my teeth sounded like castanets, and he never even moved! I mean, I'd do that for a dog or even a stranger!"

Again, the memory of those cold eyes staring at me from across the room sent shudders through my body.

"Was he always like this?"

"More or less."

"Then why'd you marry him?"

"I thought I'd change him, open him up, cut the membrane under his arm pits so he could put his arms around me. I don't know. I thought he'd change. Instead, I've changed. I dread going back to that apartment, his family and my life with him. I feel as if I've joined the living dead. I'm becoming one of them."

I remembered that a story at teenage friend once confided in me. She had married a man who wouldn't open up, wouldn't share his feelings with her. She tried everything. First, she tried talking to him. He wouldn't answer. Then she tried going to therapy alone. It didn't work. Finally, after years of tears and much pleading, he reluctantly joined her in therapy. She was jubilant, telling me.

"We'll open him up. We'll see who lives there, what there is inside of him that won't come out, that's all locked up."

She was aglow with new hope. I saw her a few months later looking smaller and more resigned. She added, as if to continue the conversation we had begun some time before, "You know, Bash, we opened him up, and you know what? There was nothing there! We lifted the lid, and the trunk was empty."

She laughed hysterically as she told me. In subsequent years, she became an alcoholic, never facing the emptiness of her marriage, in time becoming less honest, hiding behind the myth that things were wonderful. I should have listened to her, but each situation has its own tormented structure. Philosophical categorical imperatives, with which I had grappled in my philosophy classes, didn't really apply on the real human level.

"What are they frightened of?" My doctor brought me back, as he brushed a lock of gray hair out of his eyes.

"I wish I knew. It's as if they're afraid someone will discover something about them, something terrible, some terrible secret. Maybe they fear someone will find out they're not chic enough, not rich enough, not clever enough. I'm clutching at straws. There's a whole different side to them that they keep under wraps, both individually and as a family. Maybe that's it. What could be so terrible? I don't know. We all have our skeletons, and some rattle louder than others. What are yours?"

"I'm a doctor. I'm perfect. Perfect people have no skeletons taking up space in their closet. We barely have enough room for our clothes."

We were both laughing out loud as Dorothy swept into the room. She looked impeccable in a pink Chanel suit with a pill box hat perched on her freshly styled red hair. Her long pale-brown gloves matched her snake bag and shoes. Pearls and diamonds glistened in her ears. Around her neck, they rested above a beige silk blouse, which tied into a cravat.

"Hello, Bawrsha, how are you?"

"Hello, Mother! Better, thank you. You've met my doctor?"

"Yes." She extended her gloved hand and shook his.

He smiled and inquired, as he bowed ever so slightly, "How's your husband? I hear the family has two casualties here." He again gestured toward the ceiling.

"He seems to be fine, tired, impatient, but fine, thank you."

She fumbled for a cigarette and struggled with her gloves, as my gallant doctor lit one for her, ignoring the admonition against smoking. "Thank you!" She nodded to him. "How's old Bawrsha doing?" She smiled toward me. I was somewhat taken aback by her effort at intimacy.

"She'll be all right. The worst is over." He turned to me, patted my arm and became very official. "Now, young lady, you stay in bed. I have to go, but I'll look in on you later. Keep your chin up and stay as pretty and bright as you look now."

He nodded to Dorothy. "My best wishes for a speedy recovery to your husband!" He backed his way out of the room. Our conversation about her royal antecedents must have impressed him.

"That man really likes you," Dorothy observed. "Such a handsome man."

"I like him. too. He helped me through the night." I didn't want to go into the details with her. "How's Dad?"

"He's all right. I went to see him, and he almost threw me out. He was so impatient with me. I've been writing some thank-you notes from his hospital room, but it seems he wants to be alone. He said he didn't want to see me this afternoon. I didn't have to come. It's as if he were blaming me for something again. Anyway," she shook her head, as if to brush the thought away, "the tests are negative." She took a long drag on the cigarette, "I have to give these things up," surveying the cigarette between her well- manicured nails, "but I can't seem to be able to do it. Ben [the family doctor] says I must!" The smoke curled around her head as she ground the cigarette out in the ashtray.

"Does Dad know that the tests are negative?" I didn't know that the specter of cancer had raised its hooded head.

"Yes." She picked a speck of tobacco off the tip of her tongue.

"Then it must make him feel better. Who's going to work on Flower Drum Song?"

"He'll have to do it when he gets out. Dick hasn't been too well, either, I don't know what they'll do. Such bad timing. He's been at Payne Whitney Clinic since June, you know!"

After Richard Rodgers had part of his neck and face removed from a cancer operation, he grew depressed and took to drink. A stay at Payne Whitney helped him to recover.

"Maybe that's what makes Dad impatient?" I ventured, trying to lighten her obvious burden. "Maybe he needs time to think. The medication they give you here, the drugs, makes it difficult to pull it all together." I could still feel the edges of my mind lost in banks of fog.

"I don't know, dear. He's very irritable toward me." The frightened, perplexed look again settled on her face. "You look much better," She patted the bed. "That black turban makes you look like Gail Sonder-gaard, glamorous, not in keeping with the rest of the decor in here." She looked around the room. "Terrible colors on these walls." The bil-ious green wasn't my favorite, either.

"Have you seen Andy? How is he?" I wondered about my son.

"He's fine, dear. Jimmy brought him over last night, and I played with him. What a dear child he is. He kept reaching for the flowers and tipping over. You know, like he did at The Farm. Susan came over, and we both played with him on the bed. We called him Ferdinand the Bull. You know, the one who loves to smell flowers, and the other one, Thumper the Skunk! No, no, not Thumper. That's the rabbit. Flower! Isn't that the skunk's name, Flower?

Andy laughed and said "Wahwer" when we called him Flower. He's fine. Jimmy will bring him over this afternoon. I got him some clothes and a shirt that says `GRANDMA LOVES ME.' He looked wonderful when I left him. Gertrude [the cook] is so enchanted with him. She came out of the pantry and was feeding him oatmeal from a silver porridge cup that belonged to Jimmy. He got it from Lady Duckham. I must give it to you." She looked around the room. "Didn't Jimmy send you any flowers?"

"No wahwers for me, Mother." We laughed. "Jimmy's not into flowers." We both looked around the empty room.

"Oh, my, but that's terrible. Ockie's room is like a florist's shop. I'll bring some down tomorrow."

"It's O.K., Mother. No one knows I'm here! I just want to get home as soon as I can!"

"Well, Andy's well cared for, so don't fret over him." She patted the bed again. "I hear you washed the walls before you miscarried. I know physical labor makes me feel better, too. I like to wash Ockie's socks by hand when I'm upset. It settles my nerves," she commiserated with me.

"The baby died inside me. It died, and I felt that it was poisoning me. I couldn't sleep or even think. Well, maybe I'll feel better now."

"Why did it die? Does the doctor know? Did he give you any reason?" she inquired.

"No, he said that it separated from the placenta, that's all. No reason, at least they don't know. He said it was probably dead for six weeks."

"Poor Bawrsh, you'll be all right. You're made of good solid stock, you'll see. If there's anything we can do to help you, let us know. Do you need anything?"

"No, Mother, but thank you."

"See you tomorrow. Stay chipper. I'll stop in after I see Ockie!" She leaned over, and on her way out, she pecked the air over my ear, pulling on her long brown gloves as she left the room. The smell of her perfume and cigarette lingered after she was gone.

Her problems with Oscar seemed to have softened her. She seemed kinder and less concerned with the mascara on my eyelashes, or the gloves I may or may not have been wearing, in or out of bed.

For the first time since I knew her, she seemed genuinely interested in my welfare. Maybe her fear for Oscar opened up an area of compassion in her from which I, too, benefitted. Perhaps we could be friends, after all. Under all that veneer and posturing beat the heart of a woman who bore three children, who as a woman must have had some understanding for the plight of another woman.

I called Oscar. He sounded tired but concerned about my miscarriage. We exchanged pleasantries. He might have been generally more courteous than Dorothy, but he was more subtly less reachable. After comparing our battle scars, we wished each other a speedy recovery and looked forward to seeing each other at home.

Then I called my mother. "Hello, Ma, how are you?" I inquired.

She hesitated, then answered in a sad flat voice, "All right . . . Something wrong? How Andy? How Jimmy?"

"They're O.K., Ma. I've had a miscarriage. I'm O.K. How's Poppa?" I was almost embarrassed to express any concern for my father.

"Not good. He not able to eat; he very sick. I go to St. Albans Veterans Hospital every night to see him. He very small . . . very thin," she corrected herself. "When you come to see him?" My miscarriage seemed to fly by her.

"When I get out of the hospital, Ma. In a few days, maybe a week."

"Who watch my baby boy, my Andzejek?"

"He's with Mrs. Hammerstein, Ma. She's got the maids taking care of him at their house. He's all right."

"Why you no let Jimmy bring him here?" she reproached me.

"Because with Poppa at the St. Albans hospital, it would be too much trouble for you, and you're working at the store all day."

"Andzejek, he never any trouble. We find a way. I like to see him. I come to see you Saturday and visit him in their big house. O.K.? Then I come to see you?"

"O.K.. Ma. You sure you'll find the way? It's a big trip here."

"Yes, I find way, I must find way by self. I no have Poppa now."

She had always wanted to see the way the Hammersteins lived. Jimmy and I had been married for four years, and they still had not invited her and Poppa to their home. It made her feel embarrassed and socially inadequate, but she was curious and determined to see for herself.

"I come to see you after I see Andzejek. Good? How you feel?"

"Better, Ma. I'll be all right. How do you feel, Ma?"

There was a long pause. She never really discussed her life with Poppa, or how she felt.

"How you expect me to feel with Poppa in hospital?" she reproached me for asking the insensitive question. I had opened the wound she carried in her, the wound that would grow deeper and would never really heal.

"You come to see Poppa when you leave hospital?" she insisted.

"Yes, Momma, I will."

With my world crumbling around me, I had neglected her in her grief. She didn't want to complain about it, but I knew she wanted me to know I had disappointed her. Inwardly, I vowed to see more of her in the future. She had been my greatest friend and ally, and it was partially for her that I had strived and worked as hard as I did. She thought I was wonderful and could do practically anything. I wanted to prove her right. I could feel the weight of her grief, and it opened mine.

I knew that Momma had a miscarriage a few months after she had me, when she was about my age. I also remember Poppa blaming me for it.

"You killed your baby brother!" he often recalled, wagging his finger at me. "You killed my son!" I was about five the first time I remember hearing those accusations. Looking around, trying to understand my still alien world and what I had done, fearing another beating, I ran to Momma and hid my face in her apron as confusion buzzed around me. "You killed my son," he kept repeating. Momma would come to my defense.

"Andzej, I lost the baby. Basiunia had nothing to do with it." she insisted.

"You still nursed her when you lost my son. She was a big girl. She made my son die."

"No, no, Andzej," Momma explained to him. "The nursing didn't kill the baby. It just died. Basiunia was a baby herself at the time. She wasn't responsible for its death. She didn't kill your son."

But Poppa never relented. Whenever the conversation turned to children, especially to sons, he would point a finger at me and accuse me of having killed his only possible male heir. I carried the burden of that guilt and the rage of his accusations much of my young life. It's amazing how those familial cycles repeat themselves. Here I was in a similar situation. No one knew what caused my miscarriage. A generation later, I was reliving a similar anguish that my mother had gone through. When are we able to spring clear of that eternal spin? To step off that unrelenting curve of disintegration? Dorothy made the observation that my sturdy body, "made of peasant stock," she stopped herself from adding, looked strong enough to recover quickly, but why I lost the baby was "a puzzlement," a phrase Oscar had immortalized in his lyrics.

Much later that afternoon, Jimmy came through the open door carrying Andy under his arm. He threw me a furtive acknowledgment, sat in the corner chair and put Andy on the floor in front of him. Andy stared at me and clung to his father's leg, fearing to lose him again.

"Zlodko, it's me, Mommie." Seeing me in such strange circumstances must have disoriented him. He smiled at me. As I stretched out my arms to him, he hid his face in Jimmy's pant leg. Jimmy got up and, with a heavy sigh, plopped Andy on the bed next to me. My son was still a very small person, frightened by the changes occurring around him.

"How did you get him in?" I wondered, as I turned to my silent husband.

"No one stopped me. I just came up the elevator," he added absentmindedly. Andy was becoming more comfortable and was playing with the buttons on my bed jacket. GRANDMA LOVES ME rode brightly, hand-embroidered, across the top of his new outfit. I put my arms gently around him, and he settled against me. It was the first time I had any physical human contact since I lost the baby. The warmth of life flooded my body. He smelled clean and fresh, dusted with the ubiquitous Johnson's Baby Powder. Chattering in his incomprehensible language, he slid off the bed. His short legs dangled precariously in space for a split second before they hit the floor. Without waiting to right himself, he was on his way to the window to inform me that planes flew over there, as he pointed in the direction of La Guardia Airport, on the horizon. He spied boats down below on the East River and whooped for joy.

"Boat, Mommie, boat!" His chubby fingers pointed in the approximate direction of the river below.

"Pane, Mommie, pane!" He rearranged his fingers to point at the planes in the distance. Jimmy sat preoccupied in the corner, methodically cracking his fingers, one at a time.

"How are you, Jimmy?"

"O.K. . . . How do you feel?" He stared over at me.

"Better. Did you get any sleep last night?" I wanted to keep the conversation going.

"I stopped over at the club. Some of the guys were there, and we really tied one on." He yawned as he cracked his head; the sound exploded in the room.

"What'd you do today?"

"Nothing much." He looked at the floor. "Saw Dad. He looks tired but better, tired but better," he repeated.

"I know. I called him. Mother says the tests are negative. I didn't know you were all worried about that." I was already being left out of some of the family's concerns.

"Yeah, he's O.K." He didn't seem to want to talk about it. I changed the subject, looking over to Andy by the window and the brilliant summer day beyond.

"It's a beautiful day, isn't it?"

"It's a perfect day for skindiving." As I heard what he said, the anger rose in me.

"Well, I'm sorry I'm keeping you from it."

"Yeah, so am I," he answered evenly. I wanted to scream at him.

We just lost a baby. I'm in the hospital, your father's in the hospital, and all you can think about is skindiving? I had resolved to keep the peace, to bite my tongue, so I said nothing, as he added. "If it's a nice day tomorrow, would you mind if I skipped a visit?"

"Why? I'd love to see both of you again."

"I'd like to go skindiving. Some of the guys found a new hole, and we'd like to check it out before the season's over."

Through clenched teeth, I carefully said, "Your mother might need you." He yawned again. "Your father might need you." There was more silence as he stretched his legs out in front of him and slumped down in the chair. "I might need you."

"I'll leave a number on the machine." He rose, picked Andy up, tucked him under his arm and carried him over for me to peck above the ear. I wasn't close enough to give him a real hug. Then he turned and disappeared from the room. Andy looked back at me. The departure had been abrupt, and his chin began to quiver. I started to shake again. As they disappeared down the hospital corridor, Andy's wail of displeasure receded in the distance. The blood, which had stopped oozing, now spread its warmth again as it flowed into the gauze in my womb. The thundering black horse galloped through a deepening red haze.

Chapter 28

Early the next morning, a cloud of fear preceded Dorothy into the room. It was so real that I was startled by its nerve-wracking intensity. Fear or no fear, she looked impeccable in her teal-blue linen suit. Shoes and gloves matched her beige petit-point flowered bag.

"Bawrsha, have you seen Jimmy? I thought he might be here. Your machine is on. I hate those things! I didn't even leave a message. I can't talk to them," she rattled on.

"No, Mother, he's gone skindiving. How's Andy? Have you had breakfast?"

"Yes. Andy's fine. How could he go skindiving? You're in the hospital. Ockies in the hospital. Skindiving? It's inhuman."

"Mother, what's wrong?"

"Bawrsha, Oscar may need another operation. They need my permission, something to do with his prostate. I need someone to talk to. I can't find Billy, either." She looked stricken.

"Where's Susan?"

"She's at Fire Island, dear. I couldn't reach her."

"Are they sure? Is it serious?"

"I don't know, it must be. So soon after his gall bladder was taken out. I hope it's not . . ." Her voice trailed off. She couldn't say the word "cancer," and the thought was left suspended in the air.

"Mother, the tests came out negative. I'm sure it's nothing serious." I had my misgivings, but I didn't want to overburden her. It was right after Poppa had his prostate operation that he developed cancer.

"They might have made a mistake!" She gasped and gulped down some air.

"Mother, have you seen Ben or Harold [the family doctors]? They'll be able to advise you. They know Dad's history after all these years. Don't jump to any conclusions."

"Harold's still in Doylestown, but should be here in a few hours. Ben's away. Oh, Bawrsha, I'm sorry to burden you any further, but I had to talk to someone, and everyone else is gone. I became panicky and upset. I'm sorry. This will never do. I've become a bloody nuisance." She dabbed at her eyes with a lace- edged linen handkerchief embroidered with the neat "DHB" in the corner. I saw the same fear that my mother felt reflected in Dorothy's eyes.

"My father went to the hospital, too. I wish I could have been there for my mother's sake."

"Oh, my! What's wrong with him?" Her watery eyes got wider.

"He's dying of cancer." I said the word for her.

"How terrible." Her eyes got misty, and she sank into the chair. "The 'Big C.' Oh, my, your father has it?" She still couldn't say it.

"Yes, I wish I could be with my mother." I could still hear Momma's flat, grief-stricken voice on the phone.

"What a shame I never really got to know him. What a pity he has . . ." She paused. "Oh, my!" She got up again and lit a cigarette. My eyes followed her pacing across the room, and I would like to have added, "What a pity that you never invited him or my mother to have dinner with you. What a pity you never felt it was important enough to allow yourself to be chauffeured to Farmingdale and to have dinner with them. Momma finally stopped inviting you after you were not available so many times. What a pity you couldn't make that hour and fifteen-minute trip in your comfortable limousine into the suburbs. What a pity, here you are alone in your hour of fear, turning to me, who was never good enough for you to even have dinner with my family." Her voice brought me back to my bed and the hospital room.

"Oh, my, the `Big C'!" She looked at her cigarette and snuffed it out in the ashtray. "What a terrible thing it is. First Gertie [Gertrude Lawrence], then Dick [Richard Rodgers], now your father." She took a big breath, and a dry sob escaped her body. "You're right; the tests were negative. But where are my children? Why don't they care? What have I done wrong?"

She sat down in the chair at the far end of the room and poured her story out to me. I had heard bits and pieces of it before, but never completely from her, never woman to woman. It was as if she wanted to justify her children's lack of concern and the choices she had made in her and their lives.

"I blame myself," Another heavy sigh escaped above that impeccably tailored eggshell-white blouse. "But what was I to do? They say children need a stable home. Oscar and I gave them that. They never wanted for anything. They say children need their mother. If I had been more of a mother to them, I would have had to be less of a wife to Oscar. You see, I could have lost him. I don't think they ever forgave me. I know Susan never has. Jimmy never says anything. I never know what he thinks."

"Didn't he ever talk to you?" I interrupted her.

"Not much. He was always such a quiet boy."

"Did you ever talk to him?"

"No, not really. There was never any need. You know he was an ideal child. I never had to yell at him, and I never had to speak sharply to him. He was never a problem. When he was eighteen, I left a note under his pillow telling him what a wonderful considerate son he was. He brought the note into my bedroom with tears in his eyes and asked me why I had never said that to him before. I always thought he knew how much I loved him and how grateful I was. But he never did. I used to try to reassure him with my eyes, across the dinner table, when Oscar used to tease him with Sammy Goldstein. I used to try to reassure him that I was on his side. He was still very small when Oscar took him apart. When he tried to defend himself, he stuttered and stammered, giving Ockie more fuel with which to tease him. I thought he knew how much I understood." Her hands smoothed the skirt around her legs.

"You know, Ockie has always been a frustrated lawyer. He studied law at Columbia University, and he was like a prosecuting attorney around the dinner table. All the children had to do was make some kind of outrageous statement, and he would take it apart, grammatically, legally, idiomatically, analyzing it piece by piece, showing them where they were wrong. They all suffered, but I think because Jimmy was the youngest, he suffered the most. Oscar invented Sammy Goldstein and brought him into the conversation every time he wanted to show Jim Boy up. Sammy could do it better. Maybe Ockie felt he was helping him to express himself more clearly, become more competitive, but Jimmy was so young and so earnest in trying to defend himself. Oscar wouldn't allow either of his sons to get the better of him in any way. Very competitive. Maybe it hurt them more deeply than I knew. You know, he used to trip Billy when they ice-skated together in the winter, just to force him to get up, to get up on his own two feet. Billy also cried." She paused and looked at her fingers, rubbing the liver spots with trembling hands.

I recalled the summer before, when Oscar collapsed on the tennis courts from heat prostration while trying to beat Jimmy, who by then had become a very good tennis player. We all feared for him, as he turned beet red and his breathing became very shallow. He wouldn't allow his sons to beat him on any level. Dorothy took a long drag on another one of the cigarettes she was going to give up, and continued.

"Years later, I found out that he felt deserted." She gazed into space and puffed furiously on the cigarette, nervously moving it from one hand to the other.

"I know, Mother. He told me he used to cry in the tall meadow grass behind the house, after those confrontations around the table, when he was there alone with only Bruce to console him."

"Bruce? Who was Bruce? I don't remember anyone at The Farm called Bruce." She looked perplexed.

"Your golden retriever. Jimmy said that when he used to cry in the tall meadow grass, Bruce would nuzzle against him, and his big eyes would look soulfully up into his face. He felt alone and didn't know where to turn. When Bruce was put to sleep, he never really got over it."

"Ah, yes, I remember that dog. Yes, you're right; his name was Bruce. But he became a killer and ran with a pack of wild dogs. We had to put him away."

"It broke Jimmy's heart."

"I never knew that. He never said anything about it. Broke his heart. Oh, my!" Her free hand went up to her lips, then down to her chest, as another heavy sigh escaped her.

"Did he have any friends, I mean, kids he played with?" I wondered if he ever played with anyone but Buddy.

"I thought he was happy at The Farm. Stevie [Steve Sondheim] and Jennifer [her niece] were there. He seemed to be great chums with Arnie [the chauffeur]. They wanted to go into the chicken business together, you know."

I knew the story about the chicken business. Jimmy and Arnie were going to raise them together in the large chicken yard at The Farm. Once the chickens were fully grown, they would sell them back to Oscar and make some money. Since Oscar would have had to supply not only the chickens but also the feed, he declined, feeling that he was getting the short end of the deal. It nipped Jimmy's chicken-raising career in the bud.

Dorothy mused, "Stevie was so clever and so bright. Such a mature young boy. You see how clever he is, even today. He wrote <u>West Side Story</u>. Ockie advised him to do it, and look how well it turned out. He was always so talented and so eager to learn that Ockie paid more attention to him than he paid to his own sons. I guess I did, too. I remember Jimmy trying to compete with him at the dinner table and stuttering while they all laughed at him. It was funny, you know."

She looked at me, trying to justify the laughter. Then, after a moment's pause, she said, "I never knew how much it hurt him. We all thought it was just good clean fun." She paused again and glanced out the window at the airplanes that rose and landed in the distance at La Guardia Airport.

"We traveled a great deal, and had to leave him at The Farm. Mary and Josephine were there, you know, the two Polish maids," she added. I nodded. I knew <u>ad nauseum</u> about the two Polish maids who kept us in CARE packages of beef, chickens and turkeys and who raised Jimmy. I knew the two Polish maids very well.

"If I had been more of a mother to my children, I would have lost Oscar. He wanted me along with him wherever he went, all those shows out of town. He wanted me at his side. I was proud to be there; that was my place." She drew herself up with a sense of accomplishment. Then she sank down again. "How I hated all those empty hotel rooms and those long corridors. I shopped and addressed Christmas cards. There really was no choice to make. So the children suffered. I mean, in England, children are sent away to school. It doesn't seem to make that much difference to them, but here . . ."

Her voice trailed away. She didn't seem to be aware of the fact that Britain at that time had an extensive empire that could absorb the result of the rage created by the British school system. We didn't have an empire to use as a sponge for our deserted and neglected children, so they tore up their own turf and abused their parents.

Dorothy continued, "You know, they never forgave me. Susan keeps telling me I neglected her and broke up her home. She keeps bringing up something about rolling ribbons with some terrible nanny. I never can tell. Jimmy seemed to open up a bit when you first married, but now he's the same." She looked around the room. "I loved Oscar with all my heart, and I couldn't bear to be separated from him, so I sacrificed my children. My first husband loved me. Big Henry was good to me. Men are strangely overconfident. I grew lonely and bored because he was away a great deal. Instead of listening to me and trying to understand, trying to spend some time with me, Big Henry sent me off on an ocean liner, on a cruise alone, to cheer me up. The bracing sea air and all that. It was on the <u>Olympia</u> -- that's what the ship was called -- that I met Oscar. He was thirty-one, a budding playwright, on his way to London to do <u>Desert Song</u>. We fell madly in love. I was twenty-seven, a little younger than you are now."

I was surprised she had remembered my age. "It was very complicated because we were both married. Divorce was frowned upon in those days, you know. We both had children, but our love won out. It was a painful business because Big Henry loved me so. He cried when I told him I wanted a divorce, but he loved me enough not to stop me. It was more difficult for Ockie. He almost had a nervous breakdown that time."

Her voice grew harsher. "He found out that his wife Mike was having affairs, and it almost broke him. He had to enter the LeRoy Hospital to recover. It made his divorce easier." She snuffed out one cigarette and lit another.

"I'll never forget when Big Henry and I had our last lunch together. He tried to change my mind. I couldn't think of anything but Oscar. If I hadn't loved him so much, I would have stayed with Big Henry. He looked so broken, but I followed my heart. I'll never forget the day Susan, her nanny and I left him and took a cab along Fifty-Seventh Street. Big Henry walked on the sidewalk, all sad and preoccupied. The traffic was terrible, and the cab we were riding in kept pulling up alongside him. I had to look away so I wouldn't see his sad and broken face. It happened a few times. I dreaded every time the cab slowed down and there was Big Henry walking, not aware we were in the cab alongside him. It was the longest ride I ever took. I'll never forget it."

Dorothy seemed lost in her story. Her eyes grew more watery as she thought of her former husband. "I don't know what to do," she continued. "I'm sorry to burden you, Bawrsha, but I always had Oscar to turn to, and now he's sick. You're the only one who's around." She stopped, as much for a small breath as to create a small space for me to answer her.

"Does Susan know Dad's in the hospital?"

"Of course! She was at The Farm when Ockie became ill. She became hysterical over it when she found out. The only one to get that emotional." I realized then that when Jimmy and I had separated for the first time, much family business had gone on without me.

"Has she seen him since then? Maybe she feels the danger has passed."

"Still, she could call, dear. I mean, she doesn't remember the good things I've done for her. When she was a tiny baby, the doctor told me that her lungs were so congested that she might die. I did the only thing I thought would work. I held her in my arms, close to my body all night, and the poor little thing pulled through. That saved her life, but she doesn't remember that. All she remembers is that I left her father and ruined her life."

"Mother, why don't I order some tea? Maybe it'll make you feel better?" I reached for the phone on the far side of my bed.

"It's not tea time, dear. It's too early," she reminded me. "If I had to do it all over again, I would have spent more time with my children, but then I might have lost Ockie." Tears welled up again in her already watery eyes.

Into the pause of her perplexed outpouring, I interjected,

"My mother would like to see Andy on Saturday."

"That's fine, dear. If I'm out, I'll tell the butler to let her in." I found it difficult to believe she could say that. Either the woman was stupid, completely tactless, or just plain cruel. The least she could do was to be there since Momma made an effort to visit her. Not being there was a slap in my mother's face and indirectly in mine. How insensitive could she be? The old resentments that subsided after our conversation again reawakened in me. She would not have understood if I reproached her or pointed it out, so I left it alone. I returned to the issue at hand.

"Mother, has Jimmy spoken to you at all about the way he feels?"

"No, dear. He's a remote kind of boy and stays pretty much to himself. He doesn't speak to me about anything."

"Has he ever shown any love for anyone?" Except Bruce the golden retriever and Buddy, I wanted to add.

"Well, dear, we're not very demonstrative, but I'm sure Jimmy loves us. We love each other." She became slightly defensive and momentarily bristled.

"Then, maybe he's still rebelling against something?" I was clutching at straws, trying to understand him. She focused levelly at me for a moment to set me straight with her answer and then continued to circle the small room.

"He's a bit old to be a teen-age rebel. Anyway, he doesn't really have anything to rebel against. We've given him a good home, parents who love each other; we're very respectable people." She stopped her pacing to perch on the edge of the empty bed next to mine. Then she nervously stood up again, as she continued to speak. Her hands, busy like a squirrel's, broke the air before her, and her rings sparkled. She looked truly perplexed, not understanding where she had failed her children.

"When is Harold [the family doctor] due here?" I asked her, and she glanced at her diamond-encrusted watch.

"Oh, my! He may be here now!" She jumped over to me, and for the first time since I had known her, she gave me a hug. It was furtive and fast, but it was a hug. Her perfume left a halo of fragrance around me. In spite of her cruel tactlessness, I still hoped we could become friends. Andy would need a grandmother, and one as rich as she was wouldn't hurt.

After Dorothy left, I became more aware of my body. The painkillers began to settle me into a heavy sleep again, temporarily stilling the persistent hamster on the wheel. The first Oscar, the original Old Man, made a statement that echoed in my mind as I lay there, a statement shared with us on our honeymoon by Uncle Arthur as he reminisced about his father and the philosophy of the original patriarch.

"Nature has made many mistakes," he had said, "but I think her greatest mistake was in failing to equip us with a switch by which we could turn off our thoughts. We can say 'I don't want to see,' shut our eyes, and we don't see. We can say 'I don't want to hear,' stop up our ears, and we don't hear. But we can't say 'I don't want to think' and stop thinking."

I would like to have had that switch in my brain, to turn off the hamster on its infernal wheel.

313

Chapter 29

Momma came to visit on Saturday, glowing with pride that she hadn't gotten lost in the big city. New York held its perils for her, but she followed the instructions I had given her and got to the Hammerstein house without any problems. After her visit with her grandson, she took another bus crosstown and arrived triumphantly at the hospital. The sweet smell of drooping phlox filled the room as she peeped around the door frame to make sure I was there.

"City noisy and dirty! How you live here? Garbage everywhere! So much people! No good to live here," was her greeting.

To an outsider, she would have been called a comely woman, with a round and very pretty face. I would look more and more like her as I became older. My features would soften, and my body would round out as I put on weight. The family resemblance was there and grew stronger with the years. In her circles, she was considered to have very good taste. Her brown shoes matched her brown pocketbook, and she also wore brown gloves. Her dress was a light floral print with a lot of beige and orange that swayed around her body as she walked, revealing her well-shaped calves. She still shaved her legs to accentuate their fine form and crossed them before her, to show the world that her ankles were "well-turned."

She would never have passed as being chic in the Hammerstein circles. I wondered why as I looked at her. A bit too chubby, perhaps. The Duchess of Windsor and homosexual male designers had set the trend. You could never be too rich or too thin. The statement was ascribed to many very chic, very rich, and very thin women. Momma certainly was not thin. The floral print on her dress seemed too gay, too obvious, not subdued enough. The matching shoes, purse and gloves, too carefully put together, were not casual enough. The hem of her dress was ironed flat, not left soft. Was the hair too curly from an obvious permanent? Was the lipstick too red? The straps on her "well-turned" ankles were not snake skin. The pearls around the neck were fake, not even cultured. What was it that gave her away as not being chic? Her attitude, perhaps it was her apologetic attitude. As my love for her filled me with warmth, I knew it made no difference to me whether she was chic or not. She was "moia Mamusia" (my mother).

"The city isn't too bad, Momma. You get used to it." I had became a native, and my life covered the city like a blanket, having gone to high school downtown, to college uptown, worked midtown in the theater, and lived on the West Side. New York was my home. To Momma, it was a place where a strange language was being spoken by too many people, a place of a lot of shoving and pushing, and a place of a lot of noise. Her gentle soul rebelled at the rudeness and the lack of courtesy, but her curiosity brought her to the big city. It was the first time she traveled alone, away from Farmingdale, Long Island, without Poppa to guide her. She saw Andy and had been stunned by the wealth that surrounded her grandson.

"Basiu, how rich they are! I never see people so rich. Fresh flowers everywhere, lilies, lilacs. Where they get lilacs in August? I see tulips. Where they get tulips in August?" She was amazed. As a young woman, she sewed in the homes of the well-to-do in Warsaw, but even there, she never saw such wealth.

"Money can buy anything, Mamusiu, even lilacs in August."

"The curtains all embroidered by hand? The rugs? I think by hand, too."

"Yes, Momma, they call it petit-point. It's like needlepoint, but smaller."

"Oh, my! I never do that. I do only embroidery. They walk on them?"

"Yes, Momma, they do."

"Such large rooms, so many floors, all those windows to wash, and carry the vacuum cleaner up and down all those stairs." Her eyes grew wide at the thought of the strain. I laughed.

"They have one on every landing, Mamusiu. The maids do the windows, and they vacuum the rugs."

"Andzejek has room all to his self. They have two sheets on his bed! They have two sheets on all the beds? My, you lucky he have everything. He lucky little boy! I no see Jimmy or his family. You tell them I come?"

"Yes, Momma, I did."

"They strange people, not very nice. They feel better than us. We not good enough for them? Are we still good enough for you, Barbara?" She called me Barbara only when she distanced herself from me.

"Don't say that, Mamusiu. I may feel funny about Poppa, especially when he gets drunk, but not about you. Anyway, I don't think Jimmy and I are going to last."

"You sure?"

"Yes, Ma, I'm sure." I loved her and wished that I could have saved her from being humiliated by the Hammersteins. She never knew how much I loved her. We never said those things to each other. "You're my favorite Mamusia, Ma." She brushed it aside, embarrassed at my show of emotion.

"Basiu, you have everything. They may not be nice people, but they have money. Money make your life easier. You no have to struggle so much."

She paused, and I looked at her hands, working hands that filled my life with such care and love. She held them primly on her lap, as she continued, "Jimmy no better or worse than most men. He your husband, baby's father. Andzejek needs father. You need husband."

"I know, Ma, but he's not much of a husband to me."

CINDERELLA ❧ AFTER THE BALL OR, JUST KEEP GOING

"Basiu, you expect too much. They all alike. I stay with Poppa. He same as all of them."

"I want him to talk to me, to be affectionate with me."

"Maybe you want too much. Poppa get affectionate when he get older. Maybe Jimmy the same. Men not for talking and affection. Talk to friends, get affection from children."

"What are men for, then?" It was an old argument we were having.

"For to be husbands, for to take care of family, for to make you wife, give you status. Woman with no husband has no status."

How I hated that statement. It negated a woman as a human being. The no-win discussion which we had many times before only led to disagreement and anger. It lay dormant during my marriage, but now with its possible dissolution, it was resurfacing.

"Basiu, bite your tongue! You have husband; you respectable woman. Without husband, you have no respect."

I quashed the retort I wanted to throw back at her and toned down my answer. "I don't know how long I'll be able to go on with him, Ma, with all that cold silence. The meanness when I ask him anything, and the lack of affection."

I couldn't tell her that he called me a "fucking cunt" with increasing regularity. She wouldn't have known what it meant. Had she known, it would have shocked her. She also would have been shocked to learn the extent of our financial problems.

As we talked about Poppa, her face became pitifully strained, and her beautiful, large brown eyes grew rounder and more frightened. Time passed; the shadows in the room grew longer. Before she left, she kissed me, brushed a wisp of hair from my face and patted my arm. As always, when she left, the room seemed to lose its glow, as if somewhere a light had been turned off.

Late the following evening, the ringing of the phone next to my hospital bed awakened me. It was Dorothy's voice on the other end.

"Bawrsha, before you hear it from anyone else, I have something to tell you." My heart jumped into the back of my throat. What now?

"Is Andy O.K.?"

"Yes, so's Jimmy," she reassured me. "Something happened to Reggie [Oscar's brother]."

"My God, what? Did he have an accident?" My heart rose to pound in my ears.

"He had a heart attack."

"How is he?" My fears rushed in.

"Bawrsha, he's dead. Poor old Reggie's dead."

"Does Dad know?"

"He knew before I even told him. I was writing thank-you notes for all the flowers that came to Ockie, and Dick called. He asked me to take the call on the extension in the corridor, and I felt something was wrong. He told me that Reggie had a heart attack. I went back into Ockie's room, and before I said anything to him, he looked at me and said, 'Reggie's dead, isn't he?' 'Yes,' I answered him; then he asked me to leave him alone. I left the room and cried in the hall. A few minutes later, the nurse told me to go back in. He grieved alone. I never saw him cry. Poor Ockie and poor old Reggie. Now he's dead. Ockie's lost his only brother. There were close, you know."

"I know. Does Jimmy know? Where is he?"

"Jimmy's at Reggie's apartment with the police."

"Did he die alone?"

"No, dear. There seemed to have been some women with him. They'll try to keep it out of the papers."

"Is Jimmy planning to call me?"

"I don't know, dear, but Andy's fine. We'll keep him until you get home. I understand your mother visited him. I'm sorry I missed her."

I wanted to scream at her, "I bet you are!"

She started to ramble on. "I hate to sleep alone, with Ockie not in the bed next to me. I'd like to sleep in his hospital room, but he doesn't want me there. Good night, dear. Don't worry." It was hard not to worry when so much of my well-constructed world was crashing around me, crashing around all of us.

After my unborn baby, Reggie was the next one to be released from the vortex that held us all in its spin. He flew off into the void, leaving behind the remaining people who had been caught in that unraveling spiral and who needed more time to be set free from that unrelenting curve of disintegration.

In spite of the accumulating chaos of my life, I was beginning to feel "perkier," as Dorothy would say, and could go to the white-tiled bathroom alone without fainting or walking my way with the tips of my fingers along the cool green walls. Life seemed to be happening somewhere out there in the outside world while I lay in the hospital waiting for my body to heal. Now Reggie had died. I waited to hear from someone, anyone. The butler answered at the townhouse when I called, and after extending his condolences over Reggie's death, he informed me that Andy was in Central Park with one of the maids.

Jimmy arrived in the afternoon of the next day. He sat on the chair in the corner and stared at me. I could hear my heart beating in my ears again and began to breathe deeply to control the trembling that had set in. He looked haggard and unshaven. Even behind his glasses, circles ringed his eyes. His chin seemed to have receded even more. I knew he cared for Reggie and seemed shaken by his death. As he sat in that distant corner, he began to sketch in the activities of the night before. Reggie had lived a secret life away from the family, with his cronies and his prostitutes. After he and his wife Mary parted, he left the cottage across the corn field at The Farm. Once he moved to the city, he saw much less of the family and of his brother.

"Reggie died with his boots on! There were a couple of broads with him! Fuck! He might have had a attack doing `it'!" The idea perked my husband up. "What a way to go! They were paralyzed with fear, called the cops and skipped out. The detectives cracked dirty jokes with Reggie dead on the bed," he continued with no apparent emotion.

"Are you very upset?" I asked. He shrugged his shoulders. "Did Reggie's death touch you?"

"Yeah, I guess so." His voice was flat; there was no change in tone.

"What do you feel, Jimmy?" I hesitated in asking him a question. This time, there seemed to be no apparent anger at my inquiry.

"Nothing, not much." He shrugged his shoulders again.

"Do you feel anything for anyone or anything?"

"No, not really."

"Not even Andy?"

"Well, maybe Andy."

"What do you want to do?" I pressed him.

"I don't know."

"Do you want to go or to stay?"

"Both." Well, at least he felt the same way I did. Both alternatives tugged at him, just as they had been tugging at me.

"What seems stronger?"

"I don't know."

"Jimmy, we can't keep doing this! We have to talk to each other. We're both going through a lot. I need someone to share all this with, don't you? Can't you talk to me?"

He shook his head. "I have nothing to say."

"You must have something to say, You just lost your uncle!"

"It's none of your fucking business!" Sparks of light flashed from his eyes.

"Who's business is it?"

"Not yours. I don't need to discuss my life with you!"

"Then who do you need to discuss your life with?"

"No one!"

"You want to be alone?"

"Yeah!"

"Then you don't want to be married?"

"That's right!"

"Maybe we should part. There's no reason to stay together."

"You got it!" The inevitable was happening again: no yelling or screaming, just a separation, a parting; no tearing, just a separation. Life's practical aspects cut through my pain.

"I'd like to leave the hospital tomorrow. Would you get the bill?" I hoped for a last gesture.

"I have no money."

"But who'll pay for the miscarriage?"

"That's your problem! I agreed to pay for the birth of a baby, not for a miscarriage!" He got up and left. The shaking that accompanied his entrance into the room now accelerated. It was over. There was no going back. The longer I knew him, the less I liked him. Yet, I had pushed the issue. I could have left it alone. We could have drifted along for a few more months, or maybe a few more years. Who knows? I couldn't live that way.

I needed something to still my trembling body, and I called the nurse. A dark moving mountain of a woman waddled into the room, and after looking me over, she walked out again and came back with some tranquilizers.

"Why you crying? Is it the pain?" the colored nurse inquired.

"No. My marriage just ended. My husband and I just parted," I sobbed.

"Honey! There ain't no man worth one tear from a woman, especially one who leaves his wife in the hospital."

My hands shook so much that she had to steady them to get the pills into my mouth. She held the cup of water as I gulped them down.

"But what am I going to do? I have a baby, no money, and I can't sing anymore. I don't know what to do!"

"You want him back?"

"No, there's no future for us. He's a stranger."

"Honey, find someone else who'll take care of you and the baby. Someone who won't leave you in the hospital after a miscarriage." She lifted the blanket and checked the rubber pad under me. "It hasn't broken through. Don't take it out on you body. You're pretty, and you're young. Your life's before you. You're lucky to have a baby." I started to cry again. "Be easy on yourself, honey. When you going home?"

"Maybe tomorrow, or the day after."

321

"You have your own kin? I mean, other than him?" She said the last few words with barely guarded contempt as she pointed her thumb to the door and snapped her head in that direction.

"Yes, but I can't call them. My father's dying of cancer, and my mother's devastated. I'll talk to my mother-in-law. She said she'd help me."

"Honey, blood's thicker than water. Now that you split, don't count on them."

"But they're fed up with him, too!"

"It don't matter. They'll gather around him like flies around a carcass. You'll see. Don't expect too much. I knows rich people. I've seen that rich lady who come to visit you. She your mother-in-law?"

"Yes."

"Don't expect too much from her."

"But he refused to pay for the miscarriage. Who can I turn to for help? They have the money; why shouldn't they help me?" I started to cry again.

"Don't cry, honey. You going to make yourself feel worse. Listen! Get rid of him. He's not worth your tears! Rich peoples different than poor folk. Rich peoples tight as a crab's ass when it comes to parting with their money. Call your own momma. She'll help you, you'll see!"

"What's your name?" I asked the kindly dark mountain of a woman who, with concern in her eyes, was leaning over me and holding my hand.

"Verna. My name is Verna." I sent her name through the my brain, through the haze the tranquilizers were creating in me. Verna, April twenty-first, vernal equinox, equal day, equal night, to go, to stay, fifty-fifty. Just keep going. Phil Silvers' advice floated back to me. The nurse's name sounded like a good omen, a new beginning. I watched as she fixed my blanket, tucked me in and left the room. "Just keep going" echoed in my head; then my mind stilled. It seemed to go into a chamber filled with cotton. Before I sailed away in the arms of Morpheus, I called Dorothy.

"Mother, would you please lend me or Jimmy some money? He won't pay for the miscarriage. I want to go home!"

"Oh, Bawrsha, how terrible! How can he do that? I'll see you to-morrow." I placed the receiver down in its cradle. The phone had its own cradle. The baby's cradle was empty!

The next morning, I was ready to go home to face my life, and I waited for Dorothy to either lend me or her son some money so he could pay my hospital bill. It wasn't so much. Part of it was covered by my hospitalization insurance with <u>Music Man</u>. All I needed was two hundred dollars. The pain subsided. Only an empty dull ache still throbbed under the gladiator's belt on my body. They pulled out the gauze, and my stomach had flattened down. I was totally off painkill-ers, and even stopped taking sleeping pills. The tranquilizers from the night before had worn off.

My thoughts became my own again. Could all of this be happen-ing to me? Was this the way it was supposed to be? This was not what I had wanted, not what I had studied and prepared myself for. They say you have to be very careful what you wish for, or you might get it. They also say that wish fulfillment is a double-edged sword; it cuts both ways, to the good and to the bad. I wanted to sing, to be in the theater. I got that. I wanted to get a degree in philosophy and become educated. I got that. I wanted to be part of that glittering center that was show business and not be pushed to the periphery any more. I got that, but at what price? I got smack dab in the center, but I also got Jimmy and the Hammersteins. Now I was giving it all up and had to raise a baby by myself to boot.

It couldn't have happened to that wonder-filled little girl picking bachelor buttons and poppies in the wheat fields behind our house in Minsk-Mazowiecki in Poland. I hadn't dreamed those dreams then. It must have happened somewhere after that, after we landed in this country, somewhere in Jersey City, in P.S. 22, where I vowed I would show them when they laughed at me for my strange ways and my broken English.

Chapter 30

On the first day of school, after we sailed across the Atlantic on the S.S. <u>Batory</u> and landed in Hoboken, New Jersey, then moved to Union City, Poppa ushered us in before him, speaking less English than he had led us to believe. He dressed for the occasion, wearing his best dark suit with a vest, his pocket watch with the gold chain, his grey spats with the shiny buttons on the side (like black beetles all marching in a row), his felt hat and his shiny amber-topped cane. It would be all right, he said. But, it wasn't. Momma had to work; she had already found a job. Poppa pushed and pulled us reluctantly to school.

In Poland, school was held in great respect, and we brought those same feelings of respect with us to this country. Momma dressed us in our finest dark green velvet dresses, with the large white lace collars. She mended the cotton lisle stockings and made sure the garters moved up and down. My sister and I both had our hair cut in the Buster Brown style. It was as if someone had put a pot over each of our heads and trimmed in a straight line around its edges. Our foreign-looking haircuts gave the Americans kids another reason to laugh at us.

I stood bewildered and lost in front of the class with its many different faces. Some were familiar, with light brown hair like my own; others had dark hair and dark eyes, like Gypsies. The colored children amazed me, with their brown skins and curly braided hair sticking straight out from some of their heads. I had never seen a brown-skinned person before because there were no blacks in Poland. Some of the kids sitting before me had red hair and pink faces. I wondered if they were Jewish. In Poland, I had learned that only Jews had red hair. Later, I found out that the red-haired, pink-faced kids were from Ireland and Scotland, countries on the other side of the world.

Poppa clicked his heels, lifted his hat, pinched the pince-nez on his nose and kissed the teacher's hand. She giggled, turned red and looked embarrassed, while the rest of the class laughed. I spoke no English, and they spoke no Polish. The teacher directed me to a wooden desk attached to a small chair. I sat down as I was told, surrounded by curious, giggling faces. Poppa left my homeroom, dragging my reluctant sister behind him. One little girl leaned over to touch my velvet dress and white lace collar. I yanked myself away as if I had been scalded, and wanted to run after my father. But there was no place to run.

At recess time, the kids played games of Farmer-in-the-Dell, Hide-n-Seek, hopscotch and tag. In the beginning, I had trouble learning the sequence of Farmer-in-the-Dell. Who took what, after the wife took the child? With my heart beating, I muffed my lines when my turn came, and was one of the last picked when the leaders chose up sides. That was the cruelest time of all, standing with the other kids, waiting for them--the popular kids, usually boys--to choose up sides. They did, picking first their friends, then the kids who were good. As the numbers around me dwindled and as the two teams grew, I stood there in humiliation, hurt that I was always one of the last to be chosen because I didn't speak the language. In my mind, I had learned the sequence to Farmer-in-the-Dell. When my turn came, I panicked, and wrong words came out, or I stuttered and lost my place.

At that time, in P.S. 22 in Jersey City, after we moved from Union City, there was a class of retarded children. Those children were later called "special." Then, they were called retarded, and worse names were tacked onto them. There were Mongoloids with crusty eyes who dribbled, two kids with enormous heads that wobbled when they ran, and an enormous fat girl who screeched most of the time. Some sat and rocked on the cold pavement; others banged their heads on the walls. At recess, in one of the corners of the schoolyard, they circled around each other. The regular kids were warned to leave them alone and not to make fun of them.

One day, after I had gone over my lines in Farmer-in-the-Dell, I waited in humiliation until I was the last to be chosen for the team. When my turn came, I muffed my lines was laughed at, and with tears in my eyes, I stumbled around the yard by myself. One of the Mongoloid boys came over to me, bent over, looked me straight in the face and started to pat my head. I recoiled, repulsed by the gesture, partially from his difference and partially from the fear that the regular kids would see me. I was embarrassed to be seen with the retards, but I had no choice. Since no one else wanted to play with me, I reluctantly joined them in the corner of the school yard at their disjointed games. They did a lot of circling around and falling, all accompanied by a great deal of laughter. Speech was not a necessity in their games. My lack of English was not a hindrance. I had been accepted. My relief lasted for only a few days. Some of the regular boys spotted us and came around to make fun of our games. They pointed us out, mimicking the lolling heads and spastic arms. All the other kids joined them and exploded with laughter. I was part of the group being ridiculed. The teachers ran out and stopped the hilarity. The retarded kids had joined in the laughter, not knowing they had been the butt of the joke. I raged in silent impotent fury.

After ethologists began to study animals in their natural habitat, they found that dogs, apes and human beings hate being laughed at and ridiculed.

Sometime between breakfast and lunch, as I drifted in and out of sleep, Dorothy came into my hospital room. I woke with a start, in a cold sweat. A darkness had embraced me. I opened my eyes to see Dorothy silhouetted in the light, peeling off her long beige gloves, finger by finger. Her shadow fell over me as she loomed over the bed, blocking the morning sun. Instantly, I sensed that something else had gone terribly wrong in the way she busied herself with her gloves and with her beige linen jacket. It sent a chill of premonition through me. What else could have happened? Did someone else die?

"Is everything all right?" I blurted out.

"Yes, dear. I thought you were resting." Her eyes never met mine. Those watery eyes that a few days before gazed at me with such perplexed grief now darted around the hospital room. "How do you feel, Bawrsha? You look better." She threw me a furtive glance. Something was definitely wrong.

"I want to go home. The doctor says it's all right. How's Dad?" Oscar had left the hospital right after Reggie's death and was recuperating at home.

"He's at home. Harold's taking care of him."

"And Andy?"

"He's fine. We've had such a good time. The maid brings him to me in the morning while I have my breakfast tray, and we play together. Even Ockie seems to enjoy him."

"And Jimmy?"

"He brought his suitcases over. It seems you had another fight." She knew we had parted again and that he had refused to pay for the miscarriage, but to her, it was just another fight. Obviously, they had discussed the incident.

"Did Jimmy say anything?"

"No, Bawrsha. He's a remote kind of boy. Maybe he shouldn't have married so early in life. I know he tried to support you and Andy, but he's had a difficult time. Maybe he's too young for marriage. Men are strange creatures; they don't like unpleasantness and can turn their backs on it."

"Then, what do I do? I have a baby, and I'm not well. We're in debt. I can't even get out of here." I looked around the hospital room.

"Well, dear, you've both said things to each other that can't be recalled, cruel things. He is, after all, sensitive, even if he is very quiet. When you break something like a marriage or a vase, you can't really fix it. I mean, the cracks will always be there, no matter how carefully you glue them back together." She strained for the metaphor.

"Mother, all marriages have cracks in them. Memories of the muffled sounds from their bedroom at The Farm, after the Polish maids left, came back to me.

"That may be true. But Oscar and I never really said cruel things to each other, not cruel enough to break the vase. I mean, our bond. We've always had our bond. Our love was always strong enough." She continued talking, taking the end of my marriage to her son for granted. "When you get home, you should study French and get yourself another husband. Your doctor seems like a nice attractive man. He seems to like you, and he'd make a wonderful father for Andy. Is he married?"

"I never asked him." Pain filled my body, along with suppressed rage. "What are you saying, Mother?"

"Well, dear, you and Jimmy don't seem to make each other happy. You both seem to need something else. You're much more emotional and . . . basic than he is." She searched for a word and settled for "basic." I wondered what else flashed through her mind. "Jimmy needs to be left alone. Maybe he needs to grow up. You'll have Andy. He'll have no one. This separation will be more difficult for him in the long run." She already had us divorced. "Andy is such a charming child. He's clean and sweet-smelling. His nose doesn't even run." She ran her fingers through her red hair as she searched for adequate words to evaluate her grandson.

"He has a deviated septum; it all runs inside," I offered in assistance. She brushed the remark aside.

"Anyway, anyone would be lucky to get him." She paused. "And you, of course." Of course, but not you, or your son, or the rest of your family. You never felt lucky to get me. I began to understand the ramifications of the conversation they must have had with their son.

"Have you really spoken to Jimmy? I mean, is this how he really feels?" I knew it was over, but I didn't know how much he told them. She grew red, then white, put her gloves on and then pulled them off again.

"Well, yes, we spoke to him, and then Oscar called Howard Reinheimer."

"You called your lawyer? Why?" The chasm between us was growing and deepening into the Grand Canyon.

"Well, yes. You asked us to help you and Jimmy with your miscarriage, and Ockie called Howard to see what we could do. Howard said that we shouldn't become involved. It would constitute a commitment on our part. Howard said that the responsibility was Jimmy's and not ours. We'll make sure he takes care of you and Andy. It's a matter of principle. He has to grow up and assume the responsibility until you remarry or get a job." I couldn't believe what I was hearing from this impeccably dressed woman, my soon to be former mother-in-law, who stood at the foot of my bed, blocking out my sun.

"How am I going to get out of here? Jimmy refused to pay for the miscarriage!" Visions of spending the rest of my life in the hospital flashed before my eyes.

"I don't know what he said to you, but I'm sure you'll work it out. Ockie said that if you or Andy ever need a coat from Saks or something like that, you could turn to us, but Howard advised us that we can't 'keep' you." I lay in the hospital bed, stunned by what she was saying to me. If I or Andy ever needed a coat from Saks, we could turn to them for a handout? They wouldn't "keep" me! All I was asking for was for them to help me to get out of the hospital, and the bill was only two hundred dollars. It wasn't as if I asked them for a small fortune. Only prostitutes and high-priced call girls were "kept," and she knew that. Through barely controlled rage, I heard her droning on.

"We'll see that Jimmy takes care of you and Andy. He has to assume that responsibility. It's a matter of principle," she repeated, as if she had learned the phrase by heart. "Don't worry; you'll probably get a job soon and remarry."

She leaned over, and the sun blinded my eyes as she patted my hand and rose to leave. The audience was over. Her traveling royal highness made her proclamation and left the hospital room. I feared what I would say if I opened my mouth, so I lay on my cranked-up bed, shaking. Before she cleared the room, she looked over her shoulder and added, "Call me when you get home. I'll bring Andy over or have Arnie deliver him. He's such a darling boy. Chin up; things will get better! Good bye, Bawrsha!"

My heart began to thunder in my chest; my body began to shake even more than before. I rang for the nurse, pleading for a tranquilizer to put me out of my pain and out of the realization that a warm wet spot had spread out under me on the bed. The pill relaxed me as the day nurse changed the pad, but a dull ache still throbbed in my womb. I slept, drugged from the still active sleeping pills and the added tranquilizers and woke much later in the afternoon. The smoldering heat of August created a darkness on the edge of the horizon, bringing with it clouds that engulfed the city and promised a violent summer thunderstorm. The wind preceded the rain, with the tips of the trees wildly thrashing about and the leaves spiraling in gusts up to the rooftops. A carpet of black clouds rolled across the sky. Flashes of light and a crash of thunder in the distance at La Guardia Airport announced the coming of a cooling shower. The first large drops spattered on the windows, and the whole city scrunched down, waiting for the avalanche of rain to pass.

I wanted to stand there out in that cool, wet, driving rain and let it purify me, let it run down my face and body, taking with it the crusty accumulations of four years. I wanted to get Mother Nature back into me, to reconnect with the Earth and become whole again. I wanted to be part of some larger truth, part of a greater reality, more profound than my marriage and the current trivia that surrounded my life.

<u>Let the wind dry my tears. Let the rain purify me. Let the sun heal me. Let me have courage again. Let me help my son to know the joy and wonder that I had known as a child.</u>

The pelting rain died down outside of my window. The rivulets stopped their manic descent down the window panes. As the sky grew lighter, the clouds parted, and the sun burst through. Through the remaining storm that worked its way up north, up the Hudson Valley, a rainbow curved against the blue clouds. It's going to be all right I thought, ever the optimist. I don't know how long it would take, but someday I knew it would be all right. All I had to do was to "just keep going."

I called Momma to ask for the two hundred dollars to get out of the hospital. She took the day off from work to go to the bank and then to make another trip to the city to give it to me. There was little conversation between us. She realized that something must have been terribly wrong for the very rich Hammersteins not to help me, but it would have been too tactless for her to ask. I needed the money, so she brought it, without making any detours to ask for a lawyer's advice. It would have stunned her into disbelief that my in-laws wouldn't help their son with his wife's miscarriage. She had no frame of reference for that kind of indifferent, principled behavior. She was ruled more by her emotions and a sense of family.

Even after I left the hospital, back in the gathering storm of my life, I was pursued by dreams. They came back with a rush. I no longer ran alone, but held a baby high in my arms. I had to get out of the way of something terrible that was pursuing me.

These backyards seem endless. I can't see who it is, but I know they are chasing me. You look like me. No, you look like my father or more like Jimmy, but you're really The Old Man. Let's get out through the hole in the fence. Let's leave the graves behind. Look! There are black leaves on the ground. The buildings are all black, too. We have to get out of here! Can't you run by yourself? I'll hold the big iron door open for you. There seems to be no one here, but we have to run! It's a spiral staircase. Let me guide you. I think they must be on the stairs behind us now! Here's a door! Let's lock it behind us! There's no lock! Run faster, faster! Another black alley, another empty street, another faceless black building, another door with a lock that doesn't work! They're trying to get in! I can't hold them back! It's so quiet! Run, Andy, run! I'll get help, I'll hold them off!

I'd wake up shaking, alone in my bed, back in the apartment with Andy sleeping across the room in his crib. After checking the doors, I'd lie back in the bed, take the tranquilizers and watch the hamster as it ran in slow motion on the wheel of my mind until the first light of dawn illuminated the dark corners of the bedroom.

What had gone wrong between Jimmy and me? Was there ever anything right? Could it have been that our backgrounds were so different? Was it that we never connected, never meshed gears, or whatever happens to make a marriage possible? I blamed myself and my inadequacies. I didn't know how to be married. Still, I blamed him even more. He was the man. Information that had been withheld from me because I was a woman was available to him because he was a man, or so I thought. He also came from the rich; therefore he should have known better.

"You're upset, but not because I'm immoral. I'm amoral. I don't deal with morality," he often told me and laughed when I accused him of arrogance and contempt in his dealings with people. Can there be a common ground for fairness and justice if there is no awareness of morality? My sin-drenched Catholic background couldn't deal with his lack of fair play or his lack of the concept of justice. He smiled as he repeated that he was not immoral; that implied dealing with morality. He was amoral! He didn't even deal with it.

I often wondered what he felt for me when he told me he loved me. What did he want from me? Just to be there? Just to walk silently around on the periphery of his life, never asking questions, never discussing our problems? A silent presence not to be dealt with? I took the vows "in sickness and in health" but not "in silence."

I tried to get him to join me in therapy or marriage counseling, but since Oscar didn't believe in all that, he, too, refused to go. In retrospect, Oscar may have been right. I don't much believe in it anymore, but at that time, it might have started us talking, and our ultimate parting might not have been so mean, so ugly, and so vindictive. We might have been able to lighten our rage, to defuse some of it, to purge ourselves of some of our resentments, and not be left with a burden that the years of silence locked into our marriage.

I assumed that he, too, was left with a burden, but I might have been wrong. All he seemed to be left with was a vague discomfort that he had created a responsibility for a former wife and child. "A fucking drag" was the way that he referred to it. The ultimate withdrawal dealt with his hiding behind accountants and lawyers, as his father and his great grandfather had done before him. He became a shadow upon an impenetrable stone wall, like Plato's cave dwellers.

One of the things that Uncle Arthur had spoken about with pride about Oscar I was the fact that the Old Man himself never took part in any of his lawsuits. Business managers and lawyers took care of his legal affairs and finances. My father-in-law initially hid behind lawyers when I asked him for help to get me out of the hospital and eventually to "fuck me over" with his legal advisors, as Jimmy subsequently explained to our son. Jimmy also had learned his lessons well at the family knee, hiding behind lawyers and accountants, when I periodically was reduced to plead with him to pay for his growing son's needs.

Still, I was afraid to go on alone. Although I had begun to hate him, the hate itself was familiar. The world outside, with a small child, held many fears and had become unfamiliar ground to me. I would no longer be in that hallowed Hammerstein circle, no longer part of that deceptively glittering world. I had to return to my own life, not the life of a wife, the mere appendage of a man, but my own life, not realizing that I set myself up in another appendage situation, that of motherhood.

What dreams could I dream now? There were no dreams left. I had to heal my body, raise my child. The careening roller-coaster of my childhood dreams dove down to the bottom of the hill, crashed through the ice, fell to the bottom of the lake and then went even deeper, to the bottom of the well itself.

I had gotten all I had ever wanted. I had all my wishes fulfilled. Suspicious of the fickle genie of wish fulfillment, I feared to rub the vessel again, afraid to cut my fingers on that double-edged sword. Dreams that had been the companions of my youth, and which sustained my ambitions, brought me no joy. I covered that part of my life with a thick impenetrable blanket. I stopped dreaming, fearing that my dreams might wake me up to another nightmare. Not understanding the process, I turned off a vital force in myself, the force of optimism, and with it, the will to live. I started to mark time in place. Despair overwhelmed me. The financial morass into which I sank stayed with me for many years.

My health suffered from the miscarriage. The supreme self-confidence that had been mine and had become so badly bruised by my marriage to Jimmy and the Hammersteins needed time to heal. I tried singing. The panic that clutched at me only during auditions became my constant companion, even when I was alone. I would start to sing in the empty apartment, but my heart would start to beat loudly and my knees would begin to shake. I couldn't get a breath deep enough to sustain a tone. I feared fainting in the wings again, as I done in Music Man, and knew that my wounded voice wouldn't carry past the footlights, even for an audition.

After trying to take typing and steno courses at a local business school, as Momma had always encouraged me to do, I realized I couldn't continue, not only because my hands shook too much, but that kind of single focused concentration was beyond me. I got a job as a receptionist at the office of theatrical lawyers, Weissburger and Frosch. Years before at the garment center, thanks to my old friend, Max Kolmer, I had learned to operate a switchboard. It never occurred to me that the time would come when I would have to work it again, to support myself and my son.

It was ironic that people I had known socially, with whom I had long conversations at so many dinner parties, and some who had come to my home, didn't even recognize my voice. I became an anonymous person who oiled the wheels of theatrical intercourse as I answered the switchboard.

Babysitters became a massive expense. There were few day care centers that were available or affordable in the late Fifties. Jimmy stopped sending me money. I appealed to the family again (We kept in loose contact because Dorothy wanted to keep in touch with Andy), banking on the hope that they would see to it that Jimmy would fulfill his responsibility to Andy and me, as they had assured me.

The last time I saw Oscar was in the family home on the East Side. We sat across from each other, in that impeccably outfitted sitting room with its needlepoint rugs and fresh flowers everywhere. The silver picture frames holding those smiling faces were in place. My face was not among them. Dorothy had wanted to see Andy, and I, with a storm of mixed feelings, brought him over. Knowing how Oscar felt about money, I hated to bring up the issue again. Bloomingdale's had placed our unpaid account in the hands of a collection agency, and the collector had threatened to come to the office where I worked and to attach my receptionist's salary. The money I had brought to the marriage was all gone. Since I had deferred to Jimmy's wish of not wanting to be gauche when we married, I didn't even have an engagement ring to hock. My salary barely covered the rent, food and babysitters' fees.

Oscar looked tired and worn. He had aged greatly from his two recent operations. Folds of skin that hung down the sides of his face were barely concealed by the maroon ascot that circled his grooved neck. I had never seen him wear a robe during the day. He had always been meticulous about his dress. Flower Drum Song had opened. It was during the rehearsals of the show that Oscar had a dream. In his dream, the show was in trouble; it needed to be fixed by having some of the scenes cut. He realized that the scene that had to be deleted was crucial to the love story. It was the scene where boy meets girl. If boy didn't meet girl, then there would be no story. He woke up from the dream, perplexed. I wondered what he was trying to prune out of his own life at the time: his marriage, his love affair, or Jimmy's mess with me? He obviously solved the problem with the stage presentation, for Rodgers and Hammerstein repeated their "theater magic" and brought in a hit. Flower Drum Song ran for seventy-five weeks and earned a million dollars.

We had some white wine. As I sipped from my glass, I looked over at him, deeply resenting that he had gone to his lawyers when I had asked him for help to get out of the hospital. He feared for his money, for the millions he ultimately left to the government in taxes.

335

His son might have been a burden and a disappointment to him, but he was, after all, his son. I was not only his son's estranged wife, who sat facing him, hat in hand, but was also becoming more and more of a problem. I was making him uncomfortable by asking for him to intervene. He had no lawyers or accountants to hide behind in his taupe-colored living room. He had to face me.

As we exchanged civil pleasantries, he shifted his now much lighter bulk in the deep satin pillows, and I could sense his growing discomfort. He couldn't cross the street to get away from me, as he had done in the past when he had encountered a blind person or the presence of any other "human weakness." Jimmy was living upstairs in that elegant townhouse, surrounded by servants flitting around him, as the butterflies flitted around the walls at The Farm. Oscar didn't like to be reminded that his son's wife and his grandchild were in financial trouble. It was O.K. to be poor, but it wasn't O. K. to confront the Hammersteins with the fact. To Dorothy, poverty like labor, had a certain degree of nobility. But it was "bad taste," "bad form" to look poor, or to admit to being poor. Having a conversation with him about money put me in the category of using "bad form." As always, he was cordial, and even more than usually remote.

We spoke of Andy, whom he thought was a "nice kid," and he almost unconsciously moved his arms and shoulders away from the thought of physical contact, echoing his more apparent withdrawal when he had actually met him a few minutes before. The conversation turned to what I was doing. I told him about my job at the switchboard. It wasn't too taxing, I could sit all day without too much strain, and I needed the money. He seemed surprised.

"Doesn't Jimmy send you any money?"

"No. I haven't heard from Jimmy since we parted in the hospital, and he hasn't sent me any money or taken care of any of the bills."

"Can you live off what you make at the switchboard?"

"No."

"Why don't you continue your singing career now that you don't have a marriage to interfere with it?" He leaned his chin on his fingers

336

as he looked levelly at me. There was a cold detachment in his voice and more than a hint of censure.

"I can't seem to sing anymore! My breath is too shallow, and I get hoarse when I sing. I guess it'll take time. In the meantime, Dad, I need your help. Would you talk to Jimmy and ask him to send me some money? I know he works for you now, so he can't be that broke."

"He's paying off a lot of debts."

"I know, but taking care of his son is not a debt; it's a responsibility. Mother said I could come to you if I needed help. All I want is for you to see that Jimmy sends me some money, so I can get Bloomingdale's off my neck and keep Con Ed and the telephone company happy."

"Well, Basia, you'll have to work that out with him. I'll talk to him, but I don't know how much that will do. You can't get blood from a stone. Jimmy has to grow up and assume responsibility for his life. I can't keep bailing him out of trouble."

I suggested a way out. "Would it help to have some kind of legal agreement drawn up, to put him on some kind of a schedule, until we decide what to do? Maybe it would force him to confront his responsibilities better, and I wouldn't have to bother you."

"It might." He fidgeted again, not liking the direction the conversation was taking.

"I don't want to do anything to make things worse. Could you recommend someone? Maybe Howard could. Maybe he could recommend a mutual lawyer who could draw up an agreement, to put Jimmy on some kind of regimen?" Since Oscar never moved without conferring with his lawyers, bringing Howard into the mix might open an area of possible mutual accommodation.

"That would imply a separation agreement." The lawyer in Oscar surfaced.

"Yes, I think so."

"I'll talk to both Howard and Jimmy about it." He finished his white wine, and I finished mine. The Lord Chesterfield talk was over. I could hear Andy laughing upstairs in Dorothy's bedroom, so I excused myself and left. It seemed awkward to kiss even the air over his ear, so I refrained from doing so.

A few days later, a lawyer called me. The family, at the recommendation of Howard Reinheimer, had gotten in touch with him, and he would see what he could do about getting me some money. In the meantime, I was to make a list of my expenses. Letters were exchanged. No papers were signed as Jimmy remained a shadow in the background. Checks in the amount of a hundred and fifty dollars a week started arriving at my apartment.

Chapter 31

There were no more weekend treks to The Farm in Doylestown. All those doors shut behind me as I left. Instead of going west to Pennsylvania on the weekends, I now ventured east to Farmingdale, Long Island, to stay with Momma. Ever since the realization that Poppa's lingering disease would be fatal, Momma had grown more increasingly desperate.

My last visit with him, at the time of my separation, was more for my mother's sake than for his. I went because of her insistence, following her to St. Albans Veteran's Hospital. Poppa lay in a small room at the end of a long white and noisy corridor. He had shrunk and looked tiny on his narrow hospital palette. That once-towering angry presence of my life lay shriveled and wasted under the covers. The skin around his skull and face didn't sag. It stretched tightly over the high cheekbones, giving him a cadaverous look. I never really knew the color of his eyes. Sometimes they seemed a blue-gray, and at other times, they seemed hazel. Now they had shrunk so deeply into his skull that the color was indiscernible. As I gently touched his hand, the warmth of his fingers surprised me. They lay still on the covers. I looked at him, and the anger I had felt for him seemed senseless. In front of me on his death bed lay my father, another man I hardly knew. Who was it that lived behind those sunken eyes? Who was it who had raged through our house filling my youth with such fear and chaos? Another male stranger passing through my life.

Momma added the flowers she had brought to the existing display on the window sill, never taking her eyes off him. She busied herself throwing away the faded blossoms and sprucing up the remaining ones, waiting for his approval. My eyes filled with tears, as I looked at my tormentor and, now, my latest tragedy.

"How are you, Poppa?"

"Ah, Basiunia, you come to see me." I could barely hear his raspy voice. The cadaverous face looked more like Stalin's than ever. We had called him Stalin when he went into one of his towering rages. His hair had turned almost white, softening the sharp widow's peak on his forehead, but his bushy eyebrows still bristled.

"Yes, Poppa."

"Mamusia says you have trouble...big trouble," he rasped out.

"Don't talk, Tatusiu. You sound very weak."

"Is all right. I get better soon," his squeaky voice wheezed out. "Basiu, I tink about your problem. I have idea. Sue the sons-of-bitches. They have to help you. Andzejek need home. You need money to live. Take them to court, get in papers, make them trouble. The sons-of-bitches don wan papers to show them up for what cheap bastards they are. You see, they help you."

"Poppa, they aren't responsible for me. I married their son, and Jimmy has no money. At least that's what he says." My mind returned to the six thousand dollars that he was going to invest in <u>Flower Drum Song</u>, and I wondered if I could have been wrong.

"They no help him? What kind of people are they?" The raspy voice sank back into itself, as he coughed and his thin body shook under the sheet. I looked at him. In the past, I would have argued and thrown back at him. Not unlike you, Poppa; you never helped me, either! I had to put myself through school, while you made your nephew Bolek into a doctor! Now I held my tongue.

"I have idea for you," he continued. "Mamusia say you need help. Come live with us. I go home soon. We have room upstairs. Come live with us."

"Thank you, Poppa. When you get home, I'll move out there, but now I need help in the city." I played his game of hope.

"I tink about your trouble. Go to Polish Consulate, get nice Polish lady off boat. She help you, you see. Go to Polish Consulate, get Polish lady."

The raspy voice grew even more breathy and then silent. His thin blue-veined arms twitched and stood out against the stark whiteness of the sheet. He still wore his wedding ring on his right hand. It looked like an enormous ill-fitting collar on his gnarled and bony finger.

"He fall asleep now." Momma hovered over him and tucked the blankets around him. "We go."

I followed her down the long white corridor. I never saw Poppa alive again. The following day, he lapsed into a coma and came out of it only once to say to my mother, who sat at his bedside every night, holding his thin, warm hand, "Juz, Juziu, juz" (enough, Josie, enough), and he died. Up to that last moment, he never admitted he was on his death bed. It was as if he had willed himself to hold out until he could give me the last piece of advice about getting a lady from the Polish Consulate. Until the last moment. Momma brought him fresh fruit and flowers from the garden every night. She combed his hair and waited.

"What is she waiting for?" I asked my sister, not getting an answer from my mother, except for an impatient shrug. "For him to die?"

"No," my sister answered. "She was waiting for him to tell her that he loved her, that he always loved her."

"Did he ever tell her?"

"No, he died without ever letting her know that he loved her."

"A prick to the end."

I shook my head as the old anger and resentment returned. I could see Momma sitting by his bedside, waiting for those few words that would have given such comfort to her life, but he never even gave her that. Death absorbed him with those few words left unspoken, words that would have justified her devotion and loyalty to him.

Chapter 32

The spin that began its journey from the center with the death of Uncle Reggie, gathering in its sinuous return my miscarried baby, expanded another encircling coil to include Andrzej Redzisz, my father. It moved slowly and imperceptively through our lives from the point of its inception out of some dark hole to leave a red stain upon the absorbent surface of life.

After we buried Poppa, my problems with Jimmy resurfaced. History was repeating itself. The weekly checks stopped coming. My calls to the house went unanswered. After I called his theater, I found out that he had quit <u>Flower Drum Song</u> and had taken up another hit-it-big project. He was developing Hunter Mountain in New York State, for skiing.

As I was leaving one of my messages for Jimmy with the butler, Oscar, who had a habit of listening in on the phone conversations of his children, interrupted my call and confronted me with the fact that Jimmy had given them, his parents, his word that he would take care of his responsibilities. He had given them his word; why should he lie? Didn't they help me to get a lawyer to get him in line?

"But, Dad, I have nothing in writing!"

"Then maybe you should get a separation agreement, after all!" Jimmy had refused to sign anything and didn't want a separation agreement.

"But he quit his job! How is he going to help me?"

"Well, Basia, you can't get blood out of a stone!" Oscar repeated his favorite lyric. "If he has it, I'll see to it that he sends it on to you. If he doesn't, then you can't squeeze it out of him. We've decided he has to grow up."

"Dad, this doesn't involve only me; it also involves your grandson. I have to create a life for him, and my salary doesn't cover our expenses. Why are you taking a stand with him at this time? He won't suffer; he lives at home with you. I'm the one who's being hurt, and through me, your grandson. Jimmy's not going to change. I can't even go on welfare. They'd laugh us out of the place. Andy's name is Oscar Hammerstein the Third."

"I'm aware of his name, Basia." A long, long pause pushed through the silence on the telephone. "I'll talk to Jimmy and the lawyers..." Oscar's voice grew testy.

"Can't you lend him some money? I mean, you've done it in the past and bailed him out of trouble with his projects. Look at it this way; Andy is his project and he needs developing. I'll take care of his immediate needs, but Jimmy has to help me with his financial needs."

"I'll see what I can do. I can't make any promises. He has to assume his own responsibilities!" Oscar's voice sounded a bit raspy, like Poppa's just before he died. I pushed back a light that had gone off somewhere inside me. We hung up, leaving the unpleasantness and silence hanging in the air between us. I didn't know what Jimmy was telling them. The money stopped, and he never visited his son.

A few more weeks went by, and no one called me, not the family, not the lawyer, not Jimmy. I called again, and this time got Dorothy. She couldn't understand why I was still "bothering" them, as she put it. Jimmy had assured the family that he was taking care of his son.

"Ask him to show you canceled checks! He's not sending me anything!"

"He says he is, Bawrsha. It would be insulting for me to ask him

343

to show us canceled checks. I don't know what you want from us. There is nothing we can do."

We hung up angry. He was lying to them, and they believed him. There was no response from the lawyer they had gotten for me. He must have realized that the family was not going to pressure Jimmy, and he didn't want to offend them. After all, he had been engaged by the family lawyers. To get some kind of representation, I had to go outside of the family. I had to stand on my own two feet. I had to make a complete break with them. As Verna, the nurse at her hospital had told me, "Blood's thicker than water," and they were his family, not mine, even though there was a baby who needed care.

I started looking for someone else to represent me. The first divorce lawyer, recommended by a colleague at work, was Arnold Krakauer, who, after hearing my story and my meager demands, literally jumped at the chance to represent me. After failing to get through to Jimmy and his lawyer, he appealed directly to Oscar and Dorothy. They invited him to dinner, having met him casually before through his ex-wife, Kathleen Winsor, the author of Forever Amber. After his dinner with the Hammersteins, Arnold Krakauer joined their social circle, and I never heard from him again. I later learned that he was quite bitter about his own divorce. As a result, he had little compassion for most of the women he subsequently represented. I wondered what conversations Arnold Krakauer had with my former in-laws, what lawyer-client confidences he might have betrayed to ingratiate himself with theatrical royalty.

I felt trapped by frustration as I sat at the switchboard and tried to find another lawyer. Many attorneys who returned my calls were very impressed by my situation. One lawyer couldn't promise me enough. He saw no problems in getting me not only enough money to live on, but a settlement and a trust fund for my son. He went on for half an hour assuring me that everything would be all right and that he was the lawyer for me. He would get in touch with Jimmy's lawyers. My second visit with him was very different. When I asked him questions about what we had covered in our initial meeting, he denied ever promising me anything. He told me he had called the Hammerstein lawyers and learned there would be no settlement for me or trust fund for my son. It was as if I had spoken to a different person in my first conversation with him. It also felt as if he were taping the second conversation. Years later, I found out that his original confidence grew out of the fact that he had gotten one of Jimmy's lawyers his divorce and was on friendly terms with the firm. He was advised to drop me, and after not answering my calls, after a few weeks he did. Taping his interview with me was a way to protect himself after he had raised my hopes.

Then there were the lawyers who, once they realized that their fee would not be as extravagant as the Hammerstein name had promised, blatantly demanded sex as part of their payment. I was out in the world of men again. The protection for which I had sold my own birth right, my own being, dissolved with my marriage. I had to face reality on a level from which I had run and for which most women are never adequately prepared.

News about Jimmy filtered back to me through well-meaning friends. He was dating so-and-so. He was seen at this party and that dinner. I sat at the switchboard during the day and at home at night, raising his son, my health tentative, my body still raw from the miscarriage. Monthly periods that had always filled me with tension and cramps now incapacitated me. Tranquilizers filled my brain with fuzz. I sleepwalked through the days and stared at the ceiling at night.

Oscar appeared on TV interview shows. Although he looked thin and tired, he and Dick seemed excited about Sound of Music, their most current production, which was to become a perennial classic. It opened in November 1959. With that show, Oscar had written 1,589 songs. That year, he received the "Father of the Year" award. He commented that the award might be a "big surprise" to his children. I know it was to me, ranking second only to the "Kindest Man in the Theater" article, which had appeared earlier.

No matter where I turned, I couldn't get away from the Hammerstein situation. The theatrical switchboard was like a conduit of information as it passed through me before it came to rest with my employers. Endless gossip filtered back to me. The family was calling me a "golddigger." They felt I was trying to hit the family up for a great deal of money. One of my gay buddies sent an item to columnist Earl Wilson that stated,

WHAT DAUGHTER-IN-LAW OF WHAT FAMOUS BROADWAY LYRICIST AND PRODUCER IS LIVING NEAR POVERTY AND RAISING HIS NAMESAKE?

Earl Wilson ran to Oscar with the item, and the "old boy" network closed ranks behind them. Favors were exchanged, opening night tickets promised, and the "shared narrative" remained shared only by the inside theatrical community. The gay boys checked the paper daily for the item. It never appeared. After Oscar got the "Father of the Year" award and after months of silence and ugly gossip, I wrote Dorothy a letter.

Dear Dorothy:

Things said or written in anger are almost always irrevocable. It may be because they truly express what we feel. We usually hide the deeply felt emotions concerning our feelings under social constraints of politeness and good breeding. Only under the burning flare of anger are we left unhampered enough to be our more honest selves. I have put myself in a completely compromised position by turning to you with my problems and my plea for help. If I was ever in doubt about your feelings toward me, and have made any excuses about you, your ongoing reaction has made them perfectly clear.

After we spoke in the hospital as woman to woman, I thought that some kind of a bond had been established between us. It seems that I was wrong. You turned to me because your children weren't around to comfort you when Oscar needed his first operation. Now that he is out of the hospital and successfully pursuing his life, you don't need me and have reverted to your old critical, distant self.

Why at this point have you decided to cut Jimmy off from your help? Dad has been bailing him out ever since I knew him. Why, when both my son and I are at his mercy, have you decided not to help him? Are business debts more important to clear up than the debts he has toward me and his son? Jimmy is not going to change; he feels it his right to behave any way he wants to. You have fed into that by giving him a great deal of attention when he messes things up. He will keep messing up, just to get that attention. I never really understood the phrase, "the sins of the fathers are visited upon the children," until recently. Since I wasn't around when Jimmy was a child, I can't attest to his upbringing, but it seems to me that he was a lonely child. Bronchial asthma is an emotional disease, in spite of what the doctors say. Jimmy has had it since childhood. He grew up like a weed, with no guidance, no attention. You told me yourself that you hardly ever spoke to him when he was growing up. By cutting him off financially, you are only hurting me and Andy. He is getting more attention now than he has ever received in his whole life. You say that I don't trust anyone. That is only partially true. I don't trust you anymore. I have turned to you in my hour of need from my hospital bed. You turned your back on me. Is this the time to wash your hands of your son? Your timing is cruel and suspect. I don't think that it will change him, and I am desperate about not only my but my son's future.

With your tactful concern, you have informed me that to help me directly would imply that I wanted to be "kept" and that it would spoil me. You know that only call girls and prostitutes are "kept." I find your assessment of me cruel and insulting. You advised me to get a job. I have a job! I work on a switchboard trying to make ends meet, while your son is jazzing around putting together another project that will lose him money, from which you will again bail him out, in spite of what you are now saying.

You seem to forget that I started to work at sixteen and should get some respect from you, since you look so favorably on the "nobility of labor." I also put myself through most of high school and six years of college. I went to school during the day and worked at night and at matinees, all at the same time I studied singing and acting. By the time I married your son, I had a fully paid-up car, most of my furni-

347

ture, a piano, money in the bank, a wardrobe, and some stocks and bonds. My days were filled with the "nobility of labor" from dawn to dusk. When I married your son, all of my assets were absorbed by the marriage. My savings went, so did my stocks and bonds. The babysitters were paid for by unemployment insurance when I was unable to work. So you see, even Jimmy never really "kept" me. I find your allegations cruel and unkind.

Other statements you have made to willing dispensers of gossip have filtered back to me, that I am a "golddigger" and am looking for a "handout" and that I am trying to hold up your son for a fortune. You have seen my meager list of expenses; it is not a secret. It happens to be in your lawyer's hands. Less than a thousand dollars a month is hardly the demand of a "golddigger" looking for a "handout."

Working on the switchboard eight hours a day takes me away from my son. I see in Jimmy what remote control in child care does to a small baby. I would like to go back into the theater, to sing again; that's what I've prepared myself for. Until I married your son and stepped into the morass of your family, I had a bright and optimistic outlook on my life, and a promising future. It will take a while for me to recoup my strength, my lost energy, my optimism and my faith in humanity. I didn't retire from the stage to be "kept" in comfort and luxury. I worked most of the time I was married to your son, taking time off only to have the baby and the miscarriage.

While I have asked you to see to it that your son fulfills his obligations, he has been living rent-free in your home, and now he has even quit the job that Dad gave him in Flower Drum Song. I have a child to raise and quake at being at his mercy.

Dad's award as Father of the Year stopped me in my tracks. For the writing of some pretty lyrics, he has been awarded a medal for being a wonderful father. The father of the year? He never talked to his children until they were old enough to play tennis or chess! By that time, it was too late to reach them. All the patterns had been set. He seems to show little reaction except physical withdrawal even when his grandson is around him. What kind of a father or grandfather is that?

Unfortunately, I got stuck with the product of that upbringing. As Dad told me, "You can't get blood out of a stone." You can't get love and affection from a stone either. Hammerstein is an appropriate name for your family; as hard as a hammer and as cold as a stone.

Perhaps it's better for me to have really found out how you feel. The offer of a coat from Saks for me, or for Andy, I find insensitive and again insulting and will not avail myself of your generosity. I will not dishonor myself by scratching at your table for scraps anymore. As you sagely put it, it might spoil my character, and I want to keep my character unblemished. Since we will probably have a minimum of contact in the future, may I wish you many happy anniversaries and Happy Birthdays, and all the other festivities that I might inadvertently forget about!

Basia

Gleeful gossips informed me that after receiving and reading the letter, Dorothy got bumps on her chest again. I had completely burned my bridges. There would be no possibility, no weak moment to turn back. After the letter and the unpublished item to Earl Wilson, the lines had become completely drawn. The job at the switchboard would be my main source of income. Co-workers and employers thought it strange that I had to work for them, but even at that time, they knew more about the history of the family and the rest of the Hammersteins than I did.

As Spinoza said about God and our inability to perceive the whole picture while we are on the inside, so it was with me. I had been on the inside of the family while I was married to one of the Hammersteins. The reality of what the family really looked like from the outside had not been available to me. I believed the mythology, the self-serving internal stories, when I was on the inside. When I stepped out, like Spinoza's corpuscle, I saw it from a whole different perspective. I saw the hypocrisy. The Hammersteins had wonderful press based on Oscar's talent, easy charm, gifts, opening night tickets, and other favors. Most people believed that his glorious lyrics, lyrics that were filled

349

with such romantic perception, lyrics that glorified love and adored children, had to come from a man who felt that way.

After Arnold Krakauer, my temporary lawyer, became their dinner guest and a series of other lawyers arched their way through my life, I settled for one who didn't demand sex from me. He drew up a temporary written agreement that promised me a hundred and fifty dollars a week. Jimmy reluctantly signed it. The money began to arrive regularly. Part of that original agreement and all the subsequent ones that I signed was that he had to visit his son regularly.

Now that I was no longer in the closed Hammerstein circle, friends I had made along the way, who had drifted away from me while I was married, re-entered my life. Most of them were the chorus gypsies with whom I had spent the early part of my career.

Before our complete severance and my letter to her, I had asked Dorothy to help me to get Andy into the Ethical Culture Pre-school. I wanted him to begin and continue his education, not only in a school setting I admired, but one that would allow him to experience his total scholastic career under one roof at the Ethical Culture School. We as children in this new country moved eleven times in the first three years after we landed in Hoboken. I wanted to save my son from that fate and allow him to spend kindergarten through high school in one place. Dorothy hemmed and hawed when I asked her for that particular help, hiding behind the principle that they didn't use their influence or status to gain favors.

Much as I chafed at my job on the switchboard, it carried with it serendipitous blessings, for it enabled me to meet Lee Light, who at that time was the executive secretary to Arnold Weissburger, one of my bosses. Through her I was able to meet Arnold's mother, who was on the Board of Directors of the Ethical Culture Society. It was Mrs. Weissburger who got Andy into the Ethical Pre-school. He would not have made it on his own. From a bubbly sunny baby, he became a whiny, unhappy child, affected by the separation, by the loss of his father and by the despair of my life. He clutched at me wherever we went, fearing that I, too, would leave him. At our interview for the pre-school, he hid behind my chair and refused to come out. Without Mrs. Weissburger's help, he would never have made it. I will be forever grateful to Lee Light and Mrs. Weissburger.

Lynda Lunch, who had become a friend from a former show, returned to my life and arranged an audition for me for Fiorello. Hal Hastings was the conductor with whom I had worked in Top Banana. The audition was petrifying. I could barely sing, but he remembered me from earlier, better days. Over the chords of my audition song, I heard him say to the pianist in the pit, "You should have seen her when she was young. A real knockout! We all tried to get into her pants!"

I hadn't known at that time that a line had formed around the block. Did he also defer to Jack Donohue, as Phil Silvers had done, assuming I was Jack's girl? There were better singers than I at the audition. Lynda was close to Hal and prevailed upon him to hire me. I was back in the chorus where I could again hide in a group, off the switchboard, not knowing what name to use, not knowing how long my voice would last.

At about the time I got into Fiorello, I realized that a woman raising a child alone needed help. The transient unreliable babysitters were a constant problem. Cancellations were not uncommon. My desperate last-minute calls to get someone to stay with Andy disrupted my life. Poppa's advice from his death bed bore fruit. After we buried him in Pine Lawn Veteran's Cemetery on Long Island, I called the Polish Consulate, and they sent me a lady who kept me from completely going over the edge.

History kept repeating itself. Not unlike his father, my son was also nurtured through the first years of his life not only by a Polish mother but also by a Polish maid named Julia Krawiec. She came to this country, literally getting off the plane with two shopping bags. For twenty-five dollars a week, plus room and board, she took over my life and took care of both of us. I don't know if I would have survived without her. Without knowing the language, she scouted out Jewish merchants on the West Side, discovered which ones had emigrated from Poland, and then proceeded to trade only with them. Her shopping forays became a social time when she could share human contact through the time-honored custom of haggling over the price of goods. She shopped, cooked, cleaned, laundered, and generally took care of both of us. She became to me, as I had been to Jimmy, a wife, except that she got paid for it.

Having gone through all the tragedy of the Second World War, she daily regaled me with stories of the horror she had experienced. I still see her, pumping back and forth in the rocker in my living room, her eyes wide open, her hands clasping and unclasping, recounting the story of the young Jewish woman running across a field, clutching her baby. The Germans sprayed the field with machine gun fire, decapitating her. Her headless body kept running across the field clutching the baby to her breast. Both were dead. Julia rocked like a victim of autism, as tears rolled down her face. I often wondered why I had been spared the horror of war in Poland. Was I saved for some mission? Did I have some role to play? At the time, it seemed difficult to believe.

I settled into a regimen of nightly performances, daily singing lessons, and weekly sessions on the couch. The legal nightmare continued. The barrage of lawyers that Oscar's money made available for his son, in spite of his principles and Lord Chesterfield lectures about responsibility, made me feel like a tiny female David, up against a towering behemoth of a Goliath. Oscar wouldn't help Jimmy to help support us, but he could share his money and his power to fight us. The brother of the judge who had married us four years before became my legal adversary. Every single tiny point had to be hammered out. Did I really need fifteen dollars a month for the laundry? What about the expenses for transportation? How could buses add up to twenty five dollars a month? I envied Momma her widowhood. It had a clean finality to it. Divorce kept the wounds open, never letting them heal. Momma's wounds, like her memories, could fade back into the past, and maybe in time become comforting. Mine, in my separation and divorce, were scraped open almost daily.

Jimmy and I had not really spoken about an actual divorce, in spite of the outburst at the hospital. Except for the separation agreement, which Oscar obviously prevailed upon him to sign, he still didn't want to deal with any of the immediate problems. I could feel Oscar's legal training in the direction in which matters were starting to turn. Revised monthly schedules flowed from my pen, as my new young and ambitious lawyer negotiated with the family. He repeated to me pretty much what the Hammerstein lawyers said to him, partially because they impressed him and partially because he knew that ultimately they would pay his fee. His constant refrain was that I should get out as soon as possible and get on with my life. I agreed with him, but didn't want to let my husband off the financial hook completely.

After Jimmy left <u>Flower Drum Song</u> and disappeared up north into Hunter Mountain, the family lawyers spread their hands and repeated the litany. He had no money to attach. I kept telling my lawyer that I would throw myself at the mercy of the court. He adamantly advised against it and felt that reaching an agreement instead of going to trial would be better for everyone. After the Hunter Mountain project folded and Jimmy lost out again, his lawyer informed my lawyer that my former husband was filing for bankruptcy. My lawyer again advised me to settle for minimum support. I again wanted to put the matter before the courts.

The last offer my lawyer brought to me left me with no choice. He stated very clearly and very succinctly that Oscar was setting up his trust fund. He had discussed it over the years and was now putting it into effect. *If I were still married to Jimmy at the time of his death, unless I gave up all my rights to share in his estate and trust fund, Oscar would cut Jimmy out of his will.* Short and sweet. I had to give up all my possible rights to Jimmy's trust fund and inheritance, for which I would get eleven thousand dollars a year, which was three thousand dollars more than I was then getting. Andy's schooling would be paid for and all the debts incurred during the marriage would be taken care of. I would get no settlement, no reimbursements, no medical coverage, no cost-of-living adjustment. If I didn't accept it and sign on the dotted line, Jimmy would not only be cut out of the trust fund but he would be left a bankrupt pauper.

My lawyer informed me that Oscar had told his lawyers that he no longer wanted the Hammerstein money used to support all of the former wives, girlfriends and children. It seemed that Arthur, Oscar, Billy, Reggie, and now Jimmy were creating a small army of disgruntled former wives who had benefitted from the hard work and dubious largesse of the Hammerstein men.

I couldn't sleep, wondering what to do. Should I sign away all rights to the estate? Should I settle for less than a thousand dollars a month? If I didn't, I would be left with all the debts, penniless, with a former husband who probably wouldn't change and become a better businessman and father. I felt squeezed from all sides. My friends, some of whom were also going through divorces, faced similar bleak futures. The male- controlled media raged against all those former wives who fleeced their husbands, getting away with enormous settlements, while in truth, most of us barely got by. We scrimped along, raising our children, constantly calling our lawyers to get child support payments that were in arrears, while the men often remarried and continued to live comfortable affluent lives. A new class was growing in our midst, a new class of poor women, raising their often-needy children. We commiserated about the injustices, about the legal system that was set up by males for males. Mostly male lawyers, who were the legislators, created the laws. They appointed each other to carry out those laws. The women and children always suffered.

Whatever possibilities I hoped for a reasonable life vanished with the Hammerstein offer. My lawyer pressured me to sign. He wanted to get paid, reiterating the fact that a penniless, bankrupt Jimmy who had been cut out of Oscar's trust fund would be more difficult to deal with and urged me to accept the agreement he had hammered out for me. Throwing myself at the mercy of the court, as I had wanted to do, made no sense to him. It would be a futile gesture. There was no salary to attach. During our negotiations, Jimmy, the ever-present shadow, stayed unemployed and out of sight, covered by the blanket of bankruptcy.

Poppa's death affected me more than I thought. A sadness joined the rage that I had carried for him. The sadness receded in time. The rage refocused itself on the Hammersteins and their lawyers.

On August 1, 1960, I signed the divorce agreement and flew to Mexico to make it legal. A new decade had begun. I'll never forget the hot motel in Juarez. Stockyards surrounded the town, with thousands of poor beasts in their corrals, wailing in the night, bemoaning their fate, as I was bemoaning mine. I too felt I had been led to slaughter. Others seemed to make all the decisions that affected my life. I felt like a puppet on a string, trembling from every new blow.

Almost six months to the day on which my father had died, on March 19, 1959, Oscar found out from his doctor, Ben Kean, that he also had cancer. Dorothy's fears were finally realized. She would not only have to say the word but deal with it in her own life. Not a hint of my father-in-law's terminal illness surfaced in the media. When it was leaked to the press, it was called diverticulosis. He died on August 23, twenty-two days after I had divorced his son. He waited until the trust fund and money were safe and then shucked off his mortal coil.

The demise of my marriage to Jimmy in 1960 followed closely on the heels of my father' death in 1959. The spin outward accelerated as Oscar, who also died in 1960, joined his own brother Reggie, who died in 1958 in that great unraveling, adding another spiral coil accelerating its outward spin into space.

I understood my lawyer's reasoning, even though I resisted when he had insisted to have me sign the agreement. He knew more of the facts concerning Oscar and his family than he had shared with me. Without the agreement, my husband Jimmy would probably have lost his inheritance. My lawyer may not have been paid by an unemployed bankrupt Jimmy. Would Oscar really have cut his own son out of his will? I realized that the probability of his having done so was overwhelming.

In his will, Oscar canceled all of Jimmy's debts and existing I.O.U.s by stating, <u>I hereby forgive and release any and all loans which may</u>

be outstanding and owed to me, at the time of my death by my sons. He also make it clear that Jimmy was to receive no actual cash that he could squander. I have made no bequest to my son, James Hammerstein, in this paragraph FOURTH not because of lack of affection, but because I have assisted him during my lifetime and have attempted by this paragraph FOURTH to make what in my judgment is an equitable arrangement for my other two children.

Jimmy remained in the trust fund. His inheritance was safe. For the rest of his life, he would receive a hefty percentage of the legacy that Oscar's prodigious output created, which grew even more imposing over the years. Everyone in he family fared well. Oscar had left a multi-million dollar estate. Even Dorothy's children benefitted. They shared in the proceeds of the trust fund. The only person left out of the will was Oscar's namesake and grandson, my son Andy. He wasn't even mentioned. It was as if he didn't exist.

What name to use thrashed around in my brain. I had become Barbara Hammerstein on all of my legal documents. As much as the sound of the Hammerstein name rankled me and its associations always set me on edge, it's a name that gave me status and caused people often to ask, "Are you related to Oscar Hammerstein?"

"Only through tears," I answered in the beginning.

As the importance of the Hammerstein name receded in the distance, they would ask, "Are you related to Roger Hammerstein?"

In time, I would answer, "Only through my son."

As in my youth I had tried to find a first name to fit me, I now looked for a last name. The first name was still up for grabs. I was no longer Barbara Redzisz, the Polish immigrant, and not Basha Regis, the name of a stripper as Jack Entratter had teased me. I stayed with Basia, which is the proper spelling in Polish, wondering if I should attach the Redzisz to it and create a double whammy for people to spell. Basia was bad enough for Americans to pronounce, Basia Redzisz would put my life on hold, as I spelled it out for everyone. I had been called "Radish" and "Redzig" and every other possible mumble after the "Re" was tentatively pronounced by resistant American lips.

Foreign names did not trip lightly upon the tongues of Americans. They stumbled over them, usually giving up with frustration at having been stumped.

The women's movement was breaking ground and gathering momentum. I searched for a name that would attach me to my maternal roots. That didn't fare any better. My mother's unpronounceable name, Skozewska, had been her father's name. Poppa's mother's name, Klimek, had been her grandfather's name. The names of the women had ceased to exist. They had become anonymous, lost in the communal grave of <u>history</u>. Regis popped up for a consideration. Although it had regal antecedents, it sounded too Americanized. Many Polish people, after they arrived on the shores of America, shortened or changed their names to sound Anglo-Saxon. I didn't want to join their ranks.

Since I spelled Basia for everyone anyway, I decided to keep it. The simplicity of Hammerstein and its impressiveness also stayed. I became Basia Hammerstein, obviously Polish through the first name and ambiguous through the last.

My new life revolved around <u>Fiorello</u>, Andy and Momma. I made friends again, deep, enduring loving friends who to this day still return into my life and share the affection we established and enjoyed during those months.

Then the last major tragedy in that series, the terminal turn of the wheel, the outward uncoiling spinning itself out of my life, gathered in its unrelenting curve the beloved person who had been my Mother. With her passing, the point of focus that existed in space, out there, always physically real for me, ceased to exist.

Chapter 33

When I was very small, one of my great joys was when Momma and I used to go for walks together. I felt almost conspiratorial with her, leaving Poppa asleep and Jane with <u>stara</u> Baba, the old Polish lady who took care of us. Momma changed after she had my sister Jane, that child who scowled at the world from the day she was born. I watched with curiosity and fear, as Momma's skin turned yellow and she grew sad and tired. After she brought my new sister home, she spent a great deal of time in bed, and I brought her flowers, bunched together and drooping, to make her smile.

As I grew older, she taught me to read and to ice skate, holding me up by my scarf, which she had laced under my armpits. She encouraged me to try everything, even if she went pale after I, at the age of five, wrenched my tiny sled with its little seat from <u>stara</u> Baba and sent myself on a dizzying course down a snow- iced hill. Grownups on enormous sleds, like stacked giant animals, thundered past me as I, exhilarated, whizzed by them. Momma and Poppa lugged their sleds up the hill, following me with their eyes and with terror in their faces, as I came to a stop way down below at the end of the ride at the bottom of the hill. I never in my life again felt such pride, such a sense of adventure, such exhilaration, as I did on that ride down that hill when I was five years old. Even Poppa repeated the story to friends who came to dinner and to play pinochle and who sat for hours around the kitchen table.

"You should have seen her weaving her way down the hill with her galoshes on the bar of that sled, pushing it in and out of all the others. Big ones, you know how big some of those sleds can be, and when the boys stack themselves sometimes three or four on top of each other, I worry myself what would happen if they tipped over on me. Why, I'd look like potato pancake." His card-playing companions would laugh.

"How old are you, Baska?" Poppa asked me.

"I'm five, Poppa."

"Poppa made a nice sled for you, didn't he?"

"Yes, Poppa, you did." He patted me on the head and returned to his pinochle or the telling of ghost stories.

In many ways, I am more like him that I am like my mother, but I never knew who he was. About the time that my eyes reached his heart, I stopped trying. Somewhere, sometime when I reached up to his armpit, I lost my feelings for him. That is why, I explained to myself, I fell in love with very tall men. It went back to the time when I was small, when my father was still very tall to me and when I still loved him. There was love there then, a love I could draw upon, a love that went underground or ceased to exist after I grew taller. It was that juxtaposed memory that made it possible for me to love men at all, that memory of his bigness and of my smallness. That's why some of the men who towered above me awakened in me the memory of deep feelings, before I wrote my father off with much contempt. The love changed into hate, and the hate solidified into a rock of ice in me.

Momma used to read a fairy tale to me about the Snow Queen and how a shaft of ice had gotten lodged in the heart of a young boy. A little girl tried to find him and with her love to melt that shaft of ice. I felt like the little boy, and yet a part of me felt like that little girl, but the frozen heart in me was unreachable. Poppa's squinting presence was an affront to me. How often Momma told me that I had a hard heart toward him and how many times we fought because I couldn't understand how she could have loved him.

It must have been very hard for my mother to leave Poland and come to this country, as years before she had to leave Warsaw after I was born and to move to Minsk-Mazowiecki. For me, Minsk was a place of wonder that goes with being a child, but for Momma, who was a vibrant young woman who laughed and danced and enjoyed the kawiarnias (coffee houses) in pre-war Warsaw, with Mjeczyslaw Fogg singing his risque songs, which in Minsk Mazowiecki she could listen to only on the Victrola she had to wind up and keep wound, or the end of the record would sound like Poppa when he got drunk. In Warsaw, she also left behind her family, her friends and her freedom.

Watching her grow sadder and quieter and yellower after Jane was born, I decided I would never marry and never, never have children. If she hadn't married Poppa, she would have soared like the meadow lark at whom she gazed with regret and sung her own song, but having given up her freedom, she paced back and forth like a caged animal in the circumscribed limits of our compound in Minsk, left only to watch the changing seasons, cooking, cleaning and taking care of us.

In the spring, the roads in our area became filled with straining horses and cursing drivers as they plowed through the deeply furrowed black mud. Sometimes the drivers, with their short dark jackets and their little black caps, got off the wagons, took the reins from over the heads of the horses and pulled the bucking, sweating animals clear. Sometimes they pushed the rickety wagons from behind. Year after year, the same areas in the road filled in with cold rain, and year after year the same farmers, and then their sons, bogged down in the same soft spaces in the road. The mud was rich and black. It fell away in large swaths from the wagon wheels. It was also deceptively yielding. What appeared at one moment to be a solid piece of black earth parted under a bit of pressure, and a horse or a person or a wagon wheel would be sucked into soft black ooze.

We had one of those areas at the bottom of the hill, beyond the tall wooden fence armed with barbed wire, that protected us from unfriendly neighbors, beggars and Gypsies. It was a formidable fence erected by Poppa, with a large creaking gate, which not only had barbed wire on top of it but crisscrossed all over the front and back. Hard as I tried to climb it, all that I succeeded in doing was to tear my smock to shreds and scratch my arms and legs. As a punishment, Momma would apply iodine, which stung and burned. Usually, she would pick a leaf of wild plantain, spit on it and place it on my skinned knee or elbow.

A latch opened the fence from the inside, but Poppa had devised a pulley system with an overhead rope contraption, known only to Momma and him, that opened the ponderous gate from the outside and led through the garden to the French veranda. To me, the house was enormous, filled with nooks and crannies and a many-tiered black stove in the main room, behind which I slept when the frost covered the windowpanes with lacework no less intricate than that which Momma embroidered during those long winter months. We used kerosene lamps to lighten the dark winter days and went to bed early to save on fuel, Momma and Poppa into mounds of feathers and I into my fluffy blankets on the ledge behind the many-tiered stove.

The mud at the bottom of the hill usually disappeared with the warmth of summer and turned into a cloud of fine light-brown dust. Through that dust and over the fields, the cavalry rode on constant maneuvers. They were young handsome, moustached, straight-backed men in tight-fitting uniforms with bright easy smiles that flashed white in their deeply tanned faces. We went all dressed up every Sunday, with the banners flying and lances gleaming in the sun. Momma swayed as she walked, with flowers swirling around her hips on the dresses she wore. Poppa always appeared in his gray spats and amber-tipped cane. My sister and I would emerge in matching dresses and would take the doroszka (hansom cab) to the barracks, where the Ulani (cavalry men) put their horses through dressage, and played violent games with three-legged stools, horses and men vying for one less stool than there were riders, until one man was left with his horse, grabbing the stool and holding on to it in the clouds of dust that swirled around them. The yelling that came from the crowd and the sound of trumpets from the hill in the distance and ice cream pouring down our clean and starched matching dresses created memories that hooked back to a time of great pageantry.

Every Sunday, the cheers went up, and I eyed the handsome Ulani and looked forward to the day when they would click their heels, bend over me and ever so lightly kiss my finger tips as a tremor would go through me at the thought. I had to settle for spitting on the edge of my skirt and rubbing my face with it and hiding the ice cream stains folded under me. I glowed when they thundered past and tipped their caps or just touched its edge with their two fingers in homage to my beautiful mother. Poppa generally stood with his thumbs under his suspenders, filled with the pride of his patriotism, repeating over and over that the Ulani would save us if war came, for the talk of war was in the air. In fact, it was all that the men talked about when they met.

One day, in the mid-1930s, an edict came down from the president in Warsaw that all citizens had to mend their fences and whitewash them for the tourist trade. Our sturdy fence was already in great shape, so all that Poppa had to do was whitewash it and then run around the neighborhood, reporting all our neighbors who were dragging their feet and not complying with the edict.

"How will it look to the rest of the world if we don't fix our own fences?. It looks like 'cigarette alley' (Tobacco Road, something lost in the translation), and he flashed his gold teeth at the uncomprehending and unsmiling prostaki (peasants).

"Poland must look like we belong to twentieth century; otherwise we won't get any respect. We have to start somewhere. Mending fences is a good idea." They scowled at him but thought that maybe he had a point.

Whitewashed fences would not help what was in store for the country. The themes of war started to weave their melodies through our lives. The Aurora Borealis of the northern skies flamed down into Poland and formed a burning cross in the cavernous sky. I remember

Momma looking up into the heavens, heavens that I thought were so beautiful, filled with streaks of light pulsating toward some great center, and she rubbed her arms, holding them close to her. The way that she looked, I could feel the fear in her eyes. She said that the portents were ominous. Something terrible was going to happen. It always did when the Northern Lights came so far down south. In fact, they seemed to throb somewhere above Warsaw to the west of us, streaks of white, cut through with red, blood red, fiery red, like a great fire in the sky, blotting out the stars and making the moon seem pale. "Portents," Momma called them, and she shuddered as she blessed herself, pulling the sweater around her, even though it was hot and the rest of us were fanning ourselves with pleated pieces of paper. I pushed out her panic and wondered if that pulsation was the heart of God, and were we looking at it beating up there, in that cavernous black sky?

Then another edict emerged from President Pilsudzki's office. All buildings had to be camouflaged, painted olive-green, so as not to be seen from the air, if and when foreign planes flew over Poland. Windows had to be taped over with strips of paper. Blankets had to be hung over them at night to prevent any light from escaping. We taped the window with strips of newspaper dipped in that terrible smelly glue that was Poppa's favorite, and then we hung the blankets over the windows. As we finished up, Poppa got out a flashlight that grew dimmer and dimmer the farther you got into the dark. Then he ran around the neighborhood again, reporting all the neighbors who had not painted their houses the olive-green color and whose windows cast long trails of light, piercing the darkness. By the time we left Poland, the amber-headed cane was not enough to contain the wrath of our neighbors. Poppa slept with a gun under his pillow. The cane was his daily companion, but the pearl-handled revolver sometimes tumbled to the floor when Momma made the beds. Had we stayed in Poland during the war, if the enemy didn't get him, some of our neighbors would certainly have tried.

Then one day we awakened in our olive-green house, with the white picket fence around it and the tic-tac-toed windows, to the sound of the locomotive wailing in the distance and all the church bells ringing and all the sirens blasting and all the dogs howling and an eerie silence in the fields, where the birds usually sang. President Pilsudzki had died, and people readied themselves for war. Young men with packs on their backs kissed their families good-bye and marched. Some marched west toward Warsaw. Others trudged away to the east. Poppa always said that Hitler feared Pilsudzki, but when Pilsudzki died, he felt that no one was powerful enough to stop him.

Poppa left one day for Warsaw and came back a few days later with a piece of blue serge uniform material with a cigarette burn in it, claiming that he had bought it from one of Pilsudzki's adjutants. It seems that Pilsudzki was wearing it when he died, but could not be buried in it because he had a habit of putting lit cigarettes into his pockets and then crushing them out with his fingers. Poppa claimed that the piece of fabric he had acquired was a piece of the original uniform. Pilsudzki had to be laid out in another suit of clothes. Poppa passed the fabric around to the few friends he had left. They fingered the burned cloth skeptically, crumbling the place where the burn darkened the edges, wanting to believe that the cloth had touched greatness. But knowing Poppa, they were suspicious about his claims.

In the latter part of that summer, the wagons rattled by through clouds of dust, laden with vegetables, cabbage and potatoes, with leg-tied chickens and an occasional cow swaying from side to side. Women trudged with cheese and butter in baskets, or with sheets of bulging linen rolls on their backs. Boys flicked willow plaited whips across the backs of goats and sheep, or even snapped them at honking geese. All passed by on the way to the market.

I watched them go by with my nose peeking through the wooden slats of the fence. On Sundays, they came past the house on their way to church, the women in long flowered dresses with aprons, bright kerchiefs and braided hair, following the men. Occasionally, the men laughed, but more often than not, they talked of war with a kind of agitated excitement. It was the women who seemed playful and who burst out into song and laughter, as they, too, swished the children on. Momma stayed home behind that tall fence and watched them go by with her tight long skirt and high-heeled shoes. She still followed fashion magazines and copied what women in Warsaw wore and also women whom I saw in the movies from the America that Poppa talked about.

When I was very small, Momma would hide me under her coat and take me to the movies with them. When the lights went out, I would open the buttons of her coat and peek out, catching a glimpse of the paintings of swans that majestically sailed across those cinematic walls, their necks curved, staring at their own reflection in the waters below them, as they floated among the lily pads and the rose colored water lilies. A thrill always passed through me at the sight of those swans; some kind of longing began to form itself in me then. They carried with them echoes of other places. Where were those beautiful lakes they sailed upon, and where did pink water lilies grow?

It was there in that little movie theater that I saw a movie called <u>Golgotha</u> and witnessed, in scratchy, flickering black and white, the agony of Christ upon the cross and His betrayal by Judas, with blood pouring down His face and into His eyes as He dragged the cross up that hill of skulls. I clutched at Momma and hid in the folds of her coat, snuggling against her soft breasts, finding shelter there. The fear subsided in me, and tears fell over that poor man on that flickering screen who was so badly hurt. Momma said, "for my sins," and that made me feel even worse. I vowed to be good, to tell the truth, not to wander off. I didn't want that poor man to hang on the cross for me, and I didn't want to think why the vultures circled over Him. Momma rocked me and laughed and told me not to whimper because they would throw all of us out of the movie house. Children were not allowed in the cinema at night. So I cuddled down and slept while the music droned on and the vultures circled overhead.

One day, I found a loose slat in the massive fence surrounding the orchard, which someone had left hanging on one nail to get in, and which I, with much joy, used to get out. Poppa had grafted every conceivable variety of fruit onto every variety of tree, and our orchard was not only prey for boys hankering after sweets, but also the curious found their way there. Then Poppa, with branches sticking out of his hair and button holes, brandishing his pearl-handled revolver, with his hysterical dog, Bobik, yapping at his heels, descended upon them like some ancient malevolent spirit of vegetation and hauled them away to the police station. Sometimes they took flight, but missing the loose slat in the fence, the only way out, they battered their way around the orchard, trapped like sparrows in a cage, while Bobik tore at their trousers, and Poppa shot his gun wildly in the air. They were grateful when he finally took them to the police station and pressed charges against them. Momma would hide in the house, embarrassed and furious at the spectacle, peeping out from behind the curtains, while my sister and I clapped Poppa on.

When Poppa came back from Warsaw with the burned piece of serge fragment, he dropped the news that he was going to the United States and that he would send for us when he got settled there. There followed a period of fighting, long silences and much slamming of doors, until the French windows rattled. Momma cried a great deal, and Poppa whittled far onto the night, bent over the kerosine light. The smell of burnt hair filled the dark corners of the house and lingered there, even after they had been aired out. Then angry as a wasp, Poppa thrashed around the bed all day and wandered through the orchard at twilight. Momma would haul out the acid-smelling bedding and expose it to the last rays of the setting sun. It didn't help much, for that smell not only lingered in the house but stayed in the furniture, in the pillows and the throws on the couch. Poppa's color became the color of putty or the color of clay, and his eyes seemed more dark and slanted behind the glasses that arched around his high ridged brows.

It was during those last few years in Poland that I found the world beyond the gate fence so filled with miracles. Both Momma and Poppa were so preoccupied with the misery they shared that I slipped away unnoticed and ran through the vaulted pine forests, with shafts of light showing me the way, gathering me toward their dark secret caverns. I flew to the barracks where the Ulani, in white tunics and high boots, groomed their horses, brushing down billows of white foam that dripped down their flanks and left their coats gleaming in the setting sun. As they brushed their animals, they sang their melancholy songs of war and of loss.

The longing and the sadness washed over me in goose pimples, and I would sit outside of the iron fence that encircled the barracks and watch them for hours, until the owl hooted in the distance and the dogs barked their twilight greetings, like a canine telegraph on the wind. The day ended, and in the darkness, with the hair standing on my arms and at the back of my neck, I would follow the path along the railroad tracks and pray to the Virgin Mary to protect me against any wandering Gypsies or chimney sweeps who might be ready to carry me away. Then with relief, I'd find my hole in the fence and re-enter the safety of home behind that tall fence.

So great was their mutual anguish that most of the time they never even missed me, and when I returned and tried to cheer Momma up with flowers that had wilted, as often as not, she pushed me away, impatiently listening for something, waiting for something to happen, something that seemed to be terrible and sent chills up down my spine every time I thought about it.

So I ran from home when daylight dawned, far into the forests and into the fields. One of my greatest joys was the cold oozing mud in front of our fence that pushed itself through my toes after it rained. With the rain came Spring and fields of violets, blankets of lavender flowers, disappearing into the far distance, at the edge of the dark and craggy trees. Easter always came with Spring and with the purple-robed statues on the pedestals in church, with the bleeding figure of Christ covered and laid out in the center aisle, with kerchiefed women weeping over him and blowing their red noses as they blessed themselves and backed away from the crypt. The fasting and then the priest coming to the house and blessing all the babkas and the torts and the ponczki (donuts) and the kielbasy (sausages) and loaves of home-baked rye bread, and hams and little flower pots of sprouted green spring wheat, reproaching Momma for not attending Mass and for not taking Communion, and Momma, with a pink color starting at her neck and moving up on to her face, apologizing and joking with him so that he didn't press the point that embarrassed her. Then the singing and the Resurrection and Easter baskets filled with brightly colored eggs and cows and sheep made of sugar and little sprigs of boxwood stuck all around the edges of the basket reminding us that Spring was close at hand.

Then the church was filled with flowers, and the sun burst through the purple-red and blue windows, and we felt giddiness from the sitting and the incense and people singing. There were bells and the blooming horse chestnuts with their own white spires, like candles in the sun, and the processions around the vestry with the altar boys holding the priests' long skirts and the priests holding the tips of the banners that hung down from the holy pictures. They marched over the cobblestones and the old bridge, under which the ducks upended themselves in the muddy stream below, and beyond to the houses in the distance, where the Jews lived with their strange beards and forelocks, long dresses and skull caps, where the smell of fish hung in the air. On Saturdays, their wives walked with them with their long skirts and their dark red wigs on their often young heads. Then to the graveyard, with the tilted crosses and moss-covered stones, its crepe flowers and flickering candles, in tiny little amber or garnet cups and the tiny little graves of children. Then the incense, the singing, and the pigeons swooping away in waves, like airborne petals alighting in the eaves, where the bells pealed and the linden trees shimmered with flowers and bees.

It came as a surprise to me later on in life, when I was again alone, how much time I had spent by myself when I was very small and how much that must have affected my life. When all those patterns were being created, I only remember the awe, the search for those tiny little people who lived in flowers, the aching desire to talk to birds and animals, the shrines at the roadside where the chipped statue of the Mother of God sat and stared out across the fields, while we placed dying flowers before Her, imitating the solemnity of the grownups.

The wheat fields filled with red poppies and blue cornflowers, and in the winter on ice skates, following the meandering streams across endless miles of marsh, watching the sun send silver and golden shafts into the trapped leaves and fish of the glistening ice. In the autumn, <u>Babie Lato</u> (old lady summer), with strings, or webs spun of silver, shimmering in the branches of trees, catching the sunlight and then the moonlight, as the wind traced them across the sky. The air sparkled and buzzed and ruffled my hair; the mud oozed through my toes. The pines hummed with mystery and fragrance. Green fields spilled out of the earth with magic and wonder. Could any of that have been true? Could any of that have been real? Was it a dream I had dreamed, or a vision I had created?

Chapter 34

After the fighting and the silences, we went to Warsaw and visited Poppa's family. After that, in the winter of 1938, we prepared for our journey to the United States. Momma put a handful of Polish soil into a white linen handkerchief and brought it with her to this country, this place she had heard about but feared for its strangeness.

As the S.S <u>Batory</u> pulled away from the dock in Gdynia and Momma clutched that small bundle of Polish soil to her heart, we all sang "<u>Goralu czy ci nie zal, odchodzic od stron ojczystych</u>" (Mountaineer, aren't you sad, to leave your home?). She cried as if her heart would break, as if she would never return to all those upturned faces that looked like her. In tears, we watched the boat pull away from the dock to take us far, far away.

From then on, my own anguish hardened me to what she was going through. I hated the rubble-strewn lots of Jersey City and being laughed at for not speaking English and for not being understood and for being nine years old and feeling helpless. There were no more fields, no more flowers, no mud-filled alleys, no storms that started at one end of the sky and rumbled their way across to the other. There were just people who pushed and shoved and yelled louder and louder, because they felt we did not hear them and that is why we didn't understand them.

I remember just isolated incidents from those unhappy years. The war in Europe began soon after we left. Momma, in her despair, developed large bumps on her head, and some of her hair fell out. She had felt guilty for having left her own mother and sisters behind. I remember her listening to the radio almost all day and part of the night, when the German tanks rolled over those beloved fields and crushed under them, all those beautiful young men, with their beautiful horses. She lost track of her family when the mail ceased. One day, she came home with a bag filled with shoe polish, silver polish, metal polish and stove polish, proud that she had found something that belonged to her and that she recognized as Polish, thinking that polish meant that they had come from Poland. I remember her disappointment and embarrassment upon finding out that one had nothing to do with the other.

"How could that be? How can polish be my Polish and polish at the same time?" She was incredulous and pushed all those bottles into a drawer and looked at them with a sense of betrayal. How lonely it must have been for her and how frightening. Yet, for the first time, she realized she was free, that making her own money made her independent of Poppa. He could sleep all he wanted, and she might have to lie to him where the material for the curtains came from, but for the first time in her life, she bought what she wanted, and laughter came back into her life, as she discovered her own worth. She dressed us and made us clothes, me standing and fidgeting and itching, as she on her knees, with pins in her mouth, carefully pinned a hem or a sleeve or marked a pocket. At the store were she worked, they valued her for her craft and her expertise. She became proud and her own person, but she never felt quite free of the emotional bond that kept her tied to Poppa.

Momma once said to me years later, "Basiu, no matter what Poppa do, he bring us to America, and in America I am myself. Remember that, Basiu, and don't resent Poppa so much. He is, after all, your Poppa." That was many years later, when she had made her peace with him and the chasm between him and me grew wider.

Momma went to work, Poppa went to sleep, so Jane and I explored the industrial factories, deserted and demolished rotting piers,

371

and abandoned, burned-out houses with tons of rubble everywhere. It was all so alien, so strange. I kept looking for flowers and found some pushing their way through crumbling foundations and pieces of broken glass.

Momma's income didn't bring us much money, but there was always enough to spend all day Saturday and all day Sunday at the movies. It was in those movies that I formed my future self. I would learn the language, and somehow someday I would become rich and famous. Momma said that all it needed was hard work and that everything was possible in America. The only thing that I couldn't be was a president, because the president had to be born in the United States, but everything else was possible.

One day, about three years later, I had a moment of moving awareness. I was walking on Danforth Avenue in Jersey City, on the left side of the street facing south, when it flashed to me that I was no longer thinking in Polish. I had begun to think in English -- broken English, but English nevertheless. I knew I would never forget that moment, and I also knew I was on my way. There were many English words that always gave me trouble, like "through" and "though" or "bought" and "brought." To this day, I say "batree" for "battery," but I was on my way.

Then, on my birthday on December 7, 1941, we heard over a radio that the Japanese had bombed Pearl Harbor. America had declared war, and Poppa had to go to work. All able-odied men had to be mobilized for the war effort. That meant we could go home after school instead of wandering around the streets. Poppa was not too happy about the fact that he had to get his skinny body out of bed, and he coughed for anyone who was willing to listen.

His coughing always announced that not only had we awakened him, but that we were in for it. He would emerge from the bedroom, his hair on end, his suspenders hanging down his baggy pants, screaming and beating us with whatever was available, blows that fell on our heads and arms and upturned hands, blows that left welts and often bleeding sores. Momma would gather us to her and turn her back on

372

his fury, often taking some of the blows herself, but she went to work every day, and we were left alone with him most of the time. There was no place to go, so we played in the street.

The smell in his clothes and on his breath followed him everywhere, as cigarette butts sagged in every glass and flower pot. Ironically, it was Momma who died of lung cancer; she who never smoked had to die of lung cancer, which his smoking had probably precipitated.

We had left Poland ostensibly because Poppa's American citizenship was on the verge of expiring and he had to return to the United States to maintain it. Momma cried so much at the time that I partially believed it. That is the story that I remember being told, but later when my own passions dragged me around the landscape, I realized that my father came back to the United States to find the only person he probably ever loved, besides his own mother and my sister: his first wife, whom he had left behind in Denver, Colorado, when he left to go to war. Those were thoughts that Momma didn't even allow herself to think, as she sat her vigil with him, waiting for him to die, waiting for him to say he really loved her. He held out to the very end. All that he did finally say when the cancer had devoured his body and he looked like pictures from Buchenwald was "jusz (enough)," and then he died.

It was a propitious time for all of us, for we landed in America on February 14, 1938, on St. Valentine's day, and the war erupted in Poland in September of the following year. It wasn't the war, and it wasn't preserving his citizenship that brought us to this country, although they were compelling enough reasons. It was his need to find his first wife. That's why he wanted to leave us behind.

After the United States entered the war, we moved to Long Island to a town called Farmingdale, and we stayed in Farmingdale for one year, which was the longest that we stayed anywhere, while he worked at an airplane factory. We rented a large white house, at 312 Conklin Street, with two acres of woods and fields behind it, which contained grape arbors and an old apple tree. For the first time since we had come to this country, we were happy. In the summer, we searched for and picked blueberries, which Momma made into mouth-watering pies and cold blueberry soup. Then, with the apples, she baked not only pies but made cold apple soup with cold noodles, and stuffed a majestic goose with them.

One day, a short-legged, curly-haired white dog peeped in through the screen door of the kitchen, and after I fed him some leftover soup bones, he became our very own. We named him Mickey, probably after Mickey Mouse. That stray dog let us wash him and even to shave his white curly hair in the summer, in the mistaken belief that he would be cooler. What we didn't know until we had shaved him was that Mickey had black spots all over his body. We laughed so hard when we finished at the apparition that we had created, an apparition with a fuzzy head, paws and tail and a black-spotted skinny body, that Mickey took off under the porch and was so humiliated that he wouldn't come out until we apologized to him and lured him back out with some stew bones. (Dogs, apes and humans hate to be ridiculed.) Momma found him such a sight that she wouldn't let him follow her to the store. He followed her anyway, at a distance. Every time she stopped and yelled at him to go home, he plopped his speckled rump on the sidewalk and waited until she started walking again. Then he, too, would get up and, keeping a respectful distance, follow her. He loved us, but he loved my mother most of all.

I remember that, to make myself some money, I went to the fields that became Levittown after the war and picked bunches of wild flowers -- daisies, phlox and cosmos -- and sold them door to door in the neighborhood. We explored those woods around Bethpage State Park for blueberries and for mushrooms and often came home to clean and sort the <u>boletes</u> and the <u>russulas</u> onto metal grills, which Momma placed in the oven, leaving them overnight with only the pilot light on. As they dried, all the tiny white worms would work their way up and out of the floppy fungus. Then we strung the mushrooms like great wreaths, and the smell filled the house as she made clear beet <u>barszcz</u> with potatoes and dill with those big floppy mushrooms floating in them. She pickled the tiny <u>bolete</u> caps and stewed the <u>rus-</u>

<u>sulas</u> and the chanterelles, and we didn't know then what a delicacy we enjoyed as a matter of course. The onions added to the taste when she ladled the stewed mushrooms onto a mound of mashed potatoes. The memory of those meals still fills my mouth with water.

In Poland, Poppa had greater freedom for his mushroom picking. But in Bethpage State Park on Long Island, he not only had to keep his pants on (he used to take them off in Poland and fill the pant legs with mushrooms), but the state troopers and the park rangers chased him out. This came later when I was working in the garment center and taking horseback riding lessons, in memory of those Sundays in Poland when we sat in the sun and the Ulani sang their songs and put their horses through the paces. One day, an elderly gentleman, or so I thought (I was in my late teens and he was about forty), would always be there when I took my riding lessons. He was a fine horseman and offered to take me on the trails. I was delighted having progressed to the point where I was ready to take my chances outside the corral. We rode side by side. He posted, while I bounced up and down. When we walked our horses, he decided to impress me with the fact that he knew the superintendent of Bethpage State Park. I immediately jumped at the opportunity and told him how the state troopers were throwing Poppa out of the park because he picked mushrooms. I made Poppa sound like some deposed prince in search of his lost ancestral lands who was keeping busy by foraging for fungi in a foreign land. He told me that he would see what he could do. The next weekend, my riding companion was there with a personal card from the super's office. It said, "To whom it may concern: Mr. Andrew Redzisz, the bearer of this card, is allowed to pick mushrooms in Bethpage State Park until further notice." It was signed by Joseph Burbeck, Superintendent of Bethpage State Park.

Next to his veteran's pension, that card became Poppa's most prized possession. He was the only man ever to have a mushroom-picking license in Bethpage State Park. The park police, after stopping him once and looking at the card, never bothered him again, getting used to his bent-over form poking at the leaves with a long stick. After he died, I went through his things and found in his wallet, along with his Social Security card and a much-used and tattered card, which I had gotten him fifteen years before, that allowed him to pick his beloved mushrooms unmolested in Bethpage State Park.

But that joyful interlude was not to last. Poppa got into a fight with his foreman at the plant, and we had to transfer out of Farmingdale to Jamaica, Long Island. They couldn't fire him because the war was still on, so they got rid of him by transferring him.

"Psia krew, dziurawe worki. (Dog's blood, bags with holes)" was the worst thing he could call them. We left behind the potato fields filled with violets in the early spring, packed our manatki, as my mother called our junk, and trundled our way west to Jamaica, Long Island. Our new landlady initially allowed us our cat, which she poisoned within the month. I watched Kicius die on the kitchen floor. As he convulsed and stiffened, a yellow liquid spread out under him. He died on the cold linoleum, with his eyes open and his teeth showing in a grimace of death. We also had to leave Mickey behind in Farmingdale. He sat with his curly white hair all grown back and fluffy, with his ears hanging limply on either side of his head, looking at us with those bewildered eyes, as we pulled away in Poppa's square black Chevrolet. How we screamed at him not to leave Mickey behind. How we cried that we would always hate him and never forgive him, but he calmly drove away with his hat flat on top of his head, squinting forward through his eyeglasses, while Mickey became smaller in the distance and finally became just a white spot under the large trees, disappearing as we headed west on Conklin Street away from that one year of happiness that we found in this country. As we left Mickey behind in Farmingdale and screamed at Poppa, my heart congealed with the ice that even the Snow Queen could not melt.

I remember getting the full benefit of the way he not only acted but thought when I was twelve years old. We still lived in Farmingdale, and I had not yet even gotten my period. I was a very young twelve, isolated from other children by the language barrier. I had played doctor in Poland many years before, but I had not made that connection with kids in this country, so being twelve for me was very young.

After Momma and Poppa had gone to the movies, my sister and I had gone to bed. They came home around eleven o'clock that night and realized they had locked themselves out. It was a hot sultry Long Island night, and our upstairs windows were open. When they called upstairs to us and threw pebbles at the upstairs windows, I heard them. Half asleep, I came downstairs to let them in. I remember putting the light on in the kitchen and unbolting the door. Proud that I had done something useful, I went back to sleep. The next day, Momma took me by the hand and led me into the parlor. She couldn't look me in the eyes as she jerked me by the arm and demanded, "How could you have done that?"

I was flooded with apprehension. What could she have found out, that I had fought with my sister again, that I didn't do my homework? Thoughts chased each other through my racing brain.

"Done what? What did I do? I'm sorry; I didn't mean it." I was apologizing before I knew what I had done, just to cover any mistakes I might have committed.

"The way you opened the door last night, don't you remember?" Did I break it? What did I do? I thrashed around wildly trying to remember if I had broken anything because of the way that my mother was looking at me.

"You came down in only your night shirt. You had no pajamas on, and your father saw you. He thinks you are a shameless hussy, a <u>kurua</u> (whore), and that you will end up no good. Women of the streets behave that way, but not his daughter."

She kept repeating the phrases over and over again, about what my father thought, while a pain spread in my chest and up into my throat and down into my stomach, as it spasmed and I could barely explain, "But I was asleep. I don't remember doing that. All I did was to open the kitchen door when you woke me up, <u>Mamusiu</u>."

"What were you wearing?" my mother demanded. I remembered the little shirtie that came above my navel and left the lower half of my body bare.

"It was hot, and I took my pajamas off. I forgot to put them back on, <u>Mamusiu</u>. I didn't mean to do anything bad." My whole body started to shake. I wanted to run somewhere, anywhere, to hide my shame. Both my mother and my father thought I was the worst dirty creature because I had came down the stairs in that short little shirt. For many years after that, I would wake up from a dream screaming in panic and humiliation trying to cover my body with a short white shirt that reached to my navel and could not hide my shame. Even as I grew older, the image grew with me, imbedded in my store of memories, and the teenager grew into a woman trying to hide that dirty part of herself, the part that stirred such rage in my father and such recriminations in my mother. I had felt so dirty, so worthless, that for weeks I avoided my father's eyes after that night. He himself, as I grew older, called me a whore and a hussy-without-shame and most often a pig, words which in English almost sound funny, but in Polish, to a little girl, they became brands that crippled many aspects of her life. It was probably why I stayed a virgin until I was 22 years old, just to prove how wrong he had been. It was probably also why I picked at my face until it looked like chopped meat, bit my nails until my fingers bled and twirled my hair until I developed a bald spot on the side of my head.

I wanted to know a different way of being than the one my father represented, a way that I blamed on Polish provincialism and Catholic dogma. I could not understand until many years later what all that meant, but by then, the damage had been done, and I spent a lifetime trying to undo it.

Chapter 35

South Jamaica was like another Jersey City. We moved into a mixed community of Polish, Irish, Italians, and blacks, close to St. Joseph's, the Polish church. Although my parents never attended, they forced us to go to church and found comfort in the idea that they were bringing us up right, secure in our heritage. South Jamaica was also a place in transition. The groups were to be called ethnic later, but then they were just "Polacks," "Micks," "wops" and "niggers"; there was no mincing of words. The Polish were always close to the bottom of the social ladder in the United States, vying for menial jobs, furiously trying to keep ahead of the blacks, who were taking over their neighborhoods. The ethnic groups were sanding down their edges by intermarrying, but the racial lines were drawn, and there was an uneasy peace. The wars that existed were mostly between the Irish and the Italians, groups of guys staking out their turf, hanging around the Polish National Hall, because it had a bar and a pool room. The blacks usually fought among themselves. They dared not as yet to take on the white guys.

I remember walking for miles out of my way to Schimer Junior High School to avoid the empty lots that surrounded the building. After school, as often as not, some black girls would be slashing at each other with knives in the tall grass, or worse, some guys would be punching each other out, with blood spilling all over their faces, while their friends egged them on, screaming on the surrounding weed-covered dunes and drinking from bottles hidden in paper bags, passing the bags around with the liquid flowing down their faces and onto their clothes.

Once on the way home, while picking flowers and watching the clouds changing shapes in the sky, I came upon a scene, with the knives flashing and the girls screaming, the two girls in the center having it out over some guy who stood on the sidelines with a toothpick between his teeth and his pants rolled low on his hips. He was the blackest and the most beautiful man I had ever seen. He was even more beautiful even Vincent, with whom I had fallen in love with in Farmingdale, the year before. He stood tall, with a head shaped into a gentle curve, his hair cropped short, softly cupping the skull beneath, his brows wide and his nose very straight down from his temple. His nostrils flared and notched upward. He had enormous solid black eyes that swept out from the center of his face and curved around the sides to tiny little ears that sat flat back against his skull, as if listening more intently to what was going on inside rather than outside of him. His legs seemed to start at his armpits, they were so long. Along with the yelling and screaming, to come up against that face took the breath out of me. Shaking, with my heart pounding, I retreated behind a sand dune, into a patch of rag weed, away from the blood that was pouring onto the sand over him.

I saw him a few more times on the Q40 bus, and I studied him closely, obsessed by his surly dark beauty. Once we even stared at each other in silence, he at the exit door and I in my seat, while heat poured over me. When the bus stopped, he turned away and sprang into the street. As he did so, I again saw the profile, like the Greek statues I had begun to see in art books. At that time, it was beyond my wildest dreams to conceive that I could ever date a black man. First of all, not only blacks but all men scared me. Second, my family would disown me, and my family was all that I had. There were few opportunities for friendship between the races. It was all stratified, partially on race but mostly on class. Class had to do with money and the opportunity for education.

It is said that the United States is a great melting pot, where all coalesce together into one great big undifferentiated, Anglo-Saxon-influenced, American mass. It became apparent that the definition as "mass" was not appropriate. People stayed distinct and didn't flow one into the other. So the concept of a mosaic emerged. We are like an enormous bathroom tile floor, this mosaic we call American humanity. This, too, seemed like a point being stretched. So a new metaphoric definition had to emerge. It seems this great American experiment is not unlike a cluster of burrs, the sticky spines catching each other and yet not touching like in a mosaic, or fusing together, as in a melting pot. The burr suspends itself as part of and yet apart from the other. Many burrs can exist in this way, like molecules in an atom hanging together but separate and individual. With those rough edges, the burrs of individuality and background have to be rubbed off, have to be sanded down so that people don't stick them into each other and create chaos. All have to become smooth like marbles, and often as cold and hard, so that the spiny needles of the burrs don't prick, don't puncture the content of the other. There has been much resistance to this polishing down, this smoothing of edges. It raised and still raises its spiked head in schools, where children had and still have to sit, work and play together.

Being a foreigner and Polish placed me lower on the social totem pole than the blacks. The lack of familiarity, fueled by inequality, fanned into a potential flame incidents that must have been repeated a thousand times in a country trying to be a melting pot, then a mosaic, but in reality having to deal with a net of prickly burrs.

In Poland, when children misbehaved, either the Gypsies or the local bogeyman, who was usually the local chimney sweep, was called on to deal with them. The chimney sweep was always dressed in black, his face completely obscured by soot, so that only his white eyeballs gleamed. He usually wore an impressive, large-brimmed black hat and around his shoulder a coil of heavy stiff wire, which ended in an enormous round black and bristly bush. All kinds of stories were told to Polish children to keep them in line. A chimney sweep would carry them away to Hell if they were bad; that's why he was so full of soot. He brought it up with him from the fires of the underworld. A chimney sweep would throw them down the chimney, and they would get cooked like Hansel and Gretel, which had its own frightening implications concerning being eaten. He'd carry them away from the village. He'd do to them unspeakable things, things beyond even our fevered imaginations. When a chimney sweep entered a village, all the children screamed, scattered and hid. Only the dogs chased him down the dusty narrow streets and tugged at his black coat. My sister was brought up on that story, and the memory of it always stayed with her. When she went to school in Jersey City, right after we landed in America, she took one look at the black kids in her class and let out a shriek, and since no one understood her, they pegged her for a bigot.

Had they understood Polish, they would have known that her screams of panic were because she thought that the black kids were chimney sweeps and not blacks. I often had to walk home with her after school, across the litter-strewn lots of Jersey City, protecting her from a bunch of black kids who were ready to tear her limb from limb. When she made it home alone, there were times she arrived all black and blue and beaten up. She screamed at them in Polish; they screamed at her in English. Neither knew what the other was saying. Her terror of them lessened with time, but not by much. For her, they evolved as personifications of the fear we had of them as chimney sweeps in Poland.

It was in Jamaica that I first learned how to make friends. Two local Polish girls, Amy and Terry, became my constant companions. Friendship was a new and heady experience for me, and I began to see the possibility of relationships outside the family. Amy Kasperowicz lived with her family in a house built for midgets — migiks, as my father used to say. You had to stoop down to get through the doorway. As you walked up-right, your head brushed the ceiling. It was like the gingerbread house in Hansel and Gretel, and we loved it.

Amy's father was a craggy sort of a man with a large head and heavy brows, and his body leaned to the side as he shuffled by, like the hunchback of Notre Dame. One day he met Momma, took one look at her, and went bonkers. When Momma visited Amy's mother, she had to walk down a long lane with large maples lining each side, until she got to the midget house. As she creaked open the garden gate, Mr. Kasperowicz, Amy's father, would jump behind the tree closest to her, and as she proceeded down the lane, he would jump from behind one tree to behind another tree hiding and peeking, keeping abreast of her, but never saying anything to her, just jumping from behind one tree to behind another tree, until Momma knocked on the tiny door and disappeared into the tiny house. He would then retreat into the woodshed behind the house and wait until she left, to repeat the same performance, jumping behind each tree, until she reached the street and there were no more trees for him to jump behind.

My girlfriend Amy adored him, and I wondered at how lucky she was to have loved her father. He was gruff but very gentle with his daughter. I never knew what he did for a living, but guessed he was a janitor at some building somewhere and they felt it was a humiliation to discuss it.

Momma used to go over to their house to adjust the hem for Mrs. Kasperowicz's laying-out dress. Mrs. Kasperowicz had decided on the dress she was to be buried in, and Momma would adjust the hem, raising it and lowering it, as the fashion of the day dictated. After we moved out of Jamaica, Mrs. K. would take the long train ride to Farmingdale and lug the dress in a suitcase with her. Momma would redo the hem again, kneeling on the floor, with pins bristling out of her mouth.

Mrs. K. would then take a boat to Poland and wait to die. Since she didn't die, she'd get tired of waiting and came back. She repeated the procedure a few years later. The dress, although as yet unused, got very old and musty, smelling of mothballs, with a corrugated bottom where the hem was being raised and lowered, according to the latest fashion. I loved it when my mother teased her and looked at her with wide and innocent eyes.

"Pani Kasperowicz, what will happen if you die and the dress is not in fashion?"

"Pani Redzisz, that would be a tragedy." And she would lean over in mock keening, clasp her hands and rock with laughter. "But Pani Redzisz, I know that you will remember me. Even if I am as stiff as a board, you will come and make sure that I am buried in style. Won't you have pity on me and do it, Pani Redzisz?"

As she stopped rocking, she fixed Momma with a look somewhere between caution and supplication. Momma would seriously inquire,

"But Pani Kasperowicz, how can I get the right length if you are laid out in a coffin?"

"Oh, jejej, Pani Redzisz, you can put it on yourself and let Baska pin it for you, and then I'll feel better when I die. You promise me, Pani Redzisz?"

"You want Basia to pin the hem on me, if it's not the right length?"

"Tak (yes)," Pani Kasperowicz nodded eagerly.

"In case you die between hem changes?"

"Prawda (truth)."

"Dobze (good), Pani Kasperowicz. I'll do it for you, but who will pay me?" And they would both rock back and forth and laugh until tears ran down their faces.

"I'll leave the money for you in the top draw of the bureau with `Pani Redzisz' on it, OK?"

"OK." Momma died many years later, and Pani Kasperowicz, a very old lady with dental plates that danced around inside her mouth, periodically still went to Poland to die. I wondered who subsequently adjusted the hem on the dress for her.

Then came one of Momma's tragedies. After the war ended, Poppa, who was no longer needed in the war effort, took all the money out of the bank and left. With no word, he just left. She almost had a nervous breakdown. That was when I spent all my time at school, leaving at dawn and coming home after dark, accumulating more extra credits for service to the school than anyone in its history. She

CINDERELLA ❧ AFTER THE BALL OR, JUST KEEP GOING

worked at the Bon Ton and hoped to save some money to buy a house back in Farmingdale, and lo and behold, Poppa forged her signature, took all the money out of their joint bank account and flew the coop.

I was relived that he was gone. Gone was that mean smelly presence; gone were the dirty socks that ripened in the heat of the long summer evenings as we sat and listened to Gabriel Heater. Gone were the fights, the screams, the shoes thrown across the room, the clicking of his teeth as he picked through them. Momma told the ladies at the Bon Ton that he went looking for the silver mines he had invested in many years before. She stopped seeing friends, and a pained expression etched itself into her face, an expression that was never to leave it again. It was at that time that I decided that I would always take care of her, that I would take the place of Poppa, and a good riddance to him. But Momma felt herself adrift without a man. She told me later when I was getting divorced, "A woman without a husband has no status."

And she believed it. The way that society had been set up, she was right. Then about a year later, he sent her a card from California. Momma was in a rage, but she was overjoyed. He wanted to come back to her. He never spoke of his trip to us. I wondered if he ever spoke of it to her. Soon after his return, he developed a pain in his lower body. After a series of prostate operations and their eventual move to Farmingdale, he slid slowly into terminal cancer and died in 1959.

What I didn't know at that time, as I spent my weekends with my mother, dragging my son Andy east to Long Island, when his father either forgot or chose not to pick him up, that the spin that had caught so much of my life in it its unrelenting curve of disintegration was not yet finished with me. I was to receive another hammer blow before it left me either to drift without a rudder or to claw my way out of a bottomless pit of despair.

385

Chapter 36

My marriage into the Hammerstein family had distanced me even from my mother. She felt awkward around me. I don't know whether it was because I had changed so much or because she had defined me as being different. In any event, we drifted a bit apart. After my divorce, I again turned to her. She had paid for my miscarriage, and I was grateful. The truth was that I had no where else to go. My son and I visited her home in Farmingdale, and we slept in the attic room I had built when I still lived at home. This time, I had a small child with me, who was becoming as closed and as silent as I.

Then one day before Easter in 1969, my mother, who had been a gentle and patient soul, flew into a rage and threw me out. She accused me of using her home as a hotel, that I took advantage of her, that I didn't understand her plight, her loneliness. I was hard, unfeeling, insensitive. Her outburst was difficult to understand. Hurt and puzzled, I left with my son, who was as shaken as I was. Easter came and went. I had usually spent it at home, sharing it with my sister and my twin nieces, who lived also in Farmingdale. But no call came. I didn't know what to do, feeling wronged and unjustly chastised.

Then on a bright Spring matinee Saturday, when Julia was off and Andy was with his father, as I was getting ready to leave for the theater, a tentative knock came at my apartment door in New York City. I opened it to find my mother standing in the foyer before me. Her eyes were panic-stricken, enormous in her round face. She tried to say something, moving her lips up and down, opening and closing her mouth.

"Ba-ba-ba-shu," not being able to finish the phrase, or even my name, stammering, she reached out her hands to touch me, to gather me to her. We hugged. I took her arm and guided her inside, and a panic began to spread through me. She had always been the rock on whose strength I had relied; then she threw me out and now stood crumbling before me. Throwing me out because "I was bad" was one thing, but standing before me, unable to speak, was another.

"Ba-shoo-niah," she repeated, apparently unable to say anything more.

"What is the matter, <u>Mamusiu</u>?"

"<u>Nie-nie-nie v-v-veim</u> (I don't know)," she stammered out, trying desperately to form the words that got stuck somewhere inside her. She entered my apartment (from which a former tenant had plunged to her death), trying to speak, but nothing came out. I hugged her again, trying to comfort her, smelling that familiar ancient smell that belonged only to her. As I held her hands and tried to comfort her, she stammered and stumbled through a few words that informed me how frightened she was and how something so powerful as almost total speechlessness had gripped her and caused her to have violent headaches. She forgot words, lost her train of thought, was aware of it, and it not only embarrassed her but made her impatient.

I took her with me downtown to my show. It was a Saturday matinee. Doc, my dear friend, found her an empty seat down front. During the numbers in <u>Fiorello</u>, I still remember her pretty round face, drifting in the darkness beyond the footlights, looking up for me, and then smiling in recognition. Friends came to my aid. Linda Lynch, one of the dancers in the show who had helped me get the job, knew a doctor who was available to the theatrical community during matinee days, especially on Saturdays, when everything else had closed down. After the afternoon show, still with orange make-up on my face, we flew in a cab up town to Fifty-fifth Street to see the doctor, who took one look at my mother, examined her and booked her into Mount

Sinai Hospital for tests.

Then he turned to me. "It looks like she has a lesion on her brain. It may be malignant." Malignant, malignant lesion, not a scar, not a temporary spasm of some sort, but malignant, a cancer. Momma has cancer. Dear God, please, no...

"But if its malignant...?"

"Then she has it somewhere else in her body, and it has broken off and lodged itself in her brain. I'm not one hundred percent certain, but close. That's what's causing the aphasia, her difficulty in speaking."

"Then wherever it is, it must be large enough so that part of it broke away." I pictured an island of debris swept away by the current in the Everglades, part of the mainland breaking off and attaching itself somewhere else downstream.

It was difficult for her to speak, not only to form words, but something beyond that, further behind the words themselves, was impaired, Her memory was gone in places. Words would not come to her, their source obscured. She became more and more impatient with herself. The harder she tried, the more it all slipped away from her.

"When did you first notice that you couldn't speak, Mamusiu?"

"It started when Poppa die, a year ago. I get terrible headaches, and I go to doctor for check-up. He say I have spot on lung. That not new. I have tuberculosis in Poland, so I not worry. He want me to come back, but I know how they are: they take your money and not help you."

"When did you find it hard to remember words?" She looked at me, and a blankness came over her face.

"I all alone, I no speak to anyone, I no remember," she stammered out. Why hadn't I swallowed my pride when she threw me out? I might have seen her deterioration. Those few months might have made a difference. Her anger at me must have been part of the changes in her brain.

"Where are your headaches?"

"Here," and she pointed to the side of her head, gingerly touching it, almost to see if it would give.

"Do you hurt any place else?"

"No." She shook her head, making her eyes grow wider as she tried to focus on me.

On Monday morning, Julia helped her to dress, and I took her to the Mount Sinai Hospital, where the surgeon was in attendance who would operate on her. He repeated to me the same process that the first doctor had outlined about lesions and malignancy.

"We will operate tomorrow morning to relieve the pressure on her brain, and it might improve the aphasia."

"Can she be helped? I mean, do you think that an operation will help her?"

"There is no way of knowing at this time. All I'm hoping for is that it will relieve the pressure and help her speech and memory. We won't know until we go in there and look around to see how large it is and how much damage it has done." ("Go in and look around"; he's talking about Momma's head, the center of her being, not about renting an apartment.)

"Try not to jump to any conclusions. I know how hard it must be for you, but we won't know anything until after the operation and after the x-rays."

I left her at the hospital, vowing to return after the show that night. She looked panic-stricken, fearing I would leave her at the mercy of people who would not only not understand her broken English, but no English at all, as she grappled to create meaning in the shreds of words that broke through her lips. As I left her, to dance, sing and smile upon that large indifferent stage, my fear for her became as tangible as the other appendages on my body. She lay on the table with a white sheet over her, being wheeled away, looking after me like our dog Mickey did in Farmingdale, when we had left him behind so many years before.

The next day, in the evening, after the operation, the doctor told me the bad news. The lesion was large and malignant. It was a secondary lesion; the primary source of the cancer was in Momma's lungs. To some degree, the rest of her body was riddled with it. Riddled, he had said, and I thought of the holes in Swiss cheese. No, not like that, more like raisins in a cake, not holes; more like foreign matter, something different, like raisins or even nuts in a cake. He asked me if she smoked, and after I answered him, he turned his head to the side and said that it was strange for someone to get lung cancer who didn't smoke.

"My father smoked a great deal, but my mother didn't."

"How old is she?"

"Fifty-six," I told him.

"She looks younger, more in her middle forties." He looked at me. "You favor her."

"I know." I nodded my head quickly up and down, to hold down the lump in my throat.

"How long does she have to live?" I could barely form the words.

"It's hard to say in these cases. It my be a few weeks, or it may be a few months." Weeks, months and then she'd be gone.

"What is the best thing I could do for her?"

"When she's ready to go home, which should be within maybe ten days, make her comfortable and give her the prescriptions I will give you."

"Will she be in pain?"

"Post-operative, yes, and then her lungs may become a problem, but we'll deal with that as it comes up. If the lesion doesn't spread, it may become contained. We don't really know."

"Thank you, doctor." He looked at me and touched my arm.

"Do you have any family?"

"Just my sister."

"You are a very courageous woman. This may be a very difficult time for you. If you need me at anytime, please call me." He gave me his card, which said "Dr. Juan Battista."

"Could I see her? How is she?"

"She came through the operation very well, but she's still heavily sedated, so don't expect too much."

He led me through the sad despair of the hospital corridor, with its pale occupants huddled in the shadows and the white glare of TV screens lighting up their lonely faces. Some sat or lay there with healthy friends and family, talking to them with hope and cheer. Others sat or lay alone. I shrank from the miscarriage, just two years before, when I, too, lay in my own pain and aloneness, when my mother came to my hospital bed to help me.

Momma lay so small and still in her bed, in a soft green room, with blood flowing into her pale arm and her head so heavily bandaged I could barely see her face. The sides of the bed were up like in a baby's crib. There were tapes on both arms where the blood flowed in, and I thought of the holes they must have made. My body heaved and then heaved again, as I touched the blanket that covered the angle of her foot and patted the contents under it. There seemed nothing I could do. She was breathing quietly.

I called Jane and told her what the doctor had told me, that it was malignant. After I hung up, I opened the door to the telephone booth partially, so the light would go out and no one would see me as I cried.

What could I do? I had to make some plans. If Momma wanted to, she could live with me. I could put a cot in the living room for myself, and we would somehow manage. Suppose she didn't want to live with me? Maybe she'd like to stay with Jane. I doubted it. A nursing home? No, never a nursing home. Thoughts ran through my brain. I couldn't sleep. Andy came back from being with his father, with a cold and a stomach ache. The support check was late. I still had not recovered completely from the miscarriage and still shook, but not so much as before. I had to work and was grateful for the job with Fiorello, and now the worst tragedy of all: my mother with cancer.

When I went to see her at the hospital the next day, she was still groggy. As she stumbled through my name and through the words that still would not come to her, I realized the operation had not helped the aphasia. She tried to say my name, and patted my hand. Should I have told her then that she had cancer? Should I have added more to that stricken look she had on her face? I couldn't do it, so I lied and told her she had a blood clot and it had been removed, but it would take a while for her to get better. Relief replaced the look of panic. She seemed to be relieved at the news and slipped away into the darkness beyond her pain.

The next day, one of Momma's nurses called me and asked me to bring her a turban. When they unwound the head bandages, she realized, for the first time, that they shaved her head and that she was bald. That seemed to upset her as much, if not more, as the large square and livid scar that sat like a brand on the side of her head, with little black teeth holding it in place. I could understand her sense of loss over her hair, because I remembered right after I came out of the anesthesia, after I gave birth to Andy and looked down on my bare and shaven pubis. Not only did I feel bare and sore, but the lack of hair brought with it a sense of loss.

So I brought her two turbans, one blue and one white, which she wore while she stayed at the hospital. When she was finally well enough to come home, I paid Julia to take care of her, along with her housekeeping and babysitting chores that she did for me. She faced her new challenge with gratitude, for she was saving her money to bring her son over from Poland.

As Momma grew stronger, she grew restless and wanted to go to her own home in Farmingdale. I had to work, but realizing that the time was short, I moved out with her because the doctor said it was probably just a matter of a few months. Julia again rose to the challenge and packed us up. Taking Kicius, another cat, and my plants, we moved out to Farmingdale. For the next few months, I commuted to New York City to do the show. Then I drove back at night to be with her and Andy.

We often spoke about cancer at the theater. Others had gone through it with some member of their family, and the drug Kerbiozen was moving through the desperate underground. Because I felt suspicious toward doctors as a profession, having internalized my father's feelings, in spite of the care and consideration that Doctor Battista gave my mother, I now clutched at any straws to help her and felt that the medical fraternity refused to acknowledge Kerbiozen because it wasn't part of their profit loop. Since they couldn't control it through the chemical companies that endowed their research and their chairs, they wanted to restrict its use and not allow anyone else to benefit from it.

I sent away for the drug, filled with hope for the first time since the operation, but still playing the game that Momma had a clot, and to keep the clot contained, we had to give her injections. The Kerbiozen came as a yellowish murky substance, in a long slim vial, the neck of which had to be cracked off in order for the hypodermic needle to draw the contents out.

Momma slowly recovered some of her strength, but walking made her short of breath, and the aphasia remained. She grew more and more impatient, not understanding why, after all that she had been through, that her mind still wandered, and she could not pin it down. When she tried to form her ideas into words, her apparent intent would dissolve. Her eyes grew wider with despair and impatience.

With Julia's help, she took her baths, uncomfortable that some-one had to help her and would see her naked body. Julia helped her to dress, washing and ironing her things with the same care that she took care of me and Andy. We brought her many turbans that matched whatever she wanted to wear, and they slid around on her head, which was becoming covered with brown stubble.

Julia, who was never at a loss for words, now regaled my mother with her life in Poland, her relatives and the gossip which came to her though the constant letters that she exchanged with them. Momma listened, with many mixed emotions, partially grateful for her care, partially resentful that Julia, a stranger, was in her home. Most of all, Momma felt humbled that she could not hold her own with Julia, and Julia was only a servant. Her fingers worked the edge of any fabric that was near her, as often as not the hem of a flowered house dress, while her eyes rested on something in the middle distance.

Before the Kerbiozen came, I went through the doctors in the neighborhood hoping to find one who would administer the drug. Not one would touch it. I pleaded, begged, shamed, even tried to bribe some. Nothing came of it. I raged inside, knowing that everything had to be tried, no matter how flimsy the hope.

"My mother has terminal cancer, and I haven't told her." I would go through the litany, "Would you give her injections of Kerbiozen?"

"Kerbiozen is not an accepted treatment for cancer," they would answer.

"I know, but there is nothing else for her besides the painkillers, and I want to try everything. Would you please administer it to her? I could bring her in every week."

"I can't do it. It doesn't work, and if anyone found out, I could lose my license."

"I won't tell anyone, and I'd be so grateful if you would help her. It might help her. There are some people who feel they've been helped."

"They only think it helped them. People believe anything they want to believe; they believe in placebos."

"But if it helped her, it might set some precedent, and you would get the credit. Please, couldn't you do it for just a few months? She doesn't have more than that to live."

"I'm sorry, but I can't." And that would be the end of that.

Then in my continuing and desperate search, I found a doctor close to home in Massapequa, who not only agreed to give Momma the injections but was professionally curious about their efficacy.

We settled into a routine those last few weeks: a visit to the doctor, walks with Julia around the block, which left Momma breathless and tired, but she tied gay kerchiefs on her head to hide her scar. Her hair begun to lie down on her head and no longer stood up like a brush. We talked at length with the doctor, who seemed solicitous and even called to see how she was, dropping by the house to give her a weekly shot. I was so grateful to him that I turned and called him whenever anything came up. He was always there, attentive and helpful.

In spite of the fact that Momma was in pain and that the aphasia had not gotten better, she announced one day that she was going back to work. She feared that her money was running out and that she would have to face a poverty-stricken old age.

"Mumusiu, don't worry; I'll take care of you."

"You will, Basiu?"

"Of course, I will, <u>Mamusiu</u>." I ached for her that she ever doubted that I would. How far we had drifted apart in those few intervening years of my marriage.

After a few weeks, her pain grew stronger and even the Darvon wouldn't help. She kept insisting that she had to go back to work. At a loss what to do, I spoke to the doctor. He advised me to tell her that she had cancer. She had to know sooner or later, and I couldn't keep it from her forever. I couldn't protect my mother from the realization of her own disintegration.

One day, she looked at me as Jane and I were going through some pictures in one of the rooms upstairs and asked me, "B-B-B-B-Basiu, what is the matter with me?" She stammered out the phrase, and her eyes darted around the room, not looking at me, fearing the answer. Jane and I had decided to tell her and were looking for the right moment. She had opened the door for us. We looked at each other and realized this was the moment we both had dreaded.

"<u>Mamusiu, kochana Mamusiu</u> (Mother, dearest mother), you have cancer." I said it. It had to be said; those terrible words had to be uttered. Not only Dorothy feared to utter the name of the big "C"; I, too, dreaded to face its terminal claw. Now it was hers; we had shifted the burden. She looked at me with reproach, as if I had given it to her. She sat there like a pillar of stone; then she started to rock back and forth.

"<u>Boze moi, boze moi</u> (my God, my God), not only Andrzej but me, too. Cancer, Basiu are you sure? You said it was clot. <u>Boze moi</u>, what did I do? Why me? What did I do?" She kept rocking back and forth, as she stammered out the words, repeating them, losing them, coming back to the phrase, over and over again.

"What did I do. What did I do? Basiu, why me? What did I do?" She turned to my sister. "Jasiu what did I do? Why me? Why is God punishing me? What did I do? Basiu, what did I do?" I had no answer for her, not then and not ever. She clasped her hands in front of her face and unclasped them. "What did I do? <u>Boze moi</u>, what did I do?"

From that day on, until the very end when Momma no longer could talk at all, she kept asking what she was being punished for.

395

What had she done to so offend God, that He, in His divine mercy, visited cancer upon her? Julia sat with her. The plans for returning to work were dropped.

Fiorello and the people I worked with made it possible for me to get through those days, to break the feeling of hopeless despair that my mother's sickness plunged me into. I drove west into the city, facing the oncoming rush hour traffic, and on clear days, I drove into the rays of the setting sun, to be there within a half hour, to get my make-up on and my costumes, to smile and to sing, even to dance, as if there was no other thing in my life. Then after the show, stopping at the apartment, picking up the mail and heading back to Farmingdale at night, wondering at my life, at the direction that it had taken, how far from the dreams that I had dreamed. Who would have believed I would be raising the grandson and namesake of Oscar Hammerstein II by myself, for eleven thousand dollars a year, fighting monthly to get my child support check, my body drained, my ambitions shattered, my voice gone, and my mother slowly dying from cancer?

As she got worse and questioned me relentlessly about why God was punishing her, I was feeling progressively more helpless. My periods never ended, and they often lasted for a whole month. They spread under me like a hot wet puddle as I drove back and forth, or they formed into large clots that slid out and sent the blood running down my legs undeterred by any napkin I might have been wearing. I often held onto the staircase backstage, or tightly to the steering wheel, as silver stars popped behind my eyelids and swam like tadpoles in the darkness that came and went in waves. During the show when the weakness came over me, I would force my way through, and then after the last curtain went down, Doc, my dear friend, would carry me home, and he would sleep on the couch to make sure I survived the night. Then back to Farmingdale and the stricken despair of my mother and to Andy's growing unhappiness, praying to God that nothing should happen to Julia, because I would not have been able to survive without her.

We kept giving my mother the Kerbiozen, hoping it might help her. There was nothing else to turn to. Her head hurt, and her breathing was becoming more difficult. I was beside myself. Jimmy came when he wanted to, often without calling, took Andy or left him, without showing up. Andy became more and more resentful, more and more demanding. The more preoccupied I became, the more he tugged at me. I knew he needed me, but I had little to give him in those sad days. He began to get attention by falling and knocking things over or by doing destructive things, things his father had done before him. He began making demands on me that ended in my screaming at him. Then I'd run from the house to ride around the Island in my car, ending up on the beach at night, hoping for some peace and for some solace.

As I took Momma back and forth to the new doctor who was administering the Kerbiozen, we would talk. He and I became conspirators in trying to prolong her life. I turned to him with trust and with hope. There were days when Momma seemed to feel better, and I prayed that the cancer would go into remission, but when the pain came upon her and when I had to increase the dosage of Darvon, I grew panicky about what lay ahead for her.

Then one day, I came home after a Sunday matinee, with no evening performance, to an ambulance parked in front of the house. I slammed on the brakes to see two white-coated men carrying a stretcher with my mother on it, covered by plastic with only the top of her head showing. Julia was clutching Andy in the doorway and wailing out loud while neighbors peered from their windows. I ran to the stretcher.

"What happened? Dear God, is she...?" I couldn't say it.

"She's still alive. She's had some kind of a stroke. What's that scar?" The attendant pointed to her head.

"That's a scar from the operation she had a few months ago. It was cancer." I pushed down the plastic blanket and looked down on Momma's pale face, with her mouth slack and to the side. I followed the howling blinking ambulance to the hospital as they put

397

her under an oxygen tank. I could see movement in the back of the ambulance as they took care of her, and I kept as close to it as speed and traffic would allow. Her doctor arrived before us, and the other hospital staff members scurried to make her comfortable, preparing me for the worst. But the worst would have been a blessing. The doctor told me my mother had survived the stroke. That was a relief, but it had left her blind, partially paralyzed and in more pain. I looked over at her, through the window partition and could see the tubes, the plastic tent, the heavy laborious rising and falling of the blanket. Momma's doctor put his arms around my shoulders, as I mumbled my question out to him. "Is she in more pain after the stroke?"

"I don't know, but I'll talk to the staff nurse to make sure they give her some more morphine."

"The Darvon is not enough?"

"Not anymore. For a while, the morphine will quiet the pain. You realize that the stroke may shorten her life to a few weeks, even maybe days?" I nodded and started to cry.

"What happens when the morphine no longer kills the pain?"

"Then we'll do what we have to do." He looked levelly at me. "Morphine can cut her pain, but it also may end her life. We have to be careful of the dosage. For now, I'll tell the nurse to raise it."

We drove back to his office for a home supply of morphine, when and if Momma ever left the hospital. We spoke across his wide desk. It was still Sunday afternoon, but so much had happened in a few hours that as I cried I could feel the clot push itself hot and wet down my legs. As I slid out of the chair, I hit the floor. He helped me on to the cot and spread a towel under me.

"How long have you been bleeding like this?"

"Every time I have my period," I told him, as the stars swam around the ceiling and a back door seemed to open into a familiar and comforting darkness.

When I came to, I had on a clean white diaper like a baby's, but my inside felt funny, sore. I dazedly looked around the doctor's office and came to with a start. I noticed bloody gloves in the basket next to the table. The hair on my arms stood up. My mother's doctor was standing over me with a benevolent smile on his face as he announced, "You have to have an hysterectomy, or you, too, may lose your life."

Rage and fear swept over me. He had given me an internal examination when I passed out. What else had he done? I sniffed for the familiar smell of semen. None drifted around me. But I felt sore and violated, aching inside and barely dealing with the new bombshell he had thrown at me.

"There must be a family predisposition to tumorous growth in your family, so you must be very careful and not take any chances. There is a fibrous growth and some polyps in your uterus that you shouldn't take any chances with. I'll book you into the Le Roy Hospital for Monday."

My rage turned to panic and then to helplessness. Oscar had his nervous collapse at the Le Roy Hospital on Madison Avenue. I would follow him there.

"But I only passed out," I insisted.

"You exaggerate; you only seemed to pass out," and he went on to make a notation in his date book. I covered my diapered bottom with a slip and nodded. Should I rage at him; should I scream at him? How could he? How unfair it was, but I needed him to help me in case Momma came home and needed the Kerbiozen shots and some morphine. I felt trapped. He was the only one I could turn to. So, shaking, I left his office.

That evening when I got back to the theater, the girls in the dressing room took one look at me and closed ranks around me. Beverly took care of the hospital. Diane called her gynecologist, a woman, and made an appointment for me for the following day. We laughed over the diaper. They wanted to know who the creep was who said that I needed a hysterectomy. I told them only part of the story, not connecting the doctor with my mother but telling them it was just a doctor I went to with my bleeding.

Somehow I got through the show that night. The music from the orchestra seemed farther away than the pit under the stage. I followed the patterns of habit to get through the evening. Doc carried me home again that night as he had done before and slept on the couch to make sure I again survived the night. I slipped in and out of complete blackness, a blackness in which even dreams had ceased to exist.

The next day, the woman gynecologist that I went to see told me I might need a curettage in the future, but she saw nothing suspicious in my uterus. After I told her what was happening in my life, she gave me a packet of tranquilizers.

"Take these. They'll quiet you down and give your body a chance to heal."

I called Momma's doctor to tell him I had canceled the hysterectomy at the Le Roy Hospital because I had to be around to take care of her. I would have it right after the situation with her resolved itself. He accepted it without question and asked me to have dinner with him. He might withdraw his offer of morphine and not continue with the Kerbiozen, if I didn't comply to some degree with his demands, so I had to go along with him.

I saw Momma a few more times. She lay in her room with another woman who had been given up for dead. The woman's head rolled off the side of the bed trailing a mass of red hair, her eyes open, sightless, her tongue lolling out, past a sagging mouth of drooling saliva. Only raspy breathing betrayed a presence of life.

Momma had partially come out of her coma, but couldn't talk at all. The worst thing of all is that the stroke made her totally blind. I sat next to her and held her hand and patted it. She clutched at mine and rubbed her cheek against it. She seemed to recognize my footsteps coming down the hall, for she grew agitated as I approached.

The next day, I brought some alcohol and rubbed her back and arms with it. She smiled in her darkness, and I marveled at how soft her skin was, firm and white as a girl's. I massaged her body, amazed I had never before touched her with such intimacy and such sadness. Momma patted my hand as I left, and tears rolled down the sides of her face, disappearing under her turban. I wondered how much awareness there was behind those large, now sightless brown eyes. The nurses told me she was a very demanding patient, screaming for more morphine at night. Dear God, what do I do now? Talk to the doctor?

"You know the nurses won't give my mother enough morphine. She screams at night in pain when I'm not there. I don't know what to do. They say she could become a drug addict if they gave her a larger dose."

"That's true, my dear. She could become addicted, and we can't have that happen."

Why not? I wanted to scream at him. What's the difference? She's going to die, anyway. Why not make it easy for her?

"I'll talk to the nurses," he assured me. I saw her again the next day, but this time, she didn't recognize my footsteps coming down the hall. I tried to reassure her, wondering if she heard me.

"You'll be all right, Mamusiu. You had an attack, but you'll be all right."

Her sightless eyes formed a furtive momentary, "why," and it left them, just as suddenly. How much did she understand? How much did she hear? The woman in the next bed lay with her eyes open, with no perceptible sound coming from her. She looked more dead than alive. Momma grew fidgety; then she started to moan. I asked her if she were in pain. She didn't answer. Then she started to scream. I called the nurse.

"Please give her a shot." The nurse repeated that she didn't want to be responsible for Momma's addiction and that she did this all the time.

"Then she must be in pain." I shook with frustration and could picture my mother screaming in pain while they, righteous in their rationalizations, held out that they protected her from becoming addicted. "Give her a shot," I hissed. "She doesn't have much more time to live. Why not let her be comfortable? Who cares if she dies clean or an addict?"

They looked at me with ill-veiled contempt. I had to change my tactic. "Please talk to her doctor. She has cancer and aphasia. She's blind, partially paralyzed and now in pain. She can't last too long. Why let her suffer?" They seemed to soften, but I wondered by how much.

On Tuesday when I visited her, the other bed was empty. The red-haired woman had died, and they had taken her away. I glanced over to the newly made and empty bed in dread. Momma lay heavily sedated. At least someone was listening to me. Her pale hands no longer scratched at the blanket; they just lay there, white and still. I rubbed her arms with alcohol and straightened out the turban on her poor head.

Like Julia, while telling me stories about the war, rocked back and forth, I, too, keened as I spoke to my dying mother, trying if not with my words, but with the sound of my voice, to reassure her. Somehow I got through another show. Lowell, one of the dancing gypsies and my friend, came up to me and asked me how she was.

"I don't know how you do it? How's your mother?"

"In pain, in a coma." I couldn't go on.

"It would be better if she died, wouldn't it?" He put his arm around me. I nodded and started to cry. "Bash, you're a saint. You know you're a saint. I don't know if I could go through what you're going through."

"Sure you could, Lowell. Sure you could, if you had to."

In the middle of "Politics and Poker," a message came over the loudspeaker that I had a telephone call. I knew, as did everyone else backstage, what it meant. The blood gushed from me as the nurse on the other end of the phone told me that my mother never came out of the coma and died peacefully in her sleep the night before. She died on August 23, one year to the day Oscar had died the year before. Doc carried me out of the theater, drove me to Farmingdale and helped me to make the last arrangements. George Abbott, the director of <u>Fiorello</u>, offered me his home in Merriwold Park, up in the Catskills, to recuperate and to grieve for my mother in peace.

Chapter 37

<u>Fiorello</u> was like an extended family to me. There was always some kind of a party backstage: a birthday, a shower, or an anniversary. There were cakes, candles and presents. There were also vigils that were kept with people like me, who were losing parents or loved ones. The gay boys put on their feather boas and blew out the candles on their birthday cakes during intermissions. They played jokes on each other, and we laughed sometimes with such raucous abandon that the audience could hear us out front.

One cause for such hilarity was a situation that reverberated throughout all the dressing rooms in all the theaters in a matter of minutes. We had a male singer in our show who was a sponger; he never bought anything himself, but took sips out of anyone's drink that happened to be standing within arm's reach. The dancing boys brought their iced teas up to their top floor dressing room where they all changed. He would go out of his way to pass through that dressing room and partially empty most of their containers. A sip here and a gulp there resulted in an enraged dance corps.

There was an almost built-in antipathy on the Broadway stage between the dancing boys and the singing men. Most of the male singers were considered to be square and to take themselves very seriously, with one eye on the current job and another on the Metropolitan Opera. Many of the dancing boys took life as it came. And for a good reason, being called gypsies, they traveled from town to town, auditioning, decorating their apartments and splashing their bodies with Jean Nate.

The dressing rooms reflected the difference. The singers had pictures of wives and children around the mirrors, with meager little cases of make-up on their dressing tables. The dancing boys with their feather boas and glittering jewelry, fancy hats, rows of mouth wash, colognes, petit-point pillows and Chinese robes, had pictures of Judy Garland and Bette Davis struck around their mirrors.

It was the dancing boys who decided to get revenge on the sponging male singer that one very hot day in the middle of summer, when even the imperceptible cross breeze on the top floor didn't ruffle the feathers on the pink boas. They plotted with diabolical glee. It was a joint effort, as it were, so that no one person could be singled out for blame, like the Agatha Christie mystery novel, <u>The Orient Express</u>, which took place on a train and in which twelve people had been implicated in a murder.

They bought a very big clear glass and filled it with ice cubes. Then one by one, they ceremoniously peed in it, on cue, some more, some less, as the spirit moved them. With much giggling and malicious laughter, they frosted the top of the glass with granulated sugar and draped a finely sliced piece of lemon over the edge. They all discreetly wedged themselves into the john when they heard the male vocalizing his way up the stairs. He surveyed the empty room and spotted the inviting frosted drink, gulping down almost half of it, before smacking his lips and proclaiming to the apparently empty room that it was a bit salty. He then proceeded to down the rest of it, and then looked around for more. When he realized there was no more to be had, feeling triumphant that no one had caught him in the act, he turned on his heel and disappeared down to the back stairs, to the singers' dressing room below.

The dancing boys followed him down, and when the room was filled with all the male singers and some of the bit players, they announced very proudly to the assemblage that the sponger had drunk their communal pee. It's hard to say what went on inside him, but on the outside he turned white, then red. The red grew deeper and deeper. We in the girls' dressing room, under the stage, heard about what had happened and flew upstairs as an apoplectic male singer sped through the backstage and out into the street, yelling revenge and searching for the stage manager, while word of the incident tied up all the backstage phones as the story spread throughout the whole theatrical community. He threatened to bring the whole dance corps up on charges before the grievance committee at Actors Equity. He kept running around while we were all making-up, trying to get some statement from witnesses who might have seen the nefarious deed.

My friend Beverly Dixon, ever the peacemaker and union representative, instead of taking his statement, sat him down in the corner of the basement and asked him, "What are you going to say to the grievance committee at Actors Equity? That they peed in the glass and you drank it? Do you have the glass?" He shook his raging head, flanked by ears that had turned a beet red.

"No, but I know they did it. They even announced it in front of the whole dressing room."

"Did they say it was their pee, or just pee, in general?" Beverly was being very thorough.

"They said it was their pee, that they all peed in the glass."

"Are you sure? I asked some of the male singers up there. They told me you drank some pee in a glass. Anyway, that's what the dancing boys told them. No one mentioned that it was any specific pee."

"I'm gonna get them. They can't do that to me. I'm gonna bring them up on charges."

"Listen, what are you going to say, how are you going to put it? Honorable committee of peers, I have been duped into drinking a glass full of pee. Did anyone force you to drink it?" Knowing full well that no one forced him to drink anything and that he had a reputation of helping himself to other people's things, he had to face the painful reality that he had been had and that he could do nothing about it. They had humiliated him. The dancing boys may have been on next to the lowest rung on the totem pole of theatrical hierarchy, but they had brought him down to their level.

"Leave it alone," Beverly continued. "It'll blow over, and people will forget about it. If you don't, it'll get into your records and maybe even get in the papers. Do you want that to happen?"

He glared back at her. "I'll get a lawyer. They can't do that to me," he sputtered, but he left it alone and fumed inwardly, plotting some future revenge, but not having so clear an opportunity as the dancing boys had had. He might have dropped the charges against them, but no one forgot the incident, and years later whenever we met, anyone who had ever been in Fiorello would repeat the story and embroider it and expand it, until it took on the dimensions of a myth.

Then one day, Lowell, one of the more elegant dancing boys, and my friend, stood in the doorway of the girls' dressing room, downstairs in the basement, under the stage, with a tiny little Kewpie doll in his hand. Some of the singing girls looked over and remarked how pretty it was and how it had the same color hair as Lowell's (a kind of strawberry blond), except that the doll's hair was kinky and Lowell's hair was straight. (Singers were always somewhat square.) They touched its pink face and gave out such a scream that the stage manager left his post on stage right and barreled down the stairs to see what had caused the commotion.

It was at that moment that the whole dressing room went up in peals of laughter. Upstairs, on stage. Tom Bosley, as Fiorello La Guardia, was telling Marie of his love, and we below the stage were screaming so loud that the first rows of the audience must have heard us. It seems that Lowell had used his penis as the face of the Kewpie doll, painting eyes on it, and teasing his own pubic hair into a halo around the head. We all crowded around him congratulating him on his creativity, and one of the other dancing boys shook hands with the doll. What? That's what he did. Shook hands with it, while a distraught Freddie, our stage manager, trying to keep the show from disintegrating, threatened to fire all of us, if any more noise was heard from below the stairs.

It was with Lowell that I had many conversations about his homosexuality. I asked him one day, "Lowell have you ever gone to bed with a woman?"

"I don't know if I ever went to bed with one, my dear, but I had sex once in the back of a cab with a friend, who happened to be female."

"What was it like? I mean, did you enjoy it?" I tactfully inquired.

"Well, my dear, it felt like, and I don't mean for you to misunderstand and take offense, but it felt like I was wearing loose galoshes."

"Lowell, not even tightly fitting galoshes?" I laughed.

"No, my dear, I stand by my observation: Once you've known a nice tight ass hole, there is no going back, as it were."

I must have flushed crimson, for he laughed as I continued my inquiry. "Did you ever like girls?"

The controversy was raging that something in the way children were raised, problems with their mothers, caused them to become homosexual. I hoped to avoid it with my son.

"No, as far back as I can remember, when I was a tiny little boy, I looked under the john partitions to see men peeing, and played with other little boys and their little weenies." He made a sucking sound. "Such a delicacy, little weenies."

When I was in Two's Company, the Bette Davis show, I began to wonder seriously about the behavior of the gay boys and the causes of homosexuality. It was a show that had two directors. One was Jules Dassin, who had not as yet married Melina Mercouri and directed "Rififi," so he was completely unknown to some of us. The other director was Jerome Robbins, who was known in the close-knit family of the theater as a choreographer, but as yet had not become the creative power that subsequent successes made him. Since two directorial male heads are an impossible reality in any situation, instead of making the show twice as good, the show never got off the ground.

Two's Company was a revue, with Bette Davis supposedly making a comeback to the Broadway stage. Jerry Robbins was to have choreographed her musical numbers, and Jules Dassin was to have directed the comedy sketches. On paper, it must have looked like a wonderful idea. But in reality it was a disaster. Jules Dassin was no match for Bette. He was not a comedy sketch director; his forte was drama. The sketches droned on, saved only by the presence of Bette Davis and a revolving door of leading men, who came and left with increasing frequency.

It was in Two's Company that Jerry Robbins decided to make Nora Kaye, the great ballerina, into a star, not Bette Davis, but Nora Kaye. Why Nora Kaye? Because it seems they had been engaged, and he broke it off, so he felt that he somehow had to make it up to her and decided to do it in the show that had Bette as the star. This led to many complications. Bette sat around in her Confederate hat and her matching dress, waiting for some direction, while Jerry had Nora and the dancers rehearsing some of the most beautiful dance numbers that I have ever seen. One was called "Roundabout."

"You go round about and round about and round about again." There was also the "Haunted Spotlight" with Bill Callaghan and Buzz Miller. I sat in the back and watched as the dancers leaped and twirled across the stage, and all of my muscles danced with them. Jerry had with him his best people, who moved with grace and magic and who left in their wake air that resisted settling back into place for the beauty of movement that their passage had created.

It was not a happy show; it did not work. We toured around and got stuck in Detroit where we sat for many weeks, while half of the directors in the theater came out to see what they could do and then left without doing anything. We weren't sure we would ever get home, and Detroit seemed farther away from New York than it is now.

The dancing group stayed together and entertained itself as a unit, while the singers dispersed to their rooms or sat in the tacky Barlum Hotel till all hours of the night. The dancing boys threw parties, and Jerry insisted that I be invited to them. I came, not understanding why I was there and feeling out of place, as they recounted their experiences in shows I as yet had barely heard about. Jerry would sit and put my legs across his lap, and Nora would come over and take my legs off his lap, and I would be embarrassed and feel like a fish out of water. I was told I was pretty and moved like a dancer; that was why Jerry wanted me there. I dressed the place up. He also liked me. I liked him a lot and felt a great deal of confusion about what kind of a relationship I was expected to have with him. It was only my second show, and at that time I still had a great deal to learn.

On Halloween Eve, the dancing boys organized a costume party. They all came magnificently attired. I never forgot the pictures that were to etch themselves forever on my mind and to keep an avenue of questions open, until many years later some of the answers began to appear. They all came in their black leotards, beautiful lean bodies, tall and muscular, as only the bodies of dancers can be.

The four dancing boys had a variation on a theme. The theme had to do with women. One came disfigured by lumps where all the muscles and curves of a woman would be, gnarled bumps protruding from calves, thighs, arms, breasts, hips and a hag's wig, with pieces of flesh like elongated moles hanging from his pasty face. Another came as one in the throes of death, with another hag's wig with not only a painted scar, but one that was raised and from which blood seeped all the way down the front of his leotard, showing not only a gaping wound, but intricately painted flesh with veins surrounded by exposed bone and gristle. Yellow pus drained from one end, balancing out the red blood that drained from the other. He lay down his beautiful slim body from time to time on a bench and went through the death agony, gurgling and spasming, letting his head loll from side to side, splattering the catsup on the hotel room rug. Another one came as a pregnant woman with enormous lumps for breasts sagging onto an enormous belly that he kept pushing down on all night, trying to give birth.

They played a game where we were all blindfolded, one by one, and spun around. Then we were told to put out our index finger, and as we stumbled around with the extended finger, a jar of vaseline was impaled on it, eliciting squeals of revulsion from the players and squeals of glee from the participants. It was from them that I learned about Abano Oil in my bath, of its musky heady smell, and of perfumes and colognes and the ubiquitous mouthwash. The smell of the body was repugnant to many of them, and they were all almost uniformly immaculate, neat, tasteful and lacking any body odors. As their party costumes indicated, the female processes fascinated and repelled them, as did blood. They were either fascinated by blood or repelled by it, to the point of nausea. I began to see male homosexuals in many ways, as they filtered through my life, often making large decisions which affected not only my life, but the lives of the artistic community and the nation, then later I realized, the mythology of the whole world.

My mother and I never discussed this area of my life because she felt that it was dirty and that male homosexuality was a figment of my imagination. She had never heard about it; therefore it did not exist. But in the theater, I was surrounded by it, and because I was so surrounded by it and the power it weilded in the theatrical community, in time I began to ask many questions about it. Some of the answers to my questions and an immense tragedy that struck the creative world were yet to work themselves into my future.

Chapter 38

And so the last curve on that disintegrating spin flung my mother's spirit into the far (or near) reaches of space, or rearranged her spirit, so that she remained here but existed through other perceptions. Some say that death is the ultimate end. Others say that it is a passageway to judgment, into heaven if one obeyed the rules, and to hell if one didn't. Then there are those that say that death is a renewal, a reincarnation, a new push for the soul to purify itself. It seems to depend on who is in power. Some merge with the earth and bury their dead. Others merge with the sky and float away to heaven. Some re-enter the great womb of the eternal Mother, others join the father in the sky, still others seek the sun, and then there are those who reach out to the void. No one seems to know any of the real answers. But even though the answers are not known, it hasn't stopped men from killing each other, in the name of their particular answer, in the name of their particular vision of truth. I know that the body is left behind at death; that's a given. Yet a part of me holds out and hopes that something remains intact, that some silhouette remains recognizable, a tentative tracing even after the physical body releases the breath and with it whatever the breath sustains.

My physical coming here was through a great deal of water. My dreams reflect that water, seeping in, leaking in, filling my homes, my property, all that I dream about. The exit seems to be much drier; a different sort of placenta is ruptured. There is no actual physical sac

411

that bursts to cause the flooding, but if those who have touched the experience of death and have returned can be believed, then it seems to be an air passage filled with light and a sense of relief, a movement through a tiny little opening into a blissful existence filled with overwhelming brilliance. Since it is in darkness that all our fears are spawned, then the possibility of light on that ultimate journey comes as a welcome change. The repetition of bliss only echoes our arrival on this level at the time of our birth, when we first drink in the earth's air and aspire upon the journey we call life.

It was three years after Momma's death, after I had seen her through that ultimate passage, three years of trying to be healed from that shattering wound. It was then that she appeared to me. It did not feel like a dream. Whatever it was, it occupied a different space, neither dream or conscious reality, some other level for which I had no frame of reference.

One moment I lay upon my bed, in my bedroom, back in my apartment in New York City, with my hair up in curlers, wearing my white silk jumpsuit. The next moment, without even being aware of it, I had blinked, my mother stood before me at the foot of my bed. She wore the same blue turban she had asked me to bring her in the hospital, after they shaved her head and trepanned her skull on a search-and-destroy mission after the foreign attackers that had invaded her brain. The turban was a bit askew. She straightened it, not so much to hide her scar, but to hide the baldness with which the operation had shamed her. The turban shifted again, for she had little hair with which to hold it in place.

"Mamusiu, kochana (dearest) Mamusiu, what are you doing here? I thought that you had died."

She looked down at me with those large sad brown eyes. " I thought you had forgotten me," she said in a soft voice, with words that seemed to sparkle like a string of lights in the air between us.

"Mamusiu, I haven't forgotten you. I don't know where to get in touch with you. Where have you been?" The frightened child began to rise in me, and my arms and legs began to tremble.

412

"I am here where I have always been. I am here." As she answered, the blue turban slowly moved forward, over her face. She lifted those familiar hands to position it more firmly on top of her head. As she did so, I again saw the livid scar on the side of her skull, and the memories of her last days flowed over me and through me.

Through tears, I choked out, "But we buried you. I saw the earth strike your coffin. It took so many shovelfuls to cover that coffin, while we stood on that sultry August day in the pouring rain."

I wanted to leap across the bed and hide my face in her body, smell and touch her warmth, but a leaden weight locked me to the bed. "We buried you. How can you be here?"

"Oh, Basiu, Basiu, you don't understand. We die twice. The first time we die and they bury us, as you buried me in the earth, and we die a second time when everyone forgets us."

"Mamusiu, I haven't forgotten you. You took the lights with you when you left me." I reached out with one of my hands, and the tears blinded me. When I wiped my eyes, she was gone. The room hadn't changed; the same sounds hung in the same semi-darkness. I lay in my bed, in my silk white jumpsuit with my hair in curlers, my body a dead weight on the bed, and she was gone. After I had quieted down and began to think again, I wondered if she really had spoken to me. Did I make all that up, or had she come to me from some other level? If she had died and could talk to me, maybe I, too, had died and they had forgotten to bury me. Maybe I, too, was dead and my awareness of self existed only through my own pain and the filtered imagination of others. I must be marking time in place until "they," the other "we," bury me.

I had not forgotten her. The sight of her grave caused me such grief that I could not visit it. And a picture of her face in a frame or an album always broke into whatever I was doing and flooded me with memories. Would I ever forget her? Would there ever come a time when something about her would not cause my body to spasm and my face to fill with tears? She had been my greatest love. I had not loved anyone as much as I had loved her. Not my father, not the men in my life, although I wanted to find one who was like her and male, for whom I carried obsessive passions, not my nieces or my sister, not even my son. My joy and comfort around her had been complete. Now the point in space where she existed, where I knew I could always turn to, could always find, was gone, had forever disappeared. She didn't need to pay attention to me for me to feel at peace. All I needed from her was for her to be there. And now she was gone.

Chapter 39

It all happened within a period of just over two years. Most of the major players on the stage of my life were gone. My marriage had ended ,and I lost a baby through a six-month miscarriage. Almost everything that filled my life at the time was gone: my mother, my father, my marriage, my singing voice, my health. I was left almost penniless to raise my child alone. I had stepped into one of my own nightmares. Reeling from punches, not knowing which way to turn, overwhelmed by despair, I doubled over from pain and grief for Momma. Another part of me tore at my hair in rage at the remaining Hammersteins, who were hiding behind their barrage of lawyers. I couldn't sleep and awoke shaking, as the hamster in the cage of my mind raced endlessly on its wheel and the black horse of rage careened through the caverns of my life.

Looking back to that time, I think I went through a walking nervous breakdown. Not in time nor in space was there an area for me where I could unravel, lie down and check out. I had to keep going. Phil Silvers' admonition kept repeating itself in my brain. "Just keep going," he had said. "Just keep going." That's what I did. I had a son to raise, get my life back on track, begin to dream new dreams, recreate them out of the ashes of the past. Since I have always loved birds, the mythological Phoenix became my new symbol for the future. I would rise out of my own ashes. Out of the dust that filled my mouth and choked out my life, I would fashion a new me. I would emerge out of the cinders newly forged, no longer the Cinderella of old, not the ancient goose girl, but a freer bird, one not as earthbound, fired with a new strength, new purpose. I would fashion a new set of dreams.

There was no point in space to which I could turn to for comfort and protection. I would have to fully grow up. I would have to become my own mother and my own father. I would have to learn to stand alone.

The greatest awakening came to me with the realization that I was not only at the mercy of fate, the careening curve of destiny and disintegration, but also at the mercy of an alien male world from which there seemed to be no escape. Not only was the sexual game played by male rules, but so were all the others. It became apparent that men created systems for their own survival and comfort. Those games of power had little to do with women and children. The fact that I felt peripheral all my life had little to do with my shattered illusions. It had to do with the reality that existed in the world around me.

Well-meaning friends couldn't understand my apparent lack of funds. Didn't I get a settlement? Wasn't Andy part of Oscar's trust fund? How could Oscar Hammerstein III not be part of the Hammerstein legacy? George Abbott was amazed when we spoke about my apparent plight. He advised me not to become bitter.

"Bitterness puts wrinkles on your face, and it shortens your life," he said as he smiled and patted my still-smooth cheek. He lived to be a hundred and seven years old. He also wondered how I could have been so poorly represented legally. "Why did you give up all of your rights to Jimmy's inheritance?" he asked me.

"Because Oscar threatened to cut him out of the trust fund. That would have left him penniless, because he had declared bankruptcy at the time, and me with no money to raise Andy," I tried to explain.

"Would he have done that? I mean, cut his own son out of the will? Strange, you know, your father-in-law, former father-in-law, once told me that he was writing his lyrics for his grandchildren."

I filed away that remark from George Abbott with the growing list of accolades about my former father-in-law, which included "Kindest

Man in the Theater" and "Father of the Year" awards. There were no awards for hypocrisy.

The answer to why I had been so poorly represented and about which I felt that I had been given no choice clarified itself further one day during a conversation with my divorce lawyer, who also took care of my mother's estate after she died. We had grown chummy, primarily because he never made a pass at me and handled himself like George Abbott, an old-fashioned gentleman. He was getting married and invited me to meet his intended. We had some wine together. Like so many people before and since, he wanted to impress me with the fact that he, too, was held in great esteem by the Hammersteins.

"Really?" I didn't realize that he had actually met Jimmy, Oscar or Dorothy. All of the transactions had been through lawyers. "They held you in great esteem?" I inquired. His wife-to-be was preparing dinner in the kitchen.

"Yes." He rolled the clear white liquid in his wine glass. "Their lawyers offered me a partnership." My breath caught, suspended, as a wave of ice swept through my body and the warmth left it.

"Why didn't you take it?" I could barely control my voice.

"Oh, it fell through," he replied absent-mindedly, drifting into a reverie over the rim of his drink.

"When?" I planted the word as casually as I could manage, into the air between us.

"Right after you got the divorce, right after you came back home from Mexico," he mused, as he stared at the clear liquid. At this point, the dinner arrived with a look of alarm on his intended's face. They exchanged glances. He straightened up, pulled himself out of his reverie, and the intimacy precipitated by the wine left him, as he changed the subject.

The Hammerstein lawyers brought him with the promise of a partnership. When he delivered the goods, they dumped him. He had pressured me into signing the divorce agreement by impressing upon me the fact that Jimmy would be left out of the trust fund and I would become a pauper. He kept reiterating the fact that I had no choice but to sign and get out, as the plum of a partnership dangled in front of his nose. Once they had me out of Jimmy's financial picture, they got rid of him, too, killing two birds with one stone. All he got was his fee. It wasn't only his fee that had been at stake. The stakes had been much higher. It also became apparent to me that he must have known that the agreement had to be dealt with expeditiously. Had I been married to Jimmy at the time of Oscar's death, as his legal wife and the mother of his son, I would have been entitled to some of the estate. By offering my lawyer a partnership, they got me out of the picture. It was all neat and legal. Jimmy got his inheritance. I got to raise his child on an income just above the poverty level.

After the conversation, I found myself a new lawyer. Little could be done about the agreement I had signed, as my new lawyer advised me. It was foolproof and watertight. Jimmy's lawyers had served him well. I may have given up all my rights to the estate that made him a millionaire and forced him to take courses in financial management, as he gleefully told me when he visited Andy, but I didn't sign away the rights of his son to live on a relatively similar level as his father. Another Jack, this time Rosen, approached the barrage of Hammerstein lawyers. They wouldn't even deal with him and put him off with endless delays. So we petitioned the court on behalf of my son. There was no way for us to know the extent of my former husband's income. In my original separation agreement, I was to receive his income tax statements, minus the monies he received as gifts and bequests from his trust fund. Those documents were never made available to me, and I couldn't afford the accountants and lawyers that were necessary to interpret what he was getting.

Jack Rosen and I met downtown at the courthouse, and we filed into a large room in which dozens of people sat and waited for their names to be called by a court clerk so they could plead their cases before the judge. We sat at the edge of one of the rows, with only two empty seats just inside us in the same row. My lawyer reiterated that we had a problem since we had no actual knowledge about the extent

CINDERELLA ❦ AFTER THE BALL OR, JUST KEEP GOING

of Jimmy's income. We would have to make guesses, which was iffy and a problem. Since Jimmy wouldn't make his income known to me, even though our agreement demanded it, we were swimming through murky waters.

As usual, Jimmy and his lawyer arrived late. Their eyes scanned the room and settled on the two empty chairs just past us in the row in which we were sitting. My heart started to pound in my chest as the old rage began to rise. Jimmy's arms were filled with papers. The papers stuck out every which way, as if they had been grabbed at the last moment and crushed to his chest to get to the courthouse on time.

Both he and his lawyers exchanged pleasantries with me and my lawyer. As Jimmy began to climb over my legs to get to the empty seat beyond me, the papers he had been clutching to his chest fell out of his arms and landed on my lap. As they fell in my lap, they exposed a row of figures that were neatly arranged in a straight line on the right hand side of the page. The last figure that added up the long row of numbers was four hundred and sixty thousand dollars. I looked down at the miracle that had opened up before me and had "fallen right into my lap" and then up at Jimmy, who not only turned red, but began to sputter and grab at his fallen treasure, trying to get it off my lap and up off the floor around me, furthering an already uncomfortable situation. His lawyer, realizing what had happened, grabbed him. Both of them plowed over me again, missing some of his papers that remained on the floor under my seat. The financial statement that had landed in my lap was gone, but the numbers burned themselves into my brain. When I told my lawyer what I had seen and what the commotion had been about, he smiled and nodded, advising me that at least we knew the ballpark figure and that it made his job easier.

Our names were called by the clerk, and we got up to enter the courtroom. Just as we were about to open the doors to that inner sanctum, Jimmy's lawyer ran up to my lawyer and offered to draw up a new more equitable agreement. Since I had seen Jimmy's income, it would have made it more difficult for him to keep his client's son, if not me, at such a low standard of living. From eleven thousand dollars a year I had been getting, I was to receive sixteen, most of it in child support. It was all that my lawyer felt I could get. Andy's education would be secure. His father would have to pay for his books and supplies, which he had refused to do after the original agreement, hiding behind his lawyers' interpretation that tuition was the only actual cost of schooling. He would also cover my son's medical costs, which would include work on Andy's teeth. There would be no cost of living increase, and no change of status for me.

It wasn't much, but it made my life easier, and the papers having "fallen into my lap" gave me hope that perhaps some of my former good luck and blessings would re-enter my life. I returned to my studies and began my Masters in Theater and Communication at Columbia University and refocused on my career.

In the past, I had naively thought that talent had the same wellspring as truth and beauty, the three Muses having risen from the same root. The contrary seems to be true. Talent has little to do with truth or beauty. It also has little to do with the person it uses for its realization. As Oscar Greeley Clendenning Hammerstein II put it, "It is not invariably true that an artist's work is a reflection of personal characteristics, for some men sublimate their good qualities in their art and have little goodness left over to distribute among friends and relations."

It is that goodness that is missing from the planet, that goodness that ironically came to be called "family values" from another direction. It is that goodness that has to be rediscovered and renurtured into fruition. For talent does not exist as an idea in space; talent is an evolutionary expression of the fear-driven human creature clamoring for attention. We have to defuse the fear, even at the cost of compromising our creativity. In order to survive, we have to find the larger context beyond it and redefine our reality. As William Butler Yeats had said, "Talent is the commonest thing in the world; the rare thing is character."

420

Epilogue

The first title that came to mind as I began to write this memoir was <u>Hip-Hip-Hypocrisy</u>. Then <u>Mired in the Land of the Living Dead</u> popped up for consideration. Both contained thinly cloaked aspects of bitterness in them. The latter sounded like the title for a horror movie with creatures barely rising out of a deep lagoon. Since George Abbott admonished me that bitterness would put wrinkles on my face, I searched on for a more appropriate title.

Along the way, my niece Cheryl, after reading some of the text, informed me that my story sounded like "Cinderella after the ball." The appropriateness of the title stuck.

As a potential princess searching for her Prince Charming, I really thought that I had two fairy godmothers. One was the theater, which turned me from a socially suspect immigrant into a mysterious foreign persona. The other was Hunter College, which partially sated my thirst for knowledge and filled the holes of my ignorance with ever-new found facts.

But, as with Cinderella, the hour of reckoning had to arrive. Illusions had to be shattered. Her unveiling came fast. A bong! at midnight, and it was all over. My unraveling, though, came much more gradually as I was constantly found lacking in the social milieu of my newly acquired relatives. I, too, was reduced not only to actual but psychological rags. And the only "glass slippers" that ever fit my feet were the Birkenstocks I subsequently began to wear for my own comfort.

Because the despair of our constant moving when we came to this country left me with such chaotic memories, I wanted to spare my son the dislocations that accompanied a life in the theater, and we stayed put in New York City. He attended the Ethical Culture Society School, Fieldston and then Amherst College, where he honed his artistic skills to become a fine painter creating luminous landscapes of the world around him. Ironically, in time, he became the Hammerstein family archivist and historian.

After my job at the switchboard and then <u>Fiorello</u>, with my health slowly returning, the changes in musical comedy theater precipitated by the popularity of rock music, growing TV viewing and the scarcity of shows that were being produced on Broadway forced me to other related occupations.

The future seemed to lie with TV, so to get some experience, I decided to start at the bottom, beginning with radio. Becoming interested in interviewing people, I landed a job with WRVR, an FM station, initially announcing classical music. Then when the station changed its format to talk radio, I hosted my own call-in interview show. My guests included, among others, Maya Angelou, Anais Nin, Rollo May, some of the politicians who were running for office trying to overthrow the political machine on the Upper West Side, and a host of celebrities whose shows were opening off Broadway and whose movies were being shown around town.

After a year, the station switched to a jazz music format, and we talk show hosts were fired. Artie Shaw, who had his own spot, joined the ranks of the unemployed. Having acquired some hands-on experience, I now thought to follow my heroine and mentor, Barbara Walters, into the TV world of talk show hostesses and anchor women. The glass ceiling at the time was a solid concrete wall, and female talking heads were considered unacceptable for a variety of reasons: Viewers wouldn't trust women; women's voices were too high or grated on viewers' nerves; some women were too aggressive, others not aggressive enough; they were too emotional, disorganized, dumb. I wasn't ethnic enough; that, too, was one of the reasons I couldn't get a TV job. At thirty-three, I was considered over the hill, no longer "younger flesh."

My only hope was the emerging cable TV market. One of the two cable channels in New York City at the time, Channel C, gave me a non-paying spot, as I continued to interview authors. At the same time, I pursued my master's degree in Communication and Theatre at Columbia University, as a hedge against a penniless old age, I told myself.

During the summers, when my son went off with his father, I did summer stock and performed in dinner theaters around the country as I had done when I began my career, but now with a different focus. The prospect of achieving stardom no longer held me in its thrall. I performed to pay my bills, to get over my panic, to heal my faltering voice, to free myself from the demons of the past and to find some reasons for my life.

My obsession with trying to make sense of what was happening around and to me and "meaning" itself began long before I studied philosophy at Hunter College. It was part of my life when I, as a little girl, looked up at the pulsating Aurora Borealis in the northern sky and wondered if it was the heart of God beating up there in the heavens. Who were we here down below? What were we doing here? How were we to live our lives? It seems that the questions came with the package.

My marriage and subsequent divorce temporarily deflected me from my primary search. It also deepened my awareness of hypocrisy and the entrenched abuse of women, children, animals and the planet itself. It also forced me not only to stop pressing my nose against the glass pane to gaze at the world from which I had been excluded but also to transform the glass into a mirror that forced me to look at myself.

To that end, many people helped me. Friends were the most important: Beverly Dixon Wills, Anna Lista Solomon, Valerie Harper, who exposed me to EST; Werner Erhart, the flawed genius who understood the rules of the game and tried to share those rules with us ("You can be right, or you can make it work"); Baba Muktananda, who initiated me and kept swatting me with his peacock feather as I bawled every time I knelt in his presence; the Dalai Lama of Tibet as we chanted and he tied orange threads and pieces of cloth around my neck; beautiful Krishna Murti, barely civil with his ennui while answering endless questions with "Watch your mind; watch the way your mind works; there are no answers"; Joya Santanya (Ma Jaya Sati Bhagavati) in whose presence and because of her great power, I began to vibrate on another level to a kundalini experience that shattered the habitual patterns of my old self; Alan Finger (Yogi Amrit), who with his Hatha Yoga and meditation classes refocused and regrouped around the opening that had been burned through; Hilda Charlton, who forced me to ready a song for every service when we met those Thursday nights in the manse of the St. John the Divine Cathedral and I shook my way through dozens of newly learned pieces until my panic subsided.

When my son left for college, I moved to the lower reaches of the Hudson Valley. There, I immersed myself in several activities. I became an organic gardener and a champion of trees. I participated in a series of environmental organizations (after I had been Chairman of the Board of Citizens for Clean Air in New York City and had run its first awards dinner): joined the Rockland County Conservation Association, serving as a director for the Town of Orangetown; organized and ran the Championship Tree survey for Cooperative Extension after I became Master Gardener with the organization; became a member of the Garden Club of Nyack, planting flowers around many municipal buildings; was appointed to the Clean Air Task Force by our then County Executive, John Grant; served as Chairman of the Shade Tree Commission in Orangetown; worked with others on the Breast Cancer Task Force that had been organized by Harriet Cornell; joined neighbors in my town to beautify the area by planting trees along the streets and raising money for planters that flowered with annuals, perennials and ivy every summer.

Using the voice that I had found again, I kept my singing alive by creating with Josef Czyz, a fine musician and conductor, a choral group. Composed largely of Polish women who had come to America to help their families back home, we called ourselves "Singers of Polish Music." The sad Polish folk songs and laments that Peter Wilhousky felt were gauche now filled my life as we performed them in many Polish halls, churches and local organizations. Having been in this country since I was nine, I became the translator and general helper for many of the Polish immigrant families who needed green cards, rental leases, bank accounts and other documents filled out and filed.

Along the way, with a friend, Helen Lindsay, we not only sang with a group called "Encore," but we created our own series of acts and shared our music with most of the nursing homes, hospitals, hospices, historical societies, local festivals and whoever would listen to us. We even held meditation concerts with Betty Figlure, who led us as we chanted.

I became a grandmother, and my son broke the Redzisz and Hammerstein paternal tradition by becoming a wonderful, caring father to his three children.

The activities with my friends, neighbors and son kept my creative and physical juices flowing. But on the back burner, my emerging awareness of what words really meant spun around in my brain, creating possibilities for a new book that will be titled Stampede of the Natives, dealing with the shift from female to male centrality, which becomes apparent through all the languages of the world, has put everything that is native to the planet and the planet itself into flight.

That is my ongoing project as I continue to grow my vegetables, prune my shrubs, divide my perennials and enjoy my grandchildren. The Hammersteins, their layers and their kind in a strange way did me a great favor. It seems as if they were part of a greater plan, a wider spin of fate. Without them, I many never have experienced the numbing hypocrisy that is hidden behind the principled world that locks women, children and the planet itself in the shackles of suppression, exploitation, abuse and even possible eventual extinction.

While I was still married, as I did petit-point and listened during those tense but hallowed familial gatherings, trying to learn chess, bridge, tennis and croquet on the side, it furtively crossed my mind what the mythical waif sweeping the ashes around the fireplace would turn into. Would she become, as my sister-in-law had become, silent in her acceptance, or as my mother-in-law Dorothy, ever vigilant with the panic spreading out from those watery blue eyes? Where would the questions of my life have led me? Perhaps to drugs or the bottle, as they had led so many of my friends.

In retrospect, life itself looks as if it may have some meaning. There seems to have been a road, perhaps "less traveled by," that took me from there to here, and the steps along the way, the falls into crevasses, the great losses, had to be experienced to gain understanding. It's as if there had been a prescribed pattern for the journey, devastating as it often was at the time of its unraveling. Anyway, it was a journey worth taking, and as Phil Silvers once said to me: "Schmuck, all you have to do is keep going."

As I was settling into my life at the ashram of Ma Jaya Sati Bhagavati in Florida, my son Andy called me with the news that Jimmy had died of a heart attack on January 7, 1999.

It seemed propitious and strange that the number seven surfaced in our lives again. Jimmy and I had been married on June seventh, which had been Dorothy's birthday. And here he was, making his final exit on the seventh of January. If you count the death of our marriage as the sixth casualty, even though it came many years later, Jimmy's death became the seventh termination on that great vortex of unraveling that took so many of the major players off the stage of my life.

It seems that after he had experienced chest pains in his Soho loft in New York City, Jimmy walked down five flights of stairs because the elevator was not in operation. He died in the ambulance on the way to the hospital.

All that flashed through my mind were the cheese and salami sandwiches on little squares of Trisquit, followed by beer, that had been our nightly ritual when we were married; how Jimmy had resisted any fruits and vegetables I had tried to wedge into his nutritional life.

Andy's news of his father's death surprised me because Jimmy was twenty-eight months younger than I, and I always thought I would predecease him. I tried to squeeze out some feelings of sadness that would appropriate for the occasion. No matter how hard I pushed, nothing seemed to dribble out. Somewhere in the far distance, there came the muffled sound of a door closing. It seemed to float disembodied in the air, attached to nothing; but as the door closed, it left a faint echo that drifted on that ancient silence.

I sifted through all of my tormented memories of Jimmy, of his ghostly presence and the shadow he had been throughout our married life, and how that quality had intensified in the latter stages of our marriage. Subsequent studies of children have found that offspring of parents of great wealth and offspring of poor parents often grow up with similar psychological problems. Both types often seem to have been deprived of personal, intimate, hands-on parental care.

My memories of Jimmy elicited no response from my body, no shreds of love or affection, of tenderness and intimacy, of rage or hate, resentment or reproach. There was only that empty silence where once there had been such hope and multi-leveled emotion. What remained was only peace and an apparent lack of feeling, a detachment that heralded the razor's edge, the balance between compassion and indifference that would accompany me, and never leave me, on the new journey I had embarked upon that dealt with the pursuit of the quiescent life of the spirit.

The End

Breinigsville, PA USA
28 August 2009
223097BV00003B/6/P